Marketing Management for Travel and Tourism

Lesley Pender

Stanley Thornes (Publishers) Ltd

First published in 1999 by
Stanley Thornes Publishers Ltd
Ellenborough House
Wellington Street
Cheltenham
GL50 1YW
UK

A catalogue record for this book is available from The British Library.

ISBN 0 7487 2783 3

Typeset by
Northern Phototypesetting Co. Ltd, Bolton
Printed and bound in Great Britain by
TJ International Ltd, Padstow, Cornwall

Contents

Preface

The activities of travel and tourism are increasingly popular and this would seem to suggest an easy role for the marketer of travel and tourism services. The reality, however, is that the general principles of marketing have to be applied within a highly competitive, service-based and extremely dynamic context. The aim of this text is therefore to outline the principles of good marketing management, concentrating on the necessary adaptation of these for the marketing of services. The distinctive nature of travel and tourism is highlighted where this has implications for marketing.

Marketing is an important function of modern management both in theory and in practice. A theoretical perspective is thus provided and complemented by practical examples. Whilst the text is essentially British in focus, numerous references and examples are drawn from the international arena.

The relevance of marketing at all levels in tourism organisations cannot be overstated, particularly as tourism businesses rely heavily on contact between employees and customers. Marketing is also important in both the public and private sectors which provide travel and tourism services. Small firms predominate in the tourism sector and, given the current nature of the competition they face from larger organisations, marketing has increasing relevance for them.

World travel and tourism are set to continue to grow. This being the case, the industry will require even more successful marketers in the future. As businesses generally become more customer-oriented and competitive, so the role of marketers becomes more difficult. This, combined with the speed of change that characterises travel and tourism, hints at the skill levels that will be needed by the tourism marketing managers of the twenty-first century.

The approach taken in this text is strategic, as this is the area of travel and tourism marketing that has to date received least coverage in textbooks. There were, at the time that the authors set about writing this book, few other substantial texts in this area. However a number of useful sources have been published since that time. Some are used and referenced within this book. It is hoped that this text will complement those other sources. The text also provides coverage of important current issues impacting on the marketing of travel and tourism. It is recognised that any attempt at topicality in a field as dynamic as travel and tourism is likely to date quickly and so the reader is encouraged to view examples as being subject to change. We have also attempted to provide a critical perspective and hope the reader will do likewise.

The book is aimed at undergraduate and postgraduate students of tourism and allied fields such as hospitality and leisure, as well as those following general business studies courses with an interest in services or tourism marketing. The text has relevance also for managers already working for travel and tourism organisations.

The introductory chapter provides an outline of travel and tourism and is followed by a chapter which introduces marketing for those new to the subject. The remaining chapters integrate particular aspects of marketing with relevant applications to travel and tourism

A number of features have been incorporated into the text for ease of use. Chapter objectives are provided at the start of each chapter and a summary is provided at the end of each chapter. An exercise or case study follows each chapter to enable students to apply the theory presented in the chapter. References are also provided for those wishing to undertake further reading on the topics covered. Three further extended case studies drawn from the industry are included in Appendix 1.

A great many people have helped with the preparation of this work and their contribution has been invaluable. Any errors or omissions are of course my own.

Lesley Pender

Author profiles

Lesley Pender, BA, M.Sc., PGCED
Lesley is Lecturer in Tourism at the Scottish Hotel School, University of Strathclyde. She specialises in Travel Trade and Transport, as well as Tourism Marketing. Her research interests are airline marketing, tour operations and travel distribution.

Dave Abson, PG Dip., M.Ed.
Dave is Senior Lecturer in Marketing Strategy at the University of Northumbria, Newcastle. His research interests are in the area of customer care.

Philip Alford, BA, M.Sc.
Philip is Lecturer in Tourism at the University of Luton. His research interests are the role of database marketing in tourism and tourism market segmentation.

Caroline Barrass, MA
Caroline is a freelance lecturer and consultant in Marketing and Travel and Tourism. Her research interests include tourism distribution.

Michael J. Boella, MA
Michael teaches Law and International Management in the Department of Service Sector Management at the University of Brighton, whilst also running his own consultancy practice. He is interested in hospitality law, and edits a range of hospitality industry reference works which focus on the law.

Patricia Gray, B.Sc.
Patricia is a freelance lecturer and consultant in Market Research. Her research interests are in the field of customer care.

Tony Seaton, MA, Ph.D.
Tony is Whitbread Professsor of Tourism Behaviour at the University of Luton. His research interests are in tourism marketing, tourism behaviour, military tourism and the tourism history of Scotland and Iceland.

Abbreviations

ABC	Audit Bureau of Circulation
ABTA	Association of British Travel Agents
ACORN	A Classification of Residential Neighbourhoods
AIT	air inclusive tour
AITO	Association of Independent Tour Operators
ARTAC	Association of Retail Travel Agents Consortia
ASA	Advertising Standards Authority
ASTA	American Society of Travel Agents
ATB	area tourist board
ATOL	Air Travel Organisers' Licence
BA	British Airways
BARB	British Audience Research Bureau
BCG	Boston Consulting Group
BITOA	British Incoming Tour Operators' Association
BM	British Midland
BRAD	British Rate and Data
BTA	British Tourist Authority
CAA	Civil Aviation Authority
CAB	Civil Aeronautics Board
CAI	Canadian Airlines International
CATI	computer-aided telephone interviewing
CAVIAR	Cinema and Video Industry Audience Research
CCTV	closed circuit television
CIM	Chartered Institute of Marketing
CLPC	Conservation Lands Product Club
CRS	computer reservation system
CTC	Canadian Travel Commission
DLC	destination life cycle
EFTPOS	electronic funds transfer at point-of-sale
EICC	Edinburgh International Conference Centre
ET	electronic ticketing
ETB	English Tourist Board
EU	European Union
FFP	frequent flyer programme
FMCG	fast moving consumer goods
GDP	gross domestic product
GDS	global distribution system
GMTV	Good Morning Television
GNER	Great North Eastern Railway
GTO	group travel organiser
GWT	Great Western Trains

HIE	Highlands and Islands Enterprise
HRI	Hotel Representative Inc.
IATA	International Air Transport Association
IBA	Independent Broadcasting Authority
IG	interest groups
IPS	International Passenger Survey
ITO	incentive travel organiser
IPR	Institute of Public Relations
JATA	Japan Association of Travel Agents
JICNARS	Joint Industry Council Newspaper Audience Research
LA	local authority
LEC	local enterprise company
MIS	marketing information system
MMC	Monopolies and Mergers Commission
NGT	nominal group technique
NPD	new product development
NRS	National Readership Surveys
NTO	National Tourist Organisation
NTS	National Travel Survey
OFT	Office of Fair Trading
OSCAR	Outside Site Classification and Audience Research
PEST	political, economic, social, technological
PIMS	profit implications of marketing strategies
PLC	product life cycle
PMS	property management systems
PR	public relations
RAJAR	Radio Joint Audience Research
RCI	Resort Condominiums Incorporated
ROI	return on investment
RTB	regional tourist board
SBU	strategic business unit
SE	Scottish Enterprise
SI	Standard Industrial Classification
SOID	Scottish Office Industry Department
SMART	specific, measurable, achievable, realistic, time-constrained
SMO	strategic marketing objectives
SPSS	Statistical Package for Social Sciences
STB	Scottish Tourist Board
STRU	Scottish Tourism Research Unit
SWOT	strengths, weaknesses, opportunities, threats
TALC	tourist area life cycle
TIC	tourist information centre
TGI	Target Group Index
TTG	*Travel Trade Gazette*
TQM	total quality management
UKTS	United Kingdom Tourism Survey
VDU	visual display unit
VFR	visiting friends and relatives
WTO	World Tourism Organisation
WTTC	World Travel and Tourism Council

Acknowledgements

The authors and publishers would like to thank the following organisations for granting permission to reproduce previously published material in this book:

The American Marketing Association, Butterworth-Heinemann (a division of Reed Educational and Professional Publishing Ltd), Catriona Cramond, Elsevier Science, The English Tourist Board, Eurostar (UK) Ltd, Holiday Autos International Ltd, Kogan Page Ltd, The McGraw-Hill Companies, Pannell Kerr Forster, Paul Chapman Publishing and Pearson Education Ltd.

The authors would also like to thank the following for their help with the preparation of this book:

Geraldine Bell, Graham Birse (The Scottish Tourist Board), Susan Briggs (The Environment and Development Company), Gwynneth Harkus (Virgin Holidays), Noel Josephides (Sunvil Holidays), Deborah Lidgett (Edinburgh International Conference Centre), Rory Maclellan (University of Strathclyde), Alison Morrison (University of Strathclyde), Christine Sorensen (University of Northumbria), Shirley Thornley (Emirates Airline), Sandra Watson (Napier University), David Wesson (University of Northumbria); also thanks to ABTA, BITOA, BTA, British Airways, Leading Hotels of the World, Metro Centre, Norseman Travel and Thomas Cook.

In addition, the authors would like to thank the many tourism market research agencies contacted. These agencies are listed separately at the end of the book.

Every effort has been made to contact copyright holders and we apologise if anyone has been overlooked.

1 Introduction to travel and tourism

Objectives

By the end of this chapter, you should be able to:
- appreciate the difficulty of defining travel and tourism
- understand the structure and organisation of travel and tourism
- appreciate the linkages between the different components of travel and tourism.

Introduction

This introductory chapter provides the contextual framework within which the marketing of travel and tourism can be explained and examined. It introduces the many sectors which make up the industry, describing their different roles and highlighting linkages and integration within the industry. The text then draws together the main marketing management theories, illustrating their relevance to travel and tourism.

Defining travel and tourism

Despite the fact that travel and tourism-related activities have been taking place for centuries, their evolution into a significant area of economic activity, supported by a vast array of organisations and destinations, has been relatively recent. Indeed, the boundaries of travel and tourism are still growing into new forms. It is important, therefore, to understand exactly what we mean by travel and tourism before applying to it a business philosophy, such as marketing.

The *Dictionary of Hospitality, Travel and Tourism* provides the following definitions of travel and tourism.

Travel:
'To make a journey from one place to another place by any means, for any purpose, with or without return to the original point of departure'

(Metelaka, 1990)

Tourism:
'Variously defined. Umbrella term for the variety of products and services offered and desired by people while away from home...Also:

1. The relationship and phenomena associated with the journeys and temporary visits of people travelling primarily for leisure and recreation
2. A sub-set of recreation; that form of recreation involving geographic mobility
3. The industries and activities that provide and market the services needed for pleasure travel.'

(Metelaka, 1990)

Clearly, travel and tourism are two distinct but related areas and many of the definitions offered have been concerned in part with the nature of that link. Two differing perspectives can be useful in exploring this link:

- definitions in terms of the activity of travelling or being a tourist
- definitions in terms of the industry or providers of services to travellers and tourists.

Defining travel and tourism in terms of providers, such as travel agents, gives us some boundaries but runs the risk of missing other relevant activities. The following discussion examines travel and tourism separately before going on to look at travel and tourism together as both industry and concept.

Travel

Clearly the concept of travel covers a wide range of ideas. This book is concerned with travel which is linked to tourism and usually requiring some sort of intermediary service from others. Distance is often influential in this respect. Travelling in a taxi within town is different from arranging an international flight or a day trip to the seaside. In the former case, the distance travelled is short, the primary purpose is transit rather than leisure, and customers make their own arrangements. In the other two cases, the distances are greater and the relative complexity of the task can require the service of a specialist to help the customer make the arrangements. In the case of the flight, the purpose remains transit, whilst the day trip clearly involves leisure. However, if the taxi driver offers a guided tour of the town, or is hired by the tourist for this purpose, she or he becomes, however briefly, involved in tourism. The airline similarly may be transporting tourists to a holiday destination.

The travel industry includes buses, coaches, trains, taxis and air travel. A rail company's main activities may be day-to-day commuting, providing a service for travelling small distances to and from work, suggesting a broader market than that for holidays. Should the same rail company also provide longer-distance business commuting to Europe, as does Eurostar, or offer leisure excursions, it may well be in competition with other tourism providers. A fundamental issue in travel and tourism is the very difficulty of definition as the boundaries of the industry are fluid. Issues relating to the structure of the industry are discussed later in the chapter. Levels of involvement in tourism are also discussed.

Tourism

As the definition above suggested, tourism has more specific connotations than does travel. It is clearly linked both to travel and leisure. However, this still leaves difficulties.

Providing a universally applicable definition of tourism is not easy, hence many previous attempts at this have been criticised. Indeed, a considerable amount of debate has surrounded many of the conceptual definitions that have been put forward.

Difficulties emerge mainly because of the number and variety of interpretations as to what exactly tourism is. That tourism takes place away from home and so involves an element of travel has been generally accepted, but less easily agreed are details regarding the amount of time that needs to be spent away from home in order for tourism to result. Attempts have also been made to define tourism in terms of distance travelled, but there are criticisms of this approach. Where distance has been used as a determining factor, there have been inconsistencies in terms of the distances used by different countries for example. Similarly, the idea of defining tourism according to the purpose of travel or the motivation for travel have met with disagreement in some cases.

One approach is to examine tourism in context and this is something that Mill and Morrison drew attention to:

'Tourism is a difficult phenomenon to describe...all tourism involves travel, yet not all travel is tourism. All tourism involves recreation yet not all tourism is recreation. All tourism occurs during leisure time, but not all leisure time is given to touristic pursuits.

(Mill and Morrison, 1985)

Bull has similarly placed tourism in its wider context:

'It is a human activity which encompasses human behaviour, use of resources, and interaction with other people, economies and environments. It also involves physical movement of tourists to locales other than their normal living places. Although most tourism around the world is a form of recreation, thus implying use of an individual's discretionary time, some tourism is inevitably linked with obligations, such as business or health requirements.'

(Bull, 1995)

The Tourism Society in the UK has adopted a short definition by Burkart and Medlik which is now widely accepted:

'The temporary, short term movement of people to destinations outside the places where they normally live and work, and their activities during their stay at these destinations.'

(Burkart and Medlik, 1974)

Despite the debate that has long surrounded conceptual definitions of tourism, technical definitions do exist and are mainly used when tourism surveys are being conducted in order to provide statistical data.

Although most definitions do not discuss destination, place is a central aspect of tourism and often an important contributor to the purpose of travel as well as the motivation for tourist activity in the first place.

Travel and tourism

We have seen that tourism can be defined according to a range of possible criteria, including distance travelled, destination, length of stay in the destination and purpose of travel. Inevitably therefore this includes both domestic and international travellers. It also covers business and leisure tourists, those visiting friends and relatives, excursionists and others. The tourism product is extremely diverse. In summary, it is essential for any definition of tourism to be sufficiently broad whilst recognising the potential for overlap with other activities. Using the concept of travel and length of stay provides some distinctions, but the boundaries remain both ambiguous and ever-changing. There is clearly an overlap between those activities, leisure or business, that may take place at home or at work compared with those that take place during a stay elsewhere.

Whilst some tourists will be mainly concerned with business or visiting friends and relatives, they may well fit in tourist activity as well. Travel therefore becomes an opportunity for tourism.

The above discussion hopefully illustrates the abstract nature of tourism. This has impacted heavily on the design of academic courses covering the area. One outcome of the rapid growth of travel and tourism has been the proliferation of related educational courses. Although tourism is now treated as a valid subject, it is one that can fall into a number of academic fields. Tourism courses are offered within departments of Geography, Business, Arts and Social Sciences, as well as by Schools of Hotel Management, amongst others. This exemplifies the diversity of tourism as well as the extent to which it can overlap with other disciplines.

Global tourism

According to the World Travel and Tourism Council (WTTC, 1995), travel and tourism is the world's largest industry and generator of jobs. The extent of international tourism has increased greatly since the Second World War. Latham (1998) has pointed to an average annual growth rate of more than 7 per cent between 1950 and 1990 as illustrated in Table 1.1 below.

Table 1.1 International tourism trends: arrivals and receipts worldwide, 1950–1996

	Arrivals (millions)	Receipts[a] ($US billions)
1950	25	2
1960	69	7
1970	166	18
1980	288	104
1990	457	260
1991	464	268
1992	502	306
1993	512	309
1994	537	341
1995	566	393
1996	592[b]	423[b]

a Excluding international travel
b Figures for 1996 are preliminary estimates

(WTO, 1996; BTA/ETB, 1997, cited in Latham, 1998)

Table 1.1 also shows that by 1995 international tourist arrivals had reached 566 million, representing an increase of 5 per cent on the previous year. Receipts from international tourism worldwide (excluding expenditure on international transport) rose by 15 per cent in the same period to $US 393 billion.

International tourism is not evenly spread throughout the world. The regional share of international tourist arrivals, together with their respective average annual percentage changes are shown in Table 1.2.

Table 1.2 International tourism in 1994: regional summary statistics

	Arrivals (millions)	Average annual % change in arrivals 1985-94	Receipts[a] ($US billion)	Average annual % change in receipts 1985-94
Africa	18.4	7.4	6.4	10.5
Americas	107.1	5.5	95.8	12.3
East Asia/Pacific	76.7	10.7	62.6	19.3
Europe	322.3	4.8	168.5	12.0
Middle East	9.2	4.4	5.0	0.0
South Asia	3.9	5.1	2.4	6.2
World	537.4	5.7	340.7	12.7

a Receipts exclude international travel

(WTO, 1996; cited in Latham, 1998)

Major destinations for international tourism include France, Spain, USA and Italy, whilst major generating countries include Germany, USA, Japan and the UK (WTO, 1995). The importance of Europe in terms of international tourism could be attributable to a number of factors, including levels of disposable income, an established infrastructure and tourism industry, as well as shorter distances to travel. Latham (1998) provides a comprehensive overview of international tourism activities, providing worldwide coverage split by WTO regions.

Patterns of tourist flows vary at different times for a whole variety of reasons. Destinations go in and out of popularity and environmental factors, such as political stability and economic circumstances, are influential. Overall, however, tourism has proved itself to be not only reactive in the short term but also resilient in the longer term. Tourism is a robust business.

Inbound, outbound and domestic tourism

Tourism can be classed as:

- *inbound* – involving tourists visiting a country from overseas
- *outbound* – involving residents of a country travelling overseas
- *domestic* – concerned with people who travel within their home country.

These three forms of tourism constitute the three fundamental market sectors. Both inbound and domestic tourism take place internally in the country concerned and can be grouped together as *internal tourism*. Part of the industry in any one country is likely to be concerned with attracting and catering for tourists coming to the country and for those travelling domestically, whilst the other part caters for those travelling overseas.

Domestic tourism

The domestic segment is perhaps the most ambiguous, merging into the broader leisure market, yet it is still a significant part of the tourism industry. The United Kingdom Tourism Survey (UKTS) measured domestic tourism in the UK market in 1994 at £14,495 million. The number of domestic holiday trips increased by 7.5 per cent overall between 1990 and 1994, despite a fall in the number of domestic holidays of four nights or longer. This reflects a rise in the number of domestic short breaks taken by holidaymakers in addition to a main overseas holiday (Key Note, 1996).

Despite the significance of domestic tourism overall, much of this is arranged without the involvement of the industry. In the UK, 80 per cent of domestic holidays use personal transport. The purpose of the domestic trip may be to visit friends or relatives and so accommodation is often provided. Where transport and accommodation are required, it is far easier for the domestic tourist to make his or her own arrangements directly with principals than it is for their foreign counterparts to do so. The trade, despite having a pivotal role in respect of outbound tourism, has far less involvement in the arrangement of domestic tourism. Table 1.3 highlights this difference in levels of involvement.

Table 1.3 Estimated share of the UK tourism market accounted for by travel agents and tour operators by value (%), 1997

	Travel agents	Tour operators
Domestic tourism	11	5
Outbound tourism	38	32
Total	49	37

(Key Note, 1998)

Outbound tourism

Most outbound tourists from the UK are travelling to other countries in Europe, especially France and Spain, although there is a trend towards long-haul destinations. The UK outbound holiday market is highly price-sensitive and so overseas holidays can be cheaper in some cases than domestic holidays.

The majority of outbound tourism from the UK is independently arranged, as Table 1.3 illustrates. Despite the fact that the outbound market shows more willingness to use the trade when making holiday arrangements than does the domestic market, it is worth noting that both travel agents and tour operators in the UK are losing share to the growth of independent travellers and direct bookings.

The travel and tourism industry

The difficulty of defining tourism leads to a difficulty in defining the travel and tourism industry. This problem has been recognised by a number of authors including Lickorish and Jenkins (1997). This problem is discussed below.

Industry or composite of organisations?

The very existence of a tourism industry has been disputed. Middleton (1994) informs us that the industry is one which is not recognised as such by economists. Bull (1995) goes further, describing tourism as neither a phenomenon nor a simple set of industries.

Although it is common to hear reference being made to *the industry*, it might more usefully be described as a *composite of organisations involved in servicing the needs of tourists*. Certainly, activities related to travel and tourism cross more than one industrial sector. For the purposes of discussions about tourism, these organisations are often regrouped to form a notional *tourism industry*. In keeping with what has been said above, authors such as Mill and Morrison (1985) emphasise the importance of viewing tourism as a *process* rather than an industry.

For the purposes of this text, the term 'industry' is used in reference to the composite of organisations involved in the provision of travel and tourism. 'The trade' is similarly adopted to describe tour operators and retail travel agencies and other players involved in similar functions. The distinction between the different industry suppliers is discussed later in the chapter. These organisations are of widely differing types and fall into various categories, including public sector, private sector and quasi-autonomous organisations. In addition to this, they have different roles, functions, funding, etc. The majority, however, are service-based organisations and this has implications for marketing – a concept we shall return to in Chapter 2.

Describing the heterogeneous suppliers and facilitators of tourism as an industry represents an attempt to provide coherence. There have also been attempts to bring together the homogeneous aspects of the industry into clusters such as consortia. An example of a hotel consortia is provided below.

THE LEADING HOTELS OF THE WORLD LTD

The Leading Hotels of the World Ltd is a sales, marketing and reservations organisation, headquartered in New York City, with 15 regional offices in major cities worldwide.

The organisation, established in 1928 by a group of European hoteliers had 38 initial members and was then called The Luxury Hotels of Europe and Egypt. The organisation opened a New York office in the same year and called it Hotel Representative Inc. (HRI), to provide direct contact with both American and Canadian travellers and travel agents. The Leading Hotels of the World is still an HRI company today.

Following the Second World War and the subsequent travel boom of the 1950s and 1960s, HRI grew to represent 70 European hotels. Further expansion took place in the early 1970s, when it was decided that the organisation should try to attract new members. These new members were mainly luxury hotels in Europe, but as others from around the world were also being incorporated, the name was changed to The Leading Hotels of the World Ltd, to reflect their increasingly international portfolio of properties.

Further international expansion took place in the late 1970s when several offices were opened in South and Central America. The organisation today is comprised of 310 city and resort hotels in 68 countries.

The governing body of the organisation is the Executive Committee, comprised solely of European hoteliers. Each European country or group of countries elects a representative hotelier to sit on the Committee. The Committee itself nominates the Chairman and Vice Chairman.

Requirements for membership

Requirements for acceptance to become a member of The Leading Hotels of the World Ltd dictate that a hotel must be of the deluxe/luxury category and must meet the highest standards of excellence with respect to service, physical structure, management, cuisine and all aspects of guest comfort. The organisation does not solicit new members. Rather, hotels must apply for membership. Applications are carefully screened by a committee of hoteliers. Hotels which appear to meet the requirements are then inspected by two professional hoteliers who visit the hotel for a minimum of two days. This thorough inspection of all public areas, guest accommodation and food and beverage facilities, as well as the back-of-house areas, pays particular attention to the staff and service. Following this, reports are filed with the Executive Committee, members of which are asked to vote. The most eminent properties are accepted. Each member hotel is periodically reinspected.

(Leading Hotels of the World, 1997)

Different sizes of organisation

A final point to note regarding the multi-faceted nature of the industry is that there are many different sizes of organisation. A degree of polarisation can be seen, with large organisations, such as many of the airlines and hotel chains, at one end of the scale and a proliferation of small firms, such as restaurants and bed and breakfast establishments, at the other end.

The differing roles and types of involvement of a range of organisations in the travel and tourism industry are summarised in Figure 1.1.

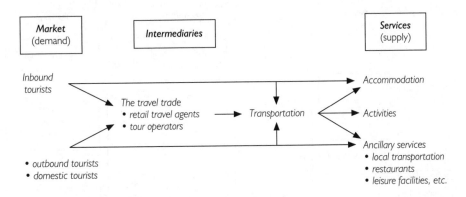

Figure 1.1 The travel and tourism industry

Tourism is not therefore an aggregate of organisations but a process which draws on many players. We will now look at the roles performed by these different players in more detail.

Tourists

Before looking at the *supply side* of tourism – the combination of organisations involved in the provision of services for tourists, it is worthwhile examining the *demand side* – the tourists. Numerous factors influence the demand for tourism and these include economic, social and cultural factors.

We have already seen that tourism involves not only those people travelling for pleasure, but also those travelling for reasons connected to work. Globally, people are travelling more than ever. The number of people travelling internationally can be illustrated by comparing the figures for 1950 with those for 1996, as shown in Table 1.1 (page 5).

Explanations for the increasing numbers of people making journeys include the following.

● People now have more leisure time than in the past.
● There is now paid holiday leave.
● Package holidays have made overseas travel in particular more affordable.
● The increase in world trade and the globalisation of many businesses has led to demand for more business travel.

Richards (in Lickorish and Jenkins, 1997) believes that tourism is best viewed through an appraisal of the demand side and the way in which the tourist spend is spread throughout a wide range of primary, secondary and tertiary industries and services as the tourist travels around. The trade contribution to the tourism industry has thus been structured in terms of the direct interdependence and level of direct earnings from tourism, as shown in Figure 1.2.

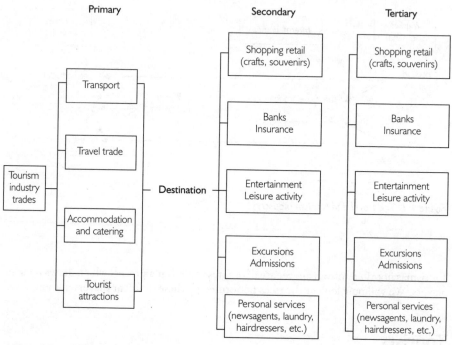

(Adapted from Richards, in Lickorish and Jenkins, *An Introduction to Tourism*, Butterworth-Heinemann, 1997: reproduced with permission)

Figure 1.2 Tourism industry trades

Unsurprisingly it is the travel trade, transport and accommodation elements, as well as catering facilities and tourist attractions, that make up the primary tourist trades. The secondary trades comprise those organisations that benefit directly from the expenditure of tourists, whilst tertiary trades are those which benefit indirectly.

We will now look at the roles performed by the primary and secondary tourism trades. A *principal* in the travel and tourism industry is the person or organisation supplying a service. Typically, these include transport or accommodation suppliers, such as hotels and airlines.

The principals

Accommodation suppliers

Accommodation is a vital element of the supply side of tourism. Tourists today are faced with a wide choice of accommodation. This accommodation stock, which is part of a vast and complex global industry, reflects the needs of modern-day tourists.

The accommodation sector is comprised of a mixture of commercial and non-commercial organisations. Commercial accommodation intends to earn profit for the provider, whereas this is not the case in the non-commercial sector. Privately-owned tents and caravans are non-commercial as are home exchanges and visits to friends and relatives. For some tourism businesses, the provision of accommodation may be a necessary part of their overall operation rather than a means of profit generation in its own right. A further distinction is that between serviced and non-serviced accommodation. Many suppliers are becoming more flexible in this respect, providing optional services.

Tourist accommodation includes hotels, bed and breakfast establishments, camping and caravaning, holiday cottages, timeshares, youth hostels, university campuses, and many others. Hotels are hugely important to travel and tourism, yet the hotel sector even in most developed countries is still highly fragmented. Many hotel companies are privately-owned companies which are not quoted on the Stock Exchange. A number of large hotel chains do exist, however, and many of these are becoming global in their ambitions. Groups such as Hilton International, Accor and Sheraton have well-known international brands.

Another popular development in the accommodation sector has been the introduction of timeshare to the market. The concept of timeshare is that apartments or chalets are sold to a number of different owners, each of whom has a right to use it for a given period each year. There are organisations such as RCI which specialise in the exchange of timeshare accommodation.

Accommodation as a central focus at a built resort has long been a popular concept, although consumer preferences for different resort types have varied. The Butlin's-style holiday 'camps' were popular in the post-war years, whilst more recently holiday 'villages' in the style of Center Parcs have gained in popularity. Resort-style hotels are currently popular in certain locations.

The growth in type and variety of accommodation provision has led to increased consumer choice. Further developments are likely in the future as competition becomes more fierce.

Transport suppliers

Road transport

The transport sector is large. Independent travellers often use their own transport, usually cars, especially when travel is domestic. As we saw earlier, 80 per cent of domestic travellers in the UK use personal transport. When travelling overseas, the addition of a second form of transport may be necessary – typically cars and their passengers will be transported aboard ferries or trains such as Le Shuttle. Buses and coaches are popular with particular types of traveller, such as groups of school children and older people. Taxis and hire cars also play a part in the transportation of tourists. Once again a combination of transport forms is possible, with holidays based on the fly-drive concept proving popular.

Air transport

Air transportation is particularly important to the overseas package holiday market. The package holiday concept really only gained in popularity following the Second World War when air transport became more easily available. The majority of overseas package holidays today include air transportation, although some are based on rail or coach travel.

Clearly, for destinations at any real distance from the generating country, the advantage of air travel is reduced journey time. High-speed trains are however competitive for shorter journeys.

The majority of air inclusive tours (AITs) use chartered as opposed to scheduled flights. Chartered flights are distinguished by charter conditions including flight times and levels of service. The operation of charter flights tends to be more restrictive than the operation of scheduled flights. Tour operators may own a charter carrier or alternatively contract for capacity on an aircraft for a finite period of time. Monarch Airlines is a major UK charter airline which is not linked to a major tour operator. Some tour operators, particularly the smaller, more specialist ones use scheduled airline capacity.

The operation of air transport in Europe is currently experiencing change following a process of deregulation since the early 1990s. This has involved the effective removal of many of the regulations surrounding air transport, including fares and route entry, as occurred in North America with the Airline Deregulation Act in 1978. The final phase of deregulation, or liberalisation as it is known in Europe, took place in the European Union (EU) in April 1997. This means any European carrier can operate services to, from and within any other European country should the necessary take-off and landing slots be available. The most significant effect of this for European travel and tourism to date has been the development of low-cost carriers such as easyJet and Ryanair. This is currently reinforcing a reduction in the distinction between scheduled and charter operations. It also means the recent development of regional routes in Europe is likely to continue. The increased competition is currently leading to a reduction in the cost of flying in Europe. Comprehensive coverage of the air transport sector is provided by Hanlon (1996).

Rail transport
The original package holiday was built around rail transport. Thomas Cook, one of the early pioneers of inclusive tours, chartered his first train, for a journey between Leicester and Loughborough, in 1841. Over the following few years Cook developed commercial excursions using chartered trains.

Rail travel is also used by independent travellers. Extended holidays travelling around Europe by train are popular amongst younger travellers in particular. At the other end of the spectrum, train journeys such as those on the Orient Express provide transportation in the most luxurious of settings. Developments in high-speed rail travel are making the train competitive with air transportation for journey times of around three hours. A significant European development in rail travel has been the introduction of the Channel Tunnel between the UK and France, offering both passenger rail services on Eurostar and Le Shuttle, a vehicle-carrying rail operation. The introduction of Eurotunnel services in 1994 produced tough competition for continental ferry routes.

Sea transport
Ferry companies are heavily involved in the tourism industry in many parts of the world offering short sea crossings. Originally operated as a fairly basic mode of transport, ferries have become more competitive in the face of competition from new forms of sea transport, including the hovercraft, the catamaran and the hydrofoil. In response to such competition generally and to the development of the Channel Tunnel in Europe, ferry companies have greatly improved their products to the extent that many offer services which can be described as mini cruises.

The cruise market in general is a main growth area in tourism. Transport is even more integral to this sort of package holiday as it is not merely the means of reaching destinations, but also integrates the accommodation as well as a variety of other services.

International Passenger Survey (IPS) data suggests that sea-inclusive holidays have diminished more as inclusive tours through Eurotunnel have increased. Key Note report that a number of ferry operators have pulled out of running their own tour operating divisions (Key Note, 1998). A major problem in recent years has been that of over-capacity in the ferry industry.

The principals described above are usually involved in some way with the trade.

The trade

The trade is comprised of those companies specialising, usually exclusively, in the organisation of travel and tourism activities. The complex structure of this part of the industry will now be examined. This will be followed by consideration of the role of related organisations such as trade bodies and official organisations.

Tour operators

Tour operators package together the different components of tours or holidays and sell these to the public, either directly or through a travel agent. Inclusive tours (ITs) are popular because they are packages of accommodation, transportation and other services offered at one price. These can remove aspects of risk and uncertainty which some people associate with overseas travel in particular. The following discussion is mainly concerned with outbound, as opposed to incoming and domestic tour operators which are covered in the following section.

The activity of packaging together the individual elements that make up a holiday involves tour operators in a variety of tasks such as researching destinations, negotiating with principals for supply, and the production of tour brochures. Brochure production is covered in Chapter 11, but the process of researching destinations and negotiating with principals require further description here.

Researching destinations is a fundamental aspect in the organisation of a tour operator's programme for any one season as it enables the company to identify the relative strengths and weaknesses of different resorts before committing resources to tour production and marketing. Factors such as tourist infrastructure, political stability, economy and market trends will all need to be considered.

Having selected appropriate destinations for inclusion in a portfolio of holidays, the next stage will be to negotiate the supply of services in order to create the tour package. It is here that tour operators use the fact that they are making bulk purchases to negotiate a price that the individual consumer could not achieve. This bargaining power increases as greater amounts of supply are contracted for and with longer periods of commitment. There are clear advantages here for the larger tour operator negotiating services at popular resorts for which their research has produced strong growth forecasts. The smaller more specialist company offering packages to less popular locations may not achieve the same discounts in contracting for services.

Negotiations with accommodation suppliers are typically for a season, although this varies. There may be a cut-off date at which rooms reserved for the tour operator are released back into general sales and there may be dates in high season when the rooms are not negotiable as the hotel can make greater returns on these themselves. Each contract will inevitably have its own particular clauses.

Negotiations with airlines are similarly varied. It may be the case that the tour operator is linked to its own charter airline and so has its own transport supply. Independent charter airlines also sell capacity to tour operators for specified time periods. Such an arrangement could be for an entire aircraft for a whole season or for a number of seats on a particular weekly flight.

Tour operators earn profit not only by charging more for the package than it cost them to create it, but also by holding deposits for as long as possible and perhaps speculating on foreign currency, as well as through the sale of additional services.

The tour operations sector includes:

- *mass market operators*, which arrange travel for the majority of holidaymakers on inclusive tours. These organisations are concerned with the achievement of high sales volumes
- *specialist tour operators*, which tend to deal with niche products and niche markets, perhaps focusing on a type of consumer, a geographic area or a particular activity.

The distinction between the two categories of operator is however blurring somewhat, as we see more and more mass market operators offering specialist products. Key Note (1998) describes several sectors of the package holiday market as having moved from being niche markets to mass markets, citing certain long-haul destinations, cruising and weekend breaks as examples.

There is a general trend towards more flexible package holidays. Specialist tour operators offer packages which can be altered. Ski specialist, Ski Independence, can alter a week or a ten-day ski package in Colorado by the addition of a city break at either end of the holiday, for example. Particularly where the airlines used have a wide network of routes in the destination country, such add-ons can be easily and cheaply arranged.

According to Key Note, there were 613 registered Association of British Travel Agents (ABTA) tour operators in July 1995. In common with the retail travel sector, the mass market end of the tour operations market is highly concentrated. The top five tour operators increased their share of the AIT market from 60 per cent to around 70 per cent between 1991 and 1994 (Key Note, 1996). Table 1.4 illustrates this concentration in terms of shares of overseas package holiday sales.

Table 1.4 The top five AIT tour operators' shares of foreign package holiday sales, by volume (%), 1996

Tour operator	Share of sales (%)
Thomson	25
Airtours	16
First Choice	10
Sunworld	5
Cosmos	2

(Adapted from Key Note, 1998, Travel Agents and Overseas Tour Operators based on Monopolies and Merger Commission (MMC) figures)

It is not only AITs that offer package holidays, coach operators such as Wallace Arnold and Shearings have long been involved in the production of package holidays, especially short breaks. Holloway (1994) offers a detailed analysis of the tour operations sector.

Incoming tour operators, ground handlers and handling agents

Incoming tour operators deal with clients from overseas who may have booked their travel in their home country, possibly through a tour operator based in that country. Incoming tour operators offer packages and sometimes tailor-made programmes as well. They are often confused with handling agents and ground handlers both of whom provide a similar service. Handling agents and ground handlers offer transfers from arrival points in a country to accommodation facilities.

In the UK, the British Incoming Tour Operators' Association (BITOA) – described below – represents the commercial and political interests of incoming tour operators and suppliers to the inbound tourism industry.

THE BRITISH INCOMING TOUR OPERATORS' ASSOCIATION

BITOA was established in 1977. The membership of the association includes national and regional tourist boards, tour operators, hoteliers, transportation companies, heritage sites, attractions and other suppliers.

The primary objectives of BITOA
- To promote tourism to Britain, and to ensure that overseas operators work with a BITOA member.
- To ensure that BITOA members adopt ethical 'best practice' procedures with clients and suppliers.
- To encourage BITOA members to adopt eco-friendly practice in their business.
- To encourage BITOA members to improve educational and training programmes.
- To represent the political interests of BITOA members in Whitehall, Westminster and Brussels.

Commercial opportunities for BITOA members
A number of opportunities are available to members including:
- the opportunity to exhibit at domestic and overseas exhibitions at reduced rates
- free unlimited use of the BITOA Legal Hotline
- subsidised educational, training and familiarisation programmes
- free listing in the BITOA Handbook distributed worldwide
- monthly updates on the travel industry through BITOA mailings.

(BITOA)

Incentive travel organisers

Travel can be used by companies as an incentive for both staff and clients. Used as a motivational tool in this way, travel can help productivity and performance. In this sense, incentive travel can be regarded as a modern management technique. Incentive travel organisers (ITOs), sometimes referred to as 'incentive houses', arrange this type of travel on behalf of companies. Specialised programmes may be designed to meet the particular needs of the employer or employee. An incentive house in Spain may liaise with employers from countries such as the UK and the USA and devise different programmes for their employees. This is similar to the provision of corporate hospitality, such as a day trip to watch a major sporting event which may have the added value of a champagne reception or gourmet lunch. Davidson (1994) provides detailed coverage of the use, by companies, of incentive travel together with the role of ITOs.

Group travel organisers

Many clubs, societies and organisations will have group outings or holidays arranged by a group travel organiser (GTO). These individuals often work voluntarily yet can generate vast amounts of business for the travel trade. Typically, retirement and social clubs, theatre groups and Women's Institute groups have a key travel organiser of this type. Schools or other educational institutions are also often involved as unpaid intermediaries in the organisation of group travel. Reaching these important individuals can be a cost-effective way of attracting a number of potential consumers at once.

Travel agents

Travel agents are involved in the distribution of both principals' and tour operators' products. Some travel agents also package their own tour programmes for sale. From a principal's point of view, travel agents offer them a network of outlets through which they may be able to sell their products. The consumer is offered a convenient, often city centre location, as well as a multitude of other benefits, including the availability of ancillary products for sale.

There are several ways in which travel agents can be categorised, but most commonly this is done by size. The main distinction here is between the multiple travel agents and the independents. The multiples are the larger groups – the well-known names in the high street. The independents are the small firms with a single branch or a small number of branches.

Another means of categorising travel agents is by type of business conducted. The main distinction is between holiday shops and business travel agents, although general agents do also exist. Business travel agents deal with travel for reasons connected with work. This market tends to display many characteristics which distinguish them from typical holidaymakers. Their needs from a travel agent are therefore also different. A number of specialist 'business houses' exist, including some which are linked to the better known holiday or leisure agents. Business travel agents tend to be part of a multiple or a well-known independent. They are usually highly specialised and in some cases establish a small branch, known as an in-plant operation, at a client's premises.

According to Key Note there were 6,994 registered ABTA travel agent offices in the UK in July 1995. Retail travel is a highly concentrated sector, with the top four travel agents increasing their share of the AIT market from 48 per cent to 54 per cent between 1991 and 1994 (Key Note, 1996). Reservations and bookings agents also exist, offering a similar but highly specialist service for a narrow product range such as hotels.

Travel agents differ from other retailers in several respects. They hold no physical stock and have no financial stake in the products they are selling. In other words, travel agents do not tend to carry a great deal of risk in comparison to tour operators. Traditionally travel agents have earned commission payments for bookings made. The exact percentage commisssion rate varies by type of product and by company, but a figure of around 9 per cent is not unusual. Additional earnings are derived from overrides (an increase in the level of commission not linked to sales performance) or incentive payments (an increase based on reaching a certain level of sales), as well as from sales of ancillary services and such like. The operation of travel agents is covered fully by Renshaw (1997). ABTA has already been mentioned and due to the public exposure currently achieved by the Association it is worth outlining (below) the role that it performs for the industry although this role is likely to change in the future.

THE ASSOCIATION OF BRITISH TRAVEL AGENTS (ABTA)

ABTA is a trade association, with both travel agent and tour operator members, which was formed in 1950. The original objectives of the organisation included 'to promote and develop the general interests of all Members of the Association' and 'to do all such things as may be deemed necessary or expedient to raise the prestige and status of Members of the Association'. These objectives suggest both a commercial and a regulatory role.

Today, ABTA members operate under strict codes of conduct. The association has both a Tour Operators' Code of Conduct and a Travel Agents' Code of Conduct which set comprehensive guidelines for members. They also apply financial checks of members and provide financial protection for consumers. ABTA has a further role in complaints resolution as they offer a low cost, independent arbitration scheme to ABTA members' clients, administered by the Chartered Institute of Arbitrators.

ABTA is concerned to solve problems such as the financial failure of, or inadequate performance by, tour operators or travel agents which can damage the reputation of the travel trade as a whole, and so it has become an independent, self-regulatory body. Financial protection for the consumer has been provided in the form of individual company bonds and funds contributed by members. Security was initially introduced by a rule in 1965 which became known as Stabiliser stating that an ABTA member tour operator selling foreign inclusive holidays and other travel arrangements through a third party could only do so through ABTA member travel agents. Similarly, ABTA travel agents could only sell ABTA tour operators' foreign holiday packages. Although restrictive, this practice was seen to be in the public interest by the Restrictive Practices Court in 1982 and was allowed to continue. Stabiliser was finally removed by ABTA in 1993 as it was no longer required following implementation of the Package Travel Regulations in the United Kingdom at the end of 1992.

(ABTA, 1998)

Tourist boards

Even when the trade and the principals in travel and tourism are taken together, they do not adequately describe the many organisations involved in the industry. It is thus necessary to consider the many other types of organisation involved in travel and tourism.

In many parts of the world, an important role in stimulating demand from overseas is performed by *national tourist boards*. In Britain the 1969 Development of Tourism Act was instrumental in setting up the national tourist boards.

The British Tourist Authority (BTA) is the statutory body responsible for the promotion of Britain overseas. In so doing, the BTA works closely with the other national and regional tourist boards in the UK. The structure of the tourist board network in Scotland is outlined in Figure 1.3.

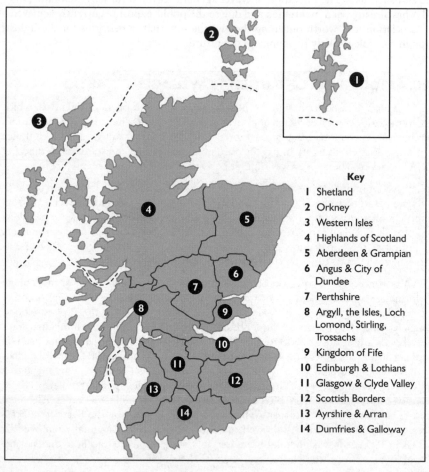

Key

1 Shetland
2 Orkney
3 Western Isles
4 Highlands of Scotland
5 Aberdeen & Grampian
6 Angus & City of Dundee
7 Perthshire
8 Argyll, the Isles, Loch Lomond, Stirling, Trossachs
9 Kingdom of Fife
10 Edinburgh & Lothians
11 Glasgow & Clyde Valley
12 Scottish Borders
13 Ayrshire & Arran
14 Dumfries & Galloway

(STB)

Figure 1.3 Scotland's area tourist boards (ATBs)

The BTA is a government sponsored agency, although in real terms there has been a reduction to grant-in-aid funding of tourist boards in recent years. The role of the tourist boards in the UK has been becoming necessarily more commercial in recent years for this reason.

The main responsibilities of the BTA are summarised by their new vision statement (see below).

A NEW VISION STATEMENT FOR BTA

To build the value of tourism to Britain

By:
- generating additional tourism revenue, throughout Britain and throughout the year
- promoting Britain as a tourist destination worldwide
- generating more value from customers in key overseas markets
- providing impartial tourist information
- gathering and disseminating market intelligence
- developing new business for the longer term
- encouraging a sustainable level of tourism for visitors and residents alike.

While:
- speaking for the whole of Britain on inbound tourism
- developing the quality of our people as a key strategic resource.

(BTA, 1998)

The public sector role in tourism is not, however, confined to the tourist boards. Taking Scotland as an example, in addition to the Scottish Tourist Board (STB) there are two other main bodies directly involved in Scottish tourism, namely Highlands and Islands Enterprise (HIE) and Scottish Enterprise (SE). All three are funded through the Scottish Office Industry Department (SOID). Co-ordination is through the Scottish Tourism Co-ordinating Group. Other public bodies involved in Scottish tourism include Historic Scotland (an organisation which protects the built heritage and operates visitor attractions), the Scottish Arts Council, the Scottish Museums Council, the Scottish Sports Council and Scottish Natural Heritage. The Forestry Commission also has some involvement in tourism, as do local authorities (LAs) and the BTA. Fourteen area tourist boards (ATBs) operate in Scotland in conjunction with STB and their relevant (LA) as well as the trade. Local tourism businesses are encouraged to become members of the ATB. The main functions of ATBs are to service visitor needs, particularly through a nationwide network of tourist information centres (TICs), and to market the area. Local enterprise companies (LECs) also exist and their role is concerned with development and stimulation of the local economy. Clearly this is not necessarily indicative of the role of the public sector in tourism elsewhere in the world, and in practice this role varies between countries.

Destinations

When examining destinations, an initial difficulty arises in that destinations are complex and come in a variety of types and sizes. Destination can describe a city, a region or a country.

Destination companies

In addition to public sector involvement in the co-ordination of tourism, tourist destinations are increasingly likely to have a *destination management* or *marketing company*. This is usually composed of a number of members and allows for a certain amount of integration between companies. A destination marketing organisation could be anything from residents with an interest in tourism to a national tourist board. Clearly, it is not easy to generalise about the role of these players. *Destination management plans* are also becoming more common, as are *tourism development strategies*.

Destination image is an important factor in the marketing of destinations. The way that consumers view a destination has the potential to influence their choice of holiday and so measurement of this has become an important aspect of tourism planning and marketing. Seaton and Bennett (1996) examine the characteristics of destinations and their images, together with some of the methods used to market them.

Visitor attractions

The visitor attractions sector is very broad. It can, however, be broken down into particular categories of attractions. A distinction is often made between 'man-made' (built) attractions and natural attractions, which are typically geographical phenomena. Popular tourist attractions include country parks, wildlife parks, theme parks, factories and other industrial sites, museums and art galleries and such like. Events can also be seen to be attractions, even past events. Certain events are natural, as say a volcanic eruption, whilst others are 'man-made', such as a festival or a concert.

Often forgotten, but highly important to the tourism industry, is a whole variety of ancillary services. Restaurants and other food outlets contribute greatly to the tourism infrastructure of a destination although often they exist primarily to serve local markets. Similarly, retail shops can derive a great deal of their income from tourist expenditure although this is often not their primary market. Some restaurants and shops are aimed at the tourist market, whilst many exist only at the periphery of tourism. Other commercial organisations, including banks, laundries and petrol stations, offer services to tourists, but seldom see them as their main market. Tourists can benefit greatly from their existence nonetheless.

As has been discussed, the different services involved in meeting the needs of tourists may also have other functions unrelated to the sphere of tourism. Each will have their own level of involvement in servicing the needs of tourists. This involvement can occur at different stages in the tourist experience. Attractions may have a broader role than the attraction of tourists. Similarly, a local festival may exist to meet the needs of a local community whilst also acting as an important attraction for tourists.

The potential tourist role of other ancillary services may be less obvious but can still be very important. As an example, a shopping centre or a local restaurant may see its primary function as serving the requirements of the local population. However, it may well play a role in supporting, even attracting, tourist activity through the sale of souvenirs or the provision of good quality local cuisine. The MetroCentre in Gateshead in the north east of England is a good example of this (see below).

METROCENTRE

Europe's largest shopping and leisure centre, the MetroCentre, attracts almost 28 million visitors annually. Although many of these shoppers are local, visitors come from as far afield as Norway and coaches regularly bring day-trippers from Cumbria, Glasgow, Sheffield and elsewhere. The centre aims to fulfil the needs of an age with increasing time for leisure. To this end, the centre contains not only 360 shops and stores but also an 11-studio UCI multiplex cinema, the first of its type in a British shopping centre, a 28-lane, 10-pin bowling centre and Metroland, Europe's biggest indoor theme park. The theme park concept came from Canada where malls such as the Woodbine Centre in Toronto successfully integrate an indoor theme park into the shopping experience. By combining shopping with leisure in this way, MetroCentre claims to be an ideal choice for a day out for all the family. The centre also has more than 50 restaurants, bars and cafes, including a 650-seater food court.

MetroCentre has three distinct target markets. The primary market consists of the one and a half million residents living within 30 minutes of the centre. The secondary market is the three million who live within one hour's travelling time and the tertiary market are those living elsewhere in the UK and in key European areas, such as Scandanavia. The centre currently has a budget of just over £1 million to support its marketing effort.

Marketing activities include spectacular decorations at Christmas which help the centre to attract more than six million visitors from throughout the UK and abroad during November and December. MetroCentre also implements a regular programme of interactive promotions and events such as a Family Festival held during the summer holidays. In addition, the centre hosts exhibitions which can be seen to be a travel and tourism activity in itself.

Each year MetroCentre welcomes more than 7,000 coach trips and many companies have become regular visitors. Airlines and shipping companies bring thousands of overseas visitors from Norway, Germany, Holland and Iceland each week for shopping weekend breaks. Many of the centre's visitors who are staying for the weekend take advantage of the special MetroCentre rates that have been negotiated at several hotels in the area.

Recognising the importance of this 'tourist' market, MetroCentre's marketing team host familiarisation tours for group travel organisers, coach operators and others in the travel and tourism market.

(MetroCentre)

The degree to which facilities such as MetroCentre might be considered part of the tourist industry will depend on how distinctive and important a role they play in supporting tourist activity. Their role as a catalyst in attracting tourists to an area is often highly regarded locally.

A service provider may straddle a number of roles in the travel and tourism industry. Although the principal role of a hotel will be the provision of accommodation, it may also provide transportation and leisure facilities for guests, whilst some even act as intermediaries, organising other tourist activities for guests. Similarly, transport operators such as rail companies may offer entire 'tour packages', whilst some visitor attractions will additionally be able to offer overnight acommodation to visitors.

A further feature of travel and tourism is integration and this is discussed next.

Integration within the industry

Integration between companies is a common feature in the travel industry. This occurs when one organisation merges with or takes over another. This process can be:

- *horizontal* Horizontal integration takes place between organisations which are at the same level in the chain of distribution, for example when one chain of travel agents purchases another.
- *vertical* Vertical integration occurs between organisations at different levels in the chain of distribution.

The concept of integration is covered more fully in Chapter 10, *Distributing travel and tourism products*.

Summary

The demand for travel and tourism increased during the latter half of the twentieth century as a result of increased leisure time availability, an increase in paid holidays, the development of air transportation and inclusive tours. The latter have encouraged more travel by offering package holidays which are often associated in the consumer's mind with fewer risks, particularly when travel is overseas.

It is all too easy to look at tourism in terms of the different sectors of the industry but, as stated above, tourism is not just an aggregate of merely commercial activities; it is a complex and multi-faceted business. The industry is highly segmented, with a proliferation of small companies. Polarisation is also evident as demonstrated by the many large and international airlines and hotels. A plethora of ancilliary services surrounds the core tourism businesses. Governments also play a role in tourism, often a co-ordinating role, whilst destination management is an area of growing importance to many tourist receiving areas. Tourism itself is becoming more global, reflecting a trend which can also be seen at the organisational level.

References and bibliography

Burkart, A J. and Medlik, S. (1974) *Tourism: Past Present and Future*, Heinemann.

Bull, A. (1995) *The Economics of Travel and Tourism*, 2nd edition, Longman

Davidson, R. (1994) *Business Travel*, Pitman

Hanlon, P. (1996) *Global Airlines Competition in a Transnational Industry*, Butterworth-Heinemann

Holloway, J.C. (1994) *The Business of Tourism*, 4th edition, Pitman

Key Note Market Review (1996) *UK Travel and Tourism*

Key Note Market Review (1998) *Travel Agents and Overseas Tour Operators*

Latham, J. (1998) Patterns of international tourism, *Progress in Tourism and Hospitality Research*, Vol. 4, pp 45–52, John Wiley & Sons Ltd

Laws, E. (1997) *Managing Packaged Tourism: Relationships, Responsibilities and Service Quality in the Inclusive Holiday Industry*, International Thomson Publishing (ITP)

Lickorish, L.J. and Jenkins, C.L. (eds) (1997) *An Introduction to Tourism*, Butterworth-Heinemann

Metelaka, C.J. (1990) *The Dictionary of Hospitality, Travel and Tourism*, 3rd edition, Delmar

Middleton, V.T.C. (1994) *Marketing in Travel and Tourism*, Heinemann

Mill, R. C. and Morrison, A. M. (1985) *The Tourism System: An Introductory Text*, Prentice Hall Inc.

Renshaw, M.B (1997) *The Travel Agent*, 2nd edition, Business Education Publishers Ltd

Seaton, A.V. and Bennett, M.M. (1996) *Marketing Tourism Products: Concepts, Issues, Cases*, ITP

STB *Promoting Excellence: Tourism in Scotland Today*, Scottish Tourist Board

WTO (1995) *World Tourism Trends 1985–1994 and Forecasts to the Year 2000 and Beyond*, World Tourism Organisation

WTO (1996) *Yearbook of Tourism Statistics*, World Tourism Organisation

WTTC (1995) *Travel and Tourism's Economic Perspective*, World Travel and Tourism Council

2 Introduction to travel and tourism marketing

Objectives

By the end of this chapter you should be able to:
- define marketing
- identify a marketing orientation
- understand the marketing philosophy
- appreciate the need for successful travel and tourism marketing
- recognise the difficulties inherent in marketing tourism services.

Introduction

This chapter introduces travel and tourism marketing. It provides an overview of the marketing process, the individual elements of which are considered more closely in the following chapters. Before we can examine the management of the marketing function, we must fully understand the marketing concept. The chapter looks at definitions of marketing and briefly considers the development of this business philosophy before going on to examine the marketing of services and tourism services in particular.

Defining marketing

Marketing is often said to start and end with the consumer and indeed this emerges as a core aspect of the many definitions of marketing. The intention here is to start by looking at a selection of these varied definitions of marketing and to attempt to summarise their key elements.

One commonly accepted definition of marketing is that proposed by the British Chartered Institute of Marketing:

'Marketing is the management process which identifies, anticipates and supplies customer requirements efficiently and profitably.'

(Annual Report)

The importance of understanding markets is evident here with the focus being on the consumer and their needs. This definition has, however, met with some objections because of the inclusion of the word 'profitably' as profit need not be an objective of a company adopting the marketing philosophy. Perhaps less contentious is the following definition, put forward by the highly regarded American marketing academic, Philip Kotler:

'Marketing is a social and managerial process by which individuals and groups obtain what they need and want through creating, offering and exchanging products of value with others.'

(Kotler, 1994)

Kotler has described marketing management as:

'the process of planning and executing the conception, and distribution of goods, services, and ideas to create exchanges with target groups that satisfy customer and organizational objectives.'

(Kotler, 1994)

Essentially marketing management describes a process of planning, organising, implementation and control. Several authors, concerned that readers may develop too narrow a view of marketing, have pointed out that the actions involved in this process described above need not be confined to typical products. Indeed, marketing activity is not restricted to physical goods. Objects of marketing activity include political candidates, charities, educational establishments, as well as the often cited examples of fast-moving consumer goods, such as baked beans, and consumer durables, such as cars.

Another important way of looking at marketing is as a process which matches the capabilities of a company with customer needs. In this way the objectives of both can hopefully be met. Exchange processes are clearly an important outcome of marketing activity. All potential customers with a particular need or want and who may engage in exchange to satisfy this need or want constitute a market. The market for travel in general could therefore be said to consist of all potential customers with a need or a want to travel. Economists describe a collection of buyers and sellers who transact over a particular product or product type as a market.

Marketing is often confused with both selling and promotion. Promotion and selling are, however, sub-sets of marketing. Although marketing involves both selling and promotion, it encompasses other activities in addition to these. Drucker explained the distinction between marketing and selling:

'Marketing is not only much broader than selling, it is not a specialised activity at all. It encompasses the whole business. It is the whole business seen from the point of view of its final result, that is from the customer's point of view. Concern and responsibility for marketing must therefore permeate all areas of the enterprise.'

(Drucker, 1994)

Some basic themes can be identified from the many and varied definitions of marketing that exist.

- Marketing is a philosophy whereby an organisation achieves its objectives with a customer orientation supported by an integrated corporate effort. Marketing decision-making revolves around the customer, their needs and wants.
- Marketing involves the management of organisational functions with a concern for customers. The crucial factor here is not the job titles given to such roles but the fact that they are managed with the correct orientation and integrated with each other and the rest of the organisation's activities.

Understanding marketing requires an appreciation of the fact that consumers are interested in products which offer them benefits, rather than in the features displayed by products. Marketing activities themselves are expensive and so understanding of them is necessary to guide expenditure.

The marketing philosophy

As stated at the start of this chapter, marketing is concerned with the 'centrality' of the customer in business decision-making. This should be viewed as a business philosophy which is at the very heart of an organisation's culture as opposed to being a departmental philosophy. As explained by Keith:

'in a marketing company (as distinct from one which has simply accepted the marketing concept), all activities – from finance to production to marketing – should be geared to profitable consumer satisfaction.'

(Keith, 1960)

The marketing philosophy clearly emphasises the importance of demand – what can be sold, to whom, when, where and in what quantities. It is therefore essential to have a basic understanding of the principles of supply and demand before studying marketing. Although beyond the scope of this book, these concepts are fully covered by Bull (1995).

Underlying this marketing philosophy is an appreciation of the fact that products simply provide a means of meeting customer needs. The difficult truth is that these needs can be met in other ways, typically by competitive products. This is one of the great challenges facing marketers.

The historical development of marketing

Marketing is often described as a relatively new phenomenon, but in fact modern-day marketing has its roots in early trade. Exchange processes have been in existence ever since any type of product has been available in excess. What has been more recent, however, is the evolution of frameworks for managing these exchanges. Today these frameworks have become extremely sophisticated.

It is widely recognised that it was the fast-moving consumer goods (FMCG) companies that first embraced the marketing concept. In the late 1990s, marketing became synonymous with business skills in the FMCG area and yet it is only more recently that the service sector has really started to take marketing seriously as a business discipline. Writers typically portray the development of marketing as having occurred in a number of key phases with significant roles played by industrialisation and, more recently, by technological innovations. The historical development of marketing in travel and tourism is covered well by Cooper et al. (1998).

As we saw earlier, marketing is not merely an activity for profit-making organisations – more recently there has been a growth in the adoption of marketing by non-profit-making organisations. Many public sector organisations have been under pressure to adopt a more marketing-oriented approach in recent years. In some cases this is due to changes in their funding structure which require them to make a profit.

The importance of marketing

There is much evidence of the success of marketing. Peters and Waterman (1982) found that 'excellent' companies were more customer-oriented. Those who are sceptical about the value of marketing would do well to look at the numerous examples of product and company failures that have resulted when marketing has been disregarded. Entire industries have suffered as a result of their failure to embrace the principles of marketing. Examples of this are often quoted from Theodore Levitt's esteemed article 'Marketing myopia' which was published in the *Harvard Business Review* in 1960. Levitt was one of the first management theorists to stress the importance of a marketing approach. His article, which still has relevance today, points to the difference in focus between selling and marketing, describing the concern of the former as being with the needs of the seller, whilst the latter is concerned with the needs of the buyer.

For most organisations, having a marketing orientation is both obvious and appealing. In practice, however, the adoption of such an orientation is absent more often than would be expected and bringing it about is not an easy task. Barriers to a marketing orientation, such as interfunctional conflict, must be overcome. The chapter returns to this following an examination of different company orientations.

Different company orientations

Reference is often made to different types of organisational orientation. Three main types of company orientation are:

- *production orientation*, where the focus is on the production of goods which the organisation then tries to sell. The management of such an organisation is concerned primarily with the achievement of production efficiency
- *sales orientation*, which has as its focus selling and other promotional activities for goods which have already been produced. This orientation is often associated with 'hard selling' techniques
- *marketing orientation*, which prioritises customer needs and wants. These will be taken into account before any decisions regarding production are made. Monitoring is continuous and results are fed back to management. A marketing orientation is held by a company wherein the marketing philosophy, described above, pervades the entire organisation.

These different orientations have often been associated with different periods in time due to their relative popularity at these times. Several authors describe:

- *the production era*, which was characterised by high demand and little competition. The consumer was a low priority on the part of organisations at this time
- *the sales era*, which saw more competition and so made more use of heavy promotional activities. There was, however, still little use made of consumer research
- *the marketing era*, which views marketing as having a central role within many organisations and so consumer needs are researched and findings used in corporate decision-making. Supply exceeding demand followed by more intense competition has led to this situation. The marketing era can be divided into two parts:
  - *the marketing department era*, with its focus on buyer needs when commencing

production. In other words, the approach is concerned with producing the correct goods and services for targeted customers
— *the marketing company era*, where the marketing philosophy occupies a more central location.

This approach, which distinguishes between the marketing department era and the marketing company era, provides a useful introduction to the concept of organisation of the marketing effort.

McDonald (1995) believes it is not essential to have a formalised marketing department, particularly in small firms. He does, however, warn against the dangers of leaving marketing to specialists, such as accountants and sales managers, who will have their own particular concerns. He further advocates that a company's marketing orientation is more important than the allocation of responsibility for marketing within the organisation. Organisation of the marketing function is discussed in Chapter 6.

Marketing and the whole business

Marketing can either be viewed alongside the other functional areas as a separate and stand-alone discipline or, more appropriately, it can be viewed in a more all-encompassing manner, as being a responsibility of each discrete area. The marketing-oriented firm would of course advocate that the entire organisation has responsibility for marketing. The extent to which this is the case varies greatly in practice. Marketing can thus be viewed in a number of different ways and Kotler does well to portray these different views of marketing within the firm diagramatically (see Figure 2.1).

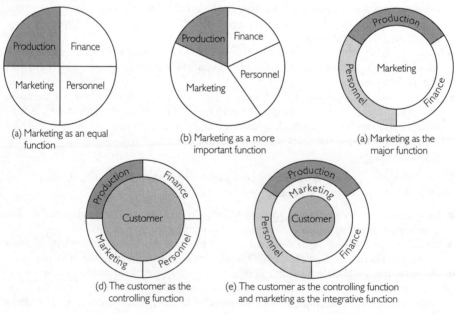

(Kotler, 1994)

Figure 2.1 Evolving views of marketing's role in the company

Barriers to successful marketing and how to overcome them

It is increasingly important that the marketing philosophy be adopted by the entire organisation as evidenced by much of the more recent literature. Different functional areas traditionally have different orientations however. Finance and accounting departments, for example, are concerned with revenue and profits. Research and development departments, on the other hand, are typically concerned with the development of the product or service. It is necessary to be aware of the different orientations that can exist. Indeed, despite its manufacturing focus, Shapiro's paper 'Can marketing and manufacturing coexist?' (1977), which looks at the marketing-manufacturing interface, has some relevance for services marketers also.

Overcoming differences in orientation is not always easy but attempts can be made to foster an appreciation of marketing throughout the organisation. As understanding of the roles performed by marketing is central to overcoming resistance to it. Improving interdepartmental communications can prove effective. One technique used involves the creation of task groups made up of members of different departments.

In some respects it can prove easier for travel and tourism organisations to overcome interfunctional conflict, especially in the many small firms where there may be fewer internal communication problems. The fact that a number of employees will have direct customer contact can further aid understanding of the importance of marketing. In larger tourism organisations, some employees will be far removed from the customers. A company-wide marketing philosophy has heightened importance where a high proportion of staff meet customers face-to-face.

Categories of marketing

Marketing activities which take place across international borders are usually referred to as *international marketing*, whilst *global marketing* is used to describe an integrated international marketing programme. This requires marketers to take some account of different local environments. There are many examples of international marketers amongst travel and tourism businesses, particularly amongst the larger hotel chains and airlines. Indeed, globalisation has been a major characteristic of some sectors of the indstry in recent years.

The principles of marketing should be capable of application whatever the product, but in practice implementation of these can prove problematic in some areas. A distinction can be made between marketing which is aimed at consumers and that which takes place between businesses. The tourism industry displays both types of marketing. We have already seen that marketing emerged in the area of consumer marketing and it is probably in this field that marketing is most established and most straightforward, if highly competitive. Industrial marketing involves marketing to industrial businesses, institutional or government buyers. Typical industrial products are raw materials and components which will be incorporated into later products and sold on. This form of marketing has a number of characteristics which are outside the scope of this chapter. A further area of marketing, services marketing, is however crucial to travel and tourism.

Marketing services

In travel and tourism we are generally concerned with the performance of service delivery as opposed to the production of physical goods, although the term 'product' can be used generically to include services. This is the approach adopted in this text. It is, however, necessary to understand the dimensions of service products. One approach is to consider goods and services as existing at different locations along a continuum as described by Shostack (1977) and shown in Figure 2.2.

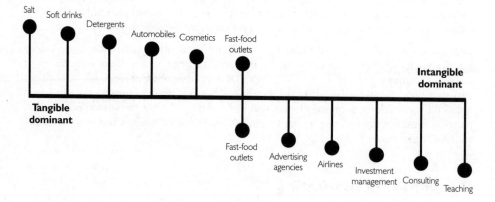

(Reprinted with permission from the *Journal of Marketing*, published by the
American Marketing Association, G. L. Shostack, April 1977)

Figure 2.2 Scale of market entities

Reference is sometimes made to 'pure' goods and 'pure' services which would clearly be located at either end of the continuum. Many travel and tourism products will be located between these extremes as they may have a tangible element in addition to the characteristics of services. The example of airlines is given in Figure 2.2.

The principles of marketing can and should be applied across the whole range of economic activity. These may, however, require adaptation to the particular industry or part thereof. In the case of services, much credence has been given to the five characteristics discussed below – intangibility, inseparability, heterogeneity, ownership and perishability – and many marketers of services have made innovative attempts to 'manage' the implications of these.

Intangibility

Services are most commonly described as being intangible. In other words, they cannot be seen, felt, heard, tasted or smelled prior to purchase. This aspect of services can make it difficult for consumers to acquire product knowledge in advance of purchase. A variety of methods are used to try to combat this difficulty. Some organisations attempt to provide 'tangible evidence' of services often through production and distribution of information sheets or free gifts which have a representation of the company or product. Shostack's continuum, described above, is concerned with different degrees of tangibility.

Inseparability

Services display simultaneous production and consumption as they are consumed directly at the time of production. Services cannot therefore be separated from their provider. For example, in order to experience a holiday you actually have to go on it. Similarly, services cannot be separated from their source and so the service provider needs to ensure successful service delivery at the first attempt.

Heterogeneity

The achievement of standardisation is difficult in services where people play such a large part in the delivery of the service. There is scope for differentiation as a result of slightly different behaviour. This adds to the difficulty of evaluating services prior to purchase. Trust on the part of the buyer is required for purchase and so the role of the salesperson takes on an extra dimension here.

Marketers often attempt to standardise service delivery through staff training, uniforms and codes of conduct or even mechanisation. Other factors, including weather conditions, are more difficult to standardise, although developments such as Center Parcs, which provides a holiday resort housed within a temperature-controlled 'dome', are an attempt to do this. An alternative, favoured by some tourism providers, is to stress the benefits of the 'individuality' of their products.

Ownership

It is often suggested that consumers own services only temporary. Indeed, in contrast to the purchase of a physical good which becomes their property once the transaction is complete, the consumer is only renting or buying access to a service such as an airline seat or a hotel room. This can be an important distinction when a consumer is choosing between the purchase of a service or a physical good. A washing machine which will belong to the purchaser for as long as they wish may seem preferable to a week in the sun, the benefits of which may be quickly forgotten.

Perishability

Producers cannot hold a 'stock' of a service indefinitely. There is a finite period only during which the sale and consumption of a service can occur. For example, an unsold airline seat cannot be sold after the flight has taken off. This spare capacity represents lost revenue and so a variety of marketing techniques are used to try to prevent this situation arising. Reducing prices shortly before a service is due to be delivered is one such technique which attempts to stimulate demand.

The above five characteristics all change the emphasis of the marketer's task when dealing with tourism services. The marketing of services has been greatly developed in recent years with knowledge of the techniques available to service marketers becoming far more widespread. The characteristics of tourism services are revisited in Chapter 8, *The tourism product and customer care*.

Marketing for travel and tourism

Undoubtedly the characteristics of services and the implications of these for marketing need to be taken into account by travel and tourism marketers. There are additional characteristics of the tourism product that require particular attention from marketers. We will now look at some of these distinctive issues in travel and tourism marketing.

Marketing in tourism has been accused of 'lagging behind' other industries and there has been an attempt by some, especially larger, tourism service providers to employ marketing managers from the FMCG sector in order to help them catch up. A popular explanation for this is the immaturity of tourism as an industry. Most commentators agree that the many small firms in some areas of the tourism industry also face problems due to limited resources. Management skills and time can be lacking in these smaller companies, as well as financial resources.

A common feature of the industry has been the development of generalist managers as opposed to specialists in fields such as marketing. This stems, in part, from the traditional training schemes used in sectors such as hospitality. In practice, many of these firms function on a short-term basis, thinking tactically as opposed to adopting a more strategic approach to marketing planning. This difference in approach is considered fully in Chapter 6. As is the case in many industries, tourism faces government regulation in some areas that also influences marketing. Consumer protection issues have become highly visible in this industry. The legal factors impacting on the marketing of travel and tourism are discussed in Chapter 12.

As was seen in Chapter 1, the tourism industry involves not just private but also public sector service providers. The public sector has not always wholeheartedly embraced the marketing philosophy for a number of reasons. Once again, a lack of resources is a common problem and this situation is worsened as many public sector organisations do not know in any one year what size of budget they will receive the next. Short budgeting cycles in themselves prevent long-term planning. These budgetary problems are compounded by the fact that public sector organisations often have to support a number of different tourism products in their area from the same budget. In addition to the public sector, there are 'not-for-profit' organisations operating in the tourism industry, such as charities which exist to organise holidays for disadvantaged children.

The disparate nature of the tourism product can lead to further problems for the public sector organisations who are unlikely to have 'control' over the products they are marketing. This can be crucial in respect of quality. A final, but nonetheless important, factor that inhibits many tourism organisations is a lack of relevant market data upon which to base marketing decisions. Although this is an area which has improved immensely in recent years, difficulties are still encountered in using data from different countries which may be inconsistent due to different methods of collection. The importance of market data is discussed in Chapter 5, together with methods for the collection of data which are both valid and reliable.

It is not only the smaller organisations involved in travel and tourism that encounter problems. There has been some polarisation within the industry, with a number of dominant organisations emerging. In some cases the growth of these organisations has been such that managers have become very far removed from their customers as a result. This has implications for marketing and must be carefully controlled.

In addition to all of the above, tourism products are high-risk products. They can be expensive, travel itself can be dangerous, and there is also a risk involved in purchasing a product that is unseen and untested. Much marketing activity revolves around minimising this risk through means such as information provision and quality control.

Many tourism organisations have yet to implement fully the concept of consumer marketing. A great deal has been done in recent years to change this, with much progress being made in some areas. There are travel and tourism organisations which have completely adopted a marketing orientation. Indeed, some of these are amongst the most successful global companies in the world. Whilst these travel and tourism organisations can therefore be seen to be highly effective at marketing, notably the larger airlines and hotel chains, it is the proliferation of smaller firms that dominate the industry that often display less impressive marketing skills for the reasons highlighted above.

The importance of marketing in travel and tourism

Middleton (1988) has pointed to seasonality as an important reason for marketing in travel and tourism. Clearly there is a need to combat fluctuations in demand. There are high fixed costs involved in providing some services which has implications when products remain unsold. Many examples of attempts to compensate for uneven demand can be cited from the tourism industry. Hotels which achieve high mid-week occupancy figures due to business tourism offer special weekend rates to try to attract business at this traditionally less popular time. Airlines publish different fares for different times of the year. This is to an extent demand-led, with air fares to South Africa and Australia increasing in price at Christmas whilst fares to some other destinations will be lower at the same time of year.

The interdependence of tourism products that was shown in Chapter 1 often requires a collaborative marketing effort and so a highly co-ordinated approach. Destination marketing companies have therefore become popular in recent years. Cooper *et al.* (1998) have argued that marketing is important in an industry where loyalty, both in the chain of distribution and in the company, is low.

As the market for tourism matures, it is becoming even more vital that managers employ appropriate marketing strategies and techniques to satisfy needs amid consumer sophistication, increased expectations and more competition. The rate at which travel and tourism is growing is evidenced not only by the number of people travelling, but also by the extent of developments on the supply side, such as new resorts and attractions, as well as a great deal of investment in technology. All these forms of investment involve risk and so there is obvious synergy in looking at both customer needs and the capabilities of the marketplace providers. The need for marketing in contemporary travel and tourism is great.

The marketing process

The adoption of a marketing orientation requires an organisation to undertake a marketing process. A number of different versions of the marketing process have been put forward and most view the activities involved in successful marketing as consisting of the following key stages.

1 *Segmentation of the overall market* Seldom is it feasible for an organisation to aim its product or products at the entire marketplace and so markets tend to be segmented (broken down) by marketers according to some relevant criteria (such as age or geographical location).
2 *Profiling consumers in each segment* Marketers like to build up a clear picture of consumers in different market segments in order to select the most appropriate segments and market to them more effectively.
3 *Selection of the target markets* Having segmented the overall market and profiled the consumers in each, organisations then select between these for the segment or segments they wish to target through their marketing activities.
4 *Development of positioning strategies for each segment* It becomes necessary for organisations to differentiate themselves from the competition in the eyes of the targeted consumers and positioning strategies help greatly with this. Positioning strategies are concerned with how an organisation chooses to position itself and its products or services *vis-à-vis* its competitors for particular markets. Many travel and tourism products continue to be promoted in similar ways and at similar times. Successful positioning strategies are valuable in creating differentiation.
5 *Development of a marketing mix for each segment* There are a number of techniques available to help with the implementation of the marketing concept and these are commonly referred to as the marketing mix. A separate mix should be created, as discussed below, for each selected segment.

Market segmentation and consumer profiling are discussed in Chapter 5, whilst positioning strategies are examined in Chapter 7 and the marketing mix is introduced below. But prior to discussion of this, the marketing environment, the context of marketing activity, is considered.

The marketing environment and the matching process

The marketing process does not take place in isolation. All companies are surrounded by a marketing environment consisting of customers, competitors and other elements, including political, economic, legal and technological factors. The marketing environment is covered fully in Chapter 3.

McDonald (1995) describes the capabilities of a firm, customer wants and the marketing environment as the three constituent parts of a *matching process* which he summarises diagramatically, as shown in Figure 2.3.

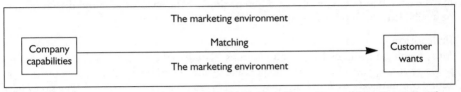

(McDonald, *Marketing Plans: How to Prepare Them: How to Use Them*, Butterworth-Heinemann 1995; reproduced with permission)

Figure 2.3

The marketing mix

The development of an appropriate marketing mix is a crucial aspect of the marketing process that was introduced above. It is this mix of marketing tools and techniques that turns the marketing concept into marketing performance.

Kotler defines the marketing mix as:

'the set of marketing tools that the firm uses to pursue its marketing objectives in the target market.'

(Kotler, 1994)

Essentially by designing a marketing mix, a plan is provided for each of these areas of business.

Cowell (1984) considers the origins of the mix in some detail, describing Borden's original list of elements of the marketing mix of manufacturers together with the market forces bearing on this. The list which derived from studies of manufacturing organisations has since been modified by others. The four Ps approach, which McCarthy proposed (Cowell, 1984), uses the following groupings.

The marketing mix groupings

Product
This grouping consists basically of the goods and services offered to the marketplace. Any one product may be offered to the market in a number of different forms. A city-centre hotel may be merely a hotel room or alternatively a room plus breakfast, lunch and dinner or even a package including particular activities, such as golf or sailing.

Place
The way in which the goods and services are made available or accessible to the market constitutes the place element of the mix, also referred to as *distribution*. The importance of careful management of product distribution is sometimes undervalued. The ways in which consumers can book the hotel accommodation in the above example will depend

on the place element of the hotel's marketing mix. Booking may be possible at travel agencies or at other hotels in the same chain, for example.

Price

The price element of the mix refers to the cost (to the market) of the product. It is often the case that a variety of prices are available for any one product. The same hotel room may be offered at different rates at different times of the week or year and discounts may be available for group bookings, etc.

Promotion

This grouping is composed of communications relating to the product. Typically advertising, public relations, sales promotions and personal selling fall under the generic heading of marketing communications. Our hotel may choose to promote itself on national television whilst also employing sales representatives to sell to corporate clients and a variety of other promotional methods. The sum of these activities will constitute the hotel's promotional mix.

The marketing mix approach recognises the interrelationship between the different elements and has, despite its apparent simplicity, become a central facet of contemporary marketing management theory.

The marketing mix for services

The origins of the mix as we have seen were based on manufacturing organisations and adaptation of the mix is sometimes suggested for services. Indeed, Borden had recognised that the framework he provided may well be adapted by others (Cowell, 1984). Booms and Bitner (1981) proposed an expanded mix for services which contains the additional elements described below.

People

It is evident from the introduction to services given above that people are an enormously important factor in service experiences. The suggested revised mix for services therefore includes the category of people to cover both staff delivering services and others taking part in service consumption at the same time. These other consumers may be 'selected' or merely others who have chosen to receive the same service at the same time. The behaviour of any or all of these people can greatly influence customer satisfaction and so require close management control. An evening in an expensive restaurant can, for example, be spoiled by the poor behaviour of other customers at a nearby table. Similarly, disruptive passengers on a flight can spoil the experience for other passengers.

Physical evidence

The problems associated with the intangibility of services suggest the importance of physical evidence. This can take many forms, ranging from photographs in a holiday brochure which provide a tangible representation of an unseen product to the physical setting in which a service is delivered, such as a restaurant. Atmospherics, which include furnishings, colour and light are seen to be highly influential by many contemporary services marketers.

Process

Closely linked to the importance of people, as an element of services marketing which requires particular attention, is the importance of processes. In service delivery we are principally concerned with the part played by customers in the procedures of service

Table 2.1 Expanded marketing mix for services

Product	Place	Promotion	Price	People	Physical evidence	Process
Physical good features	Channel type	Promotion blend	Flexibility	Employees:	Facility design:	Flow of activities:
Quality level	Exposure	Salespeople:	Price level	Recruiting	Aesthetics	Standardised
Accessories	Intermediaries	Number	Terms	Training	Functionality	Customised
Packaging	Outlet locations	Selection	Differentiation	Motivation	Ambient conditions	Number of steps
Warranties	Transportation	Training	Discounts	Rewards	Equipment	Simple
Product lines	Storage	Incentives	Allowances	Teamwork	Signage	Complex
Branding	Managing channels	Advertising:		Customers:	Employee dress	Level of customer involvement
		Targets		Education	Other tangibles:	
		Media types		Training	Reports	
		Types of ads		Communicating culture and values	Business cards	
		Copy thrust		Employee research	Statements	
		Sales promotion			Guarantees	
		Publicity				

(Reproduced with permission from Zeithamel, V. A., *Services Marketing*, McGraw-Hill 1996) delivery. The level of involvement varies greatly, particularly as delivery of some services has become highly mechanised.

Whilst these additional categories are crucial areas of services marketing, there are those who believe that there is no necessity to treat them as separate groupings. This view is based on the belief that the additional elements can be easily accommodated within the original four categories of the mix. The revised mix for services is shown in Table 2.1.

Strategic marketing planning

Strategic marketing planning involves the selection and organisation of business activities which will help the organisation to maintain health in the longer run. A variety of approaches to strategic marketing planning which are important to travel and tourism organisations are outlined in Chapter 6.

Marketing in contemporary society

As marketing becomes a more wide-spread business philosophy in general, whilst also gaining popularity in the sphere of travel and tourism, a number of relevant contemporary issues have emerged. Firstly, there has been a significant increase in ethical concerns in society. Many modern-day tourism organisations have addressed the resultant demand for more socially responsible marketing by adding so-called 'green' products to their range. This approach has been criticised for its superficiality in many instances, with products which are not truly 'green' being marketed as such. Many believe the environmental issue will continue to impact on tourism marketing in the future if indeed it does not grow in importance. Kotler (1994) refers to the societal marketing concept, a concept that enlarges the marketing concept to take account of many contemporary issues. This new concept addresses aspects such as intelligent consumption and ecological imperatives. The preservation and enhancement of both consumer and societal well-being are at the centre of this concept.

A further significant aspect of marketing in the present climate is the increasing importance of total quality management (TQM) in the delivery of services. Although this has led to the development of a variety of differing approaches to the management of quality within organisations, there are clear implications for the marketing effort.

Marketing in practice

The hotel consortia Leading Hotels of the World was introduced in Chapter 1 and information relating to the marketing activities they undertake is provided below to illustrate some of the activities involved in the marketing of tourism products. This is not intended to provide a comprehensive review of the marketing process, rather to highlight some of the more *visible* areas of marketing activity.

THE LEADING HOTELS OF THE WORLD

The main marketing activities undertaken by the organisation can be split into the following areas.

Sales activities

A team of sales staff regularly visit travel agents, tour operators and incentive organisers. In addition to strengthening business contacts in their individual areas, each sales executive keeps track of business and general trends as well as any relevant advances in travel technology. Reports of sales visits are sent to each hotel enabling that hotel to keep up-to-date with market developments.

The sales team also work with tourist boards and airlines, co-ordinating joint educational visits to member hotels worldwide. Cocktail receptions and other promotions are regularly organised on behalf of individual hotels and The Leading Hotels of the World Ltd participates in all the major worldwide trade fairs, including World Travel Market (WTM) and American Society of Travel Agents (ASTA).

Direct mail

A system of direct mail has been devised using extensive computer records, ensuring that clients receive regular, up-to-date information regarding new members, special events and promotions, etc. This system can be used directly by the company or by any individual member hotel to reach a particular market segment.

Advertising

The organisation has its own advertising company – Adluxe Advertising Inc., a subsidiary of HRI, based in New York. Advertisements are placed in trade and consumer publications on a global basis for both the organisation and its member hotels.

Public relations

Press releases are regularly dispatched from the company's New York and regional offices worldwide, thus ensuring that the media are kept fully informed of all the activities taking place within the organisation. Travel writers are provided, upon request, with reference material and relevant slides and photographs of member hotels. Occasionally press trips are organised in conjunction with an airline to promote individual properties in a specific area.

Promotional material

Directory

An annual membership directory is published as a central marketing activity. The 1997 Directory lists 310 members. The directory dedicates a half page to each property, including a full-colour photograph and a description of the facilities and services, the rate range, communications data and information regarding which credit cards are accepted.

Over a million copies of the Directory are distributed to the organisation's clients, as well as the member hotels for placement in each guest room, with copies available in French, Spanish, English, Italian, Japanese and German.

Corporate rates brochure
A corporate rates brochure, listing prices available to business travellers and covering 186 properties in 47 countries, is published for use by commercial clients.

'Great affordables'
This is a programme of specially designed weekends and holidays at 159 participating Leading Hotels which has been running for 12 years.

Meetings and incentives guide
A 338-page guide is available including entries from 119 hotels. The guide is split into two sections: meetings and incentives.

Newsletter
'Leading Destinations' is a quarterly newsletter produced in six languages for distribution to private clients. The newsletter contains news about the organisation and about special events, promotions, seasonal rates and packages offered by individual member hotels.

Conferences, incentives and meetings organisation
In addition to the above marketing activities, the organisation has set up Incentives and Meetings Departments around the world and Incentives and Meetings Co-ordinators who contact hotels on behalf of clients, organise inspection visits, plan itineraries, etc.

The reservations function
The Leading Hotels of the World Ltd makes reservations worldwide for its members through its own computerised network. Member hotels and the company's reservations, sales and marketing offices are connected to this central computer reservations system and communications network, called ResStar.

The above description of the main activities that the organisation undertakes, together with the discussion of the formation of the consortia in Chapter 1, illustrates the ways in which membership of a consortium can help to both promote and distribute the tourism product.

(Leading Hotels of the World, 1997)

Summary

We are all surrounded by marketing activities, including those initiated by travel and tourism organisations such as holiday advertisements, direct mailings and other inducements to travel. These are the highly visible side of marketing, but not all marketing activity is this obvious. An analogy with a theatre production can be made. The audience sees only that which is offered to them as an 'end product' and not the hard work behind the scenes. In tourism marketing, as in a theatre production, success depends, at least in part, on a great deal of effort before, during and after consumption. It is a framework for the planning, organisation and implementation of marketing for travel and tourism that is provided in the following chapters.

References and bibliography

Bull, A (1995) *The Economics of Travel and Tourism*, 2nd edition, Longman

Booms, B.H. and Bitner, M.J. (1981) Marketing strategies and organizational structures for service firms, in Donnelly, J.H. and George, W.R. (eds) (1981) *Marketing of Services*, American Marketing Association

British Chartered Institute of Marketing Annual Report

Cooper, C., Fletcher, J., Gilbert, D. and Wanhill, S. (1998) *Tourism Principles and Practice*, 2nd edition, Pitman

Cowell, D. (1984) *The Marketing of Services*, Butterworth-Heinemann

Drucker, P. (1994) *The Practice of Management*, Butterworth-Heinemann

Gilbert, D.C. and Banley, N. (1990) The development of marketing: a compendium of historical approaches, *Quarterly Review of Marketing*, Vol. 15, No. 2, pp 6–13

Holloway, J.C. and Robinson. C. (1995) *Marketing for Tourism*, 3rd edition, Longman

Horner, S. and Swarbrooke, J. (1996) *Marketing Hospitality, Tourism & Leisure in Europe*, ITP

Keith, R.J. (1960) The marketing revolution, *Journal of Marketing*

Kotler, P. (1994) *Marketing Management: Analysis Planning Implementation and Control*, 8th edition, Prentice Hall International

Levitt, T. (1960) Marketing myopia, *Harvard Business Review*, July/Aug., pp 45–56

McDonald, M. (1995) *Marketing Plans: How to Prepare Them: How to Use Them*, 3rd edition, Butterworth-Heinemann

Middleton, V.T.C. (1988) *Marketing in Travel & Tourism*, Heinemann Professional Publishing

Peters, T. and Waterman, R.H. (1982) *In Search of Excellence*, HarperCollins

Seaton, A.V. and Bennett, M.M. (1996) *Marketing Tourism Products: Concepts, Issues, Cases*, ITP

Shapiro, B.T. (1977) Can marketing and manufacturing coexist?, *Harvard Business Review*, Sept.–Oct.

Shostack, G.L. (1977) Breaking free from product marketing, *Journal of Marketing*, April

Zeithamel, V.A. (1996) *Services Marketing*, McGraw-Hill

3 The marketing environment

Objectives

By the end of this chapter you should be able to:

- suggest an appropriate model of the environment for a particular organisation
- analyse how the component forces influence marketing planning and decision-making in an organisation
- identify the most appropriate type of response for an organisation through the use of environmental planning and analysis.

Introduction

This chapter provides a framework by which managers can attempt to map the external factors which might affect their planning. Many authors recognise these factors to be political, economic, social and technological (PEST). It is suggested here that this framework is too narrow and if followed slavishly may lead to important factors being overlooked. Consequently, before the various external factors are considered, attention is paid to the ways the marketing environment might be modelled. Implicit in the mapping of the marketing environment is the need to monitor it and indeed forecast changes in it. To this end, Chapters 5, 6 and 7 are also relevant.

Models of the environment

As already mentioned, many authors and consultants simplify the components of the environment to political, economic, social and technological (PEST) factors. However, we need to be more sophisticated. By comparing Kotler (1994), Dibb *et al.* (1994) and Johnson and Scholes (1993), in addition to PEST we can also add demographic, cultural and competitive to the list.

In a specialist text on the marketing environment, Palmer and Hartley (1996) produce the model shown in Figure 3.1. But even this model is still not comprehensive.

By drawing on all the above sources, this text defines the marketing environment as comprising: political, interest groups, legal, economic, social and cultural, demographic, technological, competitive and physical. You should of course be aware that this list may not be exhaustive and always be sensitive to external events that might not be covered by such lists. You should be prepared to create and amend your own lists for the organisations you are interested in.

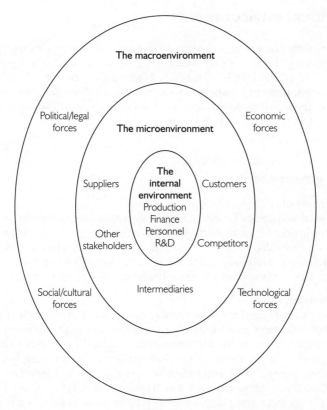

(Reproduced with permission from Palmer, A. and Hartley, B.,
The Business and Marketing Environment, McGraw-Hill 1984)

Figure 3.1 The organisation's marketing environment

Forecasting the environment

Whilst understanding the plethora of external factors that might affect an organisation can be daunting, it is crucial to realise that this modelling has to be supplemented with consideration of the future. Whether pondering the long-term (strategic) future of an organisation or the next year's operational plan, the planner needs to consider how the environment might be *in the future*. This future orientation requires forecasting. Techniques which might be appropriate for predicting future environments are covered in Chapter 7, *Operational marketing planning*.

Planners should be cautious about the certainty with which they (or others) predict the future. A much more appropriate approach is that of scenario generation. Here the planner considers what *might* happen *if* certain situations were to occur, for example, a strong sterling versus a weak sterling. This can be coupled with other possibilities, for example an increase in tourism-oriented terrorism versus a decrease. These two factors can be combined to produce four different scenarios. Clearly consideration of more events makes scenario writing a complex activity. Authors such as Mercer (1998) and particularly Fahey and Randall (1997) have recently started to focus on this approach.

The political environment

Here marketers are concerned with political systems and their impact on the markets in which they operate. To do this they might first look at the structure of governance and the mechanics of political decision-making. Marketers are concerned with who makes political decisions, how they make them and what effect those decisions might have. In this book it is impossible to do this for every market in the world and therefore it is here limited to the UK market and its association with the EU.

Levels of government

Local government
In the UK, local authorities (or councils) take decisions concerning the areas for which they have jurisdiction, for example the City of Newcastle upon Tyne. This can have great effect, not only on locally-based organisations, but also those who sell products into the area, for instance the 'Glasgow's miles better' campaign, aimed at overcoming people's negative attitudes to the city, which undoubtedly attracted tourists to the area.

National government
National government is perhaps more familiar to the majority of people. In the UK it is in the hands of Parliament which typically is controlled by one of two major parties, Conservative or Labour. At any particular time, one or other of the parties has varying degrees of power, typically relating to the size of their parliamentary majority, but also relating to the degree of control the parties exercise over their elected members. During the 1980s, the Conservatives were regarded as having great political power and were able therefore easily to enact the policies and legislation they wished to see. This led, for instance, to the deregulation of the public transport industry.

One possible way of understanding the potential impact of UK Parliament on organisations is shown in Figure 3.2.

Supranational government
Supranational government is that which comes from bodies that exist outside the nation/state. In the case of the UK this is clearly the European Union (EU). Whilst at the time of writing, the UK is not as committed a member as other EU countries, there are still plenty of examples of EU legislation that affect travel and tourism markets, such as the EU Package Travel Directive.

Interest groups

Interest groups (IGs) are seen by some as part of the political environment. However, one distinction is that interest groups (sometimes called pressure groups) work outside the political system. Palmer and Hartley argue that they:

'seek to change policy in accordance with members' interests, generally advancing a narrow cause.'

(Palmer and Hartley, 1996)

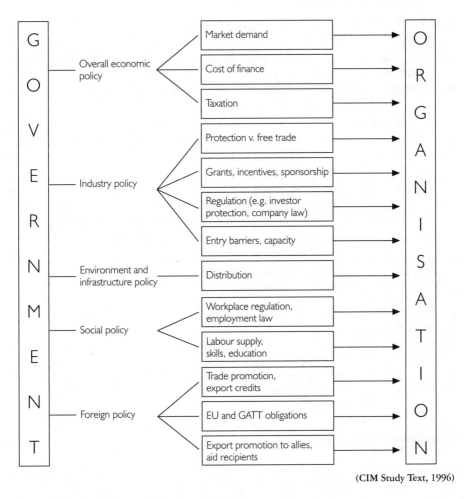

(CIM Study Text, 1996)

Figure 3.2 A framework for analysing the state's influence over organisations

They also categorise them according to their permanence, distinguishing between:

- *permanent groups*, which exist all the time and typically fight for a general cause, for example trade unions. In the airline industry, for instance, managers are influenced in what they can ask staff to do by strong union representation
- *temporary groups*, which are set up to achieve specific objectives. Once these objectives are achieved, they disband. Whilst temporary, they are potentially no less powerful.

They also distinguish between the breadth of their interests, seeing differences between:

- *sectional groups*, which fight for the common interests of their members over a wide range of issues, for example the Association of British Travel Agents (ABTA)
- *promotional groups*, which are concerned about a specific cause, for example Sustrans, who campaign for sustainable forms of transport, by the development of cycle ways for instance.

The CIM Study Text (1996) further distinguishes the sorts of relationship that IGs have with government. They identify:

- *insider groups*, which have the 'ear of government' and are consulted by politicians as a matter of course
- *outsider groups*, which are excluded from the political process and therefore resort to 'public acts' to make their point.

Implied in this distinction is that IGs only operate through the political mechanism. This is too restrictive a view of their impact – they can and do affect organisations and customers directly.

Interest groups serve to encourage some actions and discourage others. They may do so by supplying information which they have researched or by lobbying decision-makers (not just politicians). Frequently they use marketing techniques such as public relations in order to achieve their aims. A composite example of many the above is Tourism Concern who, in their publicity leaflet 'Why join Tourism Concern?' (no date), claim:

- involvement with the 'birth' of DEEGOO – an organisation to give small, local business people in the Gambia a stronger voice in tourism
- lobbying UK tour operators about hotels in Goa who had infringed locals' right to land and water
- publication of a paper on 'Tourism and trade' to draw attention to North–South trade relations in regard to tourism
- publicity of World No Golf Day to draw attention to the displacement of locals from their land to build golf courses
- encouragement of its members into a postcard campaign that secured the release of a Tibetan tour guide imprisoned for his involvement with human rights issues.

The legal environment

Due to the great importance of this area to the travel and tourism industry, a full discussion of the legal environment is provided in Chapter 12.

The physical environment

This is an area not dealt with at all by some texts and poorly by others. Kotler (1994) has the best coverage, but that is not exhaustive. Nevertheless the physical environment clearly has an impact on marketing systems. It can be split into:

- the natural environment
- the built environment.

The natural environment

Here marketers are concerned for changes that are largely beyond human influence, primarily weather, geology and geography. Changes in these areas can affect marketing decisions.

Clearly weather has a major impact on the products of the travel and tourism industry These effects might be long-term, for example if the world is undergoing global warming, then summers in the UK may become warmer and there may be less demand from UK citizens for summer sun holidays. Short-term effects are also noticeable – poor snow in an individual resort in the European Alps can have a disastrous effect on supply of skiing holidays. Operators providing holidays in this market need to have contingency plans for transporting skiers to resorts with snow.

Geological phenomena, such as an earthquake or a volcanic eruption, can provide threats and opportunities. For instance, Iceland's geothermal landscape has been an attraction for many tourists, but the recent eruption under the Vatnajokal glacier, which destroyed a stretch of the only major road in the area, proved to be a threat.

Other natural phenomena that can affect organisations are disease, for example, the bubonic plague scare that affected holidays to India in the winter of 1994–5, and fire, which occasionally destroys large areas of California, for example. It is also perhaps the traveller's fear of such factors rather than the objective risks they present that affects buying behaviour. An example of the impact of the natural environment and how it might be deal with is the case of New Zealand's Mount Ruapehu Ski Resort described below.

DISASTER STRIKES MOUNT RUAPEHU, NEW ZEALAND'S PREMIER SKI RESORT

The most striking geological features of New Zealand's North Island are the central volcanoes, New Zealand's highest. One of these volcanoes, Mount Ruapehu, exploded into life again in September 1995 affecting both residents and tourists alike. One of three volcanic mountains of Tongariro National Park, Mount Ruapehu, which reaches 2,797 metres in height, is an example of the sort of influence that the natural environment may have on tourism.

Volcanoes can tear mountains apart and at the same time affect the climate for months to come. The escape of gases when a volcano erupts can be gradual and the eruption moderate, or it can be explosive and violent, blocking out the sun and turning day into night.

Ruapehu volcanism began at least 250,000 years ago. Four main periods have characterised the active life of the volcano, which was particularly active 8,000 to 10,000 years ago. As has recently been seen, volcanic activity continues with periodic eruptions beneath Crater Lake. One eruption was first noticed when the pilot of a Union Airways plane observed steam rising from the crater in March 1945.

Possibly the most famous event associated with Mount Ruapehu occurred on 24 December 1953, when a debris dam confining the Crater Lake suddenly collapsed. The reasons for this have never been proven but are suspected to be non-volcanic. Approximately 340,000 cubic metres of water were released through the ice cave and the lake was lowered by about 6 metres. Lahar (volcanic mud flow) was sent down the Whanganehu Valley, the torrent apparently weakening the Tangiwai rail bridge above it which consequently collapsed. The untimely arrival of the Wellington to Auckland express train meant that this too was plunged into the swollen river causing New Zealand's worst ever railway disaster and killing 151 people.

A lahar warning gauge upstream now warns New Zealand Rail of any impending lahar above the bridge.

Despite Mount Ruapehu's active history, the mountain has become one of New Zealand's premier ski areas. In 1969, 1971, 1975 and 1977 eruptions generated ash and lahars that damaged the ski fields. Both the Whakapapa ski field and Whakapapa village lie in possible lahar paths. A warning system has therefore been installed to give people on the mountain advance warning of a lahar. The present system gives those people on the ski field a 3-5 minute warning of an impending lahar, hopefully sufficient time to get out of the major valley areas and water courses, if not providing them with enough time to get off the mountain. The starting point for the system is at Dome Shelter, a building on the ridge beside Crater Lake at the top of Mount Ruahepu. Signals are sent to a computer at Whakapapa Visitor Centre. Earthquakes followed by a loss of signal from Dome Shelter indicate that something volcanic has happened in the Crater area and that a lahar could be on its way. A series of alarms, including sirens on the ski field, will automatically be activated in this situation.

A recent significant eruption occurred on Monday, 18 September 1995, when an explosive eruption from Crater Lake sent a large lahar down the Whangaehu Valley on the east side of the mountain. On 23 December, the enormous Crater Lake disappeared in a series of steam and ash eruptions, so ending the ski season. It was only just as reports had been sent that the ski area was to be fully reopened, eight months after the main eruption, that the mountain once again burst into life, proving yet again how unpredictable volcanic activity can be.

Following these eruptions, the visitor centre was still extremely busy but it was noticeable that skiers were day visitors and that business in local accommodation had suffered. Attempts have been made to regain some of the lost business. For example, the Visitor Centre interprets the volcanic activity for tourists with a video show. Information is regularly provided regarding the safety of the area and tours to certain parts of the mountain are arranged when it is safe to visit them.

The built environment

Here marketers are concerned for changes in the physical environment that are the result of human action. These can perhaps be split into:

- *habitation*, such as accommodation
- *infrastructure*, such as roads, rail, airports.

These issues are important in terms of selecting countries and resorts. For instance, Spain has a wide range of accommodation ranging from the cheapest *fonda* to the grandest *parador*, providing a range of prices and quality to suit a wide range of holidaymakers. France has an excellent system of *autoroutes*, making long-distance motoring holidays feasible.

The social environment

We are concerned here with social factors in the broadest sense. Typically these include social class, educational levels, culture and sub-culture, and fashion.

Culture

Many definitions exist, typically stressing values and patterns of behaviour of large groups of people that last over time but may slowly change. In the UK, culture in recent years is thought to have become more individualistic, materialistic, youth- and achievement-oriented.

Other cultural changes taking place in the UK that affect the travel and tourism industry are the decline in the savings ethic and a reduction in 'postponed gratification', resulting in people more likely to spend on holidays than save for the future. This is coupled with a long-term decline in the work ethic, where people now value their free time and their enjoyment of that time. An increasingly positive attitude to health and fitness has meant growth in activity holidays, the provision of fitness facilities in hotels and the catering aspects of hospitality having to cater for healthier diets.

Planners need also to recognise the importance of sub-cultures whose values and behaviours are distinctly different from the majority. These may have, for example, an ethnic base – there may be opportunities to provide holidays for, say, Asian communities in the UK, or a religious base, for example MasterSun is a company which provides specialist holidays for Christians.

Social class

Most societies create social strata and some form of ranking of these strata from 'high' to 'low'. It may be determined by a variety of factors including tradition, family, beliefs, occupation, income, etc. In the UK, social class, or social group, is measured by the occupation of the head of the household. The predominant classification is that developed by JICNAR of A, B, C1, C2, D and E (see Chapter 4, page 65). Not surprisingly, there is a disproportionate number of social groups ABC1 who are consumers of tourism products, as they tend to have more disposable income. It should be recognised that social group is a very crude indicator of consumption. For example, whilst in general older people in receipt of pensions in social group E are relatively poor, there is a substantial segment within that group who are retired, rich and buying holidays.

The competitive environment

It is common for books to deal with competition at a very general level. Whilst this is important perhaps for strategic decisions concerning market entry, this approach tends to ignore the immediate impact individual competitors have on operational decisions. This text concentrates first on how we might assess the opportunities and threats presented by individual competitors (often cited as a 'blind spot' of many managers). It then looks at how the overall competitive structure of an industry can be assessed.

Understanding individual competitors

In trying to understand individual competitors, it is first necessary to define who the competition is (or might be in the future). Generally this will be companies that provide the same range of products and services as each other, for example British Airways and

Virgin. However marketers should be constantly aware of organisations who may compete for customers with a different solution to their needs, for example the Channel Tunnel rail link taking custom from the Channel ferry operators.

Questions to ask to determine competitive threat

Whilst there are some complete texts offering advice on how to understand individual competitors, Rothschild (1979) still has the best advice by suggesting marketers should try to answer the following questions.

- *Who is the current competition?* Here the planner is ascertaining which organisations are trying to fill the same needs as their organisation at this point in time, but remember to maintain a wide interpretation of this. For instance, in thinking about how people might spend a bank holiday, competition for day trips might be a compelling range of television programmes.
- This leads marketers to the more difficult question: *Who might be the future competition?* This is more difficult, as here marketers are trying to discover the plans of others. Occasionally the industry is told formally when organisations announce their plans, often in the trade press. Otherwise organisations might find out by rumour or research, but they should beware of transgressing moral and legal constraints on data collection (see Wade's classification on page 51).
- *What are their objectives and strategies?* In marketing planning it could be useful to know what the competitors' plans are. Whilst planners are unlikely to have full knowledge of these, they might be able to guess them by examining the competitions' previous actions or by studying public statements, such as their annual reports.
- *What is their commitment to existing businesses?* An organisation's plans may mean that it is about to attack the market of another. Logic might say that they are weak and will simply relinquish that market. However, suppose the organisation under attack is owned by someone who has an emotional commitment to that market (perhaps it was his or her original venture into business). They may decide to defend a position that sensibly they should not.
- *What are their relative corporate strengths and weaknesses?* If a strategist has correctly carried out the corporate audit for an organisation (see Chapter 6), then this should be easy to answer – strengths and weaknesses are relative from one organisation to another.
- *How might environmental change affect them?* Again the good strategist will be examining the effects of the other aspects of the environment, not only on their own organisation but on the competition as well. For instance, a competitor in greater debt than the strategist's organisation will suffer more with increases in interest rate charges (see *The economic environment*). This might prevent them from being too price competitive.
- *How committed is their management to the organisation?* For larger organisations where ownership and management are separate, the loyalty of the management becomes an issue. The planner needs to assess whether a competitor's management will stick with an organisation or move at an early opportunity. A high turnover of staff in a competitor may make them less able to react to market and competitive moves.
- *What is their attitude to risk?* Whether we are dealing with owners or managers (or both), strategists need to assess how they will respond to market opportunities and competitive threats. An organisation may have a track record of being hesitant in taking opportunities or conversely very reactive to, say, price cuts. These tendencies should condition how the planner's organisation should operate in the market.
- *What is their organisational structure?* The way an organisation's management and staff

are organised also gives clues as to how they might react to changes. A heavily hierarchical structure might slow down a competitor's ability to react.

- *What are the incentives given to their staff?* Here planners should try to assess the motivation of the competitor's workforce. If some sort of sales bonus system is operating, then they might be expected to fight harder to maintain their sales if threatened.
- *What is the background of their key managers?* The issue here is whether the management (and staff) have industry experience (without it they might be at a disadvantage, or indeed take unusual decisions that might surprise the industry). Strategists might also be concerned for their education and training which may affect the quality of the competitor's decision-making.
- *What is their response profile?* This could be seen as a summary of many of the above factors. Essentially, planners need to examine the competitor's past history of responding to competitive action and establish if there is a pattern. If every time prices were reduced in the past, the competitor matched that change, then it might be assumed any future changes will be met in the same way.

Sources of competitor information

While Chapter 5 describes how primary and secondary research can help answer many questions about competitors, it is worth reviewing some of the sources strategists might use. Rothschild (1979) provides a useful approach which suggests the following sources (amongst others):

- *public sources*, for example job advertisements, newspaper reports, advertising material (in the case of travel and tourism, particularly the brochure)
- trade professional sources, for example the trade press and customers
- government sources, for example, Monopolies and Merger Commission Reports
- *investors*, for example Stock Market sector analysts.

Whilst this is a good guide to published information, strategists should not forget what their management and sales force can tell them. They may well have worked for competitors in the past. It should also be remembered that primary marketing research can inform an organisation about competitors, as well as itself.

As planners become more inquisitive about competitors' activities, their activities might start to approach moral and legal boundaries. **Wade (1965)** gives guidance as to what might be unacceptable behaviour (see below).

THE WADE SYSTEM OF GRADATION OF SOURCES OF INFORMATION

1 Published material and public documents, such as court records
2 Disclosures made by competitors' employees, and obtained without subterfuge
3 Market surveys and consultants' reports
4 Financial reports and brokers' research reports
5 Trade fairs, exhibits and competitors' brochures
6 Analysis of competitors' products
7 Legitimate employment interviews with people who worked for competitor
8 Camouflaged questioning and 'drawing out' of competitors' employees at technical meeting

> 9 Direct observation under secret conditions
> 10 False job interviews with competitor's employee (i.e. where there is no real intent to hire)
> 11 Hiring a professional investigator to obtain a specific piece of information
> 13 Trespassing on competitor's property
> 14 Bribing competitor's supplier or employee
> 15 'Planting' your agent on competitor's payroll
> 16 Eavesdropping on competitors (e.g. via wire-tapping)
> 17 Theft of drawings, samples, documents and seminar property
> 18 Blackmail and extortion.
>
> The first six are generally considered ethical and legal; the remaining 12 are ranked in descending degrees of ethics or legality.
>
> (Wade, 1965)

In trying to make sense of the data collected, certain analytical methods may help. Statistical analysis of numerical data, such as sales and market share, may show trends for competitors as well as your own organisation. Key performance ratios help to analyse their financial accounts (remember to compare them over time and to others in an industry – Fame! can do this for you automatically).

Portfolio Analysis, which looks at the balance of a product range and is described Chapter 6, can indicate if the competition has a sound portfolio.

Wargames analysis, as pioneered by **Ries** and Trout (1986) and described in Kotler (1994), can not only suggest different strategies for attacking a market, but might also give insight into your competitor's actions (compare 'frontal attack' to 'guerrilla tactics').

Understanding the competitive structure of an industry
As well as understanding the strengths, weaknesses and strategies of individual competitors, it is also useful to assess the ease of entry and overall strength of competition in a particular market. Economists have long recognised different states of competition which give some insight.

- *Perfect competition* is the term used to describe an industry with many small competitors and few barriers to entry. Here an organisation could expect fierce competition with companies entering the market at will.
- *Oligopoly* describes a market where there are a few large competitors. There is limited competition and there are considerable barriers to entry, resulting in little threat of new entrants.
- *Monopoly* is where one firm dominates the market.

More recently, Porter (1980) has provided a more detailed and practicable theory for analysing competitive structure. He argues there are five forces which determine the ease of entry to markets and the intensity of competition within them.

- *Barriers to entry* These are factors such as high fixed costs of entry (consider the cost of starting an airline), and the dominance of brand names (can you name another company offering 18–30 holidays?).
- *The threat of substitute products* This is an issue that has been covered already – as a

reminder, if skiing is thought of as offering excitement, then so does white water rafting! An organisation needs to be sure to be satisfying customers' needs, not just 'selling what it makes'.

- *The power of suppliers* In some industries competition is restricted because a few large suppliers can affect what a service provider might do. It might be argued that a few airline suppliers might inadvertently collude to keep airline prices artificially high. In Europe, for instance, this may discourage tour operators from offering air travel to some destinations.

- *The power of buyers* This occurs where only a few buyers are responsible for purchasing the majority of a product. If, for instance, there were a few tour operators who purchased the majority of services from many coach operators, the tour operators would be in a strong position to make demands, such as low prices, from the coach operators.

- *Competitive rivalry* Irrespective of the number of individuals in an industry, there are industries, or periods in an industry's history, when competitive rivalry is intense. The price wars of the UK tour operators in the 1980s demonstrate the potential ferocity. In order to gain market share, prices were driven down to below economic levels. Whilst this boosted the total market size in terms of volume, it, in part, resulted in the demise of International Leisure Group, owners of Intersun. Industries such as this might be avoided by potential entrants.

The economic environment

Here strategists should examine the consequences of economic policy for marketing. They should be less concerned with *how* the economy works and more concerned with the *effect* of it on our organisations and particularly the market. The intention in this chapter is to cover the basics, but note that not all factors are relevant to all industries and there may be other factors pertinent to specific industries that are not covered here.

Planners should be able to identify the salient economic factors that might affect the travel and tourism industry, predict the probable consequences and suggest appropriate marketing action to exploit opportunities and minimise threats.

The effect of income on spending

National income
Although it is possible to measure how much a nation earns – its gross domestic product (GDP) – marketers are more likely to be concerned with what this means at the *consumer level*. The following concepts are more important therefore in ascertaining this.

Per capita income
This is how much an individual earns on average. As such, it is a broad indicator of the earnings of a nation. As tourism in particular is a luxury product, it tends to be the wealthier nations and individuals that buy these products.

Income distribution
This is just as important as per capita income, as it describes how the nation's income is split amongst its individuals. In all countries, some individuals earn more than others.

The extent of these differences can be shown by distribution statistics often published by governments' statistical services.

Disposable income
This is the amount of money a person has left after tax, National Insurance and pensions. Clearly this reduces the amount of money an individual has to spend.

Discretionary income
This is the money an individual (or household) has to spend after the essentials of life, such as rent, power and basic foods, have been paid for. It represents how much people have to spend on luxuries and so is an important concept for tourism products.

Household income and expenditure
Whilst the above concepts are easily envisaged for an individual, many purchases are done for and on behalf of a household, typically parents and children. With an increase in the number of households in which both adults work, there has been a corresponding increase in the amount of income a household has available to spend. This is compounded by essential expenditure being shared, thereby disproportionately increasing discretionary income. Superimposed on top of this, is a 'class' phenomenon where, for instance, professionals (social group A) form households. Typically individual professionals marry or co-habit and thereby create a household income that benefits from two high earnings. This generates the possibility of even greater expenditure, heightening the income distribution effect.

Business expenditure
It is usual to regard travel and tourism as a consumer product, but this is an incomplete view. There are also high levels of business travel for sales, conferences and exhibitions. Some organisations may therefore need some indicator of business income and expenditure. Some governments publish such information but it is less easy to find and use.

Other factors affecting spending

Apart from income, other factors that may affect spending should be considered.

Credit availability
Buying items with high prices may be influenced by the availability of credit. In the UK recently, the number of lending agencies and the ability of retailers to offer credit has increased dramatically. It would not be unusual now to apply to one's building society for a loan for a holiday. The increase or withdrawal of credit availability might affect tourism products.

Propensity to save
This refers to a nation's attitude to spending. Even with high discretionary incomes, people do not have to spend. For many years the British were quite cautious and tended to save, but lately there seems to be a trend to spending rather than saving.

Confidence levels
The trend to spending might be influenced by a consumer's view of the future. If redundancies are increasing, individuals may choose to save, and vice versa. Industry is similarly influenced by confidence. With a buoyant future, commerce might be tempted to expand overseas, with a commensurate increase in business travel.

Inflation

Inflation affects the value of a nation's currency. Whilst in a high inflation economy the effects of a depreciating currency are not immediately felt on purchases within its national boundaries, when its citizens travel overseas they do feel the effect. Their money buys less, acting as a disincentive to travel.

Interest rates

Whilst the availability of credit is one issue, the cost of it is another. High interest rates mean expensive borrowing for both the consumer and the supplier and act as a disincentive to borrow.

Exchange rates

Marketers must pay attention to the relative strengths of currencies which make visiting some countries more expensive and others less. Of crucial importance in this for travel amongst member countries of the EU is the European Monetary Union (EMU) which could obviate this problem.

The demographic environment

Demographics can be defined as 'the study of populations in terms of their size and characteristics' (Palmer and Hartley, 1996). This and other such definitions are then usually followed by a list of what is included in 'characteristics' – different authors including different items.

Whilst the major impact of demographics is on the market, planners should remember the effect of the demographic environment (and other external factors) on *internal* corporate resources as well. For instance, if a company relies on young workers and these are in decline due to falling birth rates, what will it do in the future to provide its service?

There are several major demographic variables to consider.

Population size

This indicates the basic size of our markets – contrast West Germany with about 60 million and Denmark with only five million. There are also trends in population change – in Europe the populations are growing slowly, giving limited market growth. In some Scandinavian countries the population size is actually falling!

Age distribution

This describes the number of people in particular age bands. In the West, with the children of the post-war 'baby boom' now in their fifties and an increasing number of people surviving to old age, there is an ageing population. This might provide tourism companies with expanded markets as the 'grey' market might be prone to travel. They may well require a different product.

Sex

Many products are segmented on the basis of sex. In travel and tourism, it might be possible to provide different holidays on this basis, for example separate holidays for boys and girls. There is also a significant tourism market for homosexuals.

Family size

This is another changing demographic factor. Typically in the West average family size has been decreasing, which might lead to a market for more ambitious holidays for smaller family units. One significant effect on family size is the growing rate of divorce.

Population location

This informs planners about where a population lives. With almost one third of the population in the UK living in the south east, clearly distribution strategies should reflect this.

Leisure time

This refers to the amount of holiday given to employees by organisations and also to the length of the working week. This has a major impact on tourism products. Annual holidays in the UK have increased from under two weeks in 1960 to over three in 1990. Similarly the length of the working week has decreased.

Education

This is measured in marketing by 'terminal education age' (the percentage of the population reaching particular exit ages from a nation's education system) and may well affect holiday choice. A more educated population may well be more prepared to travel to more unusual destinations.

Ethnicity

This reflects the racial sub-cultures that may exist in a nation. For example, the UK has a substantial percentage of people of Asian origin. This is possibly a large market segment for travel to the Asian sub-continent.

Geo-demographics

During the 1990s there were some impressive developments using conventional demographic information from the Census, combining it with the postcode system and linking it to commercial market research data. This was pioneered by Richard Webber's 'A Classification of Residential Neighbourhoods' (ACORN) (CACI).

As discussed earlier, travel and tourism products might also be bought by organisations. These too can be seen as having demographic characteristics. Consider the following.

Standard Industrial Classification

The Standard Industrial Classification (SIC) reflects the type of business an organisation belongs to. For instance, it may be that the pharmaceutical industry has specific travel needs (perhaps to the same trade shows and conferences). If so, perhaps marketers can provide special products for them, such as a package to these conferences.

Population size

Each industry comprises a number of organisations – for the pharmaceutical industry this is a small number. Conversely, for the food industry there are many organisations.

Size distribution

This compounds the previous characteristic. The pharmaceutical industry has a few organisations, but they are mostly large. The food industry has a mixture of a few large and many small participants. This has implications for communication strategies.

Organisational geo-demographics

There is a commercial organisation that performs a similar service to ACORN. Market Location Ltd provide precise geographic location of various industries and associate with it other useful data, such as products manufactured and company size. This would assist those marketing industrial travel products to specific industries to target the constituent organisations precisely.

Summary

One of the key abilities for those involved in marketing in travel and tourism is to monitor and predict the industry's changing environment. Without this, strategic and operational plans may tend to be production-oriented, miss opportunities and fall prey to threats. In order to make sense of complex environments, models have been put forward to suggest what to monitor. Such models may be inadequate for the needs of a particular organisation and a model specific to the organisation in question should be developed. Predicting the future environment is an understandably daunting task – this can be simplified by concentrating on a few highly important variables. Where accurate prediction is not possible, an alternative scenario approach can be taken and is possibly more appropriate than one which is deterministic.

Exercise: Understanding individual competitors _____

Work in a group of five.

The UK hotel industry is increasingly competitive – its biggest player is Forte Hotels plc. Consequently Forte are under constant 'attack'. Your team should adopt the role of marketing analysts for Forte. You have been asked to monitor the competition.

Each member of the team should be allocated one of the companies below. From existing secondary data sources – but without contacting the organisations themselves, except to acquire a set of company accounts (they may find the intrusion aggravating). Try to understand their strategies and possible reactions to competition.

Swallow Hotels Ltd
Novotel UK Ltd
Queens Moat House plc
Hilton International Hotels UK Ltd
Jarvis Hotels plc

Provide an A4 summary of the extent to which you consider these companies to be a competitive threat to Forte. In your group, try to come to an assessment of the competitive threat to Forte Hotels. Be sure to consider how all environmental factors might affect all the competitors, bearing in mind that external forces might affect some competitors differently.

References and bibliography

CACI Market Analysis, 59–62 High Holborn, London WC1V 6DX

CIM Study Text (1996) *Marketing Environment*, BPP Publishing

Dibb, S., Simkin, L., Pride, W.M. and Ferrell, O.C. (1994) *Marketing Concepts and Strategies*, Houghton Mifflin

Fahey, L. and Randall, R.M. (1997) *Learning From The Future*, Competitive Foresight Scenarios, Wiley

Johnson, J. and Scholes, K. (1993) *Exploring Corporate Strategy*, 3rd edition, Prentice Hall

Kotler, P. (1994) *Marketing Management, Analysis, Planning, Implementation and Control*, 8th edition, Prentice Hall International

Mercer, D. (1998) *Marketing Strategy: The Challenge of the External Environment*, The Open University

Palmer, A. and Hartley, B. (1996) *The Business and Marketing Environment*, 2nd edition, McGraw Hill

Porter, M.E. (1980) *Competitive Strategy: Techniques for Analysing Industries and Competitors*, Free Press

Ries, A. and Trout, J. (1986) *Marketing Warfare*, McGraw-Hill

Rothschild, W. E. (1979) Competitor analysis, *Management Review*, July

Tourism Concern (no date) *Why Join Tourism Concern?*

Vaitilingham, R. (1994) *The Financial Times Guide to Using Economics and Economic Indicators*, Pitman Publishing

Wade, W. (1965) *Industrial Espionage and the Mis-Use of Trade Secrets*, Advance House

Market Location Ltd, 17 Waterloo Place, Leamington Spa CV32 5LA

Tourism Concern: Patricia Barnett (Co-ordinator), Southlands College, Wimbledon Parkside, London SW19 5NN

4 Why do people travel? Introductory perspectives on tourist behaviour

Objectives

By the end of this chapter you should be able to:

- understand what tourist behaviour is
- understand the role and principal forms of market segmentation
- understand the main practitioner approach to tourist behaviour
- understand the main academic model of tourist behaviour
- understand the structuralist orientation to tourist behaviour.

Introduction

Tourist behaviour may be defined as the study of the ways in which people choose to engage in, negotiate and experience travel away from their normal place of residence in pursuit of particular goals and satisfactions.

It is a central feature of modern life and one which is continually growing in importance. Its significance lies not just in its economic impact (the aspect which is of most interest to tourism businesses, and one which has been constantly emphasised by promoters of tourism as a field of study who have frequently claimed that tourism may now be the world's biggest industry). It also occupies a social and cultural significance in modern life which entitles it to rank alongside other domains of human activity, such as medicine, law, the arts, and the physical sciences which have had a longer and more secure position in the history of western thought.

Until the twentieth century, the recreational dimensions of human experience had been largely ignored as legitimate objects of serious study. Only rarely did writers of unusual originality suggest that leisure behaviour, precisely because of its everyday ubiquity in the fabric of human lives, might be just as worthy of study, as the more traditional, legitimatised subjects of academic study. The writer, Samuel Johnson, was one of the first to recognise the authenticity of leisure behaviour when he observed that 'No man is a hypocrite in his pleasures'. The philosopher Nietzsche went further, suggesting that the activities and pleasures of everyday life, engaged in by the many, might actually be as, if not more, worthy of attention than the grander pursuits of the arts and sciences:

'These little things – food, place, climate, recreation, the whole casuistry of egoism – are beyond all comparison more serious things than anything that has been taken seriously hitherto. It is precisely here that one must begin to learn anew.'

(Hollingdale, 1981)

We start with these comments on both the economic and social implications of tourist behaviour because this chapter seeks to widen the treatment of the subject beyond the approach commonly used in marketing texts. It attempts to describe not just how tourist behaviour is managed within tourism marketing organisations, but to indicate its relationship to wider societal and social processes, traditionally explored through the social sciences, particularly in anthropology, sociology, pychology and cultural history. In short, this chapter seeks to cross-relate social science theory and managerial practice in ways which, it is hoped, will illuminate both.

The chapter is structured into three sections:

- an overview of tourist behaviour as it is approached and researched as a *problem-centred domain* in the practices of tourism organisations for the purposes of developing more effective marketing programmes
- an analysis of tourist behaviour using a *consumer behaviour model* derived from the literature of marketing theory
- an examination of tourist behaviour in relation to wider societal phenomena of ideology and social representation.

Tourist behaviour: The marketing practitioner's approach

Planners responsible for marketing tourism rarely think scientifically about the nature of tourist behaviour. With some exceptions most tourism managers have neither the time nor inclination to stand back from the context of their daily responsibilities to formulate hypotheses and build models of what tourist behaviour, as a general theoretical field, might be. They are mainly concerned with pragmatic solutions to immediate problems. They adopt rule-of-thumb research procedures designed to identify and answer questions which they see as relevent to selling their products better. No explicit, systematic view of behaviour is involved.

The practitioner approach to tourist behaviour typically involves the acquisition of data useful for four kinds of analyis:

- economic and societal analysis of the business environment
- quantitative volumetric analysis of consumption
- quantitative segmental analysis of consumption
- quantitative and qualitative explanatory analysis of consumption patterns.

Economic and societal macro data

Tourism managers assume that demand for tourism, as a commodity which is both price and income elastic, is greatly influenced by prevailing economic trends. They commonly seek to monitor and predict demand by acquiring three main kinds of macro data on:

- *disposable earnings* Since tourism is a leisure good, demand will be dependent on what the consumer has left once essential goods such as heat, accommodation, food and drink have been paid for.
- *relative prices* According to some commentators, these feed through after a year. Relative prices are particularly important in destination choices. They can be affected by changes in exchange rates, the price of competitive products, inflation, the fluctuating price of air travel and other external variables. For example, Spain has enjoyed great success as a mass tourism destination over the last three decades because of the weakness of the peseta against other currencies, in addition to the positive attractions it offers in climate, culture, etc.
- *consumer preferences* Obviously tourism choices are dependent on what people like doing with their leisure time. Tastes and wants of consumer populations change under the influence of many factors (the media, economic constraints or opportunities, education, etc). In the 1990s we saw, for instance, greater preoccupation in the West with healthy lifestyles, the environment and taking shorter holidays, all of which have impacted upon tourism demand.

It is the effect of these influences which make many large tourism organisations regularly monitor the *socio-economic environment* through compiling 'tourism barometers' – short studies which look at a range of economic and social indicators in order to assess the outlook for tourism.

Volumetric aggregate data

Since tourism management is ultimately about sales and revenue (bookings made, admissions achieved, packages sold, bedspaces occupied, etc.), practitioners are interested in quantitative measures of overall tourist behaviour. The tourism manager seeks to quantify tourist demand in order that it can be satisfied in the present or future through a supply of tourism products in a manner which produces a profit for the commercial operator, and consumer satisfaction for the public sector or non-profit-oriented tourism organisation. This means that tourism organisations are, in the last analysis, most interested in volumetric, macro-data on tourist behaviour which provide reliable indications of current performance, which can then be used as a basis for planning and managing likely future demand for tourism goods.

Most tourism agencies (for example, national and regional tourist boards) focus their main research analyses on three kinds of question:

- How many visitors/customers do we have?
- How many units of product have been purchased (bednights, air tickets, admissions, packages, etc.)?
- How much was spent?

These questions are addressed through analysis of data indicating:

- total volumes of travellers/trips/visits/bookings/bednights
- total volumes of revenue derived from them.

These kinds of data are kept on a regular basis so that trends in time can be studied as a basis for longitudinal analysis (for example, 5- or 10-year patterns of demand for a destination, airline, hotel, etc.). In addition, it is also often possible to undertake lateral analysis which involves the study of trends in different locations or places (for example, within different parts of a destination, in different hotels within the same group, on different routes flown by an airline).

Most big organisations also try to obtain competitive data on all these issues so that they can monitor the total market and the individual performance of other organisations as well as their own.

Disaggregated data and market segmentation

However, though such aggregate data represent the bottom line of tourism performance, it is insufficient to provide a satisfactory managerial understanding of tourist markets. For one thing, aggregate figures always conceal important differences in demand by market groups within the total. Secondly, aggregate data do not reveal much about the kind of tourists who constitute the overall levels of demand or the nature of the tourism experience they engaged in. For these reasons, tourism organisations commonly institute research procedures (typically through commissioning or undertaking visitor surveys) which explore both the nature of the trip and the kinds of tourists who engaged in them. This process is called *market segementation*, which has been defined as the process of breaking aggregate demand into identified sub-groups within overall populations. The identification and profiling of the market segments which may be particularly worthwhile as consumers for particular tourism products is a critical requirement in marketing planning, since in most markets a relatively small number of people may constitute the main demand for a product. It is by market segmentation that a tourism organisation defines its market, matches products to it, and promotes in media which will most effectively reach the target consumer groups

Market segmentation data come in two forms and each commonly includes some or all of the categories of data listed:

- *trip descriptors*:
  - purpose of trip
  - party size and composition
  - transport used
  - driving distance
  - activities engaged in on trip
- *tourist descriptors*:
  - place of origin – international/domestic/regional/local
  - first time or repeat visit
  - age and family status
  - gender
  - sources of information used
  - expenditure per trip and per day
  - accommodation used
  - social grading/occupation
  - education
  - lifestyle
  - satisfaction levels.

Rather than describe each of these categories individually, there is a detailed case study on New York City at the end of this chapter (page 96) which illustrates the use of many of these tourist and trip descriptors by a large international tourism organisation, New York City Convention Bureau.

Five kinds of segmentation data which are particularly important in tourist behaviour analysis deserve further comment.

Purpose of trip data and the emergence of VFR research

Virtually all tourism organisations try to distinguish what proportion of their business comes from four main categories of travel:

- recreational
- business
- visiting friends and relatives (VFR)
- other.

It is essential to understand these categories because they are associated with differences in levels of daily expenditure (business travellers spend the most per day), length of trip (international recreational travellers and VFRs stay longest), accommodation choices (business travellers stay in the more expensive hotels, while only a small number of VFRs use commercial accommodation), party size (business travellers often travel alone, while most recreational tourists travel in the company of others). Moreover, the proportions of each type of tourism category can vary widely. For example, many hotels get their main revenues from business travellers during the week but from recreational travellers at the weekend. In the UK, about a third of domestic tourism revenue is business.

Much data exists on recreational tourists, some on business tourism (see Davison, 1994, and Schlentrich, 1996, for two good studies), but until the late 1980s VFR tourism was one of the most neglected and under-researched categories in tourism analysis. In the early 1990s it began to attract interest since it was thought to be growing internationally, to be the principal kind of tourism at some destinations and there was a suspicion that its value might be more than had previously been thought. In 1997 a study based on five years analysis of VFR tourism in the UK (Seaton and Palmer, 1997) and an analysis by a UK tourism consultant (Beioley, 1997) offered a number of new insights into the category, which confirmed some of these suppositions.

- *VFR spending* Though lower in *overall* terms than in other kinds of tourism, spending by VFRs was significant in certain sectors of expenditure, notably on travel, services and retail. For carriers, retailers and, to a lesser extent, for food and beverage suppliers, VFRs were an important market in the UK, particularly at certain times of the year (especially Christmas and spring). The study also suggested that there might be hidden patterns of expenditure *by hosts* in VFR tourism which could compensate for the lower overall expenditures recorded by visitors. Moreover, a small proportion of VFRs in the UK, about 9 per cent, were found to use commercial accommodation.
- *Timing and duration of VFR trips* VFR tourism was made up of a significantly higher proportion of shortbreak trips than all tourism. It is distributed more evenly throughout the year, and peaked in months, particularly December, when tourism as a whole declines at many destinations.
- *Destination characteristics* The destinations of VFR tourism differed significantly from those visited by all tourists and particularly from those visited by holiday tourists. VFR destinations were more likely to be urban conurbations with a high population density and other smaller towns with a comparatively moderate base of holiday tourists.

VFR thus tended to reverse the normal patterns of recreational tourism being most common in high density population, urban regions, rather than rural and seaside destinations.

Social grading

One of the most important demographic predictors of tourism behaviour is socio-economic data which, in the UK, is operationalised through the JICNAR Social Grading classification, in which the population is stratified for marketing purposes into six social grades, as shown in Table 4.1.

Table 4.1 JICNAR Social Grading Classification

Social grade /group	Description	Approximate proportion of UK population
A	Upper middle class: higher managerial, administrative and professional groups	3%
B	Middle class: intermediate managerial, administrative and professional	16%
C1	Lower middle class: supervisory, clerical, junior managerial, etc.	26%
C2	Skilled working class: skilled manual workers	26%
D	Working class: semi and unskilled workers	17%
E	Those at subsistence level: state pensioners, widowers, students, etc.	12%

In 1992 a study of tourism behaviour since the war (Seaton, 1992) showed that ABC1s, though a minority of the population, consumed more tourism than the C2DEs. It also showed significant differences between the groups in a diverse range of tourism behaviour which included: destination choice, activities pursued, accommodation used and expenditure. In 1998 a new analysis based on social grading was made using data on domestic trips taken within the UK between 1991 and 1996 (Cramond, 1998). The results replicated most of the main differences identified in the previous study. Some of these differences are summarised below.

THE IMPACT OF SOCIAL GRADE ON TOURISM IN THE UK, 1991–6

Trips by social grade: international/domestic/shortbreak, UK, 1991–6

Seasonality

ABC1 holidays are less seasonal, with a greater proportion taking place in January, February, March, October, November and December. This is probably due to financial means to support several holidays, ability to decide period of travel and taste for avoiding the masses.

Destinations

ABC1s holidaying in the UK prefer large cities, small towns and cities and country/village destinations. C2DEs are more likely to prefer seaside resorts. Internationally ABC1s are more likely to holiday in Italy and France, while C2DEs are more likely to holiday in Spain and Turkey. ABC1s are most likely to be independent travellers, accounting for almost three-quarters of non-package bookings.

Accommodation

ABC1s are more likely to holiday in chalet/villas and second homes. C2DEs are more likely to holiday in holiday camps and caravans.

Table 4.2 All trips/Non-UK trip propensity by social grades in UK, 1996
(100 = UK average for all social grades)

	AB	C1	C2	DE
All trip propensity	170.9	114.3	86.4	60.9
Non-UK trip propensity	192.9	113.9	85.0	49.1

% of all domestic trips 1991–6	% of all foreign trips 1991–6
ABC1 52-57	ABC1 60-65
C2DE 43-48	C2DE 35-40

% of all UK shortbreaks 1991–6	% of all foreign shortbreaks 1991–6
ABC1 56-63	ABC1 65-72
C2DE 37-44	C2DE 28-35

Expenditures

There is a sliding scale which varies directly with social grade in terms of expenditure per trip and expenditure per day (see Table 4.3).

Table 4.3 UK expenditure by social grade, 1996, UK and international tourism

	AB	C1	C2	DE
Per UK trip (£)	155.28	145.33	143.60	130.78
Per day (£)	35.87	31.99	31.76	26.53
Per international trip (£)	776.88	647.97	650.93	668.00
Per international day (£)	71.64	62.52	59.55	57.79

Activities

ABC1s are most likely to participate in any activity and also to participate in many specific ones including hiking/rambling (index 119 v. 100 average for all social grades), visiting heritage sites (index 118), golfing (index 118) and artistic/heritage exhibitions (index 121). C2DEs are more likely to participate in swimming and visiting theme/activity parks.

(Cramond, 1998)

Place of origin and geo-demographics

Tourism planners are always interested in the geographic origins of their visitors. In international tourism, assessing the generating countries from which tourists arrive allows national tourist organisations to select their main target markets (the USA, Japan, UK, France and Germany are the five biggest generating countries of international tourism). In domestic and regional tourism, driving distance can be a major factor in the market for attractions.

In the last 10–15 years of the twentieth century, a major advance in geographic analysis was made by the development of a technique called *geo-demographics* which combines geography with socio-demographics. The basic idea behind it is that people who live in similar neighbourhoods are likely to share similar behavioural, consumption and lifestyle patterns. Neighbourhood profiles are compiled through the use of census data, postcode address files (PAFs) and a variety of other database information derived from such sources as electoral registers, credit related data, and customer databases held by companies (for example, banks, grocery chains, travel agents, tour operators). Geo-deomographic segmentation can be used for several purposes, including (CACI/NTC, 1998):

- consumer profiling by geographical area – establishing how a product may sell in a certain area
- identifying product usage across geographical areas – establishing who is buying a certain product
- defining the market potential of existing customer databases/mailing lists – targeting potential customers from consumers of other products.

CACI, a firm which markets a geo-demographic classification system called ACORN, has identified 17 major geo-demographic groups and within them 54 residential *types*. There are three groups in the A category:

A1s 'wealthy achievers, suburban areas'
A2s 'affluent greys in rural communites'
A3s 'prosperous pensioners in retirement areas'.

The groups can be further subdivided into several main residential types. For example, the A1s comprise five types:

A1.1 Wealthy suburbs, large detached houses
A1.2 Villages with wealthy commuters
A1.3 Mature affluent home-owning areas
A1.4 Affluent suburbs, older families
A1.5 Mature well-off suburbs.

CACI specify how many people fall into each group and type and what proportion of the population they comprise. Once these groups and types have been identified, it is possible for users of their system to analyse how their travel behaviour and tourism consumption varies. For example, group A1 has a high propensity to holiday in France, while group A3 has a high propensity to take a holiday of more than three weeks (CACI/NTC, 1998).

The reason why people are increasingly receiving larger and more regular loads of junk mail and unsolicited phonecalls from businesses is because someone somewhere has them down on a regional, geo-demographic database as a prime target market.

Family life cycle
The family life cycle concept has been around in sociology and marketing since the 1950s. The idea behind it is that consumption changes as people progress through different phases of the cycle and that tourism tastes and choices will change too. Tourism can sometimes be a ritual purchase to celebrate a *rite of passage* as people pass from one phase of the lifecycle to another (for example, going away on honeymoon to celebrate marital status or taking a retirement trip). The main lifecycle stages include:

- Bachelor stage – young singles not living at home

- Newly married or coupled persons without children
- Full nest 1 – couples with youngest child under 5
- Full nest II – couples with youngest child 6-11
- Full nest III – older couples with dependent children 11-18
- Empty nest I – older couples, no children at home, head of family still working
- Empty nest II – older couples, no children at home, head of family retired
- Solitary survivors in labour force
- Solitary survivor retired
- Single parents with children – includes both unmarried single parents as well as divorcees
- Same sex couples in gay relationships.

Many tourism organisations and destinations plan their marketing with particular life cycle groups in mind. Saga Holidays offer package tours for older life cycle groups. In recent years, more and more hospitality organisations from motels to pubs have realised the need to be child-friendly to attract families with children under 11. Some destinations such as Sitges in Spain have become known as 'gay playgrounds'.

Multi-dimensional measures: Lifestyle research

Psychographic or lifestyle segmentation was developed in the 1970s but only became widespread in the USA and UK in the 1980s and early 1990s. It was an attempt to go beyond segmenting markets by single variables (social grading, geography, etc.) by providing a much more holistic, multi-dimensional approach to consumer profiling which investigated, not just people's socio-demographic characteristics, but also their attitudes, opinions and values. The idea was that in populations it would be possible to identify groups who shared similar values, tastes, as well as socio-demographic characteristics – all those things which we now call *lifestyle*.

A version of lifestyle segmentation is currently (1998) used in tourism planning by Victoria State, Australia where the technique has been called 'Australia's most powerful research instrument'. It is described in detail below.

THE USE OF PSYCHOGRAPHIC SEGMENTATION BY VICTORIA TOURISM, 1995

Developed by the Roy Morgan Agency and based on annual research with 32,000 people in Australia, it identifies ten psychographic or lifestyle groups based on a combination of psychographic characteristics (tastes, beliefs, values, attitudes, opinions) and demographics (age, sex, income, socio-economic data). The lifestyle typologies are correlated with participation in different kinds of tourism activity so that the state can identify the most likely target segments for their destination.

Below is a description of each group with their percentage occurrence in the Australian population in brackets, and their most and least favoured tourism activities indexed against an average of 100.

M = the tourism activities they were *most* likely to pursue.
L = the tourism activities they were *least* likely to pursue.

The four groups marked * were chosen as the main target markets for Victoria.

*Visible achiever (17%)

Aged 40 years old, this group are the wealth creators of Australia and the biggest holiday spenders who with the Socially Aware, account for 41 per cent of all holiday expenditure. Confident and competent, they work for financial reward and job stimulation and earn above average incomes of $45,000+. Seek recognition and status for themselves and their families. They have 25 per cent of all children, with traditional views about family responsibilities. They are oriented towards a world of visible 'good living', travel, recreation, other evidence of success. Some are 'blue collar' businessmen. Demanding and smart strategic shoppers they are prolific consumers who take advantage of recessions to buy well.
M Luxurious/comfortable pursuits 169; golf 150; spectator sports events 147
L Football/cricket 68; disco/nightlife 43; backpacking 49

Conventional family life (9%)

This is Middle Australia, people whose life is centred round their families. Skilled tradesmen or middle office workers, with mortgages and small savers. Around 38 years of age on average incomes, they struggle to give their children better opportunities than they had. Not ambitious, they prefer to spend time in home with family.

*Young Optimist (8%)

The student generation, active, trendy, outgoing, mainly aged 18-24 and often children of *Visible achievers* and *Socially aware* parents. Young singles or couples living together at university or just started in profession. Relatively well-off (particularly if living at home) they collect new experiences, ideas and relationships. Trendsetters, outgoing, ambitious and very career-oriented, by far the most dynamic and active group. Some are keen investors. Financially they don't tend to plan ahead or budget.
M Snow skiing 258; backpacking 278; disco/nightlife 316
L Art galleries 85; special interest meetings 76; package tours 80

*Look at me (14%)

Young (generally between 14 and 24 years old) and unsophisticated and not politically active, this segment is peer driven and very active looking for fun and freedom away from family. Self-centred and self-motivated, they care only about living for today. Interested in jobs not careers, they are trend conscious and experiment with new fads. The weekend is for fun and excitement with a group of friends seeking high visibility. They enjoy both watching and taking part in sport. Financially they don't tend to plan ahead or budget.
M Other sports 245; backpacking 231; disco/nightlife 226
L Art galleries 49; wineries/vineyards 55; horseracing 61

*Socially aware (13%)

Predomonantly aged between 35 and 49, this is the most educated group in the community. They are generally up-market professionals earning over $45,000. Mostly married, with or without children, they take a thoughtful and strategic approach to life. They are politically and socially active and environmentally aware, pursuing a stimulating and progressive lifestyle in leisure and at home.

M Art galleries 222; arts/cultural events 186; nature experience 167
L Casinos/poker machines 70; horseracing 79; fishing/hunting 80

Something better (10%)

Upwardly mobile younger couples, building up their business, career driven. They both earn good incomes but borrow a lot to fund lifestyle (home and activities) and are financially stretched. Over half have children but the family is not central to their lives. They are confident, ambitious and progressive. Many suffered during recession but are resourceful and working hard to keep ahead.

Traditional family lifestyle (17%)

Over 50, empty nest and mostly retired version of Middle Australia. Most live in their own homes. They have strong commitment to traditional roles and values and are cautious of new things. They have time for a few more interests and manage to get away to nice places occasionally. God has an important place in their lives and they are concerned about health. Relationship with their grown-up children and grandchildren is paramount.

Real conservatism (5%)

Observers of society rather than active participants. Tend to be very traditional and religion plays a big part in their lives. More likely to be found on the land or in quiet suburbia. Very cautious about new products and ideas, they vote extreme right. Financially well-off, they are hoarders rather than spenders. Travel is popular especially caravans, fishing and other traditional holidays.

A fairer deal (6%)

This is a working-class, blue-collar group. Around 30 they are on low incomes struggling to make ends meet. They are dissatisfied and consider they get a raw deal from life. Full-time home duties for women and full-time (un)employment for men reinforce traditional roles. Money worries and employment insecurity create high levels of pessimism and cynicism. Many are union members, have only third party car insurance and smoke. Not at all active in leisure pursuits, they tend to be homebound, watching TV.

Basic needs (3%)

Older, retired workers and widows living (often alone) on a pension. Very traditional views with strong Christian ethic. They feel vulnerable, seek protection and security and follow a survival lifestyle.

An interesting feature of this psychographic system is how it correlates to both age and position in family life cycle, and to class, occupation and education. It tends to suggest that, at the end of the day, the most important data a tourism organisation needs to know about its market comprises are age, family status, education and occupation.

(Tourism Victoria Domestic Market Research)

Quantitative and qualitative explanatory analysis of tourism patterns

The main categories of data used by practitioners discussed so far comprise quantitative measures which seek to *describe* and *classify* tourist behaviour rather than *explain* why it takes place. Some organisations also seek data which provide greater insight into *how* and *why* tourists behave as they do. For example, airline companies try to find out what people are looking for when they choose one airline over another. Destination agencies try to find out what image visitors and non-visitors have of their country in order that their promotion may be better focused to exploit strengths or redress weaknesses. For example, the Scottish Tourist Board recently carried out group discussions and indepth interviews to find out how Scotland is seen as a destination by people in and outside Scotland (Seaton and Hay, 1998). However, among practitioners explanatory research is much less common than quantitative descriptive data

Summary

This section has described some of the pragmatic, rule-of-thumb techniques used by practitioners to investigate tourist behaviour. They are based on no unified, scientific view of the tourist and have emerged through heuristic processes of trial and error, as part of working assumptions about what constitutes good practice in developing effective marketing programmes.

The consumer behaviour model of tourist behaviour

The second approach derives from a more academic mode of enquiry which disregards the specific problems of tourism organisations and seeks to develop a more explicit, scientific and systematic way of conceptualising tourism behaviour which puts more emphasis on *explaining* behaviour rather than mainly *describing* it.

The basic model of tourist behaviour was adapted from models of consumer behaviour which had been developed in marketing theory since the late 1950s and have continued to be the basis of standard marketing texts ever since (for example, Assael 1987; Engel, Blackwell, Miniard, 1990; Williams, 1982; Wilkie 1990). The models applied ideas drawn from sociology, anthropology and psychology in an attempt to understand how people make consumer choices. Tourist behaviour was seen as a complex form of consumption influenced at the aggregate level by many social, economic and political variables, and at the individual level, by a whole range of psychological, social and cultural factors. The models made two main assumptions:

- that tourism choice could be conceptualised as a *temporal process* which could be broken down for analysis into *distinctive sequential stages*
- that the influences on the consumer involved in the process could be systematically studied in ways which would ultimately allow scientists to understand and even predict the outcome of their purchase decisions.

The model thus focused on the characteristics of the decision process and the characteristics of the decision-maker/consumer. Both will now be described.

The tourism decision sequence

The consumer behaviour model sees consumption as a *temporal decision sequence*, consisting of the following steps, shown in Figure 4.1:

1 *Problem recognition* in tourism might be the feeling of a family in January that they should start to decide where to take their main summer holiday.
2 *Internal search and evaluation* might be an appraisal of known options, based on previous experience and general knowledge of alternative holiday options.
3 *External search* might be exposure to press or TV advertising, or a visit to a travel agent to look at new options.
4 The *purchase process* would be the booking.
5 The *decision outcomes* would be the appraisal of the holiday experience.

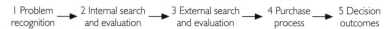

Figure 4.1 Consumer decision model

The model is based on the assumptions that, if the stages which lead to tourist decisions can be identified, and the people involved at each stage can also be identified, then it will be possible for tourism organisations to provide information to affect them (for example, by having promotional materials available at the right time and place; by locating distribution points such as travel agents or tourist information centres in appropriate locations, etc.).

However, this general model of consumer decision-making omits some important factors specific to the tourist decision process. Decision outcomes in the model are more complicated in tourism choices than in those for most other purchases. They can be divided into the following seven- or eight-part sequence of their own, shown in Figure 4.2. This revised model of decision outcomes draws attention to the fact that once a purchase has been made there is commonly a gap which may be up to three or four months before a holiday is taken and, once it has been completed, the effects may extend far into the future. Each of the phases may find the customer in very different psychological states of mind which may require intervention by the tourism organisation or provide opportunities for influence.

1 Immediately after taking decisions, especially expensive ones, customers often still feel unsure of their choice, a phenomenom known as *post-decisional cognitive dissonance*, and look for supports to confirm their choice. Tourism agencies can help to provide support with additional literature and by generally staying in touch with customers after the bookings.
2 After this comes the *trip anticipation phase* which can be increasingly excited and often occasions intense activity (reading up about the destination, buying clothes, sunglasses, or other accessories) and again the tourism organisation may contribute to this with cross-selling opportunties (for example, offering guidebooks, special offers, etc.).
3 *Travel to a destination* can also be an opportunity for influence by tourism marketers (for example, through on-ferry videos of destination features; inflight magazines offering ideas for the trip; duty free sales and other kinds of retail, etc.).
4 *The experience* itself is primarily influenced by good service and fulfilling the expectations of the customer.
5 *Travel from the destination* tends to be a 'dead' phase during which the tourist is over-

spent, still recovering from the final night party and anxious to be home; the main contribution the organisation can make is to ensure the return journey is as quick and painless as possible.

6 *The post-trip evaluation* happens within a few days of return, sometimes invoked by satisfaction questionnaires administered by the tourism organisation at the end of the trip, before people are assimilated into the routines of everyday life again, and only becomes a major issue for tourism organisations if things have gone wrong and complaints or claims for compensation are imminent.

7 The *retrospect* may extend for months, if not years (in the form, for example, of keeping photographs, mementos, etc.), and it is here that organisations may create future business through *relationship marketing* programmes with former customers on their database by invitations to reunion parties and through 'privilige offers' on new holiday products which create:

8 *Repeat purchase.*

There are many variations of tourism decision models besides the one just presented. A useful discussion of some of them can be found in Goodall (1991).

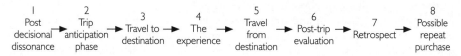

Figure 4.2 Decision outcomes sequence in tourism

The characteristics of the decision-maker/consumer

The second part of the consumer behaviour model focuses not on the decision, but the decision-maker – the tourist. The model sees tourism as a social-psychological experience which is affected, in the case of any individual, by two main sets of variables:

● external influences
● individual differences.

Another way of saying this is that a person can be seen as a product of social influences and personal characteristics. Some of the specific variables which have been studied in relation to the two are summarised in Table 4.4.

Table 4.4 Variables in consumer behaviour model

Environmental/social influences	Internal/individual differences
Culture	Motivation and needs
Class and status	Perception
Family composition	Self-image and personality
Groups and reference groups	Tourist typologies
	Learning
	Attitudes

It is impossible to provide a comprehensive inventory of each of these variables in influencing tourism choice and behaviour. Instead we shall provide a brief resume of each and for fuller discussion refer you to the works of Mayo and Jarvis, 1981; Pearce, 1982; Moutinho, 1987; Ryan, 1991; Gilbert, 1991; Seaton, 1996.

Culture

In anthropology, culture is seen to consist of patterns of behaviour and ideas developed within communities. Society itself – a nation or state – is the largest community or social grouping, so that culture may be seen as the way of life of a society. One definition of culture is:

'that complex whole which includes knowledge, belief, art, morals, law, custom, and any other capabilities and habits acquired by man as a member of society.'

(Levi-Strauss, 1978)

Culture influences how people make sense of the world which they filter through unconsciously-held values and expectations. Its effects are sometimes subtle. One writer has demonstrated from historical evidence how even tourism photography may be affected by culture. The study shows how British visitors to the Holy Land in the nineteenth century were more likely to photograph pictures of landscape and documentation, while French ones emphasised art and architecture. When both photographed the same building, the British were more likely to include some surrounding trees or hills, rather than just the building. The explanation was that the French, as Catholics, were more interested in religious buildings (Nir, 1985).

Culture is of particular importance in international tourism for two reasons. Firstly, the experience of foreign cultures is often seen as one of the main motivations of tourists. MacCannell (1976) has compared tourists to massified, amateur anthropologists for whom part of the tourism chase is 'authentic' encounters with other cultures. (It can plausibly be argued that he has the comparison the wrong way round: that tourism came first and that anthropology is only an intellectualised version of the people-watching tourists had been doing for 200 years and publishing in travel memoirs, before anthropology was invented as an academic discipline.) Nevertheless, no matter which came first, cultural encounter is an important motive of many kinds of tourism – to see other ways of life, to make contact with difference.

Secondly, since international tourism involves encounters between cultures, there is always the chance that misunderstanding and conflicts will take place through the differences in the habits and perspectives of people from different backgrounds. Different concepts of food, clothing, etiquette and other codes of behaviour may result, on the one hand, in bemused and discontented tourists or, on the other, in host populations who regard tourists as rude, ignorant or ridiculous. For tourism providers it is particularly important to understand the cultural expectations of visitors, which is why some organisations go to great lengths to research cultural expectations in order to meet them.

In the early 1990s the Australian Tourism Industry Association commissioned a major university research study into needs and tastes of the Japanese, a prime market (Platt *et al.*, 1991). Tourism Victoria also analysed how visitors from different nationalities to Australia differed in the activities they took part in as an indicator of cultural differences. The results are shown in Table 4.5.

Table 4.5 Differences in activities pursued on vacation in Australia by nationality (indices of tourism propensity)

Country of origin	Botanic gardens/ park	Zoos/ wildlife	Museums/ art galleries	Casinos	Historical parks/ folk museums	Theatre/ concerts
United States	59	58	40	14	29	19
Japan	40	74	14	23	11	8
Asia	51	47	26	24	18	10
New Zealand	44	31	20	20	10	19
United Kingdom	67	60	37	22	31	25
Europe	64	60	41	15	27	20

(Tourism Victoria: Strategic Business Plan, 1995)

Class and status

Class is the hierarchical ordering or stratification of groups within society. We have seen the impact of JICNARs social grades, as one form of class measure, on tourist behaviour and in the final section we shall return to the issue in some depth. For now, it is enough to assert that class has a great impact upon tourism choices, that destinations vary in their class profiles, that some forms of tourism are strongly associated with class membership (for example, walking holidays with the educated middle classes), and that class membership is sometimes used in tourism promotion as a way of selling specific kinds of specialist package. Despite this, class is considerably underplayed in the literature, and not mentioned at all in most of the vast output of TV travel programmes which tend to imply that we all participate equally in tourism. It is only recently, for instance, that the American Tourist Industry has 'discovered' the fact that cultural tourism is dominated by professsional, managerial groups on high incomes (TIAA, 1997).

Status is a more intangible concept than class. It can mean the relative prestige of an individual within a particular group, or the social honour accorded to particular positions within society. Research in UK and the US has over many years shown similarities in the way people in the two countries rank the prestige of particular jobs. Travel (the high status word for tourism) can be both an adjunct and expression of status. People in prestigious positions travel a lot, and in business and professional communities *rate of participation* in travel and also *distances travelled* are often implicitly used as an index of personal success (as the dinner party conversation and air terminal exchanges of executives and academics indicate).

Membership groups and reference groups

Most people travel in recreational groups of two or more, and group factors play a great part in the selection process. A useful concept is that of the *decison-making unit* (DMU) which suggests that tourism decisions may involve several people in influencing, selection, payment and consumption of the final choice. Within particular groups, some individuals may be *opinion leaders* who influence the group's activities. A student peer group may, for example, follow the tourism fashions of particular people within it, or adopt the perceived tourism practices of other student groups. People are influenced by both *membership groups* (those they belong to) and also by *reference groups* (those other groups they aspire or relate to, or regard as some kind of model of conduct). Groups may act as taste and fashion setters, and also as information networks. Friendship groups, for example, offer opportunities for tourism planners but they can also act as negative information sources which may accelerate the demise of unsatisfactory products. At the Museum of Modern Art in New York, Jo Pike, the Director of Visitor Services, estimates that a complaint from a dissatisfied customer will be amplified and transmitted to 16 friends and acquaintances (Pike, 1998).

Group and party travel is an important category of tourism which may involve both informal groups and more formal, institutional groups (school parties, OAPs, societies and clubs, etc.). For tourist attractions out of season, the group market is especially vital with museums and galleries sometimes getting over 50 per cent of their admissions from groups in winter.

Family influences on choice of tourism

The family market is the biggest one there is for recreational tourism. It also constitutes about 80 per cent of the UK VFR market (since visting relatives is much more common than visiting friends).

The family is a particularly important example of the DMU, described earlier. Main holiday decisions involve all the family so that a trade-off has to be found between the needs and preferences of mothers, fathers and children. A study of family tourism behaviour in Belgium, France, Italy and the UK showed that about 60–70 per cent of children are *consulted* to some degree about holiday decisions, but that the *final decision* is increasingly a joint one between mother and father. It also showed that in those cases where children were not consulted, there was a much greater chance of the holiday being a failure from the child's point of view (Seaton and Tagg, 1995).

Children are not always passive followers in tourist behaviour. They can be the principal influence on decisions to visit places like Disneyworld and Alton Towers. Moreover they are taking an increasingly active part in visits to attractions which use information technology. At Newsweum, the new museum of news in Washington, Eric Newton, the managing editor, has observed that children are the first to use the plentiful interactive technology and through demonstration, teach their parents how to use it later.

Motivation

Motivation has attracted a large academic literature exploring why tourists take part in tourism. No firm conclusions have been drawn but there are many theories which can only be selectively sampled here. Fuller accounts can be found, for example, in Dann, 1977 and 1981; Crompton, 1979; Mansfield, 1992; Mayo and Jarvis, 1981; Pearce, 1982.

Tourism motivation is a contradictory mix of desires – for adventure but security; for the unfamilar but not too strange; for activity but also relaxation. These contradictions have often been reflected in dichotomous theories in which tourist motivations are divided into two opposed groups. Gray's (1970) distinction between tourists motivated by wanderlust and sunlust is one example. *Wanderlust* is seen as a need for personal experiences in specific, culturally significant places, while *sunlust* is seen as a desire for rest, recreation, entertainment which is not particularly associated with the unique or distinctive properties of any specific destination.

Another dichotomous theory is that which sees tourist motivation as a function of two contrasting impulses, *pull* and *push* factors. Push factors are the *negative aspects* of the home environment which the tourist travels to avoid (poor climate, work, hassle, stress). Pull factors are the *positive images* of the destination to which the tourist is attracted (climate, culture, landscape, rest, relaxation, etc.). A similar dichotomous contrast can be found in Mannell and Iso-Ahola's notion that tourists are impelled by two needs: to *escape* from routine or stressful environments and the *seeking* of recreational opportunities for psychological rewards (Mannell and Iso-Ahola, 1987).

In addition to these dichotomous bi-polar theories, there have been longer inventories of tourism motives. Mayo and Jarvis (1981) hypothesise four main motivators – *physical motivators, cultural motivators, interpersonal motivators, status and prestige motivators*. Other theorists have produced longer lists of motives which include the need for culture, sport, relaxation, status, education, to be together with the family, and so on.

The problem is that all of them are true in some cases and not true in others. It may be less useful to look for general motivators, rather than ones which are specific to particular kinds of trips (purpose of trip segmentation described earlier remains an excellent start point to motivation). There may be as many different specific, situational motives as there are trips. Looking for general motives is rarely very helpful in allowing a tourism organisation to sell a specific product.

Finally, motivation may remain an elusive issue because the multiple choice, survey questionnaires most commonly used to investigate it may leave out motives which the researcher hasn't thought of. What diligent attraction researcher would ever guess at the motives which attracted the late Jeffrey Barnard to art galleries and heritage monuments, as revealed in a men's magazine in the 1960s?

'Where do you usually try to pull?

Well, the current top places are (a) the tea room at the Tate Gallery, (b) the American Express in the Haymarket, (c) the au pairs' pram lot at Peter Jones, (d) any park where the girls walk dogs, (e) Poets' Corner Westminster Abbey, (f) the Spitfire Room of the Imperial War Museum...

...Poets' Corner is a good place to pick up American girls. You stand by a tomb that's housing someone like Wordsworth and as the American bird walks by you heave a sigh and say, "Jesus what a loss he was. We knew him well you know. Used to drop in for tea every day..."'

(Barnard, 1967)

Perception
Perception lies at the heart of tourism. What people see, hear, feel, taste and smell in new environments constitutes the tourism experience. Perception has been studied extensively by psychologists and social-psychologists and many of their findings have been reported in texts on consumer and tourism behaviour (for example, Williams, 1982; Mayo and Jarvis, 1984; Pearce, 1982; Seaton, 1996). This section describes some of them.

Destination image
This concept has been much discussed by academics and practitioners. Destination image comprises all the associations, images and evaluations, favourable and unfavourable, which a person holds about a place, and it is thought to be a major influence on destination choice. The information on which destination images are based may derive from many sources and extend back years into childhood. Two kinds of destination image influence have been identified:

- *organic image* which is made up of destination information collected from non-commercial soures (radio, TV, film, books, poetry, education, etc,)
- *induced image* which derives from deliberately-promoted, commercial information sponsored by an organisation to attract visitors.

The former is thought to be more influential on destination choice than the latter, though in many cases people's images will be influenced by both.

Attempts to identify the key components of destination image and measure it have been widely reported by academics (see Echtner and Brent Ritchie, 1991, for a good review of the literature), but it remains a difficult area. One of the problems is that images of place may be so complex that common methods of measuring them through multiple choice questionnaires which explore a few verbal attributes may be too simple to capture the rich variety of verbal, visual and other non-verbal associations behind images. Attempts to explore the qualitative aspects of place image are much less common in research. Lowenthal and Prince have done interesting work which explores British and American preferences in landscape, claiming that they differ. The dominant aspects of American tastes in landscape are: size ('the cult of bigness'), wildness and formlessness ('casual chaos'), a relative disregard for aesthetics set against the more pressing needs of taming land for economc purposes, a tendency to sacrifice the present to the future ('building for tomorrow'), 'featurism' (a tendency for features without unity or coherence), and prediliction for the remote and the spectacular, rather than the nearby. The American visitor is less concerned whether a historic relic is real or fake, provided it is near enough. British tastes tend more to the small, the prettily picturesque, the authentic and the historic (Lowenthal and Prince, 1964; Prince and Lowenthal, 1965).

Cognitive distance and size impression

Perceptual theory suggests that physical reality is not the same as perceived reality. Much tourist experience lies in the head rather than in the real world. One instance is the difference between distance as measured geographically and distance as subjectively perceived by people. In Scotland, for example, Iceland is incorrectly perceived as further away than Italy, yet it is cognitive distance rather than actual distance which influences a travel decison. It has been said that three of the main factors affecting travel choice are budget, distance and time. Both time and distance may involve cognitive factors. Size of population and actual distance away are known to affect judgements of cognitive distance. They can also be affected by individual factors such as stress, motivation and level of activity (Cook and McCleary, 1983).

Size impression is another aspect of subjective factors in perception. Promotion, exposed to the tourist before a trip, can make a destination or tourism product seem larger or more significant than it might appear encountered 'cold'. In Villedeu les Poeles, a small theme town in France, which is famous for its brass and copper products, a group of nine small attraction managers have banded together to promote jointly in order to increase the size impression of the town. The structuring of perceptions is thus a factor in attraction management.

Another example, also in France, is the Bayeux Tapestry. This world-famous exhibit, which tells the story of the Battle of Hastings, receives over 350,000 visitors a year. Physically it is quite narrow, and could be seen in ten minutes by a visitor walking past it (as a Victorian guide book commented, 'Many persons will look upon it as a long strip of coarse linen cloth, 20 inches wide and 214 feet long, rudely worked with figures worthy

of a girl's sampler'). However, it is displayed and animated in such a way that its significance is perceptually heightened. It is housed in a three-storey building and visitors are
not allowed to see it until they have passed through a series of rooms which feature films,
models and reconstructions, telling its history, and after seeing an enlarged replica in
which every panel of the tapestry is described. After this build-up, which can take more
than an hour, the visitor finally encounters the real thing and files slowly past, listening
through earphones to a commentary which is activated by infra-red sensors in front of
each panel. In this way, a trip which might have lasted a few minutes has been turned
into heightened event.

Interpretation is thus about the creation of expectation and elevation of meaning.

Effort after meaning

Another perceptual principle, first identified in an early book on memory by Bartlett
(1932), is the process known as 'effort after meaning'. This refers to the human tendency
to seek to impose a meaning when confronted by new stimuli. One of its implications is
the importance of creating first impressions which will stimulate favourable expectations
about the tourist experience. This crucial principle means that attractions, hotels and
other tourism phenomena may only have a short time to make an impact.

At the Museum of Modern Art (MOMA) in New York, Jo Pike, Manager of Visitor Services, has said that the visitor impression is formed within six seconds. To manage it she
divides the customer perceptual experience into *processes* (how the visitor is delivered to
the product via signage, assisted information, etc.) and settings (the physical appearance
and layout of the museum). MOMA is currently redesigning the entrance and reception
to make it less intimidating and minimalist to create a more immediately, user-friendly
effect (Pike, 1998). The Townhouse, a hotel in Dublin, reminds its front of house staff of
the importance of the initial visitor encounter by placing a brass plate on the reception
desk which says, 'We are the managers of first impressions'.

Selective perception

Another major principle of perception is the process known as selective perception. This
suggest that people never 'see' all that is there, or even what they are intended to see, but
edit and interpret stimuli through filters, derived from their own backgrounds and experiences. It can be illustrated from an anecdote told by the writer Samuel Butler noting
the reaction of an Italian tourist in London:

'I once saw a poor Ticinese woman kneeling in prayer before a dentist's show-case in the
Hampstead Road; she doubtless mistook the teeth for the relics of some saint.'

(Butler, 1923)

Expectation

Perception is largely learned. We frequently perceive what we expect to perceive and are
disappointed if we do not do so. When marketing tourism products (destinations, attractions, hotels, etc.), the marketer attempts to establish desires and expectations. 'People
eat with their eyes', says Rick Abramson of the Kennedy Space Centre, which is why he
streamlined the restaurant to allow customers to see and smell the food in preparation.

Labelling and framing of objects can often be used to create expectations in museums
which may later provide retail opportunities. At the Kennedy Space Centre pieces of rock,

which would seem unremarkable without the narratives attached to them, can be sold as souvenirs when labelled as pieces of meteorite (one was sold for $15,000). MacCannell (1976) has viewed the marking process by which objects are labelled and framed as central to the tourism generating process. The importance of creating positive expectations which will later be fulfilled was also well caught in a recent advertisement for Kodak films which used the headline, 'Will the photos you look back on be as good as the time you're looking forward to?'

Closure

Perception theory comprises a principle called closure. It refers to the human desire to complete incomplete stimuli. One of its implications is the need to allow the tourist to round off the visitor experience in a satisfying manner. The best time to sell people souvenirs, for example, is not at the start, but the end of the trip so that they can 'take a piece of the experience home'. This is why gift shops are increasingly being located at the exits, rather than the entrance to attractions. It is also why Madame Tussauds encourages, and provides people with opportunities for, photography, so that they have a permanent 'signoff' to their trips when they leave.

Learning

Tourism choice is a learning process. We are not born with ideas of other places; they are acquired through experience, particularly, as we shall see in the next section, through education and family. The decision model described earlier can be seen as a learning sequence.

Once again there is a vast literature on learning. There are many theories which suggest how we learn:

- through *conditioning*, which happens as we associate particular stimuli with certain kinds of reward or response (which is why they are called stimulus/response models);
- through *gestalt* principles, by which we grasp meanings through problem-solving procedures and sudden insight rather than by programmed responses
- through *information processing*, which assumes that the brain is like some giant computer and processes data into long-term and short-term memory stores, ready for retrieval when required.

Incidental learning (learning which happens in the natural course of things, rather than by design in some formal programme like a short course on airline ticketing) is a part of, and affects responses to, many aspects of tourism. Coping with the logistics of travel and new environments is a form of learned behaviour which some are more confident of undertaking than others. It can be facilitated by clear information (good signage, tourist information centres, guides, etc.) and also through experience. Practice – or *rehearsal* as learning theorists sometimes call it – makes perfect, or at least leads to improvement. Learning is also the basis of promotional response. Tourism uses a lot of printed materials (brochures, adverts, etc.) and there are readability formulae which can be used to asssess how difficult any piece of writing is, by calculating the reading age level which would be required to understand it. Learning is a factor in responses to translated materials which are best monitored for idiom and sense by a panel of native speakers from the linguistic area involved; there are still too many stilted or plain meaningless promotional materials published by tourism agencies who thought they were saving money by doing the translation themselves, rather than checking it with nationals of the countries concerned.

Formal learning, where learning is the main goal, rather than an incidental by-product, is increasingly a tourist choice as more people seek education in their travel. Painting week-ends, flying lessons, school trips and a vast range of executive and management development courses are examples. Even in more recreational trips people are seeking some element of personal improvement (perhaps to assuage a puritanical guilt about pure pleasure, or a hypocritical delusion that they are really having fun for some higher purposes, a feature of much cultural tourism). This is why there is a growing supply of 'edutainment' products, particularly at attractions, where some notional element of education is combined with entertainment. Museums and galleries are increasingly producing school packs, often tied to national curricula, to encourage group visits, but making sure that the whole experience is fun as well.

In general, the more education a person has received the greater his or her propensity to travel – simply because the more you know, the more you want to see. Thus, for example, within a country the more people in full-time education and the longer they stay in it, the greater will be the tourism propensity.

Personality, self-image and identity

The links between personality and travel are many, but little firm evidence exists specifying their exact relationship. The importance of travel in individual biography can be inferred from the fact that when people write their CVs they often inventory the places they have visited, presenting it as evidence of their identity. Students increasingly take a year off before or after university to increase their travel experiences. And they are probably right to do so, since employers often regard travel as an indicator of enterprise and maturity.

Tourism can also be an escape from identity, a way of trying out new roles and personae. It has been suggested that two kinds of role may be sought in tourism – being 'king or queen for a day' through being waited on and treated to a life of luxury for those who have very circumscribed roles in 'real' life, or being 'peasant for a day' by roughing it and encountering a simpler, more basic existence, for those whose lives are privileged but complex (some rich Europeans, for example, pay a lot to 'return to nature' by living in primitive cabins in rural places in African countries).

Anthropologists like Nelson Graburn and Victor Turner have equated tourism with quasi-holy ritual pilgrimages in which tourists seek *liminal experiences* (roughly described as, passages across thresholds and structures of normal life into new levels of higher or less inhibited experience). Another tourist goal, according to anthropologists, is a desire for *communitas*, a feeling of oneness with others which may come from being in closed groups with them and sharing intense, common experiences during the trip. This is why holiday relationships sometimes may have profound effects on tourists and be maintained later. The potential power of travel on the individual has been caught in his most famous novel by the French writer, Jean-Paul Sartre:

'I've read that there are travellers who have changed physically and morally to such an extent that even their closest relatives did not recognise them when they came back.'

(Sartre, 1962)

For most people, tourism is nothing like so transforming. Instead it may be a short-term ego-boost, during which the tourists can play-act a few fantasies and then return back to the appointed place in the divison of labour or, if the howlings of the tabloid press have any substance, to their non-appointed place outside the division of labour. This is more the view expressed by Graham Dann, who suggests that ego enhancement and ego recognition are lynchpins of motivation:

'The fantasy world of travel seeks to overcome the humdrum, the normlessness and meaningless of life, with more satisfying experiences....Travel presents the tourist with the opportunity to boost his or her ego in acting out an alien personality.'

(Dann, 1977)

Tourist typologies
Closely related to issues of personality has been the attempt to develop typologies which distinguish between different kinds of tourist. This was pioneered by Cohen in 1972 and updated in later works (Cohen, 1972, 1974 and 1984). He classified tourists into four sociological types:

- the organised mass tourist
- the individual mass tourist
- the explorer
- the drifter.

The classification was important as a first break away from lumping all tourists together. Today it appears a little dated ('drifters' seem to have disappeared with their kaftans and cow bells as a group with anything like the presence they had at the end of the hippy 1960s) and 'explorers' are equally problematic in days where even the most apparently peripheral, liminal journey is accompanied by TV crews, radio contact, rescue ships or planes, pre-sold publishing rights and corporate sponsorship.

Another widely cited typology is put forward by Plog (1973). His two types are said to represent polar extremes of tourist personality.

- The *psychocentric* is characterised by conservatism in holiday choice, a liking for short-haul holidays by car, the familiar, low-activity levels and inclusive packages to mass tourism destinations.
- The *allocentric* prefers long-haul destinations which are accessed by air, and are characterised by activity, cultural diversity, unspoiled natural environments, independent travel and interaction with hosts.

In between are *midcentrics* who display some features of both types. A number of criticisms have been levelled against this typology, questioning whether the groups involved should be seen as personality types or sociological types, and also whether some of their characteristics are culturally-specific to the USA (Seaton, 1996).

Attitudes
Texts on consumer behaviour have devoted much attention to attitudes, opinions and values since they are presumed to be directly linked to actions. However, there have been enormous problems in utilising attitude as a construct with much explanatory or predictive use. Among these problems we may mention:

- evidence which shows that attitudes are unstable and may vary according to the specific questions asked to determine them
- that they are not always congruent with actions (a person may say he hates a particular resort but go there because his children like it)

- that they may inflate the importance of issues on the research agenda and conceal other more important ones which are not (the same problem we saw in attempts to inventory motives in multiple choice, questionnaire surveys).

Most of all there is the problem of trying to decide whether any attitude or cluster of attitudes is/are significant *independent variables*, i.e. important motors of action in their own right, or whether they are dependent variables, components or indicators of some larger construct such as personality or motivation.

In tourism research it has been implicitly assumed that they are mainly the latter. Attitude scales and monitors are normally used within studies as tools for tracking broader sets of issues rather being of interest in their own right. For example, the psychographic research in Victoria described earlier used a whole range of opinion and attitude questions as part of an attempt to identify lifestyle groups. Nevertheless, knowledge of *how* to carry out attitude research, using the different quantitative and qualitative survey methodologies described in Chapter 5, is an important sphere of competence for researchers working in tourism behaviour.

Summary

The academic consumer behaviour model is a useful way of opening up processes of tourist choice to systematic analysis in ways widely different from the practitioner model. By specifying the variety of social and individual factors which affect tourist tastes and preferences, it directs researchers to the complex sequences of, and influences on, apparently simple decisions. Despite recognising social factors, the model ultimately sees tourist behaviour as a *free individual choice* which may have particularly important *personal meanings* for the consumer.

The final model offers a very different account.

Ideology and cultural representation: The structuralist model of tourist behaviour

One of the most famous government posters of the Second World War asked the question, 'Is your journey really necessary?' The central fact about recreational tourism is that most journeys aren't. This may seem a strange conclusion for readers from societies where tourism has been naturalised to such an extent that by many it is seen as a necessity. But the fact is that until 200 years ago only the privileged engaged in recreational travel, that populations in many less-developed countries still do not, and that even today in the UK about 40 per cent of the population do not take a holiday in any one year. Moreover, stripped of its usual glamorous associations, tourism can seem bizarre, stressful or downright silly. Here are two scenarios which have deliberately been written to highlight the incongruous features of tourism which normally pass unnoticed:

- Inside a huge pile of ruined masonry a crowd of 15,000 is sitting waiting to hear a group of singers in fancy dress sing songs most of them have heard hundreds of times. Because the concert is outdoors the reception will be many times poorer than many of them are used to hearing on tape or CD.

The concert begins, but suddenly it comes on to rain and the occasion is abandoned for the first of five times during the night and the crowd have to run to buy plastic raincoats and shelter at a bar where a glass of wine costs £3.50. The concert restarts but finally takes six hours to complete because of further rain stoppages. At 3.00 a.m. the audience leaves, cold and damp, many of them having paid £90 for their evening's entertainment. Nobody asked for a refund and most go home well pleased.

The place is the Roman amphitheatre at Verona, the occasion the performance of Carmen during the opera festival which takes place every July and August.

Who were these people and what made them go home so happy?

- A young man and woman are laid out on a dirty bedroll in the precincts of the Gare du Nord Station in Paris. Exhausted after having had little sleep for two days, they lie gazing into space surrounded by thousands of hurrying passengers – and a smell of pee. They have not changed their clothes for six days and have been living on bread and cheese for the last three, a meal they hardly ever eat at home. For three weeks they have been crowding into trains, travelling round Europe in conditions of discomfort they would not accept for a day at home. Tucked into their rucksacks full of dirty washing is a poster they brought in the Louvre that will be put up in their rooms at university next term.

  When they get home they will tell their friends it has been a great trip.

  What on earth do they mean?

These cameos suggest that, looked at dispassionately, tourism can seem physically uncomfortable, expensive, and comprise activities which might be better and more efficiently enjoyed at home (listening to opera, eating properly, sleeping in a warm bed, etc.). In short they bring out the *unnaturalness* of tourism which provokes the question 'Why do it?'

Both the above scenarios might be analysed, using the consumer behaviour model just described, as *personal choices* made by people who had been shaped by many different influences but who ultimately acted as *free individuals*. The influences on them would include those just considered: motivations (desire to escape? to seek rewards abroad?), class (going to Italy as a middle-class ritual?) perceptions (images of sun, wine and history in Italy; images of 'gay, bohemian Paree' in Paris?), peer group influence (the norm that students should seek vacation adventures abroad?), learning and education (listening to opera and seeing galleries?), culture (the notion that 'travel broadens the mind' and that summer is the time to pursue it?), etc. But after all the influences had been inventoried, the underlying assumption would be that people finally made a free choice. But did they?

The third perspective offers a different view of tourist behaviour. It sees tourism more as a *product of social structure* than individual choice. Instead of making its prime unit of analysis the individual tourist and the influences at work on him or her, it takes society and *stratified group hierarchies* within society as the main focus. It conceives of the individual as enmeshed (albeit unconsciously) in a web of societal forces which mould and limit opportunities of thought and action, the result of which is to produce *collective* tourism tastes and habits which will vary, not because of freely-made, individual choices, but due to the differing location of individuals in social and societal networks. The strands of the social web which constrain and mould individual behaviour are composed of two interrelated fabrics – *ideology* and *cultural representation*. The structuralist position conceptualises tourism behaviour as a product of the *distribution of ideologies* which:

- *circulate within society* but reach different social groups within it at different levels of intensity and repetitive emphasis

- are *transmitted* through communicative networks of cultural representation operating through institutional mechanisms including the family, education, occupation and the media
- are *adopted differentially* as implicit rules of behaviour by groups who have absorbed the ideologies through the mechanisms of cultural representation.

Two notions are central to this analysis – ideology and cultural representation – which are, in reality, closely related.

Ideology

There is a vast literature on ideology and it has been used as a framework for analysis of many cultural forms, including religion, politics and leisure behaviour. In its broadest sense, ideology refers to *systems of ideas* circulating within social systems which come to act as the implicit basis of behaviour on which individuals within groups act. Ideology consists of broad patterns of ideas which underpin 'natural' behaviour. Another way of putting this is that tourism both as a general practice and in its particular manifestations is not a 'natural' activity but a *constructed form* which is socially induced within ideology, and then enters the domain of private motivation via mechanisms that are partly concealed by history because the individual rarely knows the origin of the ideas which she or he has internalised as 'normal' behaviour.

Some social analysts see tourism as a single ideological system which is particularly influenced and promoted by international capitalism whose effects include the commodification and appropriation of subordinate cultures, cultural dependency and domination – in effect, imperialism by peaceful means. This view goes all the way back to Marx who saw ideology as an instrument by which powerful economic interest groups and political elites (big business and capitalistic states) control and influence subordinate populations for their own ends. In 'weaker' versions of ideology, adopted here, tourism is seen, not as a single, homogeneous ideological system, but as a field constituted by a number of separate ideological elements, circulating among tourist populations, which may be general ones ('Travel broadens the mind', 'Everyone needs a holiday') or specific ('Italy is a great cultural centre', 'the Seychelles is an earthly paradise'). Both approaches to ideology recognise that tourism is shaped by social forces and that motivation for recreational travel (or lack of it) is never purely a matter of personal choice (though it always seem to be), but a function of the power of socially-derived ideologies and the 'vocabularies of motive' successful ideologies tend to produce in the minds and actions of individuals (including their images of, and feelings for, places and tourist activities). Tourists may think they choose; in reality they are, to a degree, 'chosen' by ideologies circulating within their social networks. Once tourist ideologies have gained acceptance those who embrace them are unaware of their origins and act on them as natural 'facts of life'.

Ideologies are visible at their birth and later when challenged and contested by different ones. Ideologies are never a static set of permanent ideas. They change, rise and fall. They are most visible at moments of transition because it is then that people see them for what they are, *contingent ideas* rather than immutable facts of life. For example, the ideology of sun, sea and sand tourism was until recently accepted as natural and virtually synonymous with the summer holiday itself, but now that it is being attacked by health critics, it is seen as just one form of tourism which came about at a particular historical moment (in the 1920s) which may eventually disappear, like religious pilgrimages in England which were thriving in the Middle Ages.

To illustrate these ideas we will look at two tourism ideologies to illustrate their social origins – Neo-Classicism and Romanticism.

Neo-Classicism

This cult of classical antiquity was an explicit, and remains a major implicit, ideological influence on tourism. It derived from the Renaissance, part of which was the rediscovery of pagan pasts and the civilisations of Greece and Rome by educated elites. Later classical studies were institutionalised in elite educational institutions, particularly in public schools, universities and the tourism form known as the Grand Tour (in which the sons of aristocrats and gentry went abroad, with Italy as their ultimate goal, to learn to be cultivated gentlemen). Knowing Latin and Greek language and culture became a badge of class membership (Oxford and Cambridge only abolished Latin as a compulsory subject in the 1960s and its decline in public schools followed). Neo-Classicism was, in short, a class-specific ideology in its origins.

Classical travel became associated with the collection of curios and 'objects of virtu' (rare and valuable works of art) which found their way into country houses built by aristocrats and their emulators, industrial millionaires in the nineteenth and twentieth centuries. Museums and public galleries developed from these gentlemen's collections and 'cabinets of curiosities'. Elite societies were founded round Neo-Classical travel and study, the most famous of which was the Dilettante Society, founded in 1734 by 'some gentlemen who had travelled in Italy'. As late as the 1920s, the Hellenic Travellers' Club, a cruising club for lovers of Greece, was limited, 'to university men and women who shall have the right to be accompanied on cruises by members of their families and personal friends'. Members paid a guinea. If they were not known to existing members, new entrants could be nominated by a vicar, a professor or headmaster or headmistress of a public school. It is worth noting that the club was called the Hellenic *Travellers'* Club, rather than the Greek *Tourists'* Club; the distinction between travellers and tourists was an ideological one which developed as tourism became more widely available and middle-class interests promoted the idea that their kind of tourism was superior to that of the masses. Some academics have contributed to the ideological elaboration of this illusory distinction (for example, Boorstin, 1963; Fussell, 1980), though one has exposed its historical origins (Buzzard, 1993).

Today, the ideology of Neo-Classicism still unconsciously motivates travel to Italy, Greece and other places, and also visits to museums, but it is a more powerful force with educated groups than others, as it always was.

Romanticism

Romanticism developed between about 1750 and 1850, initially among middle-class intellectuals and later more widely, since which it has come down in a watered-down form to a mass, international audience. It was never a homogeneous movement but rather a number of aesthetic tastes in literature, art, philosophy and, not least, travel. Among the main ideological features of Romanticism disseminated by its prime figures (who included Rousseau in Switzerland; the poets Wordsworth, Coleridge, Byron, Shelley and Keats in England; Heine in Germany) were *reverence for nature*; belief in the innate virtue of *simple people in rural locations* (Rousseau's 'noble savages'); the belief that *passion and feelings* were more important than intellect; pre-eminent belief in *individual* rather than *conventional* behaviour; and a great desire for travel to *exotic, wild or unspoiled scenery*. Landscape was a key element:

'Romanticism succeeded in placing landscape and nature at the heart of cultural interest in nineteenth-century Europe. Romantic poetry affected a style of "natural" language; water-colourists sketched and painted "from nature"; and both poets and painters as well as "sensitive" people from the middle classes sought out natural, unspoiled scenes.'

(Denvir, 1984)

Two important components of romantic responses to landscape were the concepts of the *picturesque* and the *sublime*. The picturesque was the idea that favoured travel destinations that produced views that made attractive pictures, which led to the modern idea of the scenic photostop and the 'room with the view'. Picturesque scenes were thought to include old ruins, pleasing effects of light and shadow, winding rivers and streams, moonlight on water, and peasant scenes of rural life and character. The sublime was the ideology of regarding landscapes (and other phenomena) which produced feelings of *awe* and *terror* (cliffs, roaring torrents, waterfalls, etc.) as grand and spiritually elevating which, among other things, made people cease to regard mountainous regions as barbarous and repulsive and come to see them as uplifting (the Alps became fashionable in the early nineteenth century, and mountaineering was a post-Romantic pastime which developed, mainly among university-educated young men, from the 1860s onwards) .

These changes in responses to landscape and nature produced the tourist fashion for walking for its own sake. (The Romantics, particularly Coleridge and Wordworth, were great walkers. Before them only the poor walked, not for any aesthetic reasons, but because they could not afford better.) They also popularised destinations, particularly Scotland, Wales and the Lake District, which had previously been regarded as peripheral backwaters (Seaton, 1998).

These examples illustrate how ideologies can be seen to lie at the back of tourist tastes and how their origins can be traced back to specific classes and groups. They also suggest a new way of looking at the tourism scenarios presented at the start of this chapter. Neo-Classicical ideology suggests why the Roman amphitheatre in Verona should be such a valued arena for listening to opera (a middle-class art form among most Europeans, but not, interestingly, among Italians for whom it has always been a more popular form). Romanticism suggests why a ruin under the stars (romantic nature in a picturesque, natural setting) may be even better than having a roof under one's head. The ideologies also suggest why students who mainly come from middle-class homes, like the sons of gentlefolk on the Grand Tour, see travel as a prerequisite of civilised life and why, unlike most other young people, they even take a year off to do more of it (non-students may wonder in what sense they are taking a year 'off' since student life in itself is seen as 'off', being outside the normal regimes of work most of the population engage in when they leave school. From this perspective students have never been 'on'!)

Cultural representation

The systems of ideas we have termed ideology have no power unless they are conveyed in some material form to the people they later influence. The mechanisms for such transmission are cultural representations, which may be seen as images, verbal and pictorial, carried, or mediated, institutionally. The main institutional, transmission mechanisms are the family, education, to a lesser extent occupational life, and – very important – the mass media.

Every society exposes its members to a complex range of communication, particularly technologically advanced societies which now utilise a staggering variety of media to bombard their populations with a daily deluge of messages. Cultural representation is a name given to the immense range of mediated messages, personal and impersonal, which act as conduits for ideas. It also refers to their material embodiment – buildings such as museums and galleries transmit cultural messages. The family and the education system are particularly powerful vehicles of cultural representation and thus ideologies. Cultural representation gives people ideas of how things were, how things are, and how things should be. It provides ideas about places, history, geography, and not least, normative ideas as to how one should behave, including judgements of good taste and how one should spend one's leisure. Tourism ideology occurs widely in cultural representations, including promotion, and has a profound influence, as this extract suggests:

'1913 (Summer) The affair began with some illustrated booklets on trips to Norway, wherein I saw pictures of beautiful places the very existence of which had never before entered my consciousness. "How ghastly", I said to myself almost in anguish, "that here I am forced to go on day by day frittering away my life as a museum assistant in London – in England – when all the planet remains unexplored by me." Surely it is a perfectly natural desire in a human being on first fully awakening to full consciousness of his amazing situation to set out forthwith to explore the globe.'

(Barbellion, 1919)

Cultural representation is not a consistent body of ideas. Indeed, because of the vast volume and variety of messages to which modern societies are exposed, it often results in contradictory and mutually exclusive communications. However, the contradictions are not equally balanced; they are weighted through the fact that some kinds of message are put more frequently and receive less contradictions than others (in the UK and USA, for instance, you will find few messages which suggest that consumption or tourism are bad things).

Nor is cultural representation the same for any two individuals, because the exact permutation of messages received out of the enormous potential reservoir of messages transmitted, will never be the same for any two people. Nevertheless there will be a tendency for people who *share a similar position within the overall social structure*, for example, with comparable family, educational or occupational backgrounds, to be exposed to similar forms of imagery. Research shows that people from the lower social grades watch more TV, and particularly commercial TV in the UK, than those in the higher grades. Research also suggests that people from higher social grades receive more years in education, read more printed sources of information, and are thus exposed to more ideas. The writer Jean-Paul Sartre can again be quoted to demonstrate how the educational background of an intellectual may produce unexpected images of place:

'Sometimes...it happens that I pronounce these fine names you read in atlases, Aranujuez or Canterbury. New images are born in me, images such as people create from books who have never travelled. My words are dreams, that is all.'

(Sartre, 1962)

Ideology, leisure tastes and the work of Pierre Bourdieu

Earlier we saw how social grading and class are seen as one set of influences on tourist behaviour. In the structuralist model, class and social groupings are a much greater determining factor because people are shaped by ideologies within their groups. In this final section we shall appraise the work of a writer who has theorised and demonstrated this with great originality.

Pierre Bourdieu is a French sociologist whose main work, *Distinction* (1984), has a great deal to say about ideologies and cultural representation in the production of personal choices. Its main subject is not tourism, although it is briefly mentioned, but the relationship between leisure taste (in art, music, film, style in home furnishings) and social groupings. His implicit theme is the mighty structuring power of society on our minds in those areas where we think we have greatest freedom, lifestyle choices. He sets out to analyse the relationship between social structure and cultural appreciation and acquisition. There is, he argues, a relationship between place in the social structure and the prestige of different forms of consumption of culture. Hierarchies within cultural consumption – the competences that go with them and the social status accruing from them – reinforces economic relationships of subordination and dominance.

It is impossible to produce more than a crude summary of his book which is over 600 pages long, particularly since much of its power lies in details, often witty and subversive insights into aesthetic choices scattered through its pages of meticulous analysis. Bourdieu describes his aim as an attempt to explain why certain groups are always the most likely to be fans of the 'higher' forms of culture and why others are not or, as he ironically expresses it:

'the miracle of the unequal class distribution of the capacity for inspired encounters with works of art and high culture in general.'

(Bourdieu, 1984)

Tastes, according to Bourdieu are not innate or instinctive, but a social product which derive through the main agencies of the family and the education system, but not by them alone. Leisure practices, possessions, as well as artistic and aesthetic choices, are all, often unconscious, expressions of class and group position. Taste, Bourdieu emphasises, is not some transendent quality of judgement, but a way in which individuals differentiate themselves from others:

'Tastes (manifested preferences) are the practical affirmation of an inevitable difference...Tastes are first and foremost distastes, disgust provoked by horror or visceral intolerance of the tastes of others.'

(Bourdieu, 1984)

What people like and hate are thus coded messages of status bondings.

Bourdieu set out to explore these issues empirically through a fascinating series of experiments. Between 1967 and 1967–8 he surveyed 1,217 people in France and exposed them to different exhibits relating to judgements of painting, music, home decoration, film appreciation, sport and body maintenance, and asked them to rank and discuss their preferences. He examined the sample, not just by class, but by education and occupation. The results established what he called the very close relationship linking aesthetic judgements and opinions to:

- educational capital (measured by qualifications)
- social origin (measured by father's occupation).

These were just part of the study. Bourdieu also looked at differences in the way his subjects had *acquired* their cultural judgements and the *potential usage* they were likely to make of them and here again he identified differences between class and occupational groups:

'Hidden behind the statistical relationships between educational capital or social origin and this or that type of knowledge or way of applying it, there are relationships between groups maintaining different, and even antagonistic, relations to culture, depending on the conditions in which they acquired their cultural capital and the markets in which they can derive most profit from it.'

(Bourdieu, 1984)

Not all ways of acquiring taste were equally prestigious. Tastes gained from the more subtle and 'natural' processes of family background were more valued than the more pedantic knowledge acquired programmatically through formal education. In other words, swots weren't gentlefolk and gentlefolk weren't swots. Cultural judgements acquired, as if by osmosis through 'breeding', ranked higher than the same knowledge acquired through hard-won, formal education. The true 'person of taste' seemed to have acquired his or her knowledge by instinct, rather than through conscious intention, by nature rather than nurture. Moreover, according to Bourdieu, those whose cultural perspectives had developed through education were seen as threatening to those who had done so more informally, since they were most likely to realise and analyse their real origins, in education and social position, which those holding them through family background preferred to regard as instinctive. Bourdieu coins two words to express this difference in cultural acquisition: 'mondain' meaning that kind of cultural capital which is acquired almost by osmosis through family background, and 'doctes' the more self-conscious, formal mechanisms of the schoolroom and university – book learning.

Bourdieu found that the contrast between the two modes of cultural acquisition was particularly apparent in those areas of culture which were outside the academic curriculum:

'at equivalent levels of educational capital, the weight of social origin in the practice and preference explaining system increases as one moves away from the more legitimate areas of culture.'

(Bourdieu, 1984)

This is significant. It means that recognised aesthetic tastes (for example, in art and music) which all can learn formally, are less important as social indicators than the more informal spheres of taste (for example, furnishings, food choices and leisure) which are transmitted through family and the home, and thus difficult for prospective candidates to the cultural elite to master.

Bourdieu sees the ultimate foundation of elite taste to lie in economics, not aesthetic judgement, because money buys the time and leisure necessary to acquire the repertoires of judgement which pass for good taste. He characterises this as:

'the dependence of the aesthetic disposition on the past and present *material conditions of existence* which are the precondition of both its constitution and its application and also of the accumulation of cultural capital which can only be acquired by a means of a sort of withdrawal from economic necessity.'

(Bourdieu, 1984)

It is also economic position which creates the gradual possibility and disposition to retreat from the pressing needs of material survival to a world where aesthetic preferences can be developed and refined:

'As the objective distance from necessity grows, lifestyle increasingly becomes the product of...a "stylisation of life", a systematic commitment which orientates and organises the most diverse practices – the choice of a vintage wine or a cheese or the decoration of a holiday home in the country.'

(Bourdieu, 1984)

Though much of this sounds as if Bourdieu is a left-wing radical, deconstructing bourgeois taste – and much of his book does actually read that way – his analysis is subtler than that. He differs from crude class theorists in refining his central thesis by tracing differences not just between class groupings, but by including other variables, one of which is occupation. The position of individuals within the 'taste game', he suggests, are based on generic and specific positions. Generic membership of the middle class grouping might dictate, for example, some interest in art, but specific occupational status and ambitions within that occupation might determine what kind of art would be preferred.

Bourdieu also takes pains to emphasise that nobody is outside the 'taste game' and that it is not, in any case, recent or specific to modern societies. It is found in all societies.

Bourdieu's work shows some resemblances to another sociologist Veblen, who analysed the tastes of American leisure classes at the start of the twentieth century and concluded that they were characterised by 'conspicuous consumption' (a phrase Bourdieu uses without acknowledging Veblen). But Veblen argued that elites express conspicuous consumption through overt luxury, excess and expensive purchases. Bourdieu shows how it might be through *severity* and *austerity* of taste (abstract painting rather than naturalistic ones, complex modern music rather than easy tunes). This brings us to Bourdieu's main observation about the features of tastes at the upper end of the social and educational spectrum, which is that they are characterised by preferences for those objects and experiences which are not easy, immediately pleasurable, or naturally appealing. He identifies the taste of elite groups as:

'a systematic refusal of all that is human, the common, "easy" and immediately accessible...the passions, emotions and feelings which ordinary people put into their ordinary existence, and consequently all the themes and objects capable of evoking them.'

(Bourdieu, 1984)

The highest aesthetic taste is based on distance, detachment and, almost by definition, avoidance of the popular. In art, for example, Bourdieu found, among educated elites, a preference for form over content, technique rather than theme, painterliness rather than subject. Sophisticated taste may be seen as the process of overcoming natural responses (those of children, for example, who initially like bright colours and identifiable subjects in art, but become weaned off them as they become more 'sophisicated' in their tastes through their educational experiences) and the embracing of ever more complex and abstract modes.

Summary

Bourdieu's systematic 'taste tests' have not been repeated in the UK or America and, since they did not focus primarily on tourism, we can only speculate how his findings might be applied to tourist tastes. Where might such speculations lead? If frugality rather than plenty, and austerity rather than sensual indulgence provide the high status badges then elite tourism preferences might include; not pigging out and enjoying sun and sand in Torremolinos, but wind and rain on a Scottish moor; not sweet-tasting red wine by the tumbler in an English pub in Benidorm, but a soupçon of dry white in northern Majorca; visits not to coastal Spain but rural Italy; not a comfortable lilo on the beach, but the rocking deck of an Arctic ice-breaker; not eating candy floss on a roller coaster at Blackpool, but eating berries on an ecological tour in a South American rainforest. (Notice how, as Bourdieu argues, many of these preferences are based on *nots* – not doing as other groups do.)

Bourdieu's ideas are of most interest in understanding differences in *recreational tourism choices* where the apparent freedom of taste preferences seems greatest. Other kinds of tourism are more obviously determined. Visiting friends and relatives (VFR) tourism is less free and more constrained by obligation, since the ideology of visiting family and friends largely cuts across social groups. Business travel is also less freely chosen and thus less structured by the processes of aesthetic preference analysed by Bourdieu.

The implications of the structural model

It is possible to draw up a short, structuralist definition of recreational tourist behaviour on the basis of this account:

> *Tourist behaviour is the **ideologically constructed disposition** of an individual to travel and to prefer particular travel forms, which is produced (and reproduced) differentially within class groupings through cultural representation which is transmitted mainly through the institutions of the family, education and occupation, and also through selective responses to the media which are influenced by all three.*

Its implications are as follows.

- Representation assumes a central role in tourist choice. The structural model give much greater weight to issues of representation than others. It suggests that the family, education, occupational status and the media all critically affect tourist behaviour.
- The model and Bourdieu's work puts paramount emphasis on *societal and social factors* in tourism and leisure choice. The model ignores individual factors (perceptions, learning, personality, etc.) because it assumes that all of them are shaped by the effects of the *social circulation of ideologies*. It also implicitly challenges tourist typologies such as Cohen's or Plog's, seeing them again as a product of the differential dispersion of ideologies within different population groups, rather than personal attributes (allocentric characteristics, for instance, bear a suspicious similarity to the tastes of educated, middle-class groups).

There is some empirical support for Bourdieu's class-based theories in UK and US tourism research. UK social grading studies (Seaton, 1992; Cramond, 1998) showed evidence of systematic links between tourist tastes and social class. And the TIAA study (1997) which examined the profile of people participating in cultural tourism in the USA showed the same tendencies as the British Social Grading study, concluding that: 'The profile of the head of any travelling household includes an average age in the mid to upper 40s, full time employment, a college degree and a managerial or professional occupation.' In short the US equivalent of ABC1 social status.

- Bourdieu's work has interesting and unexpected implications for unpromising destinations (those which are remote, have difficult climates and dangerous environments). Precisely because they are far removed from the kind of easy, comfortable existence the 'common man' *naturally* wants, and thus invert the canons of taste adopted by the majority, they may be coded through ideology for elites as a badge of discrimination and taste. The less obvious the attractions of a destination, the greater its potential as an object for the 'pure gaze' of the middle-class aesthete (Cohen's 'Explorer'?) – just as abstract works were in the realm of art. There is some evidence of this. The history of tourism to Iceland and Scotland and the recent development of polar tourism all offer precedents of hostile climates and environments which acquired status as highly prized, lifestyle 'badges' for elite (Plog would say very 'allocentric') travelling groups.

- Finally, it should be noted that the structural model has been criticised from several quarters. It has been seen as a deterministic one which fails to account for the complexity of human behaviour. It says nothing about how tourist ideologies originate, concentrating most of its analysis on how they circulate and to what effect.

It has also been attacked by academics working within a *postmodernist* perspective. There is no time to discuss postmodernism here, but one of its main themes is that class-based differences in behaviour are being eroded under the remorseless expansion of modern communications, which now bring all kinds of information and ideologies to all social groups. As a result, aesthetic and leisure ideologies which once circulated selectively within certain classes and groups are now crossing social barriers (mainly through the medium of television) and, as a result, there is a general merging of tastes which is eroding class-based differentiations. Three points may be made in reply to this critique. Firstly, the studies cited in this chapter on socio-economic position and tourist behaviour in the UK and America (Seaton, 1992; TIAA, 1997; Cramond, 1998) show no evidence for thinking that such a levelling of tastes is taking place; the proportions of educated middle-class groups who dominate cultural tourism has not changed in the UK since the Second World War and they exist in the USA too. Secondly, *exposure* to multi-media may be less powerful influences than family and occupation groupings. Thirdly, it may be that the media do not necessarily affect all equally. For reasons that Bourdieu has brilliantly suggested, the ultimate *effectivity* of ideologies (tourism tastes, aesthetic tastes) is not simply a function of exposure, but socially-grounded motives and self-definitions. For instance, though more people than ever before may see abstract art through the medium of TV (and even that is debatable since there is a large literature to suggest that people selectively expose themselves to media content they are already interested in), it will most engage those whose *social position* and thus *self-definition* might benefit or be confirmed by responding. What Bourdieu emphasises is that the *underlying process* of hierarchically ordered groups differentiated by taste is a constant, even though the specific *content* by which the differentiations are maintained may change.

Summary

The structural model offers a considerably more deterministic view of tourist behaviour than others, by suggesting that to a large extent people, far from making free choices, are bounded and invisibly moulded by structurally-determined, cultural forces of ideology. Just as a chess player moves his pieces freely but cannot change the rules of movement by, for example, moving a knight in a straight line, so the tourist makes free tourism decisions which have been predetermined to a large degree by social position and the invisible effect of associated ideologies whose origins lie buried in the past.

Which model?

Can the models be reconciled? The superficial answer is 'No' because they represent different ways of looking at tourist behaviour and approach it through different questions (see Table 4.6 for a summary of the main differences between them).

The practitioner model implies that it can be understood for commercial purposes by gathering data on a *limited range of questions* mainly to do with *market segmentation variables*.

The consumer behaviour model is a more *systematic and theoretical* attempt to provide a *scientific* model of *individual* tourist behaviour and investigate the main variables, both social and personal, within it.

The structuralist model takes as its start point society and social groups and, by specifying how tastes are ordered within them, suggests that tourism and leisure, like artistic and other aesthetic tastes, are a function of people's position within *social structures*.

But the three models have two significant resemblances. All three acknowledge the impact of social forces but the weight given to them varies. The first two models see them as partial influences, the latter as total determinants. Secondly, three variables – education, family position and occupational status – are elements of all three. Could it be that their common occurrence in all the models suggests that it is in these three that we should look for the mainsprings of tourist behaviour? Though the rhetoric of the tourism industry may be understandably individualistic ('give yourself a well earned rest', 'discover the real you', etc.), rather than collective ('do as all people of your class and social grouping do!'), the fact is that people engage in holidays because it is a communal ritual, activated to a great extent by society, and moulded and constrained by their place in it as managers, middle-class professionals, teachers, etc. Travel goes with the territory of living in stratified, affluent western countries because it is an ideologically-derived form of *cultural capital*, a sphere of taste discrimination which, as Bourdieu suggests, provides raw material for the differentiations and rank-orderings which are found in most societies.

The real act of individualism in modern societies may be the decision never to travel for those who can afford to do so. And even that might eventually be recoded through cultural representation, to look rather distinguished – and end up as an elite, status badge for members of the group who adopted it!

Table 4.6 The focal issues of the three models summarised

Practitioner's model	Consumer behaviour model	Structuralist model
• How many people came and how much was spent? • How many units were bought (bed spaces, air tickets, admissions, packages, etc.)? • Who were the tourists? What was their socio-economic profile? Where were they from? How did they get there? What did they do? What did they think of the experience? What psychographic/lifestyle group were they? What geo-demographic group? • Were they satisfied and will they come back?	• How did the tourist decision process take place sequentially and how was it evaluated before, during and after the trip? • Who were the people who made or influenced the decision? • What were the main motivations, perceptions, personality traits, learning experiences and attitudes which shaped the choice and experience of the trip? • How had social factors influenced the choice (culture, family, class, group membership)?	• How had the tourist's position in the social structure (class, group, occupational status) affected tourist choice? • What ideological themes were inscribed in the choice (heritage? romantic nature? classicism and the antique? sun, sea and sand? etc.)? • By what means had the ideological themes been transmitted in cultural representation (e.g. the family? education? advertising? literature? film? etc.)? • What cultural capital resulted from the tourist experience (dinner party topics? career improvement? status elevation?)?

Case study
HOW THE NEW YORK CONVENTION BUREAU MONITORS TOURIST BEHAVIOUR

The New York Convention and Visitor Bureau provides annual audits of tourist behaviour which include two major studies:
- on international travellers
- on domestic travellers.

This case study focuses on them.

(NB Many of the figures have been changed. The case is intended as a *framework for discussion* of tourist behaviour *methodology* and *uses*, rather than an accurate statement of New York's performance.)

1 International travel to new york city

This summarises the New York City results of the 1995 In-flight Survey of International Air Travellers, a survey of the nation's international travel market produced annually by the Office of Tourism Industries, International Trade Administration, an agency within the United States Department of Commerce. The results of this analysis will be used by the New York Convention and Visitors Bureau to target marketing efforts by identifying and developing a better understanding of those international markets holding the greatest potential for the city. The report reviews visitor volume, travel behaviour and demographics of key international visitor markets to New York City. The report also incorporates economic data and other trends amassed from a variety of sources, so that the survey results may be analysed in the context of changes in individual markets.

Methodology

The data on New York City's international visitors presented in this report were developed by the International Trade Administration (ITA) of the US Department of Commerce through their In-flight Survey of International Air Travelers, 1995. The survey examines travel by overseas visitors to the United States via scheduled international air carriers. The survey was conducted with the co-operation of selected major airlines on a sample of their international flights departing US airports. The survey instrument was a self-administered questionnaire, which was translated into the appropriate language for each of the different nationalities surveyed. Information obtained from the questionnaires included activities and places visited, a demographic profile of the traveller and detailed trip expenditures.

The survey was designed as a stratified, two-stage cluster sample, where flights were randomly selected by airline and international destination. Each survey response was weighted to represent actual travel volumes based on the size of the travel party of each respondent, combined with information developed from the Immigration and Naturalization Service Form I-94. This report analyses a subset of the database developed for the New York Convention and Visitors Bureau by CIC Research Inc., made up of respondents who visited New York City as part of their trip.

Illustrative results
- The total volume of international travel to New York City grew by 3 per cent in

1995, to 5.4 million trips. The increase occurred exclusively on the overseas side of the visitor market (all countries excluding Canada and Mexico), which gained 7 per cent. It was fuelled by mostly favourable exchange rates for visitors from abroad, as well as the improvement in the city's image that has taken place over the past several years. Travel from Canada declined 16 per cent due to the continuing weakness of the Canadian dollar. Mexico, beset by major economic problems, scaled back its tripmaking to New York City by 20 per cent.

- New York City captured 12.6 per cent of all international trips to the United States in 1995, rising above the 12 per cent mark for the first time since 1991.
- New York City's 7 per cent gain in overseas visitors did not match the 12 per cent increase enjoyed by the United States as a whole. As a result, the city's share of the total US overseas visitor market, a cause for concern in recent years, dipped from 21.5 per cent in 1994 to 20.6 per cent in 1995.
- Within the ranking of US cities as destinations for overseas visitors, New York City retained its number one position in 1995. The shares captured by each of the top cities changed little from 1994, with the exception of Orlando, which edged out San Francisco for fifth place.
- New York City's international visitor market is expected to be static over the next several years, with increases of less than 1 per cent forecast for 1996 and 1997.
- International visitors spent $4.7 billion in New York City in 1995, directly supporting 48,700 jobs. Maintaining their reputation as big spenders, international visitors vastly outpaced their domestic counterparts: though representing only 18 per cent of NYC's total visitor market, they accounted for 38 per cent of all visitor spending.
- Within individual visitor markets, 1995 saw some major shifts in volume and ranking:
  - France, up 38 per cent, surpassed the United Kingdom as the second largest generator (after Canada) of international visitors to New York City.
  - South Korea jumped from twelfth place in New York City's international visitor market in 1994 to eighth place in 1995, with an 84 per cent increase in travel.
  - Portugal continued its rapid ascent within the city's international visitor market, going from seventh place to fifth place in 1995 (with a 21 per cent gain) and passing both Italy and Germany. New York City replaced Orlando as the second most popular US destination for Portuguese travellers, attracting 33 per cent of the nation's Portuguese visitors.
- There were also several noteworthy losses within major markets:
  - Tripmaking from France declined 7 per cent. The loss occurred exclusively among business travellers coming to New York, and may be a consequence of France's recent economic malaise.
  - The United Kingdom slipped from second to third place in the city's international visitor market, with a 5 per cent decline.
  - Switzerland was down 3 per cent in 1995. New York City's share of the total volume of Swiss travellers has plummeted from 49 per cent in 1991 to 30 per cent in 1995.
- Among the most striking differences in the travel behaviour and characteristics of visitors from individual countries were the following:

- Japanese visitors once again led the way with the highest expenditure levels, $260 per day (compared to the average of all overseas visitors of $183). In 1994 Japanese visitors were surpassed by Brazilian travellers in the category of shopping, who spent an impressive $96 per day in this area (v. $90 spent by Japanese travellers).
- German travellers were the most likely of all nationalities to be visiting the United States for a vacation (64 per cent v. 46 per cent). German visitors made their decision to travel the furthest in advance (74 days before departure v. the overseas visitor average of 38 days).
- The profile of French visitors changed dramatically in 1995. Business travel dropped from 36 per cent of all trips to New York City in 1994 to only 23 per cent in 1995. The median household income reported by French travellers declined from $84,700 to $73,900.
- Travellers from Italy were the most likely to be on their first trip to the United States (38 per cent were first-time visitors); Japanese travellers the least likely (10 per cent).
- Scandinavian travellers, with the highest proportion of business travel of all groups (35 per cent v. 26 per cent), were the most likely to be travelling alone (44 per cent v. 39 per cent).

2 DOMESTIC TRAVEL TO NEW YORK CITY

This report presents a profile of domestic leisure and business travel to New York City for 1996. It includes both daytrips and overnight stays, and examines the travel behaviour, spending patterns, and demographic characteristics of key market segments. The report also reviews changes in visitor volumes and New York City's share of the total US domestic travel market, and includes a forecast for travel through 1997. A special feature of this year's report is an in-depth look at visitors who stayed in hotels during their trip to the city. It adopts what is becoming the standard definition of a visitor: a person travelling either overnight or a one-way distance of 50 miles or more from home for a purpose other than commuting.

Methodology

The data presented in this report, with the exception of New York City travel volumes (which were developed by the New York Convention and Visitors Bureau), are from the D.K. Shifflet & Associates DIRECTIONS database. The DIRECTIONS survey is conducted on a monthly basis, in the form of a self-administered questionnaire that is sent to 25,000 census-balanced households within the continental United States. The response rate for the survey is approximately 60 per cent. The DIRECTIONS survey asks respondents about their travel experiences over the past three months. Information is gathered about all overnight travel and day trips of 50 miles or more from home. The trip expenditure data is collected by category (transportation, food, lodging, etc.) for the entire trip, and reflects per person per day spending. For trips that involve more than one destination, total expenditures are then allocated proportionately according to the amount of time spent in each destination. For example, transportation costs such as airfare may be split among several destinations, while the total expenditure was actually made at the point of origin. Thus it is important to note that the trip expenditures cited in this report are not necessarily specific to New York City – they have been calculated on a daily basis for a trip that included a visit to New York City.

Illustrative results

Table 4.7 Total domestic visitors to New York City

	1995	1996
All travel		
Daytrippers	14,300,000	15,400,000
Overnight visitors	10,000,000	10,200,000
Total domestic visitors	24,300,000	25,600,000
Business travel		
Daytrips	5,015,000	5,655,000
Overnight	4,085,000	3,645,000
Total business visitors	9,100,000	9,300,000
Leisure travel		
Daytrips	9,285,000	9,745,000
Overnight	5,915,000	6,555,000
Total leisure visitors	15,200,000	16,300,000

- A strong US economy, along with improved perceptions of New York City as a visitor destination, provided the basis for record-breaking numbers of Americans visiting the city in 1996. The total volume of domestic travel to New York City reached 25.6 million trips in 1996, up from 24.3 million in 1995. The 1.3 million additional visitors who came to the city represented a growth rate of 5.3 per cent for the year, surpassing the 1995 growth rate of 3.0 per cent.
- Much of the growth in 1996 was in leisure travel, which increased by 7.2 per cent from 1995, to 16 million trips. The overnight leisure market was particularly strong, gaining an impressive 10.8 per cent.
- NYC business travel grew by a more modest 2.2 per cent, up to 9.3 million trips in 1996. Within the business travel market, there was a large drop-off in overnight trips (down 10.8 per cent), and a corresponding growth in business daytrips (up 12.8 per cent). This shift was most apparent in trips originating in New York State and Pennsylvania, where business visitors have the option of making day trips rather than spending the night in the city.
- New York City was again the fifth most popular US destination for domestic travellers in 1996. The city has been in fifth place the past two years, after slipping from fourth place in 1994. New York's share of the total has held steady at 0.9 per cent for the third year in a row. The first place destination, Orlando, has been steadily gaining in market share, and was up to 1.4 per cent in 1996.
- New York City's ratings have been steadily improving over the past several years. The city's rating for 'overall satisfaction' (on a scale where 1 = poor and 10 = excellent) was up to 7.4 in 1996. At the same time the average rating of all US cities has remained unchanged, trailing New York with a rating of 7.1. The average rating of the city for value made some progress in 1996 (up to 6 from 5.7 in 1995), but still remains below the average rating for US cities overall (7.0).
- The demographic profile of NYC visitors changed in several ways in 1996:
  - 'Generation X' visitors (i.e. aged 18–34 years old) made large in-roads into the city's visitor market, representing 36 per cent of all NYC domestic trips, up from 35 per cent in 1995.

- The mean income of NYC visitors declined from $61,100 in 1995 to $57,600 in 1996.
- The proportion of visitors employed in managerial or professional occupations declined from 51 per cent in 1995 to 45 per cent, while visitors in technical/sales/administrative positions were up to 23 per cent from 18 per cent in 1995. This shift occurred primarily within the business visitor market.

Overnight leisure visitors
Trips by overnight leisure visitors (which represented 25.6 per cent of all domestic trips) grew from 5,915,000 in 1995 to 6,555,000 in 1996, equalling a very impressive growth rate of 10.8 per cent. The strong growth in overnight leisure travel was well-timed, helping to compensate for losses in the NYC overnight business market.

Trip origins:
- One-third of New York City's overnight leisure visitors came from New York State (15.4 per cent) and California (15.2 per cent). California moved up from fourth place in 1995, surpassing closer East Coast origins .
- New Jersey moved up from ninth to third place, with a 5.6 point leap in market share.

Overnight business visitors
New York City's overnight business visitors include both travellers who stay in hotels or motels while in the city, as well as those who were put up by friends or relatives.

After registering an unusually high gain in 1995, overnight business travel to New York City declined by 10.8 per cent in 1996, from 4,085,000 trips to 3,645,000, still above the 1994 level. There were significant losses from two nearby areas, New York State (−5.3 per cent) and Pennsylvania (−2.5 per cent). It appears, however, that many of these overnight trips were replaced by day trips, since the total volume of business visitors (i.e. day trippers and overnight visitors) from these two states actually increased.

Trip origins:
- California surpassed New York State in 1996 as the number one generator of overnight business travellers to New York City, producing 19 per cent of the total. Because of the losses described above, New York State slipped to second place (with 10.3 per cent of the total) and Pennsylvania dropped from third to sixth place (at 5.1 per cent).
- There was a major shift in the occupational profile of all NYC business visitors (daytrip and overnight combined): the proportion in managerial/professional occupations was down from 66 per cent in 1995 to 54 per cent, while the percentage in technical/sales/administrative positions grew from 13 per cent to 20 per cent

Meeting/convention delegates
Meeting/convention delegates, who come to New York City on both day trips and overnight stays, made up 15 per cent of the city's domestic visitor market in 1996. The volume of meeting/convention delegates grew from 3,086,000 in 1995 to 3,866,000 in 1996, an increase of 25.3 per cent. This rapidly growing market represents a highly desirable group of visitors for New York City, spending more on a daily basis than any other type of visitor.

- Ninety-five per cent stayed in hotels while in the city.
- They gave New York City its lowest ratings for both satisfaction and value.

Trip origins:

- While meeting/convention delegates travel from throughout the United States to visit New York City, the two largest sources of these visitors are close-by: New York State (with 25 per cent of the total) and Connecticut (14 per cent).
- California climbed to third place in 1996, generating 9 per cent of the city's meeting/convention delegate market (up from 4 per cent in 1995). Two nearby locations, New Jersey and Pennsylvania, both lost in their shares.

Day trippers

After remaining at virtually the same level in 1994 and 1995, New York City's day tripper market took off in 1996. Of the 1.3 million additional domestic visitors the city received in 1996, 1.1 million were day trippers. The total volume of day trips (which represented 60 per cent of the city's domestic visitor market) grew from 14,300,000 in 1995 to 15,400,000 in 1996, an increase of 7.7 per cent. The rate of growth was especially strong on the business side of the day tripper market, which gained 12.8 per cent to 5,655,000. To a large extent the additional business day trips appear to have replaced losses in the city's overnight business market, most notably for trips originating in New York State and Pennsylvania. Leisure daytrips grew by 5.0 per cent for the year, from 9,285,000 in 1995 to 9,745,000 trips.

- One-quarter reported primary purpose of trip was to attend a 'special event' in the city.

Trip origins:

- Sixty per cent of all NYC day trips in 1996 originated in three nearby states: New York State (25 per cent), Pennsylvania (18 per cent) and New Jersey (14.7 per cent). Pennsylvania replaced New Jersey as the second largest generator of NYC day trips. Pennsylvania's gain in day trips also compensated for a decline in overnight travel from the state.

Hotel leisure and business visitors

Visitors from throughout the United States who stay in hotels while in New York are a key component of the city's tourism industry, representing one-quarter of all NYC domestic visitors. Hotel leisure and business visitors are sub-sets of New York's overnight leisure and overnight business markets. Hotel leisure visitors represented 44 per cent of all NYC overnight leisure visitors; the remaining leisure visitors stayed in private residences or other accommodation. Since business visitors are less apt to stay in private homes, hotel business visitors made up the bulk of the total volume of overnight business visitors: 84 per cent.

The total volume of NYC domestic hotel visitors in 1996, at just under 6 million trips, changed little from 1995 (down 1.1 per cent). Within the hotel market, however, hotel leisure trips from 2,500,000 trips in 1995 to 2,800,000 in 1996. Hotel business travel volumes went in the opposite direction, decreasing from 3,268,000 to 3,062,000 trips. The 206,000 fewer hotel business travellers represented a 6.2 per cent decline from 1995.

Table 4.8 A summary of the major categories of behaviour monitored in the two studies

Domestic travel study	International travel study
Share of total domestic market Share of total US leisure visitor market Share of total US business visitor market	Share of total US international market

| **Total domestic visitors:**
● daytrippers
● overnights
● composition of visitors by state of origin/New York Designated Market Areas (specific central cities and their surroundings as unified geographic market)
● by purpose (vacation/holiday, business, VFR, convention, study, other) | **Total international visitors:**

● composition of visitors by region/ country

● by purpose (vacation/holiday, business, VFR, convention, study, other) |

| **Domestic visitor spending:**
● by day
● by category of spend (shopping, lodging, food, transportation, entertainment, other)
● by market segment (leisure, business, leisure-overnight, business-overnight, delegates, daytrippers, couples) | **International visitor spending:**
● by day
● by category of spend (shopping, lodging, food, transportation, entertainment, other) |

| **Profile data on domestic visitors:**

● type of lodging (hotel/motel, private home, other)
● length of stay (1-8 nights+)

● occupational status (managerial/ professional, technical/sales/ administrative) | **Profile data on international visitors:**
● advance decision time (6 bands: 1 week or less to more than 4 months)
● sources of travel information (travel agent, friends/relatives, airline, travel guides, print articles, company travel dept., tour operator, print ads)
● methods of pre-booking (travel agent, friends/relatives, company travel dept., called hotel, tour operator, business association)
● use of prepaid accommodation (air/lodging, air/lodge/bus, guided tour, air/lodge/tour, air/lodge/bus/tour, air/car rental, air/lodge/car rental, cruise)
● first time and repeat visitors
● type of lodging (hotel/motel, private home, other)
● length of stay (1-16 nights)
● travel companions (alone, spouse, family, friends, business association, tour group)
● demographics (male/female, age, occupation (manager/executive, professional/tech, clerical, student, homemaker, retired, other)
● median household income ($50,000-$120,000+) |

(New York Convention Bureau)

Questions

1 What are the differences in the categories of behaviour tracked in the international and domestic visitor studies?
2 Why do these differences exist?
3 Compare the information gathered on tourism behaviour by NYCVB with that in any other destination visitor study? (For example, the United Kingdom Tourism Survey or a regional tourist board survey.)
4 This chapter has offered three main approaches to tourist behaviour analysis. Which of them does the NYCVB data *most* exemplify?
5 How do the methodologies of the international and domestic studies vary?
6 Reread the second section of this chapter on the consumer behaviour model of tourism behaviour and identify which social and individual variables *are* and *are not* monitored in the NYCVB studies.
7 What are the main trends observable in:
   a) the international study?
   b) the domestic study?

References and bibliography

Assael, H. (1987) *Consumer Behaviour and Marketing Action*, Kent Publishing Co., Boston, USA

Barbellion, W.N.P. (1919) *Enjoying Life and Other Literary Remains*, Chatto & Windus

Barnard, J. (1967) The line shooters, *Town*, April

Bartlett, F. C. (1932) *Remembering: A Study in Experimental and Social Psychology*, Cambridge University Press

Beioley, S. (1997) Four weddings, a funeral and a holiday – the visiting friends and relatives market, *Insights*, pp B1–B15, British Tourist Authority

Boechner, S. (1982) *Cultures in Contact*, Prentice Hall

Boorstin, D. (1963) *The Image*, Pelican

Bourdieu, P. (1984) *Distinction: A Social Critique of the Judgement of Taste*, Routledge & Kegan Paul

Butler, S. (1923) *Alps and Sanctuaries*, Cape

Buzzard, J. (1993) *The Beaten Track: European Tourism, Literature, and the Ways of Culture*, Oxford University Press

CACI/NTC (1998) *The Geodemographic Pocket Book*, CACI/NTC Publications Ltd

Cohen, E. (1972) Towards a sociology of international tourism, *Social Research*, Vol. 39, No. 1, pp 164–82

Cohen, E. (1974) Who is a tourist? A conceptual clarification, *Sociological Review*, Vol. 22, No. 4, pp 527–55

Cohen, E. (1984) The sociology of tourism, approaches, issues, findings, *Annual Review of Sociology*, pp 373–92

Cook, R.L. and McCleary, K.W. (1983) Redefining vacation distances in consumer minds, *Journal of Travel Research*, Fall, pp 31-4

Cooper, C.P. (ed.) (1991) *Progress in Tourism, Recreation and Hospitality Management*, Vol. 3, Bechaven Press, London and New York

Cosgrove, D.E. (1984) *Social Formation and Symbolic Landscape*, Croom Helm

Cramond, C. (1998) *Social stratification in tourism choice and experience in the 1990s*, unpublished M.Sc. thesis, University of Strathclyde, Glasgow

Crompton, J. (1979) Why people go on pleasure vacation, *Annals of Tourism Research*, Vol. 8, No. 2, pp 187–219

Dann, G. (1981) Tourist motivation: An appraisal, *Annals of Tourism Research*, Vol. 6, No. 4, pp 408–24

Dann, G. (1977) Anomie, ego-enhancement and tourism, *Annals of Tourism Research*, Vol. 4, No. 4, pp 184–94

Davidson, R. (1994) *Business Travel*, Pitman

Denvir, B. (1984) *The Early Nineteenth Century: Art, Design and Society 1789–1852*, Longman

Echtner, C. and Brent Ritchie, J.R. (1991) The meaning and measurement of destination image, *Journal of Tourism Studies*, Vol. 2, No. 2, pp 2–12

Engel, J.F., Blackwell, R.D. and Miniard, P.W. (1990) *Consumer Behaviour*, Dryden Press

Fussell, P. (1980) *Abroad*, Oxford University Press, Oxford

Gilbert, D.C. (1991) An examination of the consumer behaviour process related to tourism, in Cooper, C.P. (ed.) op.cit,. pp 78–105

Goodall, B. (1991) Understanding holiday choice, in Cooper, C.P. (ed.) (1991) op.cit., pp. 58–77

Graburn, N.H.H. (1983) The anthropology of tourism, *Annals of Tourism Research*, Vol. 10, No. 1, pp 9–33

Gray, H.P. (1970) *International Travel-International Trade*, Heath Lexington Books, Lexington, USA

Hollingdale, R.J. (ed.) (1981) *A Nietzsche Reader*, Penguin

Leiper, N. (1995) *Tourism Management*, RMIT Press, Collingwood, Victoria

Levi-Strauss, C. (1978) *Structural Anthropology*, Vol. 1, Allen Lane

Lowenthal, D. and Prince, H.C. (1964) The English landscape, *Geographical Review*, Vol. 54, No. 3, pp 309–46

Prince, H.C. and Lowenthal, D. (1965) English landscape tastes, *Geographical Review*, Vol. 55, No. 2, pp 186–222

MacCannell, D. (1976) *The Tourist*, Macmillan

Mannell, R.C. and Iso-Ahola, S.E. (1987) Psychological nature of leisure and tourism experience, *Annals of Tourism Research*, Vol. 14, pp 314–331

Mansfield, Y. (1992) From motivation to actual travel, *Annals of Tourism Research*, Vol. 19, pp 399–419

Mayo, E.J. and Jarvis, L.P. (1981) *The Psychology of Leisure Travel*, Van Nostrand Reinold

Maclellan, R. and Smith, R. (eds) (1998) *Tourism in Scotland*, International Thomson Business Press

Moutinho, L. (1987) Consumer behaviour in tourism, *European Journal of Marketing*, Vol. 21, No. 10, pp 1–44

Nir, Y. (1985) Cultural dispositions in early photography: The case of the Holy Land, *Journal of Communication*, Summer, pp 31–50

Pearce, P.L. (1982) *The Social Psychology of Tourist Behaviour*, Pergamon Press

Pike, J. (1998) Customer service: Integrating systems for a quality visitor experience, *New Horizons Conference Proceedings*, Scottish Enterprise, Glasgow

Platt, A., McGown, V., Todhunter, M. and Chalmers, N. (1991) *Japanese for the Tourist Industry: Culture and Communication*, Hospitality Press, Melbourne

Plog, S. (1973) Why destination areas rise and fall in popularity, *Cornell Hotel and Restaurant Administration Quarterly*, Nov., 13–16

Ryan, C. (1991) *Recreational Tourism: A Social Science Perspective*, Routledge

Sartre, J-P. (1962) *Nausea*, Hamish Hamilton

Schlentrich, U.A. (1996) Business travel marketing, in Seaton, A.V. and Bennett, M.M. (eds) op.cit., pp 318–49

Seaton, A.V. (1992) Social stratification in tourism choice and behaviour since the war, *Tourism Management*, Vol. 13, No. 1, March, pp 106–12

Seaton, A.V. (1996) Tourism behaviour, in Seaton, A.V. and Bennett, M.M. (eds) op.cit., pp 55–87

Seaton, A.V. (1998) The history of tourism in Scotland: Approaches, sources and issues, in Maclellan, R. and Smith, R. (eds) op.cit., pp 1–41

Seaton, A.V. and Bennett, M.M. (eds) (1996) *The Marketing of Tourism Products*, International Thomson Business Press,

Seaton, A.V. and Hay, B. (1998) The marketing of Scotland as a tourist destination 1985–1996, in Maclellan, R. and Smith, R. (eds) op.cit., pp 209–40

Seaton, A.V. and Palmer, C. (1997) Understanding VFR tourism behaviour: The first five years of the United Kingdom tourism survey, *Tourism Management*, Vol. 18, No. 6, pp 345–55

Seaton, A.V. and Tagg, S. (1995) The European family vacation: Paedonomic aspects of choices and satisfactions, *Journal of Travel and Tourism Marketing*, Vol. 4, No. 1, pp 1–21

TIAA (1997) *Travelscope Survey: Profile of Travelers Who Participate in Historic and Cultural Activities*, Travel Industry Association of America, Washington, DC

Turner, V W. (1969) *The Ritual Process: Structure and Anti-Structure*, Allen Lane

Wilkie, W.W. (1990) *Consumer Behaviour*, 2nd edition, John Wiley

Williams, T.G. (1982) *Consumer Behaviour: Fundamentals and Strategies*, West Publishing Co., New York

5 Marketing research for travel and tourism

Objectives

By the end of this chapter you should be able to:

- understand the need for and uses of valid and reliable research data
- identify the main concepts and stages involved in the research process
- identify the research problem
- understand the difference between qualitative and quantitative research methods
- suggest research techniques appropriate to the problem
- critically evaluate the research of others
- design and implement a programme of research appropriate to the problem/situation.

Introduction

Travel and tourism are complex subjects covering a huge range of issues. In conducting research in this industry one may be asked to investigate subjects as diverse as the experience of the individual tourist on a day trip in their home country to the concerns of international tour operators. Each research project poses a unique set of problems for the researcher. The purpose of this chapter is to provide an introduction to some of the main concepts and decisions involved in the research process, as well as the main techniques used. The emphasis will be on the decisions that must be made as part of survey design – from the definition of the research problem to the design of the questionnaire and data collection. The main techniques of qualitative research will also be discussed.

It is not the intention to cover data analysis here as the confines of this chapter would not allow justice to be done to the wide range of techniques and software packages available. These can be found in detail in other texts. Suffice to say that there are many computer software packages for PCs available to the researcher, such as SPSS and MINITAB, now both in Windows format. SPSS has recently extended its range of software to include a qualitative data analysis program. This is still fairly expensive and there are cheaper alternatives available, such as Sage Publications' software, QSR NUD*IST.

The purpose of marketing research

What is marketing research?

Kotler defines marketing research as:
'the systematic design, analysis and reporting of data and findings relevant to a specific marketing situation facing the company.'

(Kotler, 1994)

It is often asked if there is a difference between market research and marketing research. The difference is in the scope of the investigation, as shown in Figure 5.1. Market research is used to refer to research into a specific market, investigating such aspects as:

- market size
- market trends
- competitor analysis
  and so on.

Marketing research is a much broader concept, covering investigation into all aspects of the marketing of goods or services, such as:

- product research and development
- pricing research
- advertising research
- distribution research

as well as all the aspects of market analysis covered by market research.

Figure 5.1 A comparison of the areas covered by market research and marketing research

Why is information necessary?

Marketing research in the travel and tourism industry has, in the past, been seriously under-utilised and still represents only a very small part of the total market research turnover in spite of the massive growth of these sectors. Hodgson (1995) suggests that this has been mainly due to a combination of factors, including the need for marketers to react rapidly, therefore relying more on judgement; the restrictions imposed by official regulations, which promotes a perceived limit on the value of research; an over-reliance on price alone as a marketing weapon and weak branding in a competitive commodity market. Consumers are becoming increasingly sophisticated with higher expectations. This, combined with a more complex and fragmented market environment, means that marketing research is becoming ever more important for business success.

An understanding of the market and the needs and wants of your consumers now, and in the future, is rarely based on intuition alone. Sound market information provides the basis for marketing decisions. Marketing research, properly designed and implemented, will provide this information. In growth industries, such as travel and tourism, this is particularly relevant when considering key issues such as customer satisfaction within the hotel industry or future demand for particular holiday destinations. More recently, marketing research is being used to assess the impact (both economic and environmental) of films and TV. For example, villages used in TV's *Heartbeat* and *Hamish Macbeth*, as well as locations both used for and suggested by the films *Rob Roy*, *Braveheart* and *Robin Hood, Prince of Thieves* are now well-established tourist destinations.

Marketing research as part of a marketing information system

The wealth of information flowing into a company has to be organised so that it reaches the right people. Successful companies operate marketing information systems (MIS) to gather accurate, up-to-date information, analyse it and disseminate the results to appropriate decision-makers in time to allow the company to maximise its opportunities and to avoid potential threats. Along with other information-producing departments within the company (sales, accounts, etc.), marketing research can assist management in the decision-making process across the full range of marketing activities, from description of a market segment to prediction of future trends.

The scope of marketing research

There is no area of marketing activity to which the techniques of marketing research cannot be applied. Marketing research can provide information on the size and structure of a specific market as well as information about current trends, consumer preferences, a competitor's activities, advertising effectiveness, distribution methods and pricing research. Marketing research also plays a vital role in the development of new products and new advertising and promotion strategies. It can also monitor performance following implementation of those strategies.

The techniques used in the collection of marketing information depend largely on the nature of the research problem, but will vary from the well-known street interview to more sophisticated techniques used in such areas as motivation research.

Types of research

There are numerous research techniques available which can be applied to all areas of tourism marketing, although not all techniques are appropriate to every situation. Broadly speaking, there are two types of research: qualitative and quantitative. The use of these two types of research depends not only on the research problem but also on the nature of the information required (detailed, in-depth data or broad-based statistical data from a large sample) and the stage in the research process (for example, exploratory).

Qualitative research
Qualitative research offers the researcher the opportunity to obtain information on motivations, opinions, perceptions, feelings and attitudes in such depth that would be difficult using quantitative techniques. Essentially, the *how* and *why* of a situation, rather than *how many*, is examined. Qualitative research uses techniques such as group discussions, individual in-depth interviews, projective techniques and observation. The techniques can be very time-consuming so respondents are usually given some kind of incentive to take part which may be in the form of a small gift, shopping voucher or cash. This, of course, adds to the research costs. Data analysis may be difficult owing to its depth and complexity and so it should be carried out by experienced and trained researchers. Qualitative research is invaluable for basic exploratory studies, development of new products

or brands (for example, deciding whether 'Cumbria' or 'The Lake District' would prove more successful) and creative development studies (for example, brochure development), providing information which may be quantified at later stages of the research.

Uses of qualitative research

Qualitative research is concerned with understanding rather than measurement. It is particularly useful in a number of areas. These include:

- hypothesis formulation concerning relevant behaviour or attitudes for later quantitative testing
- assisting in questionnaire design – the variables or attributes to be examined can be defined as well as appropriate language to address those issues
- clarifying complex topics – demonstrations or interviewer explanations can be used to explain a new or complex product or service to respondents to identify any problems prior to carrying out a survey
- obtaining a general understanding of consumer attitudes and opinions at the exploratory/developmental stage of research. This is particularly useful in areas such as new product/service/strategy development and screening, creative development research and in communications research, assessing what is understood by the consumer and how
- new product development – qualitative research methods are particularly valuable at the idea generation and screening and concept testing and development stages.

Limitations of qualitative research

Due to the nature of qualitative research, which is mainly conducted prior to a quantitative survey, small samples of the research population are used. These are usually selected purposefully rather than by probability-based sampling, therefore the results cannot be generalised to the entire research population.

The other main problem with this method of research lies with the researcher. Findings may be limited by the skill and experience of the person collecting the information so it is essential that the interviewers/moderators are well trained.

Qualitative research is often considered easier than quantitative research. This may be because groups are relatively easy to set up, but they are difficult to moderate and the analysis of the database can be extremely cumbersome, even with the use of a software package.

Quantitative research

Quantitative research provides information to which numbers can be applied. Quantitative research is the best known face of marketing research and its main survey method is what most people recognise as marketing research. The chapter will focus mainly on this type of research.

An overview of the marketing research process

The collection of information is a process that must be planned. There are many different areas in which planning decisions need to be made, so good organisation is vital. This is particularly true when the questions that need to be addressed cannot be done so by one type of research alone. In reality most research projects consist of a mixture of both qualitative and quantitative methodologies. This triangulation of methods allows the researcher to gain more complete information, giving as near as possible a complete picture.

Stages in the research process

Research procedures vary depending upon the nature of the research problem, but in general, the process of marketing research is made up of a number of stages, as follows.

1 Define the research problem and set the research objectives.
2 Design the research. This includes:
   a) data sources
   b) select the sampling method
   c) select the data collection method
   d) design the data collection form (questionnaire).
3 Test the research design (pilot).
4 Collect the data.
5 Analyse the data and interpret the results.
6 Present the findings.

Problem definition and setting research objectives

Defining the research problem is the most critical step in the research process. Unless the problem is accurately defined, the information collected will be of limited or no use. Careful thought and discussion about the problem, the information needed to address the problem and the relative value of the information collected should take place before anything else. A structured, systematic approach to decision-making will also enable management (or the commissioner of the research) to set the objectives of the research. In other words, what is the problem and what do we want to find out to try to solve it? This preliminary planning is important as it has implications for the design of the research and the quality of the information collected.

Research design

There are three types of research design

● exploratory
● descriptive
● causal.

The choice of research design will depend on the problem previously defined.

Exploratory research

This is most useful in the early stages of research, particularly if the researcher is not familiar with the subject area. There is no formal structure to exploratory research as the researcher needs to look at a wide range of information sources without being restricted. The aim of exploratory research is to uncover any variables that may be relevant to the research project, as well as an investigation of the environment in which the research will take place.

Descriptive research

The purpose of descriptive research is to provide an accurate description of the variables uncovered by the exploratory stage. This could be used to investigate the market share of a company's products or the demographic characteristics of the target market (age, sex, income, etc.). Data is usually obtained from secondary data sources or from surveys.

Causal research

Causal research is used to determine the relationship between variables, such as the relationship between advertising and destination choice.

Data sources

Data come from two sources:

- *primary* – primary sources are those used for the purpose of collecting information specifically for the current research project
- *secondary* – secondary sources consist of information that has already been collected for other purposes.

Primary sources

Most marketing research projects will involve the collection of more up-to-date information than is available from secondary sources. Primary sources of information may include tourists, airline companies, travel agents, hotels, and so on, depending upon the research problem. The information is collected using the qualitative and quantitative primary data collection methods described on pages 109–10.

Secondary sources

These provide the researcher with a starting point for data collection. It may be possible to solve the research problem either wholly or in part by using secondary data, and obviate the need for primary data. This reduces the cost of a research project – secondary data are cheaper to collect than primary data.

Secondary sources of information are in the main fairly accessible, although some sources may remain confidential and others may be too expensive to acquire. Secondary sources can be separated into the two types shown in Figure 5.2.

- *Internal sources* are those that generate information within a company or organisation, for example sales figures, accounts information, etc.
- *External sources* are those that generate information outside the company or organisa-

tion. These are by far the more numerous and some examples of ext
listed below.

- *Government statistics*, for example the National Travel Survey (N'
  Passenger Survey (IPS), information from the four regional tourist boa.
  data, Family Expenditure Survey, *Social Trends*.
- *Trade information*, from the trade press, for example *Travel News, Travel Trade Gazette*
  (*TTG*).
- *Trade associations* Travel agents, airlines and tour operators all have their associated
  trade organisations which compile information on their members and their mar-
  ket, for example ABTA.
- *Financial institutions* Many major banks publish reports on regional and national
  industries.
- *Commercial research* Many market research companies undertake continuous
  research and omnibus surveys (AGB, Millward Brown). Various market reports are
  available, for example from Mintel, Key Note, Travel and Tourism Analyst,
  Euromonitor.
- *The press* It is easy to forget about such an accessible source as this, but much up-
  to-date information can be easily found in the weekly/daily press, such as *The
  Financial Times*, about an industry as dynamic as tourism.

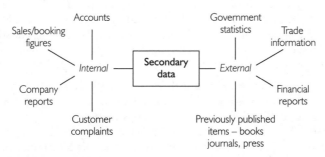

Figure 5.2 Sources of secondary data

The use of secondary data sources, also called *desk research*, can be very time-consuming
because there is such a lot of information available. Keeping the objectives of the research
in mind will help to ensure that time is spent efficiently.

Although secondary data is relatively inexpensive to use (particularly when compared to the
possible costs of a survey), there are a number of points to bear in mind. For example:

- Is the information current? (Some secondary data sources may be out-of-date even by
  the time they are published!)
- Is it relevant to your study? (Much time can be wasted simply collecting information.)
- Is it biased? (Who collected the data and for what purpose?)
- Is it accurate? (For example, how was the sample selected?, etc.)
- Can the results be reconciled with other secondary data?

If you have any doubts about the validity of the data, then using it as a basis for another
study will also result in questionable data. Although the majority of sources are reliable,
it pays to be cautious.

Practical sampling methods

In designing research, a major decision that the researcher must make concerns the selection of a sampling method. Sampling is a very important tool in marketing research. It involves selecting a small number of people from the larger survey population whose characteristics, attitudes and behaviour are representative of the larger group. Before selecting the sample, however, the researcher must first define the research population from which to draw the sample. Exploratory research can help define the population to include all the players and variables that are relevant to the survey. For some surveys, particularly if the survey population is small or concentrated in one geographic area, it may be possible to take a census, which is a useful method in some business surveys. More commonly a representative sample is interviewed as this reduces both time and the cost of the research.

Deciding sample size

Deciding how many people to include in your sample is as important a decision as how they should be selected. Factors such as cost, time and staff availability, level of accuracy required, data collection method and location of the population all play a part in deciding sample size. In reality, cost-effectiveness is the most important factor in deciding how many should be contacted in the research, followed by time and staff availability. If it is decided to select a large number for the sample, there may be insufficient staff available to contact the respondents within the time constraints of the survey, so a smaller sample size may be accepted as a compromise.

When selecting a sample, it is important that there is a high level of confidence that the sample is representative of the research population as a whole. The sample must be large enough to provide accurate results, without being so large as to increase research costs unnecessarily. It is possible to calculate confidence levels for different sample sizes and there are several texts that cover this adequately, for example Moser and Kalton (1971).

Choice of a sampling method

The two main types of sampling method – probability methods and non-probability methods – are shown in Figure 5.3.

Probability methods

Statistically speaking, these are the best types of sampling method as each respondent has a known chance of being selected, so bias is minimised. They also allow the accuracy of the results to be estimated statistically.

Sometimes probability sampling methods are referred to generically as 'random sampling' methods. In fact, this refers to a specific type of very precise probability sample. There is often some confusion over the use of the term 'random'. Selecting people in the street at random is not technically random sampling, but more often refers to selection of respondents by interviewers for quota sampling. The main types of probability sample are:

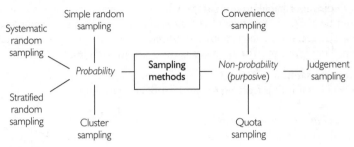

Figure 5.3 Types of sampling method

- simple random sampling
- systematic random sampling
- stratified random sampling
- cluster sampling.

Simple random sampling
Items can be selected from the sampling frame by using the lottery method, for example taking numbers out of a hat. In the UK, numbers for the National Lottery are selected by using simple random sampling. Random number tables are generated by computer and often used in marketing research.

Systematic random sampling
With larger samples, it is more convenient to divide the population by the sample size to calculate the sampling interval (n). A random starting point is selected using random number tables and every nth item after that is selected.

For example, if the sample size is 75, and the population size is 3,000, then the sampling interval is calculated as:

$$n = \frac{3,000}{75} = 40$$

If the random number picked from the tables was 35, for example, then the first item selected from the sampling frame would be 35. Every 40th number after that would be selected until a sample size of 75 was achieved. This method is sometimes called a 'quasi-random' method as the first number was selected randomly.

The advantage of these methods is that they are relatively simple to carry out and sampling error and confidence levels can be calculated statistically. The main disadvantage is that samples may be produced that do not reflect the characteristics of the survey population. For example, if a sample of students was drawn from a list of all students at a university, it is possible that all the students in the sample might be transport studies students. This is clearly not representative of the student population as a whole.

Stratified random sampling
One way to try to overcome this type of sampling error is to use stratified random sampling. This is used when it is felt that different groups within the population have characteristics that are likely to lead to different types of answers, for example in the IPS. The population

is divided into distinguishable groups (strata) who have similar characteristics. Stratification factors should be as relevant as possible to the survey (for example, consumer surveys are often stratified by age, sex, socio-economic group, etc.). A random sample is then taken from each stratum. There are two main methods used to stratify samples:

- with a uniform sampling fraction (proportionate sampling)
- with a variable sampling fraction (disproportionate sampling).

Proportionate and disproportionate sampling
A full discussion of this and the calcualtions involved can be found in Moser and Walton (1971).

Cluster sampling
Cluster sampling is a form of multi-stage sampling and may be used when the survey population is concentrated in a relatively small number of groups (clusters) that are considered typical of the market in question. A random sample of these clusters is taken first. Then a random sample of units from within these clusters is taken. If the number of units within a cluster is small, a census may be carried out.

For example, if you wanted to conduct a survey on the travel patterns of adults in the UK, you could, in principle at least, construct a sampling frame from all the electoral registers in the UK. This is clearly unrealistic. So, for the purpose of this example, you could randomly select 50 postcode areas from around the UK and then randomly select sufficient households from within those postcode areas to give the desired sample size. You would also ensure that the number of households selected from each area was proportionate to the population resident in each area. You could take it a stage further and select the chief wage earner from each selected household to interview.

There is a problem with cluster sampling that occurs if the clusters are not sufficiently representative of the survey population. For example, in a small geographical area it is likely that it will consist of people with similar housing, incomes and lifestyle.

Although cluster sampling can be more cost-effective than some other methods of probability sampling, there is a danger that sampling error will increase if the clusters are not carefully defined before the first stage of sampling.

Sampling frames
When using probability sampling methods it is necessary to use a sampling frame. This is a list of every element in the survey population. The sample is drawn from this list. A sampling frame is essential for probability-based techniques, as each element must have a known chance of selection, and so must be included in the sampling frame. According to Webb (1992), a sampling frame must have the following characteristics.

- Each element should be included only once.
- No element should be excluded.
- The frame should cover the whole of the population.
- The information used to construct the frame should be up-to-date and accurate.
- The frame should be convenient to use.

Examples of sampling frames include electoral rolls, the *Phone Book*, the Royal Mail's lists of postcodes, and other similar databases.

In practice, most sampling frames are not perfect. Not everyone with a telephone is in the *Phone Book*, for example. Finding a sampling frame that is suitable for your research can occasionally prove difficult.

Non-probability methods

With non-probability sampling methods, some element of judgement enters the selection process. The extent to which judgement is used, and therefore the element of bias introduced, varies in these methods. Non-probability methods do not require a sampling frame and the chance of each unit being selected is unknown. Statistical estimates of the size of the sampling error cannot therefore be made. The methods are:

- convenience sampling
- judgement sampling
- quota sampling.

Convenience sampling
Items are selected that are close or easily available. This is useful at the exploratory stage of research, giving the researcher a 'feel' for the subject. Despite being very cheap and quick to carry out, the level of error and bias with this method is likely to be very high and so it should be used with caution.

Judgement sampling
Items are selected by the researcher that are felt to be representative of the survey population. This method attempts to be more representative than convenience sampling. Experts also may be consulted for advice on which items are likely to be more appropriate for the survey.

Quota sampling
This is the most likely non-probability method to produce a representative sample as items selected are based on known characteristics of the population.

For example, assume that your survey population has the following characteristics:

- age: 16–29 = 27 per cent; 30–64 = 57 per cent; 65+ = 16 per cent
- sex: male = 47 per cent; female = 53 per cent.

If we wanted to interview 200 people who were representative of the above population in terms of the two quota controls (age and sex), we would calculate the quotas as shown in Table 5.1.

A survey's accuracy of representation can be increased by narrowing the bands and including more characteristics, such as social class. Interviewers are then allocated a number of interviews (quotas) with specific types of respondents.

The advantages of quota sampling are that it is relatively quick to carry out and easy to administer from a fieldwork point of view. It is also cheaper to use than probability sampling methods. The disadvantages of quota sampling involve problems of bias and sampling errors. The responsibility for selection of respondents lies with the interviewer, which may introduce bias. There is the added problem that there is no probability mechanism with quota sampling, so the sampling error cannot easily be calculated.

Table 5.1 Quota sampling frame (A): calculations

	16–29	30–64	65+	Total
Males	16–29 = 27% Males = 47% 27% of 47% of 200 = 25 Quota = 25	30–64 = 57% Males = 47% 57% of 47% of 200 = 54 Quota = 54	65+ = 16% Males = 47% 16% of 47% of 200 = 15 Quota = 15	94
Females	16–29 = 27% Females = 53% 27% of 53% of 200 = 29 Quota = 29	30–64 = 57% Females = 53% 57% of 53% of 200 = 60 Quota = 60	65+ = 16% Females = 53% 16% of 53% of 200 = 17 Quota = 17	106
Total	54	114	32	200

The figures calculated in Table 5.1 are summarised in Table 5.2.

Table 5.2 Quota sampling frame (B)

Age	Males	Females	Total
16–29	25	29	54
30–64	54	60	114
65+	15	17	32
Total	94	106	200

Quota samples are often used in surveys where fine degrees of accuracy are not required, for instance in product testing for preference between products. Although many companies who provide continuous research services use probability sampling, the majority of *ad hoc* marketing research is conducted using quota samples. If this method gave consistently biased or misleading conclusions, it would not be used.

Primary data collection methods

The researcher should not rely on the use of secondary data alone to answer the research problems. Not all secondary data are available to the researcher as some may be unavailable, for example in confidential reports, and other data may simply be too costly to acquire. The information that is available may be out-of-date or not sufficiently detailed to solve the research problem. Usually, primary data needs to be collected.

Qualitative techniques

The main techniques of qualitative research are the individual in-depth interview, the group discussion and observation. There are also a range of projective techniques available, but these present their own problems and should be used with care.

Observation

There are occasions when it is more useful to observe behaviour than to interview the respondent about it. Observation is usually used at the exploratory stages of research or to complement other research methods, rather than being used alone. When conducted in a systematic and structured way, this method can identify patterns of behaviour, but it cannot provide information on the reasons behind that behaviour.

There are a number of methods available for the observation of behaviour, and these are described below.

Personal observation

The researcher observes behaviour and records it as it occurs. The skill and the objectivity of the researcher play a key role in the collection of unbiased data. The audit data are collected by taking an inventory of certain products or brands (for example, travel brochures) at the premises (at home or office) of the respondent.

Mechanical observation

Recording devices may be used either in laboratory settings or in natural settings. In natural settings, in-store video cameras may be used to record behaviour, with the film being used later for analysis, such as researching passenger flow in airports. Video cameras or CCTV are the most widely used mechanical recording devices. Laboratory-based devices include the eye movement camera that detects the movement of the eye over an advertisement, identifying the visual aspects of the advertisement that gain attention. There are more complex devices that may be used in the laboratory, such as the psychogalvanometer, which is used to measure the respondent's level of perspiration (and so the level of arousal) following exposure to, say, a brochure cover, brand name, company logo, or other stimuli. This particular device, while useful in many areas of marketing, is not widely used by commercial tourism research organisations.

'Mystery guest'

This form of systematic observation has become extremely popular in recent years (as has its retail research counterpart, the 'mystery shopper'). Essentially, the observer takes on a relevant role in a specific situation and observes the actions of others as the situation develops. This is extremely valuable when researching customer satisfaction in hotels or for establishing levels of quality in staff training. Holloway and Robinson (1995) give the example of an American hotelier who made it a practice to stay as a guest in his own hotels, checking on the levels of service provided. He would ask a member of staff (such as a porter or lift operator) to recommend a good place to eat and was usually directed somewhere other than the hotel restaurant. In this way he identified weak areas in the sales training of his staff.

Group discussions

The group discussion is a technique that grew out of group therapy used by psychiatrists. It is based on the idea that individuals who have a particular problem will be more willing to discuss it in a supportive atmosphere with others who share the same problem. It offers the researcher the opportunity to obtain in-depth information on a variety of subjects within a discussion group framework. It is a very flexible technique as each group discussion is led by a moderator who ensures that the conversation is kept flowing within the boundaries of the 'interview guide' (a list of the main subject areas to be covered) without restricting the flow of information from the respondents.

Maintaining a suitably conducive atmosphere can be extremely difficult, so the skill of the moderator is the key to success of the group discussion. Proper interpretation and analysis of the data also depends largely on the skill of the moderator, who must have a knowledge of group dynamics, interviewing techniques, as well as the subject under discussion. This form of qualitative research is often used as a preliminary to survey research.

In the UK, group discussions usually consist of between six and eight respondents. In the USA, the groups (known as focus groups rather than group discussions) tend to be larger (around 10–12 respondents) and the discussion is less informal, with the course of the discussion more pre-determined. Groups may meet in a variety of locations, ranging from the home of the moderator (who may also have recruited the respondents), hotel conference rooms to specialised viewing facilities with one-way mirrors. In the case of the latter, the skill of the moderator is backed up by the interpretation of other researchers and possibly also the client.

The increase in awareness of the use of qualitative techniques has resulted in an expansion in the number of research companies that specialise in providing this type of research to a wide range of industries.

Nominal group technique
The nominal group technique (NGT) is a variation of the group discussion. It involves gathering a group of experts together with a moderator. These experts may be executives of a tourism company, for example, discussing the direction in which the company ought to diversify. The participants are asked to reflect on the issue and record their responses on paper. The group moderator then selects a participant at random to state one of their responses and explain it briefly, so that the meaning is understood by the other group members. This process is repeated until all participants have expressed a response. Subsequent rounds of this process may follow, depending upon the number of different ideas identified by the participants.

After the moderator has checked to ensure there are no duplications, participants are asked to establish the relative importance of each of the response ideas. Finally the results are compiled and ranked in order of importance by the participants.

This technique is a systematic consensus approach designed to produce a list of ideas whose relative importance to both the individual participants and the group as a whole is known. This technique falls somewhere between the flexible, unstructured group discussion and structured survey methodologies. It may be used to resolve both organisational planning issues and consumer research issues, such as identifying the key factors that define different countries as travel destinations and establishing the relative importance of quality and service factors in a hotel or resort.

The Delphi method
The Delphi method is a theoretically similar technique and well-documented for its use in forecasting (for example, Ritchie and Goeldner, 1994; Smith, 1995). The main difference is that the participants are not brought together as a group. It is therefore useful when the 'experts' are geographically dispersed. It is also more structured, as questionnaires have to be sent out to the participants at each stage. Although this method allows the participants more time to reflect on their responses, the usual problems associated

with mail questionnaires start to apply (for example, there is no control over who actually completes the questionnaire).

Although both methods are considered useful for consulting 'industry experts', they are not widely used by commercial tourism research organisations in the UK.

Depth interviews

The depth interview is conducted on a one-to-one basis and designed to encourage the respondent to express freely his or her ideas on the subject under investigation. As with the group discussion, there is no questionnaire as such, but a semi-structured interview schedule containing a list of topics to be covered. Again the relationship between the interviewer and respondent is important, with the interviewer trying to create and maintain an appropriate atmosphere in which to conduct the interview, which may last for anything up to an hour or even longer, depending on the subject and the depth of information required. This technique is particularly useful when the nature of the data to be collected is of a confidential nature, so it is particularly useful in business-to-business research.

Projective techniques

Projective techniques are indirect methods of investigation again originally 'borrowed' from clinical psychology. Rather than asking direct questions, these techniques ask the respondent to interpret a situation or the actions of others. In so doing the respondent will project his or her feelings, attitudes and opinions into their responses, providing insight into their underlying attitudes and motivations. There are a number of techniques available to the researcher. These include role-playing, association tests (word association and sentence completion) and cartoon completion (the respondent provides the caption for the situation depicted in the cartoon). The analysis of data obtained by these methods is complex and ideally requires a background in psychology. However, these methods are very useful for idea generation, brand image research and customer satisfaction research.

Quantitative techniques

Quantitative data collection is usually done on a larger scale than qualitative research, generally in the form of a survey of some kind, whether *ad hoc* or continuous. Survey research is the most well-known of the research approaches and is widely used for descriptive research. As Smith (1995) points out, surveys are the single most important source of information for tourism analysts. Surveys collect information from a representative sample of the survey population on such topics as consumer behaviour, attitudes and beliefs, as well as buying intentions. The strength of these beliefs, attitudes and intentions are measured and the results extrapolated to the population as a whole. If a survey is to be conducted, there are a number of methods available for the collection of data and each has its relative advantages and disadvantages. The main methods are by personal interview, telephone interview and mail questionnaire.

Personal interview

Face-to-face interviewing is still the most widely used method of primary data collection in the UK, although telephone interviewing is becoming increasingly popular. This method is labour-intensive and costly, but is more likely to result in a satisfactorily completed questionnaire than any of the other methods. This is particularly true if the questionnaire is long, complicated or covers sensitive subjects. Respondents have the opportunity to build a rapport with the interviewer, who can elicit full and accurate answers to questions without biasing the responses. In a personal interview there is the opportunity to show supporting material such as examples of a product or still photographs from advertisements. Open-ended questions can also be included in the questionnaire design as the interviewer is present to record the answers verbatim. The interviewer or fieldworker also plays a vital role in the selection of respondents for interview when using quota sampling. This, however, may introduce bias into the survey, the level of which can be reduced by thorough interviewer training.

Telephone interviewing

The development of computer-aided telephone interviewing (CATI) has greatly increased the extent to which telephone interviewing is undertaken. Interviewing is done from a central location, cutting the costs of fieldwork considerably, providing the sample size is large. It is not a cost-effective method for small samples. With the increased demand for immediate information, particularly for commercial omnibus surveys, CATI is ideally suited for the provision of a very fast turn-round of data as the results are recorded and processed as the questions are answered. The sample also can be drawn from a wide geographical spread, as the fieldworkers do not have to travel.

There are disadvantages to this method of data collection. It is difficult to establish a rapport with the respondent by telephone, which is partly why this method is not successful for the researching of personal or embarrassing topics. Many respondents are fearful of 'sugging' – selling under the guise of marketing research – and expect the interviewer to try to sell them double glazing and the like. With a disembodied voice it is also easier for a respondent to refuse or end an interview prematurely. The telephone interview demands the use of very structured, pre-coded questionnaires that may be completed quickly without having to rely on examples of supporting material. An ideal telephone interview will last no longer than 15 minutes on average.

Mail (postal) questionnaire

If the survey population is widely dispersed, it may be more useful to send the questionnaire by mail than to have an interviewer call on the respondent. Mail surveys also have the advantage of a reduction in field staff, and if there is a high response rate, the cost per questionnaire is low. A high response rate is more likely if the survey population consists of members of a special interest group (for example, mountain bikers or hill walkers) and the questionnaire relates to their area of interest. Otherwise, a response rate of between 30-40 per cent is not uncommon.

In a similar vein, mail questionnaires are useful for follow-up research, again to interested parties. This is widely used in tourism research. One such example of this was as a follow-up to a nation-wide TV advertising campaign by the STB. All those people who had responded to the brochure request phone number given in the STB's 'Autumn Gold' advertisement in 1997 were sent a questionnaire asking about short breaks in Scotland. As an incentive, all completed questionnaires were entered into a prize draw with the chance to win a luxury weekend break in the Scottish borders.

The main advantage of mail questionnaires over the telephone interview is that the questionnaire can be lengthy and ask for detailed information. The disadvantages (apart from the low response rate) are several. A mail questionnaire has to compete with the increasing amounts of junk mail that pour through our letterboxes. If there is a high non-response rate, the cost per questionnaire is high, particularly if a reply-paid envelope is included. There is no guarantee that the selected respondent will actually complete the questionnaire, and in spite of careful design, the control of the question sequence is removed. If the respondent does not understand any of the questions, there is no interviewer present to clarify the problem. There also may be a long time-lag between sending out the questionnaires and receiving completed forms.

Self-completion questionnaires

This form of data collection is used extensively and as its name suggests, this form of questionnaire is completed by the respondent themselves. It is really an extension of the mail questionnaire as it has many of its features (anonymity, lack of control over question sequence, etc.). It is not usually posted to the respondents, however, saving something on costs. It may simply be handed to them by the researcher but, more commonly, is placed at a convenient point (such as at a hotel reception, on the table at a restaurant, by an aeroplane seat, in tourist information centres). These questionnaires can vary in length from postcard size, asking only a few simple questions, up to several pages long requiring more detailed responses. There will also be instructions for the return of the questionnaire, such as details of a collection box or reply-paid envelopes/cards, etc. Self-completion questionnaires are very widely used in quality management, customer care and customer satisfaction research, which are vital to the travel and tourism industry.

Questionnaire design

Questionnaire design is an aspect of research in which many people automatically assume expertise, even those without prior research experience. The questionnaire is a vital part of most surveys and great care must be taken with its design. To the novice, the problems inherent in designing a questionnaire tend not to become apparent until the pilot stage of the survey. Many factors will affect the design of the questionnaire, such as the nature of the data required (qualitative or quantitative) and how the questionnaire is to be administered (by personal interview, telephone, mail or other self-completion). However, most questionnaires tend to lie between two extremes – between the highly structured questionnaire used, for example, in telephone interviewing, where the question wording is fixed and responses are limited, and the unstructured interview schedule used in qualitative research, which consists of a list of topics to be covered, with the actual wording of the questions left to the trained interviewer.

A well-designed questionnaire will provide the researcher with complete, accurate and unbiased information using the minimum number of questions and allowing the maximum number of successfully completed interviews.

The decision areas

Questionnaires are notoriously difficult to construct, but Tull and Hawkins (1990) suggest that a convenient way of tackling the design is by breaking up the task into a number of decision areas, namely:

- preliminary decisions
- question content
- question wording
- response format
- question sequence
- questionnaire layout
- pre-test and revise.

Preliminary decisions

These include decisions on what information is required, who will be included in the survey and how they will be contacted.

Question content

This section is concerned with the content of individual questions – what to include, rather than how to phrase the question. Points to consider include the following.

Is the question necessary?
The first decision to be made here is to decide whether or not the question is actually necessary. If the question is not necessary for the purposes of meeting the survey objectives, then leave it out. If the question is necessary, one must take care that the information you elicit will answer the question without ambiguity.

How many questions are needed?
This is a very commonly asked question when designing questionnaires. The questionnaire must include enough questions to fulfil the objectives of the research, but not be so long as to be inappropriate to the data collection method.

Has the respondent the information to answer the question?
Sometimes respondents are asked questions on subjects about which they are not informed. A husband may not have the necessary information if asked how much his wife spends a month on clothing, for example. Some respondents will attempt to answer questions without being adequately informed, which will affect the validity of the results.

Is the respondent able to articulate the response?
Even if the respondent has the necessary information to answer a question, they may not always be able to articulate their responses successfully. If asked to describe the type of person who might visit particular tourist attractions, many respondents would find difficulty in phrasing their answers or expressing themselves fully. It is easier for the respondent if they are presented with a set of alternatives from which they can choose the response that they feel to be the most appropriate. Using aids such as descriptions and pictures makes it easier for the respondent to answer the questions, and so complete the interview.

Asking questions beyond the memory span of the respondent
Asking questions about behaviour over a long time span may not produce accurate information. An example of such a question would be 'On your last trip abroad, how much did you spend on average per day in your hotel restaurant?'

Question wording

Great care must be taken with the wording of questions. Decisions about question wording include the following.

- Does the word mean the same to all respondents? For example, some words, such as 'dinner' and 'tea' mean different things in different parts of the country. Words should be chosen to mean the same to all respondents;
- The use of vague or ambiguous words also should be avoided. For example, 'How did you find the hotel you stayed in on your last trip abroad?' This is vague – does it mean 'how did you locate the hotel?' or 'what was your opinion of the hotel?' (and if so, what *specifically* about the hotel do you require an opinion on?, etc.)?

Are the questions loaded?
Some words or phrases should not be used in questionnaire design as they are likely to result in bias. Emotive words or phrases invite particular responses. For example, 'Are you in favour of taking a holiday in a country that deliberately exploits children in the hotel industry?'

Response format
There are a number of types of response format that may be used. The most commonly used are dichotomous, multiple choice and open-ended formats. Most questionnaires contain a mixture of these.

Dichotomous
Only two responses are allowed, such as 'yes' or 'no', 'male' or 'female'. A neutral 'don't know' category is sometimes included. The advantages are that these questions are quick to ask and the responses easy to record and analyse. The disadvantages are that they do not allow for any shades of meaning to be included in the responses, and many questions would have to be asked to derive information of any detail by using this format alone.

Multiple choice
Here the respondent is presented with a choice of several possible answers to the question, such as a list of holiday activities available at a resort. Frequently, the list of choices is shown to the respondent on a card. The order of the alternative answers should be rotated to avoid bias. Again, the questions are quick to ask and the responses easy to record and analyse. This format also allows for more shades of meaning and the respondent has more freedom of choice in the response. The difficulty of this format is that it is difficult to ensure that the list of possible responses is complete.

Open-ended
The respondent has complete freedom of choice in the response given with this format. This format is often used where little information exists to construct a multiple choice list, or when great detail is required. The advantage is that the information produced is extensive and is free from any bias of suggested answers. The main disadvantage is that the responses are slow to record as they must be recorded verbatim. This can lead to interviewers selecting what they think are the most important points, resulting in bias. These responses are also difficult to analyse as coding frames must be constructed for each question after the fieldwork has taken place. Coding of responses at a later stage requires grouping of responses, which can lose some shades of meaning.

Question sequence
The questions need to be organised logically to avoid introducing error or bias. Generally, you should move from general questions that the respondent finds easy to answer, to more

specific or difficult questions about attitudes or behaviour. In some surveys, it is possible to ask classification questions, which may appear personal or embarrassing, at the end of the interview. If a quota sample is being used, some of these questions will need to be asked at the start of the interview, as they may form part of the quota control. To overcome this, show-cards may be used, for example with age or income bands (see Figure 5.4).

A 15–24 B 25–34 C 35–44 D 45–54 E 55+	A under £5,000 p.a. B £5,000–£9,999 p.a. C £10,000–£14,999 p.a. D £15,000–£19,999 p.a. E £20,000+ p.a.

Figure 5.4 Sample show-cards

Questionnaire layout

The overall aim is clarity. There are some procedures that can aid clarity. These include ensuring that all questions are numbered; filter questions (ones that may be omitted in certain situations) should be clearly marked, instructions to the interviewer should be in block capitals; arrows or visual aids may be used. If the questionnaire is to be completed by the respondent (mail, self-completion), then clarity and ease-of-completion is vital.

Pre-testing (pilot) and revision

The questionnaire must be thoroughly tested, using respondents similar to those who will take part in the final survey. This is known as the pilot stage and is vitally important to the reliability and validity of your survey results. Once this has been done, any modifications needed can be made, and the questionnaire tested again.

Attitude measurement and rating scales

Attitudes are measured in scales and are used to quantify the strength of a response.

Types of attitude scale

Nominal scales

These classify individuals into two or more groups, for example, male/female, agree/disagree.

Ordinal scales

These simple scales rank individuals according to certain characteristics. For example, the top five European holiday destinations listed by a respondent in order of preference may be:

1 Spain
2 France
3 Greece
4 Turkey
5 Italy.

If there are a large number of items, this process may be done in stages, sorting items into low, medium and high ranks first. The items within these three categories will then be sorted and ranked in order.

Interval scales
These scales have regular calibrations, as in Figure 5.5 for example.

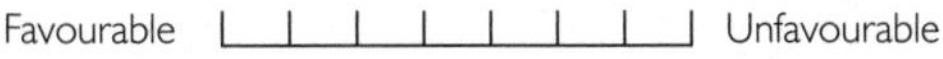

Favourable └─┴─┴─┴─┴─┴─┴─┘ Unfavourable

Figure 5.5 Interval scale

The advantage of this scale is that it can be used to measure the strength of particular attitude. It also allows the use of statistical measures, such as standard deviation, correlation coefficients and significance testing.

Ratio scales
These scales have a fixed origin or zero point, which permits the use of all arithmetical functions. e.g. measurement of length or weight. Measurements of market size, market share and number of consumers are also examples of ratio scales.

The two scales most commonly used in tourism research for attitude measurement are Osgood's semantic differential scale and the Likert summated rating scale.

The Likert scale
Respondents are asked to indicate their level of agreement or disagreement to a series of statements about a subject or object. The statements used are identified as either positive or negative and scores are allocated for particular responses. The list of possible responses is usually:

- Strongly agree
- Agree
- Don't know/neutral
- Disagree
- Strongly disagree.

The Likert scale is not an interval scale, so it is not possible to infer that 'strongly agree' is twice as strong an attitude as 'agree'. The scores achieved by individual respondents are only relative to those achieved by other respondents. Likert scales are popular as they are easy to construct and give reliable information about the degree of respondents' feelings.

The semantic differential scale
A series of bipolar (opposite) adjectives or descriptive phrases are presented to the respondent at opposite ends of a five- or seven-point scale. Respondents are asked to indicate where on the scale best describes their feelings towards the subject or object, or resort, for example. An example is shown in Figure 5.6.

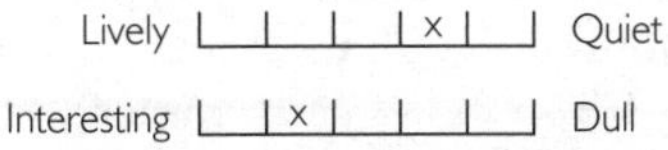

Lively └─┴─┴─┴─┼─x─┼─┘ Quiet

Interesting └─┴─x─┼─┴─┴─┘ Dull

Figure 5.6 An example of the semantic differential scale relating to a resort

Semantic differential scales have been used successfully for such investigations as corporate image, brand image, product image, etc. It is often difficult for consumers to articulate their feelings in these areas, and the semantic differential scale offers them an easy way of expressing themselves. These scales are widely used in marketing research as they obtain information about consumer behaviour that may not be obtained with the same degree of success by direct questioning.

Summary

This chapter has outlined the main research techniques and applications to the areas of travel and tourism. Although it is impossible to guarantee success in highly competitive and dynamic areas of business, such as travel and tourism, having the 'right' information and enough of it can certainly make a positive contribution to success.

The travel and tourism industry has previously been seen as entrepreneurial, with business decisions being made mainly from an operational standpoint and based mostly on judgement. More recently, research data has been increasingly valued as an aid to that judgement, especially by organisations who recognise the need to become consumer- or market-led. Research cannot only define existing markets for consolidation, but can also identify potential new markets, gaps in the market for new products, as well as helping to develop those new products and brands essential for continued market success.

    CASE STUDY
ROUKEN GLEN PARK VISITOR SURVEY

This case study aims to give an insight into issues arising from market research in travel and tourism. It is not intended to be representative of all market research practice in travel and tourism, rather it provides a real example of a survey of visitors to a specific tourism/recreational facility over a twelve-month period. The methodological focus of the case study is on the problems associated with sampling, although general comments are made on other methodological issues arising from this type of visitor survey.

Background
Rouken Glen Park is a major outdoor recreational resource, comprising 225 acres, located on the outer edge of the city of Glasgow. The park contains a range of natural, historical, landscape and recreational features making it a valuable resource in terms of natural environment and community amenity assets. In addition to serving local community needs, the park is a significant recreational amenity for Greater Glasgow and beyond. An unusual feature is the diverse range of products within the park and the mix of commercial and non-commercial operations. The park has a large garden centre, a restaurant and a small art gallery within its boundaries. Clearly certain visitors may be in the park purely to use one or more of these commercial facilities and this has to be taken into account in devising the sampling methodology. The park also has potential to attract a limited number of day visitors and tourists from further afield, in particular for events and festivals held in the park. Although there are no accurate recorded visitor numbers, an estimated 500,000 visits are made to the park annually.

The recreational facilities have evolved over almost a century and much of it has occurred on an *ad hoc* and opportunistic basis. Initially developed for local use, the range and quality of resources has enabled the park to attract visitors from a much wider catchment area. This, together with the establishment of a major events programme, gave the park significant potential to attract tourism revenue for the local economy. The responsible authorities therefore prepared a development plan centred upon fulfilling the development potential of the park both as a community asset and visitor destination attraction.

The Scottish Tourism Research Unit (STRU) of the University of Strathclyde, was commissioned by the local authority (with operational responsibility) and the local enterprise company (responsible for economic development) to carry out a survey of visitors to the park. The need to establish visitor data was a recognised part of the overall development plan.

The aims and objectives of the research
The overall aim of the market research was to establish a profile of visitors to the park.

The specific objectives for the survey were to:
● To profile visitors to the park
● To identify tourist activity within the park based on existing 'attractions'
● To estimate levels of spending in the park
● To measure satisfaction levels of both tourist and local community users
● To identify potential development opportunities for the park.

Information needs
The survey had to include a representative sample of *all* users of the park and therefore had to cover all seasons, days of the week and times of day.

Information needed to meet the objectives included:
● the origin of visitors
● their frequency of visits
● reason for visit
● sites visited
● duration of visit
● mode of transport to the park
● the number of people in the party
● an approximate level of expenditure
● satisfaction level
● what they would like to have/see in the park in terms of attractions.

Methodology
It was decided to carry out personal interviews, at a carefully selected range of locations in the park, over a twelve month period.

The extent and depth of the survey was determined by the detailed requirements of the clients, the finances available to cover survey costs, the time-scale available and the experience of the researchers in conducting similar surveys. The availability of an experienced and flexible team of field interviewers was an additional consideration in choice of methodology.

The interview team

The interviewers were introduced to the general aims and methodologies of the survey and were given training in particular aspects of selecting respondents and implementing the questionnaire.

To ensure appropriate sampling of individual respondents and to avoid the tendency to ask the 'easiest', most approachable visitor, the technique used was to ask the next individual passing after completing, checking and filing the previous questionnaire. In the case of a group passing, rather than interviewing the group or the most vocal member of the group, the individual respondent was selected on the basis of who has the next birthday. This again helped to avoid bias. The interview team reported very few individuals unwilling to be interviewed. The representativeness of the sample was periodically tested against the socio-demographic characteristics of the local population and the population within a 60-minute drive time, and was shown to be broadly in line.

In addition to information derived from the questionnaire, a qualitative element was included in the final report, built up through structured observational techniques used throughout the survey period. The interview team were trained in this technique and debriefed in a series of meetings over the course of the year. In this way, the data derived from the questionnaires could be supplemented and enriched by the additional commentary based on observations made by interviewers. The meetings also served the purpose of quickly identifying technical problems arising in the course of the research. Clearly it was important to avoid confusion between quantitative and qualitative findings in the final analysis and reporting.

The pilot test and survey modifications

The project manager and key members of the team were involved in the pilot survey, lasting one week, which assisted in identification of visitor flows within the park and in bringing to light any ambiguities or other problems with the questionnaire. As a result of this, and in consultation with the clients, a number of modifications were made. For example, the wording of questions was changed, show cards, thought necessary to assist respondents in replying to precoded questions, were dispensed with, the weighting for interview locations was modified and some points abandoned for practical reasons, such as visitor congestion, and the range of precoded responses was increased to cover a wider variety of answers.

The final questionnaire was agreed with input from one other important player in the process. It is often more efficient, in terms of cost and accuracy, for market researchers other than large companies, to subcontract the inputting of data on to computer, for analysis and processing, to specialist database companies. The expert views of this company were essential in devising the final questionnaire, as the costing of data inputting is based on the number of keystrokes. Therefore, the more open-ended questions, the more keystrokes and the greater the cost. The more precoded responses there are, anticipating all likely answers to questions, the less need there is for lengthy open-ended, costly replies. This had the added advantage of reducing the time required for each interview, as interviewers had, in most instances, only to tick rather than write out responses. The average duration of each interview, with experience, was reduced from around five to around three minutes. The cost factor also concentrated the mind and assisted in the simplification of over-complicated questions.

Analysis and reporting

On completion of the data gathering stage, the paper questionnaires were given a final check before being sent to the database company, where the data was put on computer in an agreed form, suitable for processing using the Statistical Package for Social Sciences (SPSS). In STRU's experience this was viewed as more effective than inputting the data in-house. The analysis using SPSS produced tables and raw data on the basic frequencies of responses for each question. These were reviewed and in some instances simplified to become more user-friendly for the client. In many cases, this involved deleting superfluous detail, leaving only numerical frequencies and percentages. The data was then compared, where possible, with other statistics, such as Census data, for comparative purposes and as a check on representativeness.

Responses to open-ended questions were printed in full, then categorised into clusters of similar responses. This assisted in analysis and reporting of what would otherwise have been a long, sometimes confusing, list. Open-ended questions on likes and dislikes in the park fell into ten broad categories which covered the majority of cited responses. The open-ended responses provided useful qualitative data which assisted in devising 'typical' profiles of park visitors and in making conclusions and recommendations.

A number of cross tabulations were then carried out, first to identify significant cross-correlations and, second, to highlight variables which may have been of particular interest to the client. A simple cross-tabulation was where visitation patterns were compared with age group of visitors. This example identified some clear variations depending on age of visitor.

(University of Strathclyde)

Questions

1 Suggest possible reasons for the choice of personal interviews as opposed to telephone interviews or self-completion postal questionnaires in this particular survey.
2 Design an appropriate sampling methodology for the survey to include the following:
   a) an outline of factors that need to be taken into account to ensure the sample is representative
   b) sample size and justification for this
   c) selection of a probability or non-probability sampling method and details of actual method chosen
   d) justification for your choice of sampling method.
3 The case study is based on an outdoor recreational facility. How might the methodology vary for a survey of visitors to:
   a) an indoor tourist attraction?
   b) a heritage town?

References and bibliography

Brent Ritchie, J.R. and Goeldner, C.R. (eds) (1994) *Travel, Tourism and Hospitality Research: A Handbook For Managers and Researchers*, 2nd edition, John Wiley & Sons

Chisnall, P.M. (1997) *Marketing Research*, 5th edition, McGraw-Hill

Collins, M. (1986) Sampling, in Worcester, R.M. and Downham, J. (eds) *Consumer Market Research Handbook*, 3rd edition, Esomar/McGraw-Hill

De Vaus, D.A. (1990) *Surveys in Social Research*, 2nd edition, Unwin Hyman

Holloway, J.C. and Robinson, C. (1995) *Marketing for Tourism*, 3rd edition, Longman

Hodgson, P. (1995) Travelling so fast they can't stop for research?, *Research Plus*, Market Research Society, June 1995

Jefferson, A. and Lickorish, L. (1991) *Marketing Tourism: A Practical Guide*, 2nd edition, Longman

Kent, R. (1993) *Marketing Research in Action*, Routledge,

Kotler, P. (1994) *Marketing Management, Analysis, Planning and Control*, 8th edition, Prentice Hall International

Middleton, V.T.C. (1988) *Marketing in Travel and Tourism*, Heinemann

Moser, C A. and Kalton, G. (1971) *Survey Methods in Social Investigation*, Heinemann

Moutinho, L. and Evans, M. (1992) *Applied Marketing Research*, Addison-Wesley

Oppenheim, A.N. (1984) *Questionnaire Design and Attitude Measurement*, Heinemann

Pearce, D.G. and Butler, R.W. (eds) (1993) *Tourism Research: Critiques and Challenges*, Routledge

Ryan, C. (1995) *Researching Tourist Satisfaction: Issues, Concepts, Problems*, Routledge

Seaton, A.V. and Bennett, M.M. (1996) *Marketing Tourism Products: Concepts, Issues, Cases*, International Thompson Business Press

Smith, S.L.J. (1995) *Tourism Analysis: A Handbook*, 2nd edition, Longman

Tull, D.S. and Hawkins, D.I. (1990) *Marketing Research: Measurement and Method*, 5th edition, Macmillan

Walker, R. (ed.) (1985) *Applied Qualitative Research*, Gower

Webb, J.R. (1992) *Understanding and Designing Marketing Research*, Academic Press

6 Strategic marketing planning

Objectives

By the end of this chapter you should be able to:

- create a strategic marketing plan for a travel and tourism organisation
- describe, apply and critically evaluate the various concepts and models used in the formulation of travel and tourism marketing strategy
- recognise that terminology used in management writing has varying meanings.

Introduction

This chapter considers how to plan an organisation's marketing activities for the long term. Depending on the precise dynamics of the marketplace, this time scale is generally recognised as being three to five years ahead. In the volatile travel and tourism environment, there is the temptation to argue that it is not possible to plan so far ahead and that managerial time would be better spent on other activities. Whilst it is agreed that it is impossible to forecast the future exactly, it is felt that it is beneficial for management to consider events that might happen and so be better prepared to face them.

Terminology

Terms used in management and marketing do not always have commonly agreed definitions. The word 'strategy' itself is a typical example – to some it simply means 'a means of achieving something', to others its definition will include an 'objective' and a 'plan'. Similarly, not everyone will agree with the time scale it covers. Corporate planners may consider 'strategy' for the next five years, but sales representatives may legitimately work out their 'strategy' for the next sale.

Whilst authors and managers increasingly have agreed meanings for words in the language of management, there is still plenty of scope for misunderstandings. It is important to be aware of the variability in meanings of words in all management writing.

Definitions of strategic marketing planning

In defining strategic marketing planning, it is useful to consider, at the same time, its relationship to other aspects of planning. Managers are not unanimous in how to classify their activities, so some definitions help understand the differences in what they do.

Greenley (1986) provides a useful discussion of how planning activities may be classified and suggests a framework which separates planning activities into 'strategic' and 'operational'. His explanations are a clear and useful way of understanding the differences and relationships between the two activities. This is the framework adopted in this text. Accordingly, Greenley characterises strategic marketing planning as having the following features:

'● Exploiting opportunities
● The future shape, size and posture of the firm
● An examination of the firm as whole
● Assessing the effects of environmental variables
● The responsibility of top management
● Developing overall objectives and strategy
● Enduring consequences for the firm's future.'

(Greenley, 1986)

Greenley's characteristics of operational planning are presented at the start of Chapter 7.

An overview of the strategic marketing planning process

Before planning can commence, it is necessary to recognise that an organisation may comprise more than one business. For example, Forte operates in the hotel industry as well as the restaurant market. These separate businesses can be termed strategic business units (SBUs).

For each SBU, the strategic marketing plan should contain objectives that the organisation wishes to achieve in the *long term* and the plans to achieve these objectives. The objectives are typically about the organisation's 'mission' and growth, the latter usually defined as growth in sales. Objectives should only be formulated after the process of analysing the organisation's internal capabilities and its external environment. This process may be termed a *corporate audit*. The plans at this level should be less detailed than the operational plan, which typically deals with issues up to one year ahead.

In creating strategic plans, management may be guided by a variety of models and techniques, such as the product life cycle, and portfolio planning. However in using these aids, decision-makers must be aware of the limitations of them. Managerial judgement should be supplemented by, rather than replaced with, theory.

Managers should also recognise that planning in itself may create problems for individuals in the organisation. Many employees will not find it easy – some may be threatened by the process. Plans that are imposed from 'the top down', in particular, may cause more problems than they solve. The involvement of a wide range of people in the planning process is generally thought to be beneficial, but this may require the organisation to develop planning skills in its staff.

The strategic marketing planning process for an individual SBU is shown in Figure 6.1.

Figure 6.1   The strategic marketing planning process

Criticisms of the planning process

Whilst this text adopts this and other 'logical' frameworks for planning, it should be noted that there is much interesting work which both supplements and criticises this approach. Mintzberg *et al.* (1995) suggest that, far from being a rational, periodic process, planning is more characterised by smaller incremental decisions and that strategy emerges *from* decisions taken, rather than decisions being taken to meet overall strategic objectives. They also provides useful insight into the politics and culture of strategic thinking.

Identifying strategic business units

The strategic marketing planning process can be made simpler by considering organisations as collections of SBUs. An SBU has been described by Kotler as having three characteristics:

'1 It is a single business or collection of related businesses that can be planned separately.
2 It has its own set of competitors.
3 It has a manager who is responsible for strategic planning and for profit performance and who controls most of the factors affecting profit.'

(Kotler, 1997)

This may help managers recognise that even a small business is not necessarily a homogeneous one and within an organisation several 'businesses' may exist, all of which could need strategic marketing planning.

Corporate audits

Before managers can decide 'where we want our organisation to go' (setting objectives and devising plans to achieve them), they must first of all understand 'where it is now' – sometimes known as a situation analysis. Whilst here the concern is for the long-term *marketing* plans, it is necessary for the marketing planner to understand not only the organisation's marketing abilities, but also the strengths and weaknesses of *all* the functions of the organisation. Many non-marketing aspects of the organisation can have a dramatic effect on its marketing strategies. The corporate audit is the process by which an organisation's abilities and its external environment may be analysed.

The internal analysis

It is necessary to consider the internal resources of the organisation in their entirety. This allows the strategist to analyse the contribution which all functions within the organisation *currently* make to its marketing ability and also to consider what *might* be possible in the future. For instance, a relatively cash-rich organisation might wish to consider price discounting as a means of selling. Another, with retail outlets in convenient locations and well-trained staff, may consider achieving growth by offering excellent customer advice and service. The outcome of this internal analysis should be to recognise the business strengths and weaknesses in comparison with those of its competitors. Johnson and Scholes (1993) suggest examining resources which are:

- *physical*, for example, premises, vehicles, fixtures and fittings
- *human*, for example, quantity and quality of all employees
- *financial*, for example, cash flow and relationships with sources of finance.

They also stress the importance of assessing *intangibles*, such as customer loyalty, good contacts, for instance hoteliers that will meet a tour operator's exact requirements. Another intangible is corporate image. To this list of 'resources' should be added *systems*, such as reservations and bookings which, for hotels for instance, can have a dramatic effect on customer satisfaction.

The external analysis

As in-depth coverage is given to external factors affecting the travel and tourism industry in Chapter 3, it will not be examined in any more detail here. It is worthy of note that, taken together, the corporate audit should produce the SWOT analysis (strengths, weaknesses, opportunities and threats). It should be remembered that in planning corporate strategy, forecasts of the future environment are needed. Chapter 7 includes details of techniques that can help in this difficult area.

The management implications of auditing

Internal barriers to planning

Whilst there is an obvious logic to an audit, managers must not underestimate the problems they might face in doing it. When a manager from one function starts to examine the work of those from others, there can be understandable tensions. However, with skill, this problem may also be turned into an advantage. It can bring people from separate functions together, drawing on many differing skills and people, for instance, in comparing a business's financial position to the competition. Accounting staff could make use of their skills of financial ratio analysis.

Similarly, examining corporate image may bring the marketing staff and their marketing research techniques into play. Trying to assess employee skills and flexibility might best be done by discussions with Personnel. Sales staff may be able to provide an excellent analysis of competitors' pricing strategies. Whilst this task of the audit may seem daunting, it can have the added advantage of increasing the 'ownership' of the eventual plans, overcoming the problems associated with 'top down' planning where plans are decided at a high level in the organisation and simply imposed on those lower down.

Who should do the audit?

This is a difficult problem to solve, but there are many alternatives. Some recommend the management themselves, arguing that they know the business, but their objectivity in reflecting on their own past decisions might be questioned. Others suggest external consultants who are likely to be objective, but may be expensive, time-consuming and lack an understanding of the organisation's special situation. In multi-product organisations, it might be possible to use the management of one SBU to review the operation of another, and vice versa. No one approach is without advantage or criticism; clearly it depends on each organisation's individual situation as to who is an appropriate auditor.

Setting strategic marketing objectives

Objectives are statements of 'where we want our organisation to go'. In strategic marketing planning, they should have an appropriate time scale (probably three to five years ahead) and be at an appropriate level of detail, i.e. not too precise – this is done at the operational level. Without objectives, plans become difficult to write – how does a planner decide what is needed without knowing what is to be achieved? Also the later stage of control (establishing whether what was achieved was what was planned – and if not, why not?) similarly becomes unclear.

The potential for complexity in setting strategic marketing objectives (SMOs) should not be underestimated. Organisations may have many stakeholders, all with their own desires as to the direction for the organisation. Whilst, politically, all stakeholders need to be considered, in doing so there is a danger that the strategist generates far too many objectives. Often these become mutually incompatible. For example, stakeholders with a financial interest may want a quick return on their funds invested, whilst managers are more concerned for their own long-term survival. A solution to this dilemma is suggested later; now we need to consider the main objectives that should be set.

The mission statement

Mission statements are made to benefit the organisation by guiding and motivating staff. They are perhaps best defined by Johnson and Scholes as:

'a general expression of the overriding premise of the organisation, which ideally would be in line with the values or expectations of major stakeholders.'

(Johnson and Scholes, 1993)

This question of establishing organisation purpose may be addressed by asking 'what business are we in?' This approach has been common for many years, but the alluring simplicity of the question does not mean there is a simple answer, neither is the process of answering the question easy.

Some organisations with many SBUs manage to produce a single mission statement that applies to all the units; others find that the diversity of their SBUs is such that they require a separate mission for each. Common faults in producing mission statements include:

- defining the business too widely, for example 'We are in the leisure business' (imagine all the activities that might be construed as 'leisure')
- defining the business too narrowly, for example 'We are a coach operator' (coaches are not the only form of 'transport')
- defining the mission in too complex a way, including every possible opportunity open to an organisation. Such statements tend to be lengthy and often give far too little focus to managers in their decision-making.

Business Week (1980) provides the example of Holiday Inns Inc. who, in the USA, widened its definition from being in the 'hotel business' to the 'travel industry'. Following this it bought Trailways Inc. – a bus company – and Delta Steamship Lines. Unfortunately, these companies were so different from the original business, that Holiday Inns were unable to run them successfully and they were subsequently sold off. Holiday Inns now define themselves as being in the 'hospitality business'.

An example of a good, succinct mission statement is that of British Airways (no date), which is 'To be the best and most successful company in the airline industry'.

It should not be thought that the mission statement is the prerogative of large organisations. Bransgrove and King (1996), in a study of 544 small tourism businesses in the state of Victoria, Australia, found 95 per cent were able to describe the mission of their businesses.

Growth

Most organisations set themselves an objective of 'growth'. Arguments for this are that:

- it motivates staff (who wants to work for a stagnant or declining organisation?)
- those financing the organisation like growth (if it is growing they feel they will get returns on their investments).

Care should be taken in not setting growth objectives high when there is no real possibility of such growth. It is debatable whether such plans do motivate; they may have the opposite effect of demoralising staff. It could be argued that realism is better than unfounded optimism, and even planning to 'shrink' is necessary on some occasions. Nevertheless it is recognised that humans seem to want an optimistic future and it is a brave strategist that provides plans to 'decline', however objective these plans may be.

Growth objectives are frequently expressed as growth in sales, sometimes as growth in market share, less frequently they may be expressed as growth in profits. Decision-makers should recognise the differences between *sales* and *share*. For instance, in a declining market, it is possible to increase your market share whilst your sales still decline! Similarly there is a difference in growth objectives set in terms of *volume* – for example a ferry operator may wish 'to increase the *number* of passengers by 5 per cent' – and *value* – for example, the operator wishes 'to increase *revenue* by 5 per cent'. The latter could be achieved by simply increasing fares, the former may require more substantial actions, for example by attracting customers from competitors.

Finally, particularly for commercial organisations, perhaps more thought should be given to setting profit growth objectives. It can be a misconception by managers that growth in sales and/or share equates to growth in profits. This is not necessarily so – organisations can sell more by reducing prices, but usually with a penalty for profits.

It has been suggested already that growth objectives should be *achievable*. Similarly the strategist should be sure that the organisation will be able to cope with the level of planned growth. Growing too fast can inflict long-term damage on an organisation by stretching its resources too far.

In a few exceptional circumstances, an organisation may be trying to slow down or prevent growth. For example, many National Parks are faced with a surfeit of visitors to 'honey pot' locations. In such situations, planners may attempt to protect these assets and plan to demarket them – effectively planning negative growth.

How to set strategic marketing objectives

To avoid the potential complexity identified at the start of this section, Wilson provides useful advice. He suggests that setting strategic marketing objectives can be simplified by answering the following questions:

'1 What business do we want to be in?
2 What profits do we want to make?
3 How fast do we want to grow?'

(Wilson, 1980)

To answer the first question (essentially setting the *mission statement*), he suggests management looks, not just at what is currently supplied to current customers, but also at other markets that the product could satisfy. For instance, many university accommodation services are aware that their economical and functional residences, often marketed to the conference market, also appeal to other cost-conscious customers such as Saga Holidays.

This principle can be taken further by encouraging managers to ask 'What needs does the service satisfy?' rather than 'What service do we supply?' Following this advice, skiing holiday providers, for instance, might recognise that they satisfy the need of customers for exhilaration (amongst others) – this might lead them to offer mountain bike downhill racing. This satisfies the same need but with different technology (and incidentally overcomes the problem of poor snow conditions!).

Lastly, in asking 'What business do we want to be in?', an organisation might consider how it satisfies customer needs better than its competitors. So, if an organisation's strength is that it is prepared to tailor package holidays to meet individual customer needs and does this better than the rest, this could be incorporated into its mission statement.

In setting *profit objectives*, it is recognised that it is extremely difficult to gauge exactly what level of profit might be made. However, setting a minimum acceptable level is a sensible precaution. Thereafter, the needs of all the organisational stakeholders should be considered and balanced. For example, it may be necessary to forfeit short-term profit (possibly an expectation of investors) in order to gain market share (possibly the preferred objective of the management).

The question of *rate of growth* should be carefully considered. Most people involved in organisations will probably want to see growth, but care should be taken in growing too fast. Similarly managers need to be explicit about what it is they want to grow – it is usually sales, but do not forget this might be achieved at the expense of profit.

These three objectives should be set jointly, as changes in any one can affect the others.

Clearly the organisation's strategic marketing objectives can only be sensibly set with sound understanding of the organisation's abilities and in the light of its changing environment – issues we have considered earlier in this text.

Alternative strategies for growth

Whatever mission an organisation develops for itself, it is usually accompanied by the simpler objective of 'growth'. Generally this is stated in terms of sales, but for commercial organisations could also involve a statement about profits.

In an attempt to classify the ways in which growth can be achieved, Ansoff (1968) devised the growth vector matrix, which shows that, by considering products and markets and the 'newness' of these to an organisation, the alternative strategies by which it might achieve growth can be identified (see Figure 6.2). Within each quadrant of the matrix there are further sub-strategies that give clearer guidance as to the marketing actions required to achieve growth.

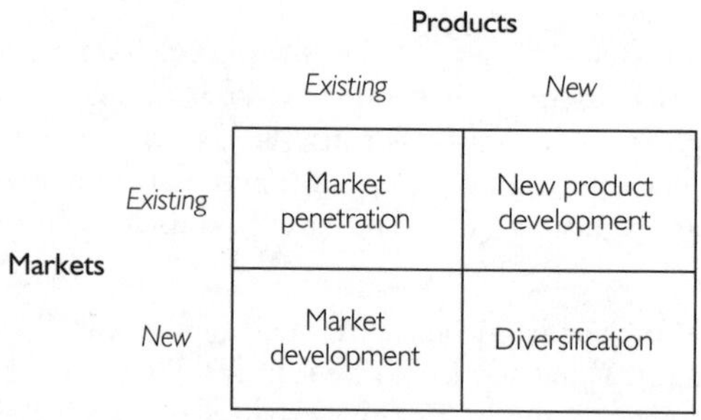

		Products	
		Existing	New
Markets	Existing	Market penetration	New product development
	New	Market development	Diversification

(Ansoff, 1968)

Figure 6.2 The directional policy matrix

Market penetration

This is essentially a strategy of selling more of your current 'products' to your current customers. In the travel and tourism industry this might be achieved in several ways, for example a tour operator might try to sell longer holidays, thus increasing the revenue from an individual customer. Encouraging more frequent use of the product also falls into this category. For instance, in competitive public transport, one operator might maintain customer loyalty by selling books of tickets – almost guaranteeing re-use of their service. Care should be taken in this quadrant of the matrix not to achieve extra volume sales by incautious use of pricing; an organisation doing this might increase its volume sales but decrease its profitability.

Market development

Here the organisation goes into markets that are new to it. Conventionally, this has been seen as exporting, but a more sophisticated interpretation of 'new' can lead to further opportunities. Some might see a segment which a company has not previously tackled as new. For example, Saga, who typically concentrate on the 'grey', over 50 segments, might regard the 18-30 segment as a market into which they could develop (although they should do so with appropriate care!). Also within this box of the matrix are geographic growth strategies. Organisations may expand nationally within their current country, for instance Stakis Hotels from Scotland expanding into the rest of the UK. They may also expand internationally across national borders, for instance Novotel moving from France into the UK.

New product development

This strategy means providing services to our current customers that we have not previously offered. With database marketing, this becomes a particularly important strategy, as current customers are readily accessible by methods such as direct mail. Ski Chamois, a Northern UK specialist ski operator, used this strategy to offer its existing winter skiing customers the opportunity to take a new 'Guinness and Gears' holiday, i.e. supported cycling holidays in Eire during the summer.

Diversification

This is the riskiest strategy and care should be taken not to put an organisation in an unmanageable situation. With it the organisation loses not only knowledge of its customers but also of the products. There are, however, companies that do well at it – Virgin perhaps is one of the best examples. Having diversified from records and retailing into transatlantic airlines, they have more recently moved into financial services.

There is little criticism to be aimed at Ansoff's model, although in use, the differences between new products and diversification become subtle. Some find these inconsistencies frustrating, but the benefits that the matrix brings of a logical and systematic approach to planning should outweigh this problem. The systematic approach should make planners consider less risky, but potentially successful, strategies rather than being tempted too quickly into perhaps dangerous strategies of diversification. Another criticism is that the matrix is a threat to creative approaches to marketing, but in practice the model often stimulates creativity. Planning and creativity should not be seen as mutually exclusive human faculties.

Integrative growth

The matrix of growth alternatives is supplemented by strategies of integrative growth. This is where the organisation considers acquiring other parts of the marketing system in which it exists. The marketing system consists of suppliers, competitors and distributors.

- *Backward integration* entails taking over a supplier, for example a tour operator buying an airline.
- *Horizontal integration* involves taking over competitors.

- *Forward integration* involves acquiring distributors, for example tour operators buying travel agents.

Many strategists fall into the trap of designing far too complex strategic marketing plans. The example below shows how Club Mediterranee took a simple concept, and with few problems, developed their markets internationally.

CLUB MEDITERRANEE GOES INTERNATIONAL

Club Mediterranee is one of the most successful international holiday camp companies. Founded in 1950 by a Frenchman, Gerard Blitz, the company is still run from Paris headquarters. By 1977 the club provided holidays for well over 500,000 people (called *gentils membres* or GMs by the organisation). Of these, around 50 per cent are French, 18 per cent from North and Central America, and 27 per cent from other Western European countries.

The holiday camps are run by a staff of over 11,000 (called *gentils organisateurs* or GOs), in addition to over 1,100 sport instructors. The GOs are largely recruited in France from the French student population; in the Caribbean they are recruited from the American market. The sports instructors are the main full-time members of the organisation, remaining under contract for several years at a time. Each camp has a permanent staff of two or three that handle day-to-day administration. All resorts are based around two key elements of Mediterranee philosophy – informality and easy access to a wide range of sporting activities.

The first is achieved by insistence on sharing meal tables, group activities and youthful staff who encourage the holidaymakers to participate. All meals and wine are included in the holiday price; only drinks at the bar are extra, and these are paid for by beads which are universal currency in the village complexes. Sport is emphasised, with the large number of instructors and the range of sporting activities possible at the Club Mediterranee sites.

Most of the holiday camps in Mediterranean or tropical locations are huts accommodating four, built amongst trees leading down to the beach and restaurant area. Facilities in the huts are fairly basic, in line with the appeal of the Club Mediterranee of 'going back to nature'.

By the late 1970s, the in arrival of the Mitterand government in France meant that the amount of money French holidaymakers could spend abroad was seriously reduced. This led the group to concentrate on building up the number of holidays taken by non-French nationals at Club Mediterranee centres. With certain exceptions, this policy has proved highly successful.

The development of Caribbean resorts for the North American market significantly changed the pattern of Club Mediterranee sales and profitability, which continued to grow at around 10 per cent per annum. Overall, the club had been one of the growth companies in France and the shareholders remain content with the progress of the organisation.

The success of the American venture had been due to various factors:
- concentration on a particular geographic and socio-economic market, especially the ABC1 East Coast urban dwellers

- emphasising the large number of sporting facilities available at the Caribbean club Mediterranean centres
- attracting a specific 18-28 age group.

Following upon its successful American venture, Club Mediterranee strategy continued to concentrate on markets with considerable untapped potential. Of these the UK supplied a likely source of growth. Based on gross domestic product comparisons, the market for Club Mediterranee holidays in the UK would be around two-thirds that of Germany – in the region of 26,000 holidays. Though the percentage of French speakers in the two populations is fairly similar, the fluency of the English population was reported to be steadily dropping, even with the increasing investment in language laboratories in schools.

(Reprinted by permission of Paul Chapman Publishing and adapted from West, A. *Cases in Marketing Techniques*, 1988)

The product life cycle

The popular concept of the product life cycle (PLC) suggests that the sales of products have slow beginnings in terms of sales which then reach a plateau and eventually decline. Profits follow a similar pattern but lag behind sales.

The stages are:

1 *introduction*, where sales are low and growth slow. This is because initially only a few innovative customers are convinced the product is worth purchasing
2 *growth*, where sales increase exponentially as greater numbers of buyers rapidly adopt the product
3 *maturity*, the stage at which growth rates slow as the market saturates and the mass of the target market is purchasing
4 *decline*, where consumers switch their allegiances to other products and sales start to fall.

More importantly, the model has implications for how marketing activities should change over time (see Figure 6.3)

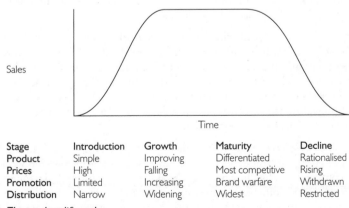

Stage	Introduction	Growth	Maturity	Decline
Product	Simple	Improving	Differentiated	Rationalised
Prices	High	Falling	Most competitive	Rising
Promotion	Limited	Increasing	Brand warfare	Withdrawn
Distribution	Narrow	Widening	Widest	Restricted

Figure 6.3 The product life cycle

Using this model, we might diagnose that the European package holiday market is possibly in maturity, whilst long-haul customised holidays are in their growth stage. British holiday camps have perhaps gone into decline.

It may be helpful to consider the distinction between class, form and brand in life cycle analysis.

- *Class* is the product at its widest level – in travel and tourism we might see family holidays as a class.
- Within the class, we can distinguish *form*, for example one form of family holiday is the holiday camp.
- Similarly, within form there are *brands*. Brands within the holiday camp form could be Butlins, Pontins and Centre Parcs.

Clearly each of these is at a different stage. Family holidays are probably in maturity, whilst holiday camps are in decline. However, at the brand level, there can be subtle differences. Butlins may be in decline, but Centre Parcs are growing.

The PLC has its critics, such as Smith and Thomas (1981) who suggest it is a self-fulfilling prophecy and Mercer (1993) who claims it does not exist. More recent work by Hooley (1995) suggests that it is still a popular and useful tool. The primary danger in using it is that the strategist mistakenly anticipates decline and withdraws marketing resource. The debate then becomes whether the decline would have happened anyway or whether withdrawal of expenditure forced a decline that may not have otherwise occurred (the self-fulfilling prophecy).

The profit implications of marketing strategies

This work, which was pioneered by General Electric and developed at Harvard Business School in the USA by Schoeffler *et al.* (1974), is based on an analysis of the pooled business experience of thousands of SBUs over more than 20 years and has produced much guidance for the strategist. The profit implications of marketing strategies (PIMS) has correlated profitability (measured as return on investment – ROI) with factors such as quality, market share and marketing expenditure. Originally, its most significant finding was the strong, positive relationship between market share and profitability – this led many strategists to 'go for share' with their plans.

The service is available by subscription in Europe. PIMS Europe (1992) has recently started to concentrate on the service companies in the database. They have discovered an even stronger relationship between market share and return on capital employed, claiming market leaders in the service sector are likely to earn 40 per cent on capital, whilst returns for the second in the market fall to about 23 per cent. Of course, caution should be exercised projecting from services as a whole to the travel and tourism industry, but the claim is worthy of further investigation.

The real power of PIMS comes from its ability to compare SBUs within an industry. This allows them to offer powerful benchmark standards against which an individual organisation can compare itself, allowing it to make better informed strategic decisions. Moutinho *et al.* (1996) offer an interesting use of PIMS data in their suggestions for designing expert systems for planning tourism strategy. Abell and Hammond (1979), who offer the best textbook coverage of the service, observe PIMS' limitations by quoting its founder Dr Sid Schoeffler who said, 'Don't ignore what the model says – but don't believe what it says either'. This is perhaps sound advice for all such models.

Multiple product planning models

Some organisations have many SBUs and this creates the need to plan the complexity of multiple product ranges. This is now known as product portfolio planning. The PLC dictates that all products will eventually decline and that others take time to generate profits. A danger of this is a boom and bust pattern of profits from a product portfolio where all the product's life cycles are synchronous. Portfolio planning models have been developed in an attempt to make sure that the products in the portfolio are in differing stages of their life cycles and so produce a manageable cash flow.

The Boston Consulting Group product portfolio matrix

The most common of the models is that developed by consultants, the Boston Consulting Group. Their product portfolio matrix requires the strategist to position the various SBUs on a two-dimensional matrix, according to their relative market share (defined as the SBU's share of the market compared to their nearest, biggest competitor) and the rate of growth of their markets (see Figure 6.4).

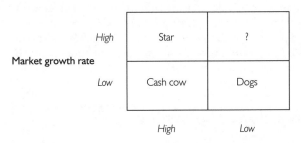

(Reprinted from *Long Range Planning,* Heldey, B., Strategy and the Business Portfolio, February 1977 with permission from Elsevier Science)

Figure 6.4 The product portfolio matrix

- *Cash cows* are SBUs with a high relative share of slow-growing markets. As such they can be given just enough funding in order to maintain their share, whilst their dominance will ensure good revenues. Hence they are cash-rich and can provide funds for investment elsewhere.
- *Question marks* are SBUs with a low relative share of fast-growing markets. They may, with investment, become stars. The funds for this would come from the cash cows. Conversely, they may be in such a weak condition as to be not worth gambling with and should be divested, i.e. sold off to an organisation into whose portfolio they do fit (or closed down).

- *Stars* have a high relative share of fast-growing markets; they require cash to maintain their position, but also generate enough revenue to cover their costs. They are important because, as the market growth rate slows, they will be the cash cows of the future.
- *Dogs*, with a low relative share of slow-growing markets, can be managed to generate a little cash (then called cash dogs). If they become problematic and start to consume cash, they should be divested.

Portfolio management therefore consists of maintaining a balanced range of SBUs that both generate and consume cash, a flow of SBUs from question marks to stars and then cash cows needs to be maintained.

Whilst the theory, with its memorable boxes and names, has the appeal of simplifying decisions in a complex situation, it does have problems. Clearly it requires information about market growth and relative share that may not be available or accurate. Furthermore, the definition of 'market' is open to interpretation, for example, for long-haul flights is the market world-wide long-haul air flights? Or should it be more narrowly defined into flights to the different continents, for instance, the USA, Asia, etc. For an SBU flying only to the USA, the first definition will produce a smaller market share than the second, perhaps resulting in the inappropriate withdrawal of funds.

It has been suggested by Morrison and Wensley (1991) that some SBU managers may, in their own self-interests, define markets narrowly. The effect of this could be to produce an artificially large market growth figure and so attract corporate funds to their SBU.

Nevertheless the BCG matrix is a popular way of planning complex portfolios. Those who think it too simplistic may find the more sophisticated General Electric model better. This model uses dimensions of industry attractiveness and business strength to produce a similar matrix. However, this has greater problems of information requirements. Both models are described in greater detail in Kotler (1997)

The human dimensions of planning

Some of the arguments for planning focus on the beneficial effects it may have on the people in an organisation. Good planning is claimed to motivate and direct individuals in their labours. It should also be recognised that planning may have a dysfunctional effect as well. For some people it may mean a significant change in the way they work; whilst this can be stimulating and motivating, it can also be threatening and stressful.

The literature of *change management* can give an understanding of the possible problems and solutions. Whilst it may be open to debate whether planning creates stress, it is important to recognise even the best plans will not succeed without the efforts of the people in the organisation responsible for implementing them. Perhaps the best marketing author to deal with this issue in a marketing context is Piercy, arguing:

'We have begun to recognise that it is not enough to have a service strategy and the systems to deliver it, we have to think about the people who deliver it, and the people who receive it.'

(Piercy, 1992)

He goes on to cite Marriott Hotels as being a superb example of service success by empowerment of its employees.

Empowerment is essentially giving line employees real power to take decisions that improve customer service. For example, a waitress may be given the authority that allows her to choose how she handles complaints – she may decide to waive a customer's bill if they have complained about the quality of their food.

However an organisation chooses to manage its employees, strategists must not lose sight of the human consequences of their planning.

Organising for marketing

Whilst it is beyond the scope of this text to discuss the pros and cons of the various structures that might be used to organise a marketing department, some consideration of the issue is necessary. The way people in a company are organised can have a significant effect on how successful marketing planners are likely to be. Whilst even small organisations, such as a family running a bed and breakfast, can have problems of mutually agreed strategies and responsibilities, the problems become greater with larger size and start to involve the issue of internal politics.

Hierarchical or pyramid structures

Here responsibility and authority is conventionally organised in layers of decreasing numbers with the Chief Executive Officer at the top of the pyramid and the Board of Directors the next layer down, with pyramids of staff reporting to the Board members (see Figure 6.5, note that not all posts are shown, for clarity).

Figure 6.5 Hierarchical organisation of a marketing department

This structure has the advantage of clear line of communication and responsibility, but is felt to be production-orientated and loses focus on what the customer wants.

Product manager/matrix structures

To overcome the latter point, organisations sometimes move towards product management roles and combine this with a matrix structure – see Figure 6.6, again some detail
is suppressed for clarity.

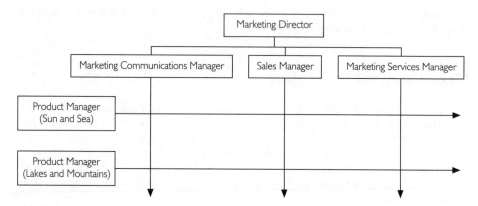

Figure 6.6 Product manager/matrix structure

This structure has the benefits of product managers committed to satisfying their segments of the market, but leads to problems with these individuals squabbling over
resources. Whilst product managers may create plans which are closer to the needs of the
market, they lack the authority to implement such plans. For greater discussion of these
and other structures, see Kotler (1997) and, in particular, Middleton (1988).

Summary

The diagrams that explain the process of strategic marketing planning give a good
overview of what is required, but the hidden complexity makes it a time-consuming
process. One fault in strategic (and opposed to operational) planning is trying to plan
too much detail too far into the future. Avoiding this may help overcome a big barrier
to planning on this time scale – that is, that others involved in the process may be reluctant to participate. Whilst marketing people see the need for such plans, others may
see them as, *inter alia*, wasteful of resources, unnecessary and threatening. There is a
variety of tools and techniques to help plan strategically, but it is important to try to
evaluate the validity of the concept in use and remember how in practice they might
be abused. Finally, this sort off planning tends to be the domain of the larger, mature
business. Smaller organisations – and those in more entrepreneurial situations – may
plan in different ways.

✎   CASE STUDY
SWALLOW HOTEL GROUP

Over the years Swallow developed from a small and friendly northern hotel group to a national chain with a distinct brand identity. In 1998 they were in the UK's top twenty hotel companies and own hotels in the three-, four- and five-star range. The other competitors are Granada Forte, Holiday Inn, Regal Hotels, Mount Charlotte/Thistle, Stakis, Marriott, Millenium Copthorne, Queens Moat Houses and De Vere Hotels. The list changes from year to year in content and order, as groups merge and de-merge. (Ranking is generally in number of rooms as opposed to number of hotels.)

Swallow Hotels were established by the Sunderland-based brewers Vaux Group plc. Initially hotels evolved from the established pubs within the brewing group which were able to offer accommodation and had no separate identity. The company operated 15 hotels in city and country locations when it established the name Swallow as a marketing aid. They could be characterised by the description 'small and friendly'.

The company decided to develop into a major hotel company, as opposed to a brewery which owned hotels. Their initial strategy included the purchase of a small chain of eight hotels (Usher Hotels of Scotland), and in 1972 they formulated plans for more investment in new hotels. Swallow Hotels Division was formed and in 1974 became Swallow Hotels Limited, an incorporated wholly-owned subsidiary company of Vaux Breweries Limited. Swallow had extended to 32 hotels with approximately 800 bedrooms. It was seen as major northern hotelier with hotels from Edinburgh to North Yorkshire.

They achieved both their growth and status with a number of objectives but primary influences were:

- Standardising the product – ensuring that the original diversity in standards of the acquired hotels was overcome by establishing a minimum standards level for the group and continually re-investing and up-grading. Strategy was based on a stringent review of those properties which in the long-term would be unable to meet the standards criteria. These would be disposed of and new properties acquired or built to the Swallow standard.
- Differentiating the product – Swallow identified at an early stage the growing interest in leisure facilities (swimming pools, saunas and spa baths, gym equipment). In addition, the changing attitudes towards fitness provided an opportunity to add to the consumer benefits and differentiate the group. Swallow were able to boast that they were the chain with the largest number of hotels with leisure facilities.

Swallow has continued to invest in leisure facilities and continually seeks to up-date them. They are a primary consideration for some segments, primarily the corporate market and the short-break market in the UK.

Their mission statement is currently,

'Swallow Hotels will operate "full service" hotels which provide quality and value for money with the highest standards in hospitality, food and comfort.'

The company continues to have an ambitious development programme and their main long-term objective is to be a truly national company.

Swallow's property portfolio is now quite strong, with a majority of four-star units and one five-star unit, following years of disposal of older and three-star properties.

Swallow is probably perceived by the stock market as rather less dynamic than some other hotel groups in terms of growth, but it is also considered a financially strong and stable company. There are other demands on group resources which have contributed to limiting growth, for example from the brewery and inns divisions. There has been a history of hotel groups contracting in size in the past, for example Stakis, and more recently Queens Moat Houses – this is often the result of rapid but unsustainable growth.

Personnel at all levels are very loyal and well-trained. More than 60 per cent of Swallow staff are in their share option scheme resulting in a relatively low staff turnover.

The market is roughly segmented as follows:

UK *business* With the end of the recession, this segment looks set to grow. Swallow are competitive in this sector and it is responsible for a significant proportion of Swallow's turnover.

- *Residential conference* This segment is also growing but only hotels with relatively modern buildings and facilities can really compete in it. Due partly to population and industry distribution, this market segment assumes more significance in the hotels based in the Midlands and southern England.
- *Tourism/discretionary leisure* UK tourism accounts for around 15 per cent of business of which the majority is short breaks. UK week-end break spending is inevitably tied to UK real disposable income (RDI).
- *In-bound overseas tourism* is most significant for hotels in the prime tourist destinations like London and Edinburgh where it is a very sizeable proportion of the total business. To many northern hotels along the tourist routes, for example Durham and York, it is very important in specific seasons. It is also very volatile business due to fluctuating exchange rates and terrorism. Swallow do sell internationally.

Swallow's business philosophy is that it believes in decentralisation as a far as possible; each hotel manager is trained and expected to be an entrepreneur in their own right. Each hotel is regarded as a separate business unit and head office attempt to interfere in the running of the unit as little as possible.

(Caroline Barrass)

Questions

1 Suggest a set of strategic marketing objectives for the Swallow corporate group.
2 Consider the alternative strategies for growth that face the group.
3 Discuss the influence that Swallow's business philosophy might have on the development of their strategies.

References and bibliography

Abell, D.F. and Hammond, J.S. (1979) *Strategic Market Planning*, Prentice Hall International Editions

Ansoff, H.I. (1968) *Corporate Strategy*, Pelican

Business Week (1980) Holiday Inns: Redefining its Focus to Food, Lodging and More Casinos, *Business Week*, 21 July, pp 100–4

Bransgrove, C.E. and King, B.E M. (1996) Strategic marketing practice amongst small tourism and hospitality businesses, *Proceedings of the Spring Symposium*, International Association of Hotel and Management Schools

British Airways plc, *Annual Report and Accounts 1990–1991*

Greenley, G.E. (1986) *The Strategic and Operational Planning of Marketing*, McGraw Hill

Heldey, B. (1977) Strategy and the business portfolio, *Long Range Planning*, February, Elsevier Science

Hooley, J.G. (1995) The lifecycle concept revisited: aid or albatross?, *Journal of Strategic Marketing*, No. 3, pp 23–39

Johnson, G. and Scholes, K. (1993) *Exploring Corporate Strategy*, 3rd edition, Prentice-Hall

Kotler, P. (1997) *Marketing Management, Analysis, Planning, Implementation and Control* 9th edition, Prentice-Hall

Mercer, D. (1993) Death of the product life cycle, *Admap*, September, pp 15–19

Mintzberg, H., Quinn, J.B. and Ghoshal, S. (1995) *The Strategy Process*, Prentice Hall

Morrison, A. and Wensley, R. (1991) Boxing up or boxed in? A short history of the Boston Consulting Group Share/Growth Matrix, *Journal of Marketing Management*, No. 7, pp 105–29

Moutinho, L., Rita, P. and Curry, B. (1996) *Expert Systems in Tourism Marketing*, Routledge

Piercy, N. (1992) *Market-Led Strategic Change*, Butterworth-Heinemann

PIMS (1992) *Services in Focus*, PIMSletter No. 49, PIMS Europe Ltd

Schoeffler, S., Buzzell, R .D. and Heaney, D. F. (1974) The impact of strategic planning on profit performance, *Harvard Business Review*, March–April

Smith, R. and Thomas, M. (1981) The product life cycle: An assessment, *The Quarterly Review of Marketing*, Summer, pp 22–7

West, A. (1988) *Cases in Marketing Techniques*, Paul Chapman Publishing

Wilson, M. (1980) *The Management of Marketing*, Gower

PIMS Europe Ltd, 7th Floor, Moor House, 119 London Wall, London EC2

7 Operational marketing planning

Objectives

By the end of this chapter you should be able to:

● prepare an operational marketing plan that is in harmony with a longer term strategic marketing plan. This will involve, *inter alia*, forecasting sales and setting operational objectives in line with good practice.

Introduction

There can be confusion over the differences between strategic and operational planning. Greenley (1986) summarises well the many views on the differences. As stated at the start of Chapter 6, this text follows his classification. Greenley characterises operational planning as being concerned with:

'● Projecting current operations into the future
● Projections into both the long and short run
● Labelling short-range operational planning as tactical planning
● Manufacturing and marketing current products
● Deploying the current base of resources
● The modifications of business functions only
● The responsibility of functional managers.'

(Greenley, 1986)

These characteristics suggest in the main that operational planning concerns itself with the short term; this is in keeping with the distinctions made by others. Essentially, for many organisations, operational planning will be concerned for planning 12 months ahead and the production of the annual marketing plan.

Typical contents of a marketing plan

Wilson provides possibly the best guide to what we should expect to see. He argues marketing plans usually include the following (our comments in square brackets):

'● A statement of basic assumptions with regard to long- and short-term economic, technological, social and political developments. [See Chapter 3 for greater detail.]
● An analysis of external opportunities and threats by market and product.
● A review of past sales and profit performance of the company's major products [for example, for a tour operator: Winter Sun, Summer Sun, Skiing, Cruise, etc.] by mar-

ket [for example, 18-30, Grey and Family] and geographic areas [for example, for an international hotel chain: Europe, South East Asia and the USA].

● An analysis of the company's and competitors' strengths and weaknesses in facilities, products, finances, customer acceptance, distribution, personnel, pricing, advertising, sales promotion, etc. This analysis often includes assessments of indirect competition [for example, the UK channel ferry operators and the Eurostar service through the channel tunnel].

● A statement of long-term objectives [marketing, financial, growth, etc.], and the strategies for achieving them.

● A statement of the objectives and strategies for the next year, with a detailed break-down in units and revenue for each product, each market, each geographical area, and each unit of the company's marketing force.

● A programme schedule which is carefully co-ordinated with the budgets for the units involved and which shows the sequence of all marketing activities for each product in each market and geographical area so that public relations, advertising, product publicity, sales promotion, and field selling can be co-ordinated.

● Statements of objectives for each of the following years similar to the statements for the next year but less detailed.

● A summary of how the company intends to capitalise on its opportunities and correct its weaknesses; key priorities, etc.'

(Wilson, 1980)

You will notice that the above list contains elements that are also included in the strategic planning process. This should be of little surprise – strategic issues do affect operational plans and a common fault is that operational plans tend to bear little relationship to strategic plans. It should be seen as good practice therefore to include relevant issues from the strategic planning process in the confirmation of the operational marketing plan.

Forecasting

In this book, forecasting is covered in this chapter on operational marketing planning, as one of the main operational activities of the marketing function is to forecast what the organisation's sales may be in the immediate future. The future in this context may be next week, next month, next quarter or next year. However, at all levels of planning, managers are often forecasting (whether they realise it or not!), hence some of the techniques that this section examines may be utilised at the strategic level, for instance in forecasting possible changes in the environment.

The relationship between forecasting and planning is sometimes confused, not only in theory but also in practice. If forecasting is regarded as an objective prediction of what will probably happen and planning as a subjective desire to make something happen, then perhaps the distinction and relationship between the two concepts can be seen.

Figure 7.1 may help you understand the relationship between forecasting and planning at both the strategic and operational levels. It may also help understanding of the relationship between many of the chapters in this book.

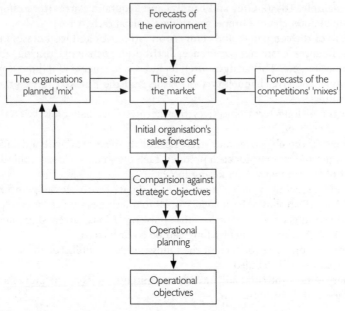

Figure 7.1   The relationship between forecasting and planning

The need to forecast the environment is easily understood. However, the relationship between our plans, competitors' activities and market size is less so. Kotler (1997) in his chapter on 'Managing marketing information and measuring market demand' does quite well to explain this complex relationship. Basically it should be realised that combined industry expenditure on marketing activities may expand the market size. In forecasting terms – as managers are often trying to forecast market size (and their organisation's share of it) – they cannot just rely on extrapolation of the past growth (or decline!) in a market, but must also account for what the industry's activities might do to the market, too.

Market share, of course, is related to the relative attractiveness and promotion of our products, compared to the competition. Put simply, a manager may have to perform several iterations of the forecast, considering what will happen to market size and share if the organisation puts into practice one set of mix decisions and simultaneously how competitors will behave.

Not understanding this perhaps led to the price wars in the UK tour operations market in the late 1980s, when in order to increase market share, prices were reduced by first one then another tour operator. It is questionable whether the market size expanded – market shares did not necessarily change. Eventually some operators were shaken out of the market – be warned!

The importance of sales forecasting

Whilst companies are clearly concerned to make an accurate sales forecast for their own marketing purposes, it will lead to the marketing objectives they set themselves later. The sales forecast is also important to other areas of the business. For instance, it could be that a package operator will be buying airline seats and purchasing accommodation in hotels on the basis of it. It is also of importance for finance, as it is the basis for managing cash flow and predicting future profitability.

It should not be assumed that forecasting is only required by large organisations. A small hotel, for example, should also try to forecast sales, if only to ensure correct staffing levels. These two examples should serve to illustrate the relative importance of forecasting, and consequently the time and resources that might be allocated to it.

Issues in selecting and using forecasting methods

Time scales

As this chapter considers forecasting in general, it should be noted that the chosen method needs to be appropriate for the time scale being considered. For example, forecasting a precise sales figure in the short term might be best done with one method, whilst considering long-term environmental forecasts would probably require a different one.

Turning points

Forecasting changes in growth also means that managers need to identify the points when change may become discontinuous – events rarely continue into the future as a straight line. Considering the curve of the product life cycle (see Chapter 6, page 143), there are three points in it that can be identified as turning points:

- where sales turn from introduction to growth
- where growth levels into maturity
- where maturity turns to decline.

The forecaster therefore needs a method to identify these turning points when dramatic marketing actions made be required. Simple extrapolation would miss these crucial points.

Data requirements

Some of the more sophisticated forecasting methods, such as multiple regression, require that the organisation has access to a lot of data, such as disposable income, price elasticity, industry advertising expenditure and even weather conditions. Others require no more than the mental ability of the forecasters. Clearly the forecaster must ascertain whether the organisation has access to the data required or can afford to purchase it.

The cost-accuracy trade-off

Like many managerial activities, the accuracy of a forecast can be increased by committing more resources to it. The amount of resource to be committed, for example, management time, computers, computing software and data, should depend on the importance of the accuracy of the forecast to the organisation. For instance, a tour operator who consistently overestimates sales and overpurchases accommodation may wish to invest more in forecasting than a small hotel owner who has to wait on tables because of an underestimate of restaurant occupancy which gave waiting staff the night off.

The methods of forecasting

A common misconception of forecasting is to think of it as a purely mathematical process. Whilst mathematics and statistics can be involved, forecasters should not ignore more qualitative human information processing. Any forecasting text which ignores the latter makes a serious omission. One of the best and most comprehensive texts on forecasting is Wheelright and Makridakis (1985) which provides an in-depth treatment of the subject.

Forecasting methods

The main forecasting methods available are quantitative methods, which typically use mathematical and statistical processes, and qualitative methods which are more the product of human thought.

Quantitative techniques

Here data is processed using mathematical techniques; most good forecasting or spreadsheet software packages provide facilities to perform these processes.

Simple moving averages
For this method, several figures over a period of time – for instance, monthly sales figures – are added together and divided by the period of time selected, for example three months. The trend is produced by adding on the new month and subtracting the original starting month.

This method can be used to provide a short-term forecast of sales. It can also be used to predict further into the future, for example the trend in the environment of personal disposable income might also be analysed by this method.

Whilst simple, this method can be quite effective. The skill lies in choosing an appropriate period of time over which to average data (for example, three months or twelve months). This period of time should depend on the underlying nature of the marketplace. For instance, in rapidly changing markets a shorter period of time is suggested.

Exponentially weighted moving averages
Whilst this method may sound daunting, in reality the mathematics is quite simple. The method puts more emphasis on more recent data, which may reflect a common-sense approach to how markets work, that is, consumers are more influenced by current fashions in destinations, for instance.

The skill in using this method is to choose a weighting factor which reflects the characteristics of the forecast situation. This might be done, for example, by looking at the pattern of sales in previous years, for instance a travel agent may find that a weighting factor of 0.6 (putting quite a lot of emphasis on more recent data) 'fits' last year's sales data quite well. Knowing this, the agent will be able to predict the current year's future sales on the basis of the current year's recent sales.

Linear regression analysis (time series)
Linear regression assumes that things change according to one factor and do so at a constant rate. In the case of time series, the assumption is that the factor, for example sales, increases (or decreases!) with the passage of time (see Figure 7.2).

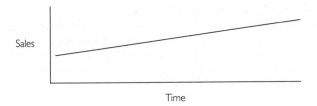

Figure 7.2

Linear regression analysis (other causal factors)

Here the assumption is that the factor we are interested in changes according to some other factor. As one factor changes, for example the population's real disposable income (RDI), then so the other factor, for example the market size for holidays, changes at a constant rate (see Figure 7.3).

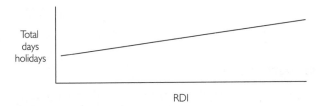

Figure 7.3

Multiple regression analysis

The forecaster may be fortunate and discover simply one variable that will affect another, as in the two examples above. It is much more likely that the factor to be forecast is affected by many other variables. Multiple regression can help us in this case; it produces a forecasting equation such as the following:

$$\text{Sales} = (1.8 \times \text{Air temp.}) + (2.1 \times \text{RDI}) + (0.193 \times \text{Advertising expenditure}) - (0.240 \times \text{Price}) - 181$$

This hypothetical example might predict visitors to an outdoor theme park, where the weather and disposable income would be the outside variables that affect demand. It is interesting to note that it also includes factors within the control of management, i.e. the expenditure on advertising and price, thus making it a budgeting tool – a point pursued later in this chapter.

It is not necessary that the forecaster be able to perform the mathematics, but he or she may need to guide a more expert mathematician in deciding which factors to take into consideration.

Econometric models

These are very complex, interrelated equations that model the effect that many factors have on a dependent variable. They are commonplace in trying to forecast the state of economies – the UK government has its Treasury model and there are several independent models available as well. Two of the best are run by the Henley Centre for Forecasting and National Westminster Bank. Increasingly, larger organisations are trying to use similar models to forecast their own marketplaces, but for most organisations, the mathematics involved will be beyond the ability of those involved in marketing.

Leading indicators
Occasionally, managers are fortunate enough to know that as one variable changes (for example, RDI), then some time after this variation, the factor we are trying to predict (for example, sales of cruises) changes. This is known as a leading indicator.

Surveys of buyers' intentions
This is a method carried out by market researchers and, as such, its accuracy should be seen in the light of any survey technique (see Chapter 5). For high value items which are planned well in advance, purchasers can tell us what and when they will be buying. This could be a particularly good method in the case of expensive, long-haul holidays.

Qualitative methods

These are sometimes known as judgmental methods, as they rely on human thought processing. Whilst more subjective than objective, they are frequently used – perhaps because little else is available – and indeed can be as good as a quantitative forecast. At minimum, some judgement should be applied to any quantitative technique to ensure common sense is not ignored.

Expert opinion
This can range from true experts who have a deep understanding of particular issues, to unofficial experts who still need to make a prediction about the future – usually the managers concerned with forecasting. Their success is variable, but their insight useful. A word of caution is needed when experts work in groups – the effect of the group can be to take riskier decisions or to develop a feeling of invulnerability (sometimes known as 'groupthink' – see Janis, 1977; Wheelwright and Makridakis, 1985). To overcome such problems, the Delphi method can be used (see Chapter 5, page 120) – here the members of the group never actually meet (avoiding therefore, *inter alia*, peer pressure). Their deliberations are collected, summarised and redistributed to the members by a moderator – the process continuing until agreement (or stalemate!) is reached.

Sales force composite
Here the aggregate view of sales staff is sought as to what sales might be achieved in the future. This is more likely to be of use in the shorter term and, of course, there are managerial issues concerned where the forecast will affect sales objectives – to which a salespersons remuneration may be related. Put simply, sales staff may be pessimistic when, by being so, they later exceed their targets (which were based on their forecasts) and so achieve greater commissions!

Interrelating strategic and operational planning and forecasting

Clearly these three managerial processes should interrelate; unfortunately they often do not! The way this could be done in organisations will vary. What follows is a possible sequence of events that should serve to connect these three processes correctly.

1 The future market size is estimated by extrapolation of past market figures and expert consideration of external environmental factors that may change the market size.
2 The sales force forecast sales using their knowledge of the market, past sales trends and the external environmental factors as predicted above. They may be assisted in this process by those responsible for the overall forecast.
3 The forecaster is now in a position to prepare an initial company sales forecast. This then needs to be considered in the light of the organisation's basic objectives as set by the strategic planning process.

There will be almost inevitably a shortfall between what this initial sales forecast predicts and the basic objectives the organisation wishes to achieve. (If there is not, then perhaps the operational planners are more confident about the future than the strategic planners, and the basic objectives need revising upwards!) At this point, the planner can consider marketing mix activities that will remedy this shortfall. Of course, we need to consider how the competition will react to our mix activities and how total industry efforts may affect market sales.

When all these factors have been taken into consideration, we will then have a new sales forecast. Again this can be compared to our basic objectives – if it is close enough, then our operational plans can go forward. If the shortfall is too great, then we need to reconsider our marketing plans and the cycle described above must be repeated. It is important to recognise that if operational plans cannot generate sufficient sales and profits to meet the sales and profit objectives suggested by the strategic planning process, then perhaps the *strategic* plans are too ambitious and need to be revised downwards.

Assessing the accuracy of sales forecasts

Depending on the importance of forecasting, the organisation should have committed more or less resources to it. If the amount of resource committed is large and/or the importance of the forecast is crucial, we may wish to assess how accurate the forecasting procedure has been.

This can be done quite simply by comparing the forecast figure with what happened in reality. A simple graphical examination of the two sets of figures will show to what extent the forecast is accurate. It may show that consistent optimism or pessimism, or that the errors are random. It is also possible to analyse the variance statistically and quantify its accuracy. In Table 7.1, the differences between actuals and forecasts gives a total variance of 69, and a standard deviation of 2.5. This indicates quite a precise forecast. A count of the signs of each month's variance shows six positive and six negative, indicating no serious optimism or pessimism of the forecasting procedure.

Table 7.1   Sales forecasts and achievements for last year

Month	Forecast	Actual	Variance
1	91	93	+2
2	106	109	+3
3	99	101	+2
4	94	91	−3
5	102	101	−1
6	105	106	+1
7	101	99	−2
8	97	100	+2
9	93	91	−2
10	104	101	−3
11	99	103	+4
12	106	103	−2
Total variance			69
Standard deviation			2.5

Forecasting and management: a final word

It should be apparent from some of the above discussion that the role of forecasting can be blurred and that it perhaps cannot be seen as a purely objective management process. As the forecast leads to sales objectives and targets, then a certain amount of wishful thinking and internal politics can corrupt the process. Management science is increasingly trying to deal with these issues. For those interested in improving and organising forecasting, or for those wishing to make a more detailed academic study of forecasting and management, a good starting point is the work of Fildes and Hastings (1994).

Setting operational marketing planning objectives

Following on from the setting of strategic marketing planning objectives in Chapter 6, and maintaining Wilson's (1980) hierarchy of basic objectives, goals and targets, the planner should now be at the stage of setting goals (perhaps at the level of department heads, such as Marketing for a tour operator, or hotel unit managers) and targets (perhaps at the level of front line staff, such as sales or receptionists). The basic objectives should have been set and agreed by the strategic planning process, but note the interrelationship between the three.

Whilst at the *strategic* planning level, the planner was restricted to few basic objectives (a level of growth, profit and the business we wish to be in), at the operational level planners are likely to create many and varying objectives ranging, for example, from occupancy rates for a hotel manager to newspaper sales for receptionists. Before examining the diversity of such operational objectives, there are some basic principles to consider – which incidentally should also apply to the setting of strategic basic objectives.

The role of objectives in management

A major role of any objective, but particularly *operational* objectives, is to motivate the employee for whom it is set. There is always the danger that managers develop a belief that setting an objective is the only motivation needed for staff and that the bigger the objective, the greater the motivation! The consequence of this approach (in most managerial cultures) will be to frighten, de-motivate and eventually lose an employee. Whilst it is beyond the scope of this text to consider all the human resource implications of objective setting, you should be aware of good practice in human resource management, to be found in many recent texts on the subject.

Objectives should also direct an employee's efforts, suggesting areas to concentrate on and areas to play down. They also help others understand what different departments and individuals' roles are within the organisation. Well-set objectives will also allow both manager and employee to appraise the employees' performance and plan improvements.

General principles in setting objectives

There are many acronyms that help set objectives correctly. SMART is a simple and common way of understanding that all objectives (strategic and operational) should be:

- *specific* to a named post, for example the Marketing Manager, the Head of Conferencing, the Night Porter. There may, of course, be subtle differences for different individuals – a new sales representative might be given a lower target than a well-experienced one
- *measurable* – the objective should be capable of being objectively assessed. Compare 'Achieve 60 per cent room occupancy' with 'Achieve good occupancy rates'
- *achievable* – this re-states the underlying theme of all we have said about planning – it should be based on what is possible, not wishful thinking
- *realistic* – it should relate to whether the person concerned could be expected to do the task asked. For instance, it is realistic to expect hotel receptionists to 'trade up' guests to better rooms, but not to expect the same of porters
- *time-constrained* – the employee should know what period of time the objective is to be achieved in.

Whilst this and other acronyms help avoid fundamental errors in setting objectives, there may be occasions where these rules are worthy of suspension. For example we may require staff to be well dressed – but this requires a subjective interpretation of what well dressed is.

Typical operational marketing planning objectives

In an industry as diverse as travel and tourism, there are likely to be a very wide range of industry-specific objectives. However, by looking at typical operational marketing planning objectives, we can get guidance as to the sort of objectives we should see in such a plan.

The work of Bluell (1966) and Cravens (1982) suggest the following five generic areas.

Sales volume
This is a commonly used objective and can be applied from the Chief Executive down to individual salespeople. Similarly it can relate to the organisation as a whole or to specific products, for example 1,000 weekend breaks in a hotel chain, increase leisure centre

membership by 10 per cent or increase restaurant meals from 100 to 120 covers. It might also be applied to specific markets, for example sell more to the USA, or to segments – sell more to the business traveller. The notion of sales *value* should be added to this concept, i.e. the revenue that is generated, not just the number of units sold. For instance, we may achieve the target number of rooms booked, but they may all be the cheapest ones. If we concentrated on sales value we would look at the revenue generated – this could be achieved by selling fewer, higher tariff rooms.

Market share objectives

Here the goals and targets become shares rather than volumes. It is worth remembering that we can increase sales volume, but actually decrease our share if a market is growing quicker than we are expanding our sales (and vice versa!) There is evidence from Schoeffler *et al.* (1974) in their profit impact of marketing strategies (PIMS), that 'share is all' in terms of generating profits. There is little doubt that managers like to be associated with organisations with a large share of the market. Care must be taken as to how this is measured; if it is measured in volume (units) alone then there is a danger of profit being sacrificed to gain share. For instance, it would be possible for a trans-Atlantic airline operator to take a greater share of the seats sold in this market, but if this is done by selling at discounted prices, there is a danger of lowering profits.

Marketing cost objectives

In some instances, the factor an individual is responsible for can only be measured as a cost. Chefs and restaurant managers are all familiar with the importance of portion control in keeping food operations profitable, but market research and advertising are equally difficult to set objectives for, except in terms of costs. A more sophisticated approach is not to control costs in absolute terms, but to control them as a ratio to revenues. For example, management may allow conference salespeople entertainment expenses as a ratio of the business they book. This would prevent them from not being able to buy a potential client a drink because they have run out of expenses.

Profit objectives

It is perhaps a common fault not to ascribe to anyone the responsibility for profit. Many organisations remedy this by setting profit goals at departmental levels, for example the restaurant in an hotel. It could be argued that the profit objective might be set at all levels. Although it can get difficult where the individual is not responsible for both revenue and cost, it is unfair to hold people responsible for things not within their control.

Marketing mix objectives

An operational plan should detail actions to be taken in the areas of which marketing is in charge. It should be expected to set goals and targets in each area of the mix, for instance:

Product

Here managers may consider not just increasing sales (that has been covered already), but issues such as new product development, for example to develop a package holiday to suit an emerging segment. Quality may also be targeted here; planners may set standards of care, such as maximum queuing times or room service response times. A company may also look at objectives to differentiate ourselves – Swallow's goal of a swimming pool in every hotel allows it to distinguish itself from other up-market chains.

Price

Much of what has been discussed about sales volume and profit impacts on pricing decisions, but there are other factors to be considered, such as using prices to balance out
demand – a common practice on buses and ferries, but also in hotels with weekend prices.

Promotion

It has been suggested that it is difficult to measure advertising, etc. in any other way than
by cost. However it may be possible – for example, measures of brand awareness, message comprehension and perhaps attitude change might be used (for more detail see
Chapter 11). For the specific case of sales staff, there is a wide range of non-financial measures, for example number of calls made, conversion rates of enquiries to sales, and new
accounts opened. Greene (1987) provides some excellent examples of sales objectives for
the hotel and restaurant markets. Tucker (1961) provides a myriad of suggestions for sales
objectives in general.

Place

Place needs special consideration in the travel and tourism industry. For example, hotel
chains often try to fill in geographic gaps with new units, and some tour operators may
try to target the distributors that do not 'stock' their product.

Contingency planning

Even at the operational level, with shorter time scales, managers may be in a situation
where they are uncertain how the future might develop. So that they are not surprised
by changing external events, they should plan for alternative courses of action known as
contingencies. An example of this might be planning what to do if the competition low-
ers prices. It may be hoped this will not happen, but it is best to be prepared in case it
does. Planners might consider reducing prices and the consequential effect that might
have on profits. Of course, it is possible to consider meeting this competitive action with
a non-price action such as 'free' meals.

Budgeting

It is tempting to assume that budgeting is the responsibility of finance. Whilst Piercy
(1982) suggests marketers have a duty to be irresponsible when planning spending, arguing there are plenty of others in the organisation who will control it, most companies will
expect the marketing department to put a cost on their planned actions. There may be
some joint activity at this stage. For example, we might, with finance staff and others,
look at the impact of our decisions in terms of break-even analysis.

Some of the more sophisticated forecasting techniques, such as multiple regression (see
page 157), can predict the sales impact of marketing decisions, for example the impact
of increasing advertising spend. At a simpler level, a manager might produce simple cash
flow forecasts on a monthly basis. Stapleton (1989) suggests the proforma shown in Figure 7.4, which might be adapted for travel and tourism.

Prior year actual		Activity	J	F	M	A	M	J	J	A	S	O	N	D	Full year	
£	%		£	£	£	£	£	£	£	£	£	£	£	£	£	%
		Budgeted sales														
		Total expense														
		Ratios														
		Salaries and wages														
		Management and supervision														
		Administration														
		Salespeople														
		Clerical														
		Other														
		Total														
		Total headcount														
		Average remuneration														
		Other expense														
		Assisted labour benefits														
		Rent and rates														
		Communications														
		Travel and entertaining														
		External commissions														
		Media advertising														
		Sales and literature														
		Public relations														
		Exhibitions														
		Samples														
		Sales force commission														
		Miscellaneous expense														
		Total other														
		Grand total														
		Expenses per head														

MARKETING BUDGET

Date: Prepared by:

(Stapleton, 1989)

Figure 7.4 Proforma for a marketing budget

For understandable commercial reasons, organisations are unwilling to let their operational plans and budgets into the public domain. Middleton (1988) however presents a hypothetical example that demonstrates the slightly idiosyncratic approach in the tour operations industry (see Table 7.2).

Table 7.2 *Marketing budget calculations for a British tour operator*

Budget summary	Year (£000s)	%
Total turnover @ £179 (arsp)[1] on 750,000 sales	34,250	100
Less cost of tour components,[2] say	−96,375	100
= gross trading surplus	137,875	28
Less targeted operating profit before tax @ say 9% of turnover	−12,000	9
= maximum sum to cover all administration and marketing costs	25,875	19
Committed costs of operation (fixed)		
Reservation system and overheads[3]	3,000	
Non-marketing administration costs[4]	2,025	
Marketing staff and overheads[5]	2,500	
	7,525	6
Marketing campaign costs (fixed and variable)		
Advertising	500	0.4 ⎫
Sales promotion	650	0.5 ⎪
Brochure and distribution	3,000	2.2 ⎬ 12.1
Other[6]	150	0.1 ⎪
Sales commission to retail agencies (@ 10%)[7]	12,000	9.0 ⎭
	16,300	
Contingency reserve[8]	2,050	
	25,875	

Notes
1 Arsp = average retail sales price, per tour sold
2 Accommodation, transport, transfers, resort staff
3 Includes computer systems, staff and all communication costs and depreciation
4 Office expenses, rates, staff equipment, etc., including general administration
5 Includes any salesforce costs, on-going market research costs, product development and all marketing department costs
6 Workshops, PR, familiarisation visits, etc.
7 Assumes 90 per cent of all sales commissionable, others booked direct
8 Held in reserve especially for tactical discounts to promote unsold capacity

(Middleton, 1988)

Implementation

At this stage of the planning cycle, managers move from planning, which despite its complexity will have merely created something on paper, to action where things get done. Putting it as simply as that belies the actual difficulty of this stage. Some authors have suggested that marketing planning fails, not because of poor plans, but because of the ability and attitudes of those expected to put the plans into practice. McDonald (1989) summarises the problems well and at the same time suggests that the 'people problem' may in fact be a barrier to planning in the first place.

Greenley (1986) suggests five interrelated areas that condition how well plans will be implemented:

- delegation
- participation
- motivation
- leadership
- integration.

Delegation

This is the extent to which we give staff lower in the organisational hierarchy the respon-sibility and authority to take action. It might be quite extensive, for example a brand manager is often given total responsibility for all mix decisions for their brand and is mea-sured on the sales and profitability of that brand. It may be a restricted but significant responsibility of, say, allowing reception staff to negotiate prices. It might be a minor but significant responsibility which (as part of a customer care policy) allows a waiter to offer a free drink to diners that have to wait too long.

Whatever is delegated and the amount of delegation, it is important to realise that it is impossible for one manager to do everything, and some level of delegation is inevitable. Recent management literature suggests it is desirable, and tends to rename it 'empowerment' – although it will be argued that there is more to empowerment than just delegation.

Participation

It was earlier argued that participation in planning is a good thing (people are more likely to achieve objectives if they helped in setting them). Most authors stress this aspect when discussing participation. Clearly, it is axiomatic that staff need to participate in imple-mentation of plans.

Motivation

This describes all the factors that cause people to try to achieve the various objectives they have. It is something clearly connected to other areas. As stated above, it is argued that participating in setting objectives motivates people to achieve. We need to recognise the wide range of motivational factors. Marketing managers may well be motivated by the job satisfaction of planning. It is understandable that some sales staff are motivated by commissions on sales. Of course, there is job satisfaction involved in sales and some mar-keting managers are motivated by profit-related bonuses!

Leadership

This is a characteristic of people that allows them to get others to achieve objectives. There is a large literature on this topic and there are fashions in styles of leadership. Per-haps the best guide as to which style is appropriate is the Tannenbaum and Smicht (1958) leadership continuum. This suggests leadership style can be selected between the extremes of autocracy (where managers simply tell people to act in a certain way) and democracy (where managers ask the group if it thinks a problem should be considered at all before working on a solution). The appropriate style depends on the nature of the man-ager (can he or she tolerate involving others?), the nature of the problem (group discussion of plans can be good – but would you use the same mechanism to decide who to make redundant?) and the nature of the other staff (do they want to participate in decisions? some may not).

Integration

This concerns itself with disparate parts of the plan needing to work together. Sales staff may be ready to sell a new product, but if the advertisements have not run, the demand will not be there. Clearly someone needs to make sure things happen when they should. Much integration will be solved by well timetabled plans and clear objectives, but during the implementation period we should not ignore the need for constant communications (vertically and horizontally) so that everyone knows what is happening in the various departments.

Control

This is the stage at which objectives are compared to achievements. Depending on the aspect of the plan being evaluated, this process may take place daily, weekly, monthly quarterly or annually. For instance, management may wish to examine bar takings on a daily basis, room reservations on a weekly basis, conferences on a monthly basis and profits quarterly. The overall success of the plan might be assessed annually. Selecting the appropriate monitoring period is important. If measurement is taken too frequently, an organisation may develop 'paralysis by analysis', where remedial action is not taken, as all effort goes into measurement. Similarly, by measuring too frequently, managers may fail to identify trends by being too close to the data.

The success of control depends greatly on well-set objectives; assuming our objectives were SMART, as suggested earlier, the following method will help determine corrective action.

1 Measure variance
Managers need to compare the objective and actual performance, but not over-react to every variance. They may set tolerances, for example, if performance is within 5 per cent of planned budgets, no action is taken. It is worth remembering that a variance only indicates something to be investigated. (Sceptics might suggest zero variance should be investigated as well, arguing that people may stop trying once an objective is met!)

2 Investigate cause of unexpected variances
Managers should investigate positive, as well as negative variances – in most cases it will help to have the individual whose performance is being reviewed participate in this investigation. Causes can be:

- Objectives set at too high a level
- an unanticipated change in the environment, for example a competitor going out of business
- under (or over) performance of the individual.

The difficulty of such an investigation should not be under-estimated. Wilson (1980) demonstrates the discipline of thought required to diagnose the causes of declining profitability (see Figure 7.5).

Question	Measurement
1 Is profitability falling?	$\dfrac{R}{CE}$
2 To what is this due?	$\dfrac{R}{S}$ or $\dfrac{S}{CE}$
3 If $\dfrac{R}{S}$ what could be the changes in one or a combination of causes?	– unit volume (V) – price (P) – costs (C) – mix (M)
4 If it is a change in the interrelationships, how can it be identified?	Price change $\dfrac{S \text{ by product}}{V \text{ by product}}$ (average price per product group) Mix change $\dfrac{S \text{ by product}}{S \text{ in total}}$ (% sales accounted for by each product group) Cost/volume change $\dfrac{S\text{ - }R}{V}$ (cost of goods sold)
5 If falling profitability is due however to $\dfrac{S}{CE}$ what could be the causes?	$\dfrac{S}{\text{Fixed assets}}$ or $\dfrac{S}{\text{Working capital}}$
6 If $\dfrac{S}{FA}$ what are the likely reasons?	Either under-utilisation (utilised capacity as % of total capacity) or new fixed assets not yet producing a return $\dfrac{\text{Fixed assets}}{\text{Total assets}}$ as %
7 If $\dfrac{S}{WC}$ what are the likely reasons?	Either $\dfrac{\text{Sales}}{\text{Stocks}}$ or $\dfrac{\text{Sales}}{\text{Debtors}}$ or $\dfrac{\text{Sales}}{\text{Work in progress}}$

Key: R = return; CE = capital employed; S = sales

Figure 7.5 Seven key questions for diagnosing declining profitabililty   (Wilson, 1980)

3 Decide on action

Where there is variance, some short-term action may be needed, for example if sales are down, perhaps the weight of advertising needs increasing, or if customer care measurements are falling, then maybe reminder training is needed for the staff concerned. It may be a longer term issue – if an organisation is not meeting the annual plan's sales goals, perhaps plans are too ambitious and need amending next year.

Various measures for control

Most measures of variance are heavily derived from finance. Much of what has been suggested above relies on straightforward measures of variance and as such could be measured graphically. Some things might best be measured as ratios – for instance, finance suggests that profitability is perhaps best measured as a rate of return on assets employed. This principle can be used elsewhere, for example an organisation might measure the percentage of enquiries that are converted to sales or allow expenses as a ratio to business earned. Rodgers (1984) provides a good overview of the possible ratios (see Figure 7.6). Tucker (1961) gives a comprehensive treatment of what is possible in this area.

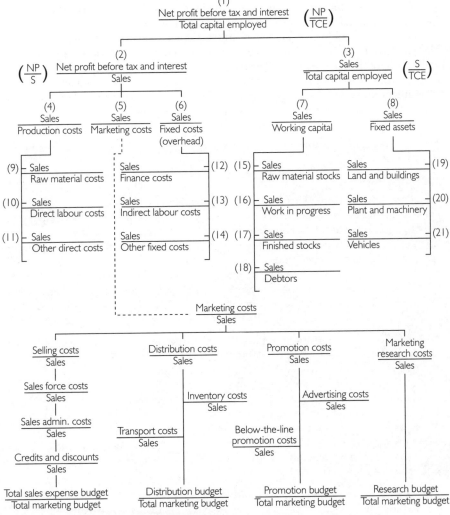

(Reproduced with permission from Rodgers, L. W., *Statistics for Marketing*, McGraw-Hill 1984)

Figure 7.6 Ratios for marketing control

Whilst these approaches are very useful and highly quantified, managers should not ignore the more subjective approaches. For instance, it might be impossible to quantify whether reception staff are presentable, but this should not dissuade them from attempting to encourage and assess it.

Summary

Operational marketing planning, i.e. plans that are usually for one year, should be made in the light of the bigger picture painted by strategic plans. They are usually less contentious than strategic plans, as many can see the logic of planning of year's marketing activities. Problems tend to arise when setting objectives. Done properly, the objectives will help the organisation to prosper in light of market needs and the competition. Objectives should flow from forecasting, which in itself should be as objective a process as possible. There is a tendency for others to have wishful thoughts about marketing objectives, usually wishing them to be bigger. The temptation to inflate objectives too much in order to meet others' ambitions should be fought. It may well lead to demotivation of people in the organisation and a failure to perform. Forecasts, objectives and plans are usually improved by open and frank discussion with everyone involved.

✎   CASE STUDY
THE ROYAL COUNTY HOTEL

The Royal County Hotel, part of the Swallow Group, is a luxurious and historic hotel situated in the heart of Durham city; it has 150 bedrooms. Durham is a popular tourist and leisure destination for the UK short-break market and as a stop-over destination for round-Britain tours from overseas. There is a healthy business or corporate market and conference trade. The Royal County is the only sizeable hotel in the heart of the city. Swallow also own another, smaller, three-star hotel in the city centre. Other competitor hotels lie outside the city and include a range of styles and standards. Newcastle, which is the nearest largest city, has a wide variety of hotels, some of which are also owned by nationally known chains, including Swallow.

Room facilities at the Royal County include private bathrooms, satellite TV, direct dial telephone, alarm, tea- and coffee-making facilities, trouser press, mini bar, hairdryer and iron and ironing board. General facilities include:
● Swallow Leisure Club, with heated indoor swimming pool, fitness room, spa bath, solarium steam room, sauna, plunge pool and relaxation area
● choice of à la carte restaurant or brasserie
● cocktail bar and lounge area
● extensive conference facilities, with main conference suite capable of handling 140 delegates, and five meeting rooms adaptable to suit a wide range of events
● free parking for 120 vehicles.

The history of the Royal County Swallow Hotel and its current situation
(Key: SB = single-bedded room; TB = twin-bedded room, DB = double-bedded room)

The hotel has developed gradually to match the Swallow criteria. In 1969–73 the

UK's Development of Tourism Act allowed a £1,000 grant for every new hotel bedroom built, to encourage an increased capacity for tourism in what were considered underdeveloped cities with the potential to develop tourism. Swallow expanded the hotel from 28 rooms (10 SB and 18 TB/DB) to add a further 43 SB and 33 DB/TB rooms, giving 104 rooms in total. In 1989 Swallow decided to develop the hotel again in line with the new company standards to include leisure facilities; a further 46 rooms (11 DB and 35 TB) were added in a new block which was built alongside the river.

The room mix at the hotel is particularly important in determining the yield of the hotel and the Royal County suffered from a number of problems relating to the mix of rooms. Prior to 1988 the high proportion of single rooms was just over 50 per cent, by 1989 it had just over a third of its rooms as singles.

The director/manager undertook a detailed analysis of the history of the hotel's current client base. He found that yields were significantly low in some quarters, complaints were sometimes high and often based on expectation as opposed to real problems in quality of service. There were specific occupancy problems which had been resolved in such a way as to affect other business in the hotel.

On the basis that at one time the hotel had a high proportion of singles, deals had been agreed which featured single occupancy at low inclusive rates affecting both food and room revenue. Coach tours were a significant proportion of the business which the hotel accommodated on both weekday and weekend nights. Because of the room mix, the majority often ended up accommodated in the block which housed the largest number of twin and double rooms – the newly built Riverside block close to the leisure facilities and conference rooms.

The detailed analysis of the historic development of the hotel, its yields and client base was followed by a detailed analysis of all complaints, no matter how small, and some research into the needs of each consumer segment. This revealed that because of the current room mix and design of the hotel, each consumer segment was often not being fully satisfied with the type of room allocated. For instance, tours on one night stopovers were not very concerned with views of the river from the new block, the hotel was not chosen individually by them on its merits, but by the operator on its location in the heart of Durham and the historic nature of the hotel – much of the original building is furnished with antiques and has a rich history.

Leisure-break clients and business house or corporate clients on longer stays often requested riverside rooms, but these were frequently already allocated to tours because they housed a majority of twins and doubles. Corporate clients additionally wanted to be close to conference rooms and leisure facilities.

The operational plan

Following are some of the details of the operational plan for the Royal County Hotel. Normally the plan begins with a summary of the current position of the Royal County and an outline of the intended direction representing the general manager's vision. It would also include an action plan for each operational area of the hotel representing their contribution to the objectives. Team members responsible for the implementation of various initiatives would be highlighted and target performance levels and time-scales outlined along with the various financial and non-financial objectives.

Hotel objectives

- To maintain the hotel's position through providing a level of service and quality in line with its four-star rating.
- To achieve the company's profit budgets each year and to safeguard the long-term profitability of the hotel.
- To deliver consistently the anticipated level of customer care, thus ensuring satisfaction and repeat business.
- To be totally committed to the Investors in People programme by achieving accreditation, and thereafter carefully monitoring all training needs and striving to meet these needs through a planned employee development programme.
- To ensure that the fabric of the building is maintained in a first-class condition so that it projects an image appropriate to its four-star rating.
- To provide and maintain a safe and healthy establishment for the benefit of customers and employees. Health and safety will continue to be a high priority.
- To be aggressive in marketing the hotel through good practices in all departments.

Plans

- To make the Royal County Hotel the best four-star hotel in Swallow Hotels and in this area by improving standards throughout.
- To improve the Average Room Rate significantly.
- To introduce a completely new concept in the brasserie.
- To look at the possibility of closing the brasserie after breakfast until lunch in the afternoon.
- To introduce a pyramid style of management.
- To increase the responsibility of heads of departments and management, giving them objectives and measurement methods.
- To create a highly motivated and professional workforce that interact positively with customers.
- To practise multi-skilling.
- To improve the physical product, specifically the bedrooms.
- To up-grade the back-of-house area.
- To introduce a new car park system and turning area at the front of the hotel, with a feature.
- To identify more car parking facilities.
- To increase the size of the leisure club in the gym area.

(Caroline Barrass)

Question

Using good operational marketing planning practice, how would you improve on the plans suggested above?

References and bibliography

Bluell, V.P. (1966) *Marketing Management in Action*, McGraw Hill

Cravens, D.W. (1982) *Strategic Marketing*, Irvin

Fildes, R. and Hastings, R. (1994) The organisation and improvement of market forecasting, *Journal of the Operational Research Society*, Vol. 45, No. 1, pp 1–16

Greene, M. (1987) *Marketing Hotels and Restaurants into the 90s*, 2nd edition, Heinemann

Greenley, G. (1986) *The Strategic and Operational Planning of Marketing*, McGraw Hill

Janis, I.L. and Mann, I. (1977) *Decision Making: A Psychological Analysis of Conflict, Choice and Commitment*, Free Press

Kotler, P. (1997) *Marketing Management, Analysis, Planning, Implementation and Control*, 9th edition, Prentice-Hall

McDonald, M. (1989) *Marketing Plans: How to Prepare Them, How to Use Them*, 2nd edition, Butterworth-Heinemann

Middleton, V.C. (1988) *Marketing in Travel and Tourism*, Heinemann

Piercy, N. (1982) Cost and profit myopia in marketing, *Quarterly Review of Marketing*, Vol. 7, No. 4, pp 1–12

Rodgers, L.W. (1984) *Statistics for Marketing*, McGraw Hill

Schoeffler, S., Buzzell, R.D. and Heaney, D. F. (1974) The impact of strategic planning on profit performance, *Harvard Business Review*, March-April

Stapleton, J. (1989) *How to Prepare a Marketing Plan*, 4th edition, Gower

Tannenbaum, R. and Schmidt, W. H. (1958) How to choose a leadership pattern, *Harvard Business Review*, March-April

Tucker, S.A. (1961) *Successful Managerial Control by Ratio Analysis*, McGraw Hill

Wheelwright, S.C. and Makridakis, S. (1985) *Forecasting Methods for Management*, 4th edition, Wiley

Wilson, M. (1980) *The Management of Marketing*, Gower

PIMS, Moor House, 119 London Wall, London EC2Y 5ET +44 171 628 1155

8 The tourism product and customer service

Objectives

By the end of this chapter you should be able to:

- understand the characteristics and elements of the tourism product
- identify issues relevant to the English tourism product
- understand the processes of product branding and positioning
- apply a number of product planning and design techniques
- understand the importance of good customer service.

The importance of the product in the marketing mix

The product is a crucial element within the marketing mix. 'Quality' has been one of the buzzwords in the 1990s and without a high quality product and good customer care, the marketing planning process is doomed to failure. The English Tourist Board's (ETB) consultation document, entitled *Action 2000: Shaping the Future of English Tourism*, will embrace the views of potentially 30,000 businesses and individuals and eventually lead to a concrete action plan for England's tourism industry. The document contains five consultation papers on key issues, two of which are 'Product development' and 'Quality'. *Action 2000* proposes that:

'For [England] to remain competitive in the world tourism market, much needs to be done to develop and raise the quality of the English tourism product.'

(ETB/BTA, 1997)

What is the tourism product?

The tourism industry incorporates many different sectors, including transport (airlines, airports, cruise ships, train operators, ferry operators, car hire firms), destination management organisations (convention bureaux, tourist information centres, public sector destination marketing organisations), travel trade (tour operators, travel agents, event management companies), accommodation (chain and independent hotels, self-catering, B&Bs, timeshare), attractions (theme parks, museums, historic buildings). Within each of these sectors there are a multitude of products on offer. Given the diversity of the tourism product it is helpful to consider some characteristics common to all tourism products. Tourism products are services and Lovelock (1996) offers some useful guidelines to distinguish services from physical goods.

The nature of the tourism product

Lovelock cites Berry in differentiating the nature of the service product:

'A good is an "object, a device, a thing", in contrast to a service which is "a deed, a performance, an effort".'

(Lovelock, 1996)

In the British Tourist Authority's (BTA) tourism marketing workshops, designed to train regional tourist board (RTB) staff, the tourism product is defined as:

'A complex experience, created and delivered by you [RTBs] and a diverse bunch of partners in a highly fragmented industry.'

(BTA Marketing Workshops, 1996)

A section of the workshop entitled 'Customising/designing the product' advises the participant against thinking of the product in narrow geographic or single entity terms. The product is not Britain, Scotland, Torbay, a hotel in Dyfed, Alton Towers, the Festival of Arts and Culture or the Edinburgh Festival; although of course these elements provide components of the tourism product. In other words, although the tourism product contains some tangible elements, the overall tourism product is an *intangible experience*.

Customer involvement in the production process

In the tourism industry, customers will often be involved in the creation of the service, for example at a carvery in a hotel where customers help themselves, or an electronic ticket kiosk at an airport. There are different levels of customer contact depending on the nature of the product. For example, in a fast-food restaurant the contact is minimal, whereas in a full service luxury hotel the level of customer involvement is very high. This concept of customer involvement has clear implications for customer service, a theme which will be considered later in the chapter.

People as part of the product

The tourism industry is often described as a 'people industry' and most job descriptions stress the importance of interpersonal skills. People skills are particularly important as the production and consumption of a service often take place simultaneously, for example when a guest arrives for check-in at the hotel reception. Services are delivered under real-time conditions (Lovelock, 1996), thus raising quality control issues and again emphasising the importance of the employee and good customer care. People are also part of the tourism product in so much as they often become synonymous with the product itself. For example, the type of people who occupy the VIP airline departure lounge and first-class cabins help to define the nature and image of the product on offer. Maintaining the perceived exclusivity of the service will be an integral part of the marketing strategy.

Harder for customers to evaluate

Physical goods are relatively high in *search qualities* – tangible attributes which help a buyer to evaluate his purchase. For example, a car buyer can test the car's driving position, stereo system, passenger comfort and overall performance, before deciding whether or not to part with their money. Someone buying a package holiday or reserving a weekend at a country house hotel will only be able to experience the product as they consume it. This creates an element of risk for the consumer and one of the marketing challenges is to reduce this risk. This is often done by providing visual and textual information in the tourist brochure. However, brochures create expectations and it is very important that the actual product meets, and preferably exceeds, those expectations. Thomson Holidays have recently started a 'what you see is what you get' policy with their holiday brochures. For example, they will show the true location of a resort hotel which may be 100 metres from the beach as opposed to being 'a stone's throw away'. This may appear like a risky advertising approach, but honesty and trustworthiness are absolutely essential in building up a long-term customer relationship.

No inventories for services

Physical goods can be stored to allow for the inevitable fluctuations in customer demand. This is impossible with a scheduled flight or a 200-bedroom hotel. In an industry which is characterised by seasonality and fluctuating demand, the tourism marketer must try to smooth demand levels to match capacity. Many hotels use computerised property management systems (PMS) for this purpose. Guest trend data is held on the PMS and is used to forecast when the quiet and busy periods are likely to be. This allows decisions to be made on stock control and staffing. A PMS also gives a better insight into the behaviour of different market segments. Different hotel products will be targeted at different segments. The system might forecast that a particular week is likely to be busy with business and convention guests, therefore reminding reservation and reception staff that they should not be tempted to sell executive rooms at a lower tariff during this period. Airlines have similar systems to help the market analyst in deciding when business class seats should be 'released' at an economy fare.

Importance of the time factor

Many tourism services are delivered in real time and customers have to be physically present to receive the service. Increasingly demanding customers are unwilling to wait a long time for a service to be delivered. This presents particular challenges for the transport sector.

Diversity of the product

This is not one of Lovelock's factors and could be considered unique to certain sectors of the tourism industry. For example, a tour operator commonly packages a number of products and sells the finished package to the customer, usually through a travel agency. However, it is unlikely that the tour operator will own all or even any of the different elements (travel agency, charter flight, coach transfer, guided tours, hotel, restaurants) which constitute the customer's overall experience. This creates quality control problems for the tour operator and partly explains why some of the larger tour operators are pursuing a strategy of vertical integration.

The product planning process

The tourism industry operates in a dynamic market and in order for organisations to retain a competitive edge they need to evaluate constantly the relationship between their products and their markets. There are a number of potential product/market options available to an organisation, as illustrated in Figure 8.1.

Market

	Existing	New
Existing	Introduce new product to present market	Launch of new product to new market
New	Modification to existing product for present market	Reposition present product to attract new market

Product (row label on left: Existing / New)

(Reproduced with permission from Holloway, C. and Plant, R., *Marketing for Tourism*, Pearson Education Ltd 1992)

Figure 8.1   Product options in new and existing markets

Increasing product segmentation within the hotel industry illustrates some of these product strategies. Product segmentation within the hotel industry can be defined as:

'The development by hotel companies of new accommodation concepts designed to meet the needs of specific target markets without depleting their existing core products.'

(Pannell Kerr Forster Associates, 1990)

Product segmentation began in the US and was a direct response to a market which had become saturated and which was characterised by falling profit margins and limited opportunities for expansion on historical lines. The product segmentation strategies followed by a number of hotel chains had the following specific aims:

● to maintain corporate growth in an otherwise saturated market
● to provide product identity to existing customers and to attract new customers previously missed due to economic or geographical reasons
● to capture a larger share of the hotel accommodation market by providing a range of accommodation facilities (as opposed to a single 'core' product) and services at different tariff levels and in a wider variety of locations.

A good example is Marriott International which traditionally has operated in the first class full-service sector. However, this sector has become very competitive and Marriott has extended its product range to meet increasing demand in a number of markets. Table 8.1 lists the positioning of the group's product portfolio along with that of its competitors.

Table 8.1 *Marriott International and its competitors: Market segmentation by product/brand name*

Market segment	Bass hotels and resorts	Marriott International	ACCOR
Luxury **First class**	Inter-continental Hotels and resorts	Marriott Hotels, resorts and suites	
First class	Crowne Plaza Hotels and resorts Holiday Inn Select	Renaissance Hotels	Sofitel
Middle **Market**	Forum Hotels Holiday Inn Core Brand Holiday Inn Garden Court	Ramada Hotels Marriott Courtyard Hotels	Novotel Mercure Pannonia
Economy **Budget**	Holiday Inn Express	Fairfield Inn	Ibis Etap Motel 6 Formule 1
All-Suites **(Extended stay)**	Staybridge Suites	Execustay Residence Inn	

(Pannell Kerr Forster 1999)

Marriott's Courtyard and Fairfield Inn are examples of new products which have created new markets. Marriott has identified *market gaps* and designed new products to fill these gaps. As Table 8.1 illustrates, both products are uniquely positioned with no direct competitors. The full-service hotel concept has reached a watershed and the new products offer choices to those consumers who are more room-oriented (as opposed to service-oriented) and who are seeking a better room price/value relationship. This type of new product development constitutes approximately 10 per cent of new product development (Teare, 1994).

Another product/market option (see Figure 8.1) involves repositioning the present product to attract a new market. According to Teare (1994), repositioning accounts for approximately 7 per cent of product development. An example of this is the ETB's 'Tourism for All' campaign, which aims to make England the market leader in Europe in providing facilities for disabled people. There are an estimated six million people in Britain with some form of disability and over half of this group never go on holiday. It therefore represents a massive untapped market. The outbound disabled market in Europe is estimated to be worth around £17 billion. The ETB have been at the forefront of the 'Tourism for All' initiatives, providing guidance on how businesses can upgrade their facilities for disabled people. They have also set up a disability inspection scheme, although the take-up rate so far has been disappointing. Another challenge is to make tourism businesses aware of the Disability Discrimination Act which came into force in 1996.

SWOT analysis

The strengths, weaknesses, opportunities and threats (SWOT) analysis often forms the bedrock of any product planning process. It provides a simple yet effective framework for analysing both internal resources and external trends and competitors. Organisations sometimes employ outside consultants to conduct their SWOT analysis. Apart from the expertise which they bring to the exercise, they also provide a more objective and 'non-political' viewpoint. This was the case in the SWOT analysis of England's tourism undertaken by the consultancy firm Deloitte and Touche (see Figure 8.2).

SWOT ANALYSIS OF ENGLAND'S TOURISM	
Strengths	**Weaknesses**
• Sought-after scenery and heritage are natural attributes • Wide range of character accommodation by tariff and location • Superb access to international markets	• Permanent loss of growth sectors of main holiday domestic market to sun destinations • Commercially unstable accommodation sector unable to service inbound demand • No clear means of distinguishing the good from the bad, especially for low-tariff serviced and self-catering accommodation and attractions
Opportunities	**Threats**
• Exploit the growth of independent travel in overseas markets to increase volume of low-tariff inbound tourism • Become Europe's No 1 non-sun destination thus improving image of 'at home' holidays • Create activity holiday products in cities and rural areas to secure domestic second/third holidays • Stabilise and strengthen the accommodation sector by reducing capacity	• Lack of professionalism in the independent accommodation sector means operators will not be able to deliver to the requirements of the inbound market • Powerful package holidays operators read the same trends and develop new product offers in sun destinations, and thus more 2nd and 3rd holidays are taken abroad

(© The English Tourist Board; reproduced with permission from Wason, G., *Effective Tourism Policy ETB Insights*, September 1996)

Figure 8.2 SWOT analysis of England's tourism

The SWOT analysis is a 'means to an end' and should be seen in the wider context of marketing trends and objectives. The SWOT analysis of England's tourism reveals a weakness in the accommodation sector. Accommodation accounts for at least one third of domestic and overseas visitors' expenditure on average and therefore the standard of accommodation is vitally important in terms of giving the visitor value for money. There is over-supply in this sector and there are problems with quality and service delivery. Customer satisfaction studies in this area reveal that standards are inconsistent and in some instances very low. For example, one study found that 30 per cent of overseas visitors to London claim to be dissatisfied with the standard of serviced accommodation (ETB/BTA, 1997).

Research has also revealed a great deal of confusion about the tourist boards' crown scheme. These weaknesses make it difficult for England to exploit the opportunities presented by changing holiday patterns: the growth in the number of second and third short holidays; increasing numbers of independent inbound tourists; and more ABC1s seeking country pursuits and culture. In response, the ETB has identified *accommodation rating* as a priority quality issue. It has announced a new scheme which will run in harmony with the AA and the RAC schemes. This new scheme will incorporate the quality of the property as well as the level of facilities offered. Hotels will be rated on a scale of one to five stars.

A harmonised rating scheme for bed and breakfasts, guesthouses and other types of serviced accommodation which do not qualify as hotels has been agreed in principle between the ETB, the Scottish and Wales Tourist Boards and the AA and RAC. The ratings will be based entirely on quality. An effective rating scheme is essential for two key reasons. Firstly, it is a means of encouraging accommodation providers to aspire to certain standards. Secondly, it is a way of reducing the intangibility of the tourism product and offering product consistency to the customer.

Positioning

The concept of product positioning is central to the planning process. If Marriott did not position the Courtyard and Fairfield Inn products accurately in the market, there is the danger that these products would 'cannibalise' sales from other products in the range. In other words, instead of adding to overall group sales the new products would simply displace customers from, say, the Residence Inns brand. Positioning is a detailed step-by-step approach, as illustrated in Figure 8.3.

The positioning of the Courtyard product by Marriott (Teare, 1994) followed a rigorous development process along the lines suggested by Lovelock's framework. Competitors in the budget, mid-price and luxury lodging segments were assessed, revealing a gap in the leisure and business markets for a cheaper hotel product priced $2 to $3 below the typical Holiday Inn. An extensive market analysis was undertaken, consisting of focus group interviews and a segmentation study which took over a year to conduct. This analytical process enabled Marriott to develop a framework for the product: Courtyard would be focused on the mid-priced market segment; it would be relatively small (150 rooms or fewer) to project a residential image; it would serve a limited menu and offer fewer public spaces than competitors; it would be a standardised product managed in clusters of five to eight hotels in one area; the Marriott name would be attached for recognition purposes.

Having identified the market segments and the benefits to emphasise, Marriott were able to develop a positioning statement:

'Courtyard...was to serve business travellers who wanted moderately priced hotels of consistent high quality, and pleasure travellers who wanted an affordable room that was a safe base of operations.'

(Teare, 1994)

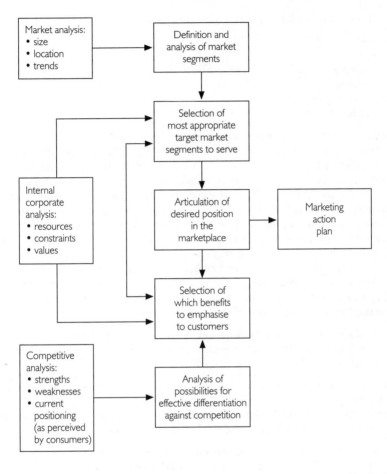

(Lovelock, 1996)

Figure 8.3 Developing a marketing positioning strategy

New product development (NPD)

In the dynamic and information-driven tourism environment of the 1990s, organisations are often keen to get new products to the market quickly to try to obtain a competitive advantage. Teare (1994) lists four main steps in the product development process:

1 Genesis and evaluation
2 Early development
3 Introduction
4 In-market evaluation and advanced development.

There are generally considered to be six categories of new product (Teare, 1994):

- new-to-the-world products
- line extensions
- repositioning
- cost reductions
- improvements and revisions
- new product lines.

Improvements and revisions are otherwise referred to as *product innovations* and constitute about 26 per cent of new product development. Great Western Trains (GWT) have recently pursued a policy of product innovation. GWT were the first InterCity operator to be privatised (Rogers, 1998). Their NPD team accompanied consumers on their journeys to gain an insight into the behaviour of different market segments – from businessmen to senior citizens to young mums with children. The exercise taught GWT that they need to consider the whole journey, door to door, and not just the portion spent on the train. As a result the company has started testing a service whereby its customers have exclusive taxis waiting for them at Paddington station when they arrive. This product innovation would appeal to young mums who are perhaps struggling with children and have just arrived at a busy London station. GWT is also testing a service with Avis, where a representative meets the consumer from the train and takes them to their hire car. This will appeal to the business traveller where convenience and time-saving are likely to be the priorities.

Considering that only one in 20 new products succeed, it is important to take a strategic approach to NPD (Lee, 1998). Lee suggests that truly innovative products adhere to three basic principles of NPD:

- *relevance* – the product should offer something relevant and motivating to the target consumer
- *differentiation* – it should be sufficiently new and different from existing products
- *delivery* – does the brand actually deliver what it promises?

The first principle underlines the importance of market research and understanding the consumer's needs and attitudes. To find out what motivates the customer and then to offer them something relevant requires in-depth research. The ETB have identified a number of product development priorities and the first one mentioned in their *Action 2000* consultation document, entitled 'Providing products for today's consumers', recognises the need for product relevance.

The underlying proposition is to:

'Promote the use of market research (including segmentation and benchmarking) as the basis for continued investment in tourism businesses to ensure that present and future market needs and opportunities are met.'

(ETB/BTA, 1997)

Core, actual and augmented product

According to Kotler (1994), the planner needs to think about the product in three stages:

1   The basic level is the *core* product, in other words: What is the buyer really buying? What is the core benefit the product will provide to the consumer? Kotler quotes Theodore Levitt's example that customers 'do not buy quarter-inch drills; they buy

quarter-inch holes'.

2 The planner then builds an *actual* product around the core benefit. Actual products can have up to five characteristics: a quality level, features, design, a brand name and packaging.

3 Finally, the planner *augments* the product by offering additional consumer services. It is often at the augmentation level where differentiation takes place and where the battle for the customer is won or lost.

During 1998, Great Western Trains built additional features into their product, including the provision of taxis and car hire on arrival, a business club service, a chauffeur-drive scheme and a bistro catering service. They are aiming for high-quality customer care. Brand awareness has been built with a £1.5 m annual advertising campaign with the theme 'Building a model railway' and a carefully segmented direct marketing campaign targeting businessmen and families. The Merlin loyalty scheme will help to augment the product, offering quarterly special offers for frequent travellers. GWT's advertising campaign in March 1998 was customer-focused and talked about what the customer is getting and 'how the trains interact with the individual'.

This level of marketing activity was unheard of in the days of British Rail, however there is one problem – the trains still don't run on time. What is the core product? What is the buyer really buying? These questions can be answered with one word – punctuality. Travelling customers want to get from A to B in a given time. This holds true for any form of transportation. Figures recently released show that more trains operated by the 25 private companies ran late or were cancelled in the fourth quarter of 1997 than in the same period in 1996 (Rogers, 1998). In terms of punctuality, three operators performed so badly that discounts were imposed – Virgin's Cross Country, Great North-Eastern and GWT. The cruel reality for the train operators is that however many features they build into the actual product and however many benefits they add on top, if customers miss meetings or are late for work they will disembark with a sour taste in their mouths.

Product life cycle

The product life cycle (PLC) provides a framework for analysing the performance of a product over a period of time (see Chapter 6, pages 143–5). One of the key strengths of the PLC is its simplicity. It is a fairly straightforward mapping of a product's sales and profit performance over a period of time. Each stage is easily described. For example, in the maturity stage there is little opportunity to gain new customers, sales decrease and profits level off or decline as more resources are allocated to defending against competitors.

However, the PLC's simplicity is also its weakness and there are a number of factors which must be taken into account when interpreting the PLC.

● The performance of a product has to be viewed against the backdrop of the market in which it performs. According to the market intelligence specialists, Mintel, the proportion of independent holidays is predicted to increase from 13.8 million in 1998 to 15.3 million in 2002. On the other hand, package holidays will see only marginal growth from 15.2 million in 1998 to 15.3 million in 2002 (*TTG*, 1998). It could be argued, in this context, that a mass tour operator's traditional sun, sea and sand packaged product which shows a levelling off of sales in this period is actually outperforming its 'go as you please' product which shows only modest growth.

- The length of the life cycle will vary, depending on whether it is describing a *product class* (winter sports), a *product form* (snowboarding) or a *brand* (Thomson Ski and Snowboard). Product classes have the longest life cycles and often stay in the maturity stages for long periods of time. Product forms tend to conform most closely to the standard PLC shape. For example, the traditional Mediterranean beach product packaged for the British market since the 1960s has passed through introduction, rapid growth, maturity and decline. The individual brand exists in a more turbulent environment and its life cycle can change quickly depending on the company's own marketing activity, competitors' actions and market trends.
- Not all products follow the traditional S-shaped life cycle, such as fads or fashions. Skateboarding and BMX bicycles are both examples of products which were introduced quickly and then died just as fast. However, BMX are enjoying something of a renaissance – testimony to the often erratic behaviour of products.

Most marketers agree that the PLC is not suitable as a forecasting tool. It is not possible to predict the level of sales at each stage, the length of each stage, or the shape of the curve. Many people claimed that snowboarding was a fad which would die quickly. However snowboarding has become an established winter sport, epitomised by its presence at the 1998 Winter Olympics, and is threatening the sales and profits of ski operators.

Despite its shortcomings, the PLC is a useful framework for marketers wishing to analyse the relationship between their products and markets. A tour operator, whose European ski product is in the maturity stage and experiencing declining profits, may want to consider developing a new snowboarding product or introduce ski packages to North America, in order to give its business a kick-start.

The life cycle concept has also been applied to tourist destinations, referred to as the destination life cycle (DLC) or tourist area life cycle (TALC). In many respects it is even more difficult to apply the life cycle to destinations than it is to tourism products such as skiing. This is due to the diversity of businesses in the area and the fragmentation of products and markets. Haywood (1986) poses the question, 'Can the tourist area life cycle be made operational?' He raises a number of questions. Which market is the life cycle referring to? Most TALC studies have assumed the area has one homogeneous market. On the contrary, a tourist area is likely to serve a number of markets and while one may be in decline (day trip segment), another (convention and meetings segment) may be very healthy.

How can the planner tell when the area has moved from one stage to the next? A number of criteria could be used to help answer this question – number of first time versus repeat visitors, profit levels of tourism businesses, visitor arrivals, visitor spend. However this type of detailed information is rarely available to the tourism planner. Haywood concludes that the TALC is not appropriate as a forecasting or even as a planning tool and that a more structured framework of analysis is needed.

Nevertheless, as with the PLC, the TALC provides a useful framework for analysing the different stages of a tourist area's development. William's (1993) work in Minorca has led to an extended version of Butler's destination life cycle model (Youell, 1998) and, although developed retrospectively, is a useful reference tool for tourist area planners. It provides some pointers to identify when an area might be moving from one stage to the next and highlights some of the problems associated with the stagnation and decline stages. Choy (1993) concludes that the roles of national tourism organisations will vary according to which stage of the life cycle the area is in. For example, at the stagnation stage the NTO needs to adopt an innovative role, focusing on product development.

Branding

Hankinson and Cowking provide a useful definition of branding, drawing on the contributions of several authors:

'A brand is a product or service made distinctive by its positioning, relative to the competition, and by its personality...Positioning defines the brand's point of reference either by price or by usage. Personality consists of a unique combination of functional attributes and symbolic values with which the target consumer identifies.'

(Hankinson and Cowking, 1995)

This definition provides a tangible framework for understanding branding and also provides a frame of reference for taking into account competitor brands. For example, in terms of price and usage, Marriott positioned their Courtyard and Fairfield products $2 to $3 cheaper than Holiday Inn and aimed them on a limited service concept at customers who were more room-oriented. The importance of a brand's personality is discussed later in the chapter.

We have already seen that a brand name is one of five product characteristics. Branding is being used with increasing frequency and expertise within the tourism industry, from the established practice of branding hotels and airlines to new applications, such as branding regions and countries. Kotler offers the following definition of a brand:

'A brand is a name, term, sign, symbol, or design, or a combination of them, intended to identify the goods or services of one seller or group of sellers and to differentiate them from those of competitors.'

(Kotler, 1994)

Branding therefore applies equally to a service industry, such as tourism, as it does to the marketing of manufactured goods. In fact it could be argued that, due to the intangible nature of tourism services, branding is more significant in the tourism industry in terms of helping customers to get a clearer mental image of what the product has to offer. Branding and positioning are closely related concepts, with a key objective being competitive differentiation. A brand strategy is likely to evolve from an extensive positioning analysis.

The meaning of a brand

According to Kotler (1994), a brand can deliver up to four levels of meaning:

'● *attributes* – a brand contains certain product attributes
● *benefits* – it is important that attributes are translated into functional and emotional customer benefits
● *values* – the brand must identify with its customers' values and ensure that the package of benefits delivers at this level

● *personality* – a brand projects a personality. In market research focus groups, researchers often ask, 'If this brand were a person, what kind of person would it be?'

Values and personality are the most important dimensions to a brand. It is at these levels where competitive advantage and customer differentiation can be achieved. Virgin has established itself as a household name, in no small part down to its founder Richard Branson, and has used this to maximum effect in its *brand-extension* strategy, which can be defined as:

'Any effort to use a successful brand name to launch new or modified products in a new category.'

(Kotler, 1994)

A well-regarded brand name makes it easier and less costly for companies to move into new markets and also affords greater advertising efficiency. Virgin has extended its branded products into, amongst others, retail (Virgin Megastores and Virgin Cola), air transport (Virgin Atlantic) and financial services (Virgin Personal Equity Plans).

A brand-extension strategy does have associated risk. If the extension fails, it might harm other products carrying the same brand name. Virgin trains is perhaps Mr Branson's greatest risk so far, involving massive levels of investment. Rail journeys are still plagued by delay. Although Railtrack, the company that owns the UK's tracks and stations, is responsible for nearly 60 per cent of delays, the fact remains that customers will blame the train operator with whom they are travelling. Richard Branson admitted on national radio that the poor service offered by his West Coast line has damaged the Virgin brand name (Rogers, 1998).

However, despite this potential threat, Virgin is breaking all the traditional rules surrounding brand extensions. What is most interesting is that customers are accepting Virgin's extensions across diverse sectors. It is claimed that this is largely due to the personality and values associated with the brand. With each new product launch, Virgin is re-affirming itself as a risk-taker, prepared to challenge the 'established' players in the market, who are often portrayed by Virgin as the 'big bad boys', for example British Airways, Radio 1, Coca-Cola, Smirnoff and the entire financial services industry. Traditional marketing literature often points to the danger of extensions diluting the brand. However new Virgin launches appear to be adding new core values to the brand:

'The brand now conveys fun, excitement, quality, value for money, innovation and much much more.'

(Mihailovic, 1995)

The value of a brand name is known as *brand equity*. When anyone points to the fragility of the Virgin business, in terms of its level of debt, Richard Branson points to the intangible benefit locked up in his brands. When calculating the value of Virgin Atlantic, a multiple of 14 times earnings would be applied to take into account the value of the brand. This would value the carrier at over £500 m, although Mr Branson claims that with the brand equity the airline is worth £800-1.2 billion (*The Economist*, 1998).

Branding tourism destinations

The most recent application of branding in the tourism industry is the attempt to brand tourism destinations. This is perhaps not surprising, given the increasing competition between tourism offices to market their respective regions. However, creating and maintaining a successful brand is a complex process, involving in-depth customer research and the allocation of resources to ensure the consistent delivery of the brand's core benefits and values. The fragmentation of the tourist region, with a range of suppliers offering several products to several markets, creates a particular challenge to the marketer.

'It is a marketing contradiction to try to establish one single brand image which can communicate many different product attributes to several different markets at the same time.'

(Cooke, 1996)

Despite this contradiction, BTA has invested a lot of resources in developing a branding strategy for Britain. According to James (1997), the priority is to establish core values for Britain and its constituent brands, London, Scotland, Wales and England. The BTA conducted extensive research among tourist board staff in Britain to generate ideas for brand values. Twenty-one focus groups were then conducted in Britain's key overseas markets to test these values. Participants included non-visitors as well as people who had visited Britain before, and represented carefully identified market segments. The research resulted in the brand architecture described in Table 8.2.

Table 8.2 The brand architecture of Britain

Brand	Positioning	Rational benefit	Emotional benefit	Personality
Britain	Island of traditional heritage and the unconventional	Traditional heritage and pageantry, landscape, arts and culture, people	I feel stimulated by the enriching, often paradoxical, experience of Britain. I feel at ease in the friendly, open culture of the British people.	Great/soiled, yet accessible. Cold in appearance, yet deeply friendly. Ordered, yet quirky. Traditional, yet innovative.
London	City of pageantry and pop	Diverse cultures, arts, pageantry, heritage, nightlife, music, glamour, shopping, safe, cosmopolitan, fashion leader	I feel liberated by the vibrancy of London. I feel stimulated by the wealth of heritage and culture of a great city.	Open-minded, casual, unorthodox, vibrant, creative

Table 8.2 Continued

Brand	Positioning	Rational benefit	Emotional benefit	Personality
Scotland	Land of fire and stone	Rugged, unspoilt wilderness, dramatic scenery, romantic history, heritage and folklore, warm and feisty people	I feel in awe of the elements in Scotland. I feel embraced by the warmth of the people. I feel rejuvenated by the experience of Scotland.	Independent, warm, mysterious, rugged, feisty
Wales	Land of nature and legend	Natural dramatic beauty, poetry and song, legend and mystery	I feel inspired by the lyrical beauty of Wales. I feel uplifted by the spirituality of the natural environment.	Welcoming, romantic, down-to-earth with passion
England	Lush, green land of discovery	Afternoon teas, quaint village pubs, cathedrals, country houses, rolling countryside, meandering roads, hedgerows, rivers, canals, coastline, piers, fêtes, morris dancing, cricket, rugged country, moorland, lakes, industrial heritage, B&Bs, rugby	I feel fulfilled by experiencing the quaint culture and history of England. I feel relaxed by the harmonious countryside and bracing walks along the coast. I feel warmed by the hearty, down-to-earth character of England. I feel soothed by the open, unspoilt outdoors.	Conservative, pleasant, refined, civilised, eccentric, down-to-earth, approachable, hearty, humorous

(© The English Tourist Board; reproduced with permission from James, G., Britain: Creating a Family of Brands, *ETB Insights*, September 1997)

The research has certainly generated some interesting perceptions of Britain. However are they the basis for developing and positioning genuine and meaningful brands, or are they just advertising slogans? James states:

'Although the different core values of England, Scotland and Wales may seem artificial, if we consistently promote them the differences will, through time, become established.'

(James, 1997)

It is certainly possible, through promotion, to reinforce the values of a product. As Ries and Trout observe:

'Positioning is not what you do to a product. Positioning is what you do to the mind of the prospect. That is, you position the product in the mind of the prospect.'

(cited in Hankinson and Cowking, 1995)

However, a brand consists not only of values and a personality, it must also deliver core customer benefits through a set of attributes. Kotler reminds us that:

'A brand is essentially a seller's promise to consistently deliver a specific set of features, benefits, and services to the buyers. The best brands convey a warranty of quality.'

(Kotler, 1994)

The London brand identifies no such features or benefits. It is questionable whether the vast range of product attributes delivered by the multitude of tourism suppliers in London could consistently deliver the benefits of a liberated feeling and cultural stimulation listed in Table 8.2. The issue of quality at destination level is also an important one. At the 47th AIEST Congress, discussing quality in tourism, delegates concluded that it was not possible to ensure quality of a destination in the same way as that of a corporation (Keller and Weiermair, 1997).

Perceptual mapping

Perceptual mapping is a product design technique used by the BTA, the ETB and the regional boards. It works by finding out what people think about three things:

- the ideal product
- your product
- your competitors' product.

Perceptual mapping helps an organisation to prioritise the allocation of its resources. It is a relatively simple technique and has the advantage of representing the findings visually in the form of a map. There are a number of steps involved:

1 Ask a representative sample of the target segment what they look for in the generic product. Expect around 25-30 different answers, however big the sample.
2 Rank all answers by the number of times they have been given, ignoring price.
3 For the axes of the perceptual map, use the top two answers, as long as they are not related to each other.
4 Ask the same sample to rate the ideal product, your product and your competitors' products using these two attributes, using a scale of 0-10.
5 Plot the results.

Figure 8.4 maps UK 'empty nesters' perceptions of weekend breaks in three-crown country hotels. This segment was asked, 'What do you look for when choosing a weekend break?' The top two answers were 'comfort' and 'food quality'. Comfort includes welcome, service, courtesy, cleanliness, quiet and warmth. As these two are not connected they were used as the axes. The ideal product was ranked as: Food 7, Comfort 8. People in the segment were then asked to rank a 20-bedroom three-crown country house hotel (the hotel conducting the exercise) and its leading competitor. The results for the property were: Food 6 and Comfort 9, and for the competitor: Food 8 and Comfort 6.

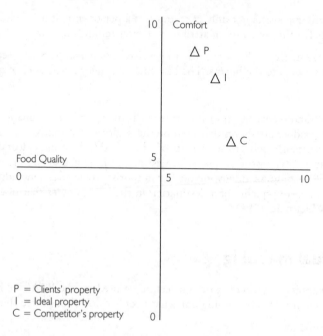

(BTA Marketing Workshops; reproduced with permission from The English Tourist Board)

Figure 8.4 A perceptual map showing the perceptions of UK 'empty nesters', living in the Heart of England Region, of weekend breaks in three-crown country hotels

The perceptual map in Figure 8.4 provides a number of insights which will assist in developing product and promotional strategies. There a number of rules for interpreting the map.

- The nearer you are to the ideal point, and the further away your competitors are, the more successful you will be.
- You can use promotion to show your market segment that you are close to the ideal point. In this example the hotel could promote its high levels of comfort.
- Promotion will create expectations and it is important that the product is developed so that it comes closer to the ideal, otherwise customers will have a negative experience. The hotel would have to improve its food quality before it could be confident of promoting this element.
- You have to research continuously, because all the points will move with time.
- The most effective way to use resources is to develop and promote your product so that it intercepts the ideal point.

This exercise can be undertaken for more than one market segment. Market segments will, by definition, be distinct from each other with their own separate preferences and therefore each segment will have its own perceptual map. For example, young families with children may have 'facilities' and 'location' as their axes.

Customer service

The phrases 'competitive advantage' or 'product differentiation' are often used when discussing product strategies. However, in a study of the airline industry, Philip Festa, a UK-based customer service consultant, points out that product innovations can be quickly copied by competitors. Airlines must look to other areas to secure long-term advantage:

'It is the people, not the procedures and products, that promise to be the ultimate differentiators between the average and the truly excellent.'

(Festa, 1997)

The airline business, as with all tourism businesses, is a people business and its staff are its most valuable asset. Therefore, a company may invest millions in new product development to try to obtain competitive advantage, yet invest relatively little in customer service where, in fact, the most effective competitive differentiation can be achieved.

Customer service in the airline industry

Increasing pressure to cut costs and maintain margins is threatening the airlines' levels of customer service. British Airways (BA) has stated that it needs to improve business efficiency by £1 billion (US$1.6 billion) by 2000. Swissair is cutting costs by 20 per cent. Lufthansa's chairman has called for a wage freeze as well as longer working hours to improve productivity. The question is: at what price? These airlines offer a core product which can be described as a 'high-margin, high-service travel experience' (Festa, 1997). Festa lists *outsourcing* as one of several challenges which airlines will have to tackle if they are to maintain their levels of customer service. Outsourcing is becoming an increasingly popular response to cost cutting pressures.

BA's Business Efficiency Programme involves 'stopping doing things we do not need to do and outsourcing where someone else can do it more efficiently'. Catering, cleaning, baggage handling, ticket processing, information technology, aircraft maintenance and flight operations have become targets for outsourcing. However, some or all of these areas may directly or indirectly impact on the customer service experience and an airline will not have the same level of control over the operating standards of the outside contractors involved. Maintaining employee morale in the face of downsizing and outsourcing is another challenge which airlines must address.

Effective communication with the customer is essential in taking a proactive approach to customer service. This involves a partnership approach with all players in the airline industry who have an impact on the customer's travel experience – the airline, reservations and airport authorities – with the aim of creating a one-stop shopping concept for the customer. Canadian Airlines International (CAI) realise that decentralisation is another necessary approach when dealing with customer service. For example, if a flight is delayed, CAI will have its representatives at the airport to deal with customer concerns, rather than waiting until after the event and conducting a damage limitation exercise. This level of service is becoming a necessity in an industry where competition for customer loyalty is intense.

At Air New Zealand, staff follow a set procedure when dealing with customer complaints (Lima, 1997). First, they apologise and 'own' the problem, as customers are not interested in debating about whose fault it is. They aim to do this within 72 hours of the problem occurring and have estimated that up to 50 per cent of customers will defect to another airline if they take longer than five days to respond. The next step is assuring the customer that something is being done about the problem. Lastly, staff discuss the problem with the customer to determine what difficulties were encountered and if compensation is appropriate. Again, communication is key to handling customer complaints. The Customer Relations Department at United Airlines believes in looking at customer dissatisfaction as an opportunity not an obstacle, in that the airline can demonstrate their level of customer care.

The cost of poor customer service

The benefits of providing effective customer service are well documented. Research shows that 70 per cent of customers who take their business elsewhere do so because of poor customer service, whereas only 20 per cent defect for reasons of price and quality. Consumer studies reveal that a customer who has a poor experience with a business may tell up to ten other people about it and a small portion (13 per cent) may tell more than 20 people. On average, 90 per cent of dissatisfied customers will not speak directly to the company about the problem but will speak freely to other customers or potential customers (Lima, 1997). The problem is that, despite these studies, managers sometimes fail to see any direct cost associated with customer dissatisfaction. This stems from the intangibility of the cost of service errors. For example, what is the actual cost of a lost customer? How much does staff time actually cost in dealing with a customer complaint?

A service-quality audit

One way of answering these questions is to undertake a service-quality audit. The audit involves a six-step process:

1 Identify each error and determine what happens.
2 Determine the frequency with which each error occurs.
3 Assign the specific costs involved for correcting each error.
4 Establish the probability of the consequence of each error.
5 Determine the total daily and annual cost of each error.
6 Identify the specific steps of the prevention or recovery process.

The audit is best undertaken by forming a task force to focus on a specific department. The results may reveal that a service error costs the organisation relatively little and may only need minor steps to correct it.

In their audit of a large hotel in New York, Luchars and Hinkin (1996) calculated that a service error involving checking guests into the wrong category of room cost the hotel $5,694 per annum. This relatively small amount could be remedied by the improved flow of information between departments and would not require a costly measure such as a training programme. On the other hand, failure to post the correct charges (for example, minibar, telephone) to the guest's room bill cost the hotel $246,302 each year. The size of this cost is due to the frequency with which the error occurs. The researchers advised in this instance that a quality management system be implemented, given the gravity of the problem. Refer to Luchars and Hinkin's (1996) article for details of how costs can be calculated.

Customer service issues in England's tourism industry

The ETB have identified a number of critical issues affecting the future quality of English tourism.

Training

The ETB recognises that the people working in the industry are its most valuable asset. With this in mind they make the following proposal:

'The ETB should continue to work with tourism and hospitality training organisations to develop training and human resource programmes, to improve service standards and business competitiveness, and to enhance the image of the industry as an employer.'

(ETB/BTA, 1997)

Consumer studies have found standards to be variable. Lack of consistency in the delivery of the product creates serious problems for the marketing planning process. Unlike a fast-moving consumer good or a fast-food service, many tourist products require a high level of guest-host interaction and therefore are much more difficult to control. The poor image and low pay of many tourism-related sectors make recruitment of high quality school and college-leavers difficult. In 1996 the Department of National Heritage set out a report addressing some of these human resource issues.

The ETB is aiming to increase the delivery of its Welcome Host and Welcome Management programmes. Welcome Host was started in 1992 and has trained in excess of 85,000 participants. Some of the issues covered in the course include: making the right impression, active listening and communication process, handling complaints and treating customers effectively. Welcome Management was launched in 1995 and addresses key issues in managing customer service, for example, creating the best service strategy, and how to recruit, retain and motivate staff to improve productivity, performance and involvement. In recognition of the growing significance of the disabled market, the ETB has launched the Welcome All programme. This course covers areas such as awareness and personal understanding and personal actions to improve accessibility.

Benchmarking

Another technique for attempting to ensure consistent product quality is benchmarking. This is aimed particularly at smaller businesses and starts with the premise that businesses in all sectors share common characteristics that ensure repeat visits. Benchmarking is about identifying, quantifying and qualifying these characteristics so they can be used as a yardstick by other businesses. Identifying a code of best practice for the quality and efficiency of a hotel reception would be an example of benchmarking in the hotel sector. This could be extended to areas such as security and breakfast service. The objective of the exercise is to enable businesses to establish their weak points, to raise standards, and to provide better value for money.

An increasing number of firms in the manufacturing and service sectors have successfully implemented benchmarking. The government and the Confederation of British Industry believe that it can be applied to the tourism industry. However there are some important questions to be answered before benchmarking can be fully implemented. Should the assessments be carried out by the businesses themselves or by independent inspectors? Who would be responsible for the independent inspections? The Cumbria Tourist Board feels that it should be a Business Links role rather than an ETB initiative. How would standards be established? The London Tourist Board thinks it is only really worthwhile if applied internationally, by comparing best practice in major cities across the world. How can the process be carried out without burdening small tourism businesses? These issues highlight the difficulties in trying to establish consistent product standards in an industry as diverse as tourism.

Future trends

Social, economic and technological trends will result in the development of new tourism products in the next millennium. The increasing consumer interest in environmentalism will see an *increase in green tourism*. The ETB proposes that in the future:

'All future tourism developments, from improvements to existing caravan parks to the creation of new attractions, should incorporate the principles of environmental sustainability.'

(ETB/BTA, 1997)

BA sponsors awards for best practice in environmental tourism. The World Travel and Tourism Council (WTTC) have developed an internet site, ECoNETT (www.wttc.org), advocating more responsible tourism and providing information on green tourism projects. The World Tourism Organisation (WTO) is developing the EU's Blue Flag standard for coastal quality as a model for application worldwide. The Japan Association of Travel Agents (JATA) has adopted a 'Declaration of Earth-Friendly Travellers', to be distributed through JATA's members, and has set up a fund for conservation projects.

Long-haul holidays stand out as one of the main growth areas, along with independent holidays, cruises and activity holidays. Defined by Mintel (1997) to take in all holidays outside Europe and the Mediterranean area (i.e. excluding Turkey, North Africa and Egypt), long-haul had a 13 per cent share of holidays abroad in 1994 (measured by volume of visits), rising to 17 per cent in 1997 and forecast to reach 20 per cent by the year 2000. This growth can largely be explained by the increasing popularity of the long-haul beach holiday.

By the end of 1998, the UK *ocean-going cruise market* is likely to have grown by 50 per cent in two years, reaching an annual total of 625,000 passengers (Peisley, 1998). There is a trend towards the consolidation of large companies in the global luxury cruise market, characterised by the proposed merger between Cunard and Seabourn Cruise Line following its sale to the US operator Carnival Corporation.

Summary

The service characteristics of the tourism product present the tourism marketer with a number of challenges. With the often seasonal and perishable nature of the product, how do you smooth out the demand curve? How do you make the product tangible and, in the process, reduce the customer's perceived risk? Are your staff sufficiently aware that they are in fact part of the product purchased by the customer? These challenges make product planning and innovative marketing vital in a highly competitive industry. There are a number of planning tools and marketing techniques at the tourism marketer's disposal. These include SWOT analysis, product/market matrix, product segmentation, (re)positioning, new product development, product augmentation, product life cycle, branding, perceptual mapping and benchmarking. Regardless of which product planning techniques are employed, a consistently high level of customer service will be the ultimate weapon in gaining a competitive advantage.

✎   CASE STUDY
PRODUCT CLUBS IN CANADA

The Canadian Tourism Commission's (CTC) Industry Enhancement Committee is responsible for the product clubs initiative. This is an on-going initiative and you can keep up-to-date with developments through the Canadian Tourism Commission's (CTC) newsletter, *Communique*, at the CTC's internet site (http://www.ctc-ctx.com/tourism/). The programme is designed to help small and medium-sized businesses pool their efforts and increase the range and quality of tourism products. The aim is to encourage co-operative ventures and partnerships between traditional and non-traditional partners in the tourism industry. The idea of the club is to create a critical mass of industry suppliers on a regional or national scale. Any examples of best practice will be communicated to the rest of the industry.

Almost 20 product clubs have been formed, based on a cohesive tourism theme or activity. For example, the Western Canada Golf Alliance product club is a partnership between the Tourism Alliance for Western and Northern Canada Inc. and the CTC. It will work over three years to build linkages between golf courses, resorts, tour operators and other tourism sectors to increase the range of products available to golf travellers. The club aims to produce a golf development strategy, improve distribution channels and build linkages with the travel trade. Of the total $287,500 investment in the project, the CTC share will be $135,000, while the club will contribute $152,500. Overall, the CTC invested $700,000 in partner funds for each of the 1996-7 and 1997-8 financial years.

Product club application criteria
There is an application procedure where a number of questions have to be answered, including:
● To what extent will the club *directly contribute or leverage funding* from other sources?
● Is the product club application focused on *small or medium size businesses*?
● How will *best practice models and success stories be shared* with the tourism community across Canada?
● How *unique or distinct* is the proposed product club from other existing organisations?
● Does it address *critical issues for the sector* that are barriers to tourism growth, such as seasonality, financing and packaging?

Applicants must also address the following elements.
● What are the club's key objectives over a three to five-year period?

- Who is the targeted customer segment and how will their needs be met?
- A financial plan for the club which highlights its financial requirements and proposed sources of funding.
- What industry sectors and types of businesses would be involved?

The Conservation Lands Product Club

The Conservation Lands Product Club (CLPC) is a partnership between the Grand River, Halton, Hamilton and Niagara Peninsula Conservation Authorities. These regions are all based in the watersheds of major rivers. The club operates under the name 'The Conservation Lands of Ontario' and describes itself as 'a public and private sector model for co-operative marketing and provision of sustainable ecotourism in an urban fringe area'. The club markets the four regions using the ecotourism theme and acts as the liaison for different sectors. The club believes the key stakeholders will benefit. The conservation authorities need to cross-promote their watersheds to increase revenues and to promote the importance of the natural environment. Visitors need an access point to obtain information about ecotourism and soft adventure destinations. The private sector, such as accommodation providers, restaurants, outfitters (suppliers for fishing, boating, camping, etc.), and guiding companies need to be linked with new clients. Tourism companies need new destinations and products to expand their business.

Target markets

The primary target demographic includes middle-income families who are outdoor enthusiasts, live in the watersheds, and are not aware of the range of ecotourism and soft adventure available in the region. The target age range is 25-50 years. The club is also interested in attracting similar segments from the Greater Toronto area (one hour drive time) and inbound tourists at Niagara Falls (one to two hours drive time). Secondary demographic groups include younger families and single people (18-25) with less disposable income who have an interest in the 'harder' end of the soft adventure market. Another secondary market is the 'over 50' group that is interested in the softer end of the soft adventure spectrum.

Business partnerships

Business partnerships will be created with the private and public sector. The tourism area product has been divided into the following sectors:
- land-based attractions (public sector, private sector, NGO/museum)
- accommodations (hotel chain, country inns, bed and breakfast, farm vacations)
- tour operators (large company or small eco-tour company)
- suppliers (retail chains, independent outlet, outfitters)
- destination marketing organisations (visitor and convention bureaux, chambers of commerce, tourism associations)
- corporate/media sponsors.

A partner will pay a membership fee, agree to abide by sound ecotourism practices and support the environmental policies and goals of the Conservation Authorities. In return they will be able to display the 'Conservation Lands Partner' watermark and receive referrals from the club's offices, enabling them to increase their client and revenue base. Part of the funds generated by the club will be directed to environmental projects such as trail maintenance.

Marketing activities

An identifiable brand, logo and slogan have been established to enhance the product club. The brand name, which has been registered, is 'The Conservation Lands of Ontario'. The brand's statement is, 'Working together for sustainable tourism'. The club's mission statement is borrowed from the WTO's guide to local planners:

'To manage the natural and human resources so as to maximise visitor enjoyment and local benefit while minimising negative impacts upon the destination site, community and local population.'

The club has designed a logo featuring the brand name in green and brown lettering against the silhouette of an eagle in flight. This logo will be used on letterheads, envelopes and promotional material. Business partners will be able to display the logo on their premises. Promotional straplines such as 'Spectacular by nature' link the club and the notion of ecotourism.

The club has established an office in Cambridge, Ontario. It features a freephone number for callers from Ontario, Quebec, New York State and Michigan. This inquiry line gives staff the opportunity to give a wide range of information on the destination's products. This provides an opportunity to encourage the visitor to stay longer in the conservation area. It also provides data that will be used to determine visitor demographics and will provide data for further research.

The office has set up a number of databases, run on the Microsoft Access program, which the club describes as 'the basis of our office'. Information held on the databases include the following:

- visitors and convention bureaux
- chambers of commerce
- tour operators
- associations, for example hiking, fishing
- services, for example restaurants
- suppliers and outfitters, for example canoe companies, clothing companies
- sites and attractions
- media
- travel writers
- government (municipal, provincial and federal representatives).

In addition, an eco-talent bank is being built to assist in future product development. This will include a listing of all available experts to serve as 'step-on' guides and advisers, for example interpreters, historians and story-tellers.

(http://www.ctc-ctx.com/tourism/)

Questions

1 The objective of this exercise is to design the axes of a perceptual map for the following segments:
- middle-income families (age range 25–50) who are outdoor enthusiasts, live in the region, and are interested in a range of ecotourism and soft adventure activities
- younger families and single people (18–25) with less disposable income who have an interest in the 'harder' end of the soft adventure market

- over-50 age group that is interested in the softer end of the adventure spectrum.
  a) List as many product attributes and benefits as you can, which you feel these segments would be interested in, explaining your choice.
  b) Decide for each segment which two are likely to be the most important. These two will form the axes of the map.
2 Identify the core benefit each of these segments would be interested in. Then design an actual and augmented product which would appeal to them.
3 What 'values' and 'personality' do you think the Conservation Lands Product Club should be portraying? How would these assist in the marketing of the product?

References and bibliography

BTA Marketing Workshops (1996) *The Tourism Marketing Workshop*, BTA

Choy, D. (1993) Alternative roles of national tourism organisations, *Tourism Management*, Vol. 14, No. 5, October

Cooke, P. (1996) The branding and positioning of tourism destinations. *ETB Insights*, November

ETB/BTA (1997) *Action 2000: Shaping the Future of English Tourism*, English Tourist Board/British Tourist Association

Festa, P. (1997) Wheeling out the service, *Airline Business*, January

Hankinson, G. and Cowking, P. (1995) What do you really mean by a brand? *Journal of Brand Management*, Vol. 3, No. 4

Haywood, M. (1986) Can the tourist-area life cycle be made operational? *Tourism Management*, September, Vol. 7, No. 3

Holloway, C. and Plant, R. (1992) *Marketing for Tourism*, 2nd edition, Pearson Education Ltd

James, G. (1997) Britain: creating a family of brands, *ETB Insights*, September

Keller, P. and Weiermair, K. (1997) A review of the 47th AIEST congress: Quality and quality management in tourism: Towards a synthesis of the Congress, *The Tourist Review*, No. 4

Kotler, P. (1994) *Marketing Management: Analysis, Planning, Implementation and Control*, 8th edition, Prentice Hall

Lee, C. (1998) Buck your ideas up, *Marketing*, 5 February

Lima, E.P. (1997) Hurdling service problems, *Air Transport World*, No. 1

Lovelock, C.H. (1996) *Services Marketing*, 3rd edition, Prentice-Hall

Luchars, J. and Hinkin, T. (1996) The service-quality audit, *Cornell Hotel and Restaurant Administration Quarterly*, February, Vol. 37, No. 1

Milhailovic, P. (1995) Time to scrap the rules: Entering Virgin territory, *Journal of Brand Management*, Vol. 3, No. 1

Mintel (1997) *Long Haul Holidays*, Mintel Marketing Intelligence, March

Peisley, T. (1998) The cruise market in mainland Europe, *Travel and Tourism Analyst*, No. 1

Rogers, D. (1998) Are the railways on track? *Marketing*, 5 February

Teare, R. *et al.* (1994) *Marketing in Hospitality and Tourism: A Consumer Focus*, Cassell

The Economist (1998) Behind Branson, 21 February, pp 81–6

TTG (1998) Mintel predicts independent holidays to match packages, 4 February, *Travel Trade Gazette*

Wason, G. (1996) Effective tourism policy, *ETB Insights*, September

Williams, M. (1993) An expansion of the tourist site cycle model: The case of Minorca (Spain), *Journal of Tourism Studies*, Vol. 4, No. 2, December

Youell, R. (1998) *Tourism: An Introduction*, Longman

9 Pricing travel and tourism products

Objectives

By the end of this chapter you should be able to:

- list the factors affecting pricing decisions and demonstrate how such factors affect those decisions
- describe the different pricing policies that are available and explain why these might vary from industry to industry and company to company
- understand what the consequences might be of different chosen policies
- evaluate the appropriateness of a chosen policy in specific instances
- suggest a price for a particular situation given costing and other information.

Price in the marketing mix

The pricing element of the marketing mix is unique in that it is the only one that directly affects an organisation's revenues and hence profits. The disciplines of finance and economics have much to contribute in setting prices, but on their own perhaps do not lead to the best pricing decisions. This chapter describes a number of theoretical approaches to pricing and suggests an approach to setting which draws on them all.

Inevitably textbooks consider each element of the marketing mix separately, but you need to remember that in fact they interact. Before looking at pricing decisions in isolation, here is a reminder of how other mix decisions might interact with pricing decision.

Product quality (both real and perceived) needs to be considered in the light of price. Often referred to as the *price-quality trade-off*, decision-makers need to recognise that consumers might accept that a better quality product will cost more. Similarly with brand image, lesser known brands might command lower prices. Brand image, of course, is in no small part the consequence of marketing communications decisions. Lastly, pricing decisions need to consider the needs of the distributor (place) – they have to be offered a good enough margin of profit to make it worthwhile them selling the operator's products.

The travel and tourism industry – like many industries – displays peculiarities of pricing. These arise partly from custom and practice, and partly from the idiosyncrasies of the industry. The intention in this chapter is firstly to introduce the basic concepts of pricing, and then consider the rather more complex pricing situations of the travel and tourism industry. As introductory examples, those companies without adequate financial resources should think hard about pricing for market share. Others cannot go for volume sales and the implied, lowered margins if it substantially alters dividends to shareholders. Companies with substantial borrowings may not be supported by banks if they pursue perceived risky policies, as the bank may 'pull the plug' at the wrong time.

Impact on pricing of corporate objectives

As the approach of this text to travel and tourism marketing is a planning approach, it makes sense to consider first the objectives of organisations and how these might affect the setting of prices. It should be recognised that not all organisations will have stated these objectives explicitly. However, if and when they do exist, they can have a significant impact on pricing (as well of course as other elements of the mix). The most common objectives are as follows.

Profit maximisation

Classical economics strongly suggests that managers in organisations take decisions in such a way as to maximise profits. Where organisations do so explicitly, pricing decisions may appear to be relatively simple. However the complexity of the marketplace and internal costs in travel and tourism make this approach difficult in reality. For instance, unless managers know precisely the extent to which reducing prices will increase their sales, they cannot predict that the reduction will maximise profits.

Target rate of return

This objective aims to achieve a particular return on the assets employed in an organisation, for example 20 per cent on average net funds employed. It has a greater feeling of the reality of decision-making. It is suggested that, rather than looking to maximise profit, owners/investors in a business may simply set a target profit with which they will be happy. This in turn may make life simpler for those taking pricing decisions – they will not need to agonise about whether each and every decision may have been taken in such a way as to maximise profit, they simply need to know (or estimate) whether the decision will meet the target rate of return.

Market share

For some organisations, market share is the be all and end all. There may be a variety of reasons for it, ranging from managerial 'ego-boosting' to strategies calculated to put others out of business. Others may be following the advice of the consultants PIMS (see Chapter 6, page 144). They correlate business success with market share more than any other factor. Whatever the reason, it is an objective likely to suggest aggressive pricing strategies.

Survival

In the worst case of marketing planning, decision-makers are forced to consider the short-term survival of the business. In this case, pricing decisions may be lead by the immediate requirement of staying in business and may result in desperately low prices.

Growth

Whilst remembering that growth of sales is not the same as increase in market share (the industry may be growing faster than your sales), the objective of growth is still very popular. It should be remembered also that growth can be achieved not only by selling more of a product, but also by selling the same volume but at higher price points. (Again for a fuller discussion of these points, see Chapter 6.)

Social

For some organisations, objectives are not only commercial in their nature. Just as the Health Education Council tries to demarket smoking as it is detrimental to society, so a travel or tourism organisation may demarket some destinations (for example, hot-spots in a National Park), for instance, by punitive car parking prices.

Basic concepts in pricing

There are several fundamental approaches to pricing. They are dealt with here in no order of priority and no one method is better than another, indeed a combination of methods may well be the best approach. The combination will depend on the internal and external information available to the decision-maker.

Cost-based methods

These methods draw heavily on the accounting discipline of costing. This approach has a lot to recommend it, in as much as if an organisation's costs are covered, then at least it is in a position to make a profit. Furthermore, these methods are often seen as fair by consumers.

To use this method, it is necessary to understand the differences in the nature of costs. At the simplest, level costs can be split into two types.

- *Fixed costs* are costs which do not vary with output, i.e. the amount of the service provided. Hence, a hotelier has the fixed cost of owning the hotel to bear, whether it is empty or full of guests. Similarly, a coach operator has the fixed cost of owning the fleet, whether or not the vehicles are in use.
- *Variable costs* are those which do increase as more of a service is provided. For example, the energy costs of a hotel increase as guests occupy the rooms and start to use heat and light. Similarly, a coach operator's costs rise as the vehicles are driven, thereby consuming fuel.

These two cost elements can be combined with *revenue*, which should increase as the service is sold, to give a picture of when an operation becomes profitable. Known as *break-even analysis* or *cost/profit/volume (CPV) analysis*, the interaction of these elements can be shown graphically. Considering costing a hotel for example. It typically has a high fixed cost as shown in Figure 9.1, which shows a hypothetical hotel's break-even point.

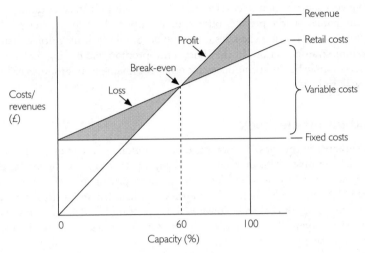

Figure 9.1   The break-even point for a hypothetical hotel

Costing issues and marginal cost pricing

Even where costs are known and accurate, there is often a case for selling at prices which do not fully cover the cost of providing the service. Take the example of aircraft seats. An airline may have planned a flight from Newcastle to Paris to be profitable at a price of £200 when the aircraft is 90 per cent full. At what price should it sell the remaining seats? A strict cost-accounting approach would be to say that all seats should cover their fair share of fixed costs and therefore be charged at the same price as the others. A market-oriented approach could say that, as the fixed costs were covered at 90 per cent capacity, all that is necessary is that the seat price covers the extra costs of having an additional person on board, for example the cost of additional fuel. The opportunity exists therefore to sell the product cheaply compared to the initial seats sold.

For conventional, manufactured products there are strong arguments against this, one being the fairness of some paying one price and others paying less. This can lead to complaints and prospective buyers delaying purchase and waiting for discounts. However, in the travel and tourism industry, where the timing of consumption of the product is critical, the market seems to accept the principle of paying less for a service consumed at short notice, hence the common practice of selling seats via teletext and at discounts for holidays booked at the last minute.

Some companies are able to calculate unit costs and estimate the changes to those costs according to volume. In tour operations, deciding upon a percentage mark-up is still extremely difficult. It is unlikely that these will ever be standard for the differing products in a tour operator brochure, not only because differing market conditions occur and maintaining product range may be more important, but also because there is a problem with allocating overheads. For instance, brochure costs and staffing cannot easily be allocated between holiday products.

Pricing to give a contribution to cost (marginal cost pricing) is an acceptable proposition for some companies, as the product offered may support the sale of other products, for example holidays supporting the sales of insurance. Similarly, it may utilise spare capacity, for example transportation. In the short term, promotional pricing, i.e. a temporary price reduction, may be the springboard for other complementary products or be used to destroy rival products.

Demand-based methods

Pricing techniques in this classification have the common feature of giving major consideration to the consumer. This does not necessarily equate to giving the lowest prices. In fact the opposite may be true. Consider ferry operators pricing journeys across the North Sea. There is a given capacity of possible journeys – when demand is slack, typically during school term times, prices can be lowered to try to stimulate demand. However, when demand picks up, typically during the first few days and weeks of school holidays, then prices can (and usually are!) increased.

The above is an example of segmentation using time as a basis. Other bases of segmentation may also be appropriate in pricing travel and tourism products. Age is often used with transport operators, for example giving discounts to both older and younger travellers (for more about market segmentation, see Chapter 4). Remember that segmentation can be a creative process and could be imaginatively used in pricing.

Deeper understanding of the way consumers perceive prices can lead to *psychological pricing*. This usually manifests itself as prices which avoid barriers, for example a £1,000 holiday may seem psychologically cheaper if offered at £999. Similarly, in order to present a simplified choice of product to the consumer, *price lining* may be employed. Here a range of prices is created with meaningful gaps between them. For example, in marketing day trips a standard trip may be priced at £50 but not include lunch. A special trip may include lunch and some other features and be priced at £65 – even though lunch can be provided at a low cost, £15 is added to make the offer clearly different. Similarly the deluxe trip may include free drinks, but be priced at £100. As long as the consumer perceives the gaps as representing a clear difference of price and quality, they should accept the distinction. The mistake not to make is to price many products with marginal differences and prices – this may lead to confusion.

Perhaps the ultimate in demand-based pricing is *negotiating*. Whilst this is possible at the level of the final consumer, for instance some hotel customers may try to negotiate a cheaper rate, it is much more common in organisational buying. As will be seen in the examples later in this chapter, a lot of hotel space and transport seats are block-booked by tour operators. Prices and other conditions are arrived at by managers and executives discussing volumes to be bought and the costs and prices they can afford. However, mere knowledge of the relative amounts of a commodity in supply and demand is not enough to secure a good deal. Do not assume that particular personality types are more suited to negotiation – tough negotiators can still be pleasant people. Negotiation is not an inherited trait – people can be trained to negotiate and even people naturally inclined to the process can benefit from training. For those looking for self-help in this area, Winkler (1981) provides a useful text.

Competitive-based methods

In some situations an organisation's prices are guided by the competitions' prices, where prices are set at the same level as others in the industry – this is known as *going rate pricing*. The arguments for this approach are that the industry will have developed prices which are acceptable to the marketplace and there is little to be gained by offering different prices (so called following 'industry wisdom'). The counter to this is that there may be the opportunity to offer different prices (and therefore achieve better profits) that the majority of the industry has ignored (this regards industry norms as the decision of a 'ship of fools').

Some will use competitors' prices as a target to be undercut. Those adopting this approach will need to be sure of their cost structures compared to others. This will be a difficult position to sustain if the price cutter does not have lower costs in the long term. It may also lead to price wars.

Some organisations may be competitive-based to the extent that they use prices to try to drive out competition (perhaps to give themselves a longer term monopoly). There is a view in the travel industry that 'destroyer' type pricing leads to a decline in safety standards and quality. Companies like airlines would be reluctant to pursue pricing policies that may affect their credibility for safety. However, third parties like tour operators are less reluctant when the responsibility for the provision of standards and safety is largely left to their suppliers, for example hotels and airlines. The trade tends to be moderated by the third parties like travel agents who must give feedback on consumer responses to falling standards or concerns on safety.

A prime example of this was the European coach market in the 1980s. In order to provides cheaper fares, some UK coach operators began to use coaches and drivers from countries where labour rates were cheaper and vehicle maintenance standards less rigorous. Passengers were being met by non-English-speaking drivers with run-down coaches in other company liveries. Eventually, passengers were not prepared to tolerate the reduction in quality, and agents selling the service were reluctant to support the sales of products which were at most dangerous and at least alienating customers and damaging their own reputations.

Some companies are in a position to be price leaders in a market and achieve a premium price over others. There will need to be reasons for this – perhaps, for instance, providing a higher quality service, such as the Orient Express.

Competition should be defined in the widest terms – consumers may look wider than other organisations offering the same product in comparing prices. Someone looking for a wind-surfing holiday in Hawaii may consider different destinations and/or different activities if prices for their first choice are not acceptable.

The contribution of economics to pricing

An in-depth treatment of economic pricing theory is beyond the scope of this text – for greater detail, refer to a general economics text, such as Bull (1995). Holloway (1997) has a detailed consideration of the contribution of economics to airline pricing.

The interaction of supply and demand

Economists contend that producers of a commodity are more likely to provide that commodity if the price for it in the marketplace is high. This is coupled with the suggestion that buyers are more likely to purchase more of the commodity if prices are low. From this comes the idea that the quantity produced and consumed, and the price acceptable, to each party will be in equilibrium at some point. This is most easily seen in Figure 9.2.

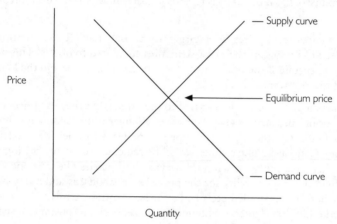

Figure 9.2

There are certain conditions that need to be present for this process to occur and it is these conditions which make this simplistic model unlikely to be useful as a mathematical way of determining price. One assumption is that consumers have perfect knowledge, i.e. they know all prices from all producers. One only has to consider the plethora of holiday products to see the unlikelihood of this in reality – consumers would need to collect all the information on holidays and then understand the differences between them. In other sectors, however, such as the English channel ferry market, knowing all prices is conceivable. Another assumption of the model is that there are many, small producers. With the exception of small hotels and guest houses, it is difficult to think of a travel and tourism sector that conforms to this criteria. The consequence of this is that competition may be reduced and therefore prices are less free to move than the model suggests.

Although the model does not help pricing decisions in a mathematical or graphical way, it does not mean that the concept is completely redundant. For instance, if a producer has a feeling that the market is undersupplied, they may tend to increase prices. Similarly, if a buyer senses that the market is oversupplied they may try to negotiate lower prices – as happened in UK hotels in the late 1990s.

This situation may change in the future. Barrass (1998) suggests that the technological environment that heralds the increasing use of the internet for marketing products might mean that perfect information is more possible. She suggests in the future, for the passenger shipping industry, consumers will be able to obtain information about all fares easily because they will all be on web sites.

Elasticity of demand

This refers to the rate at which the demand for a product rises or falls as prices alter. This is perhaps more easily seen in physical products – the demand for petrol, for instance, is relatively unaltered by price changes, hence it is called an *inelastic* product. (It is not surprising therefore that inelastic products are favourite items to be taxed – the demand, and therefore the tax revenue to the Chancellor of the Exchequer, will not fall even though the effect of the tax is to increase price.)

Transferring this concept to the travel and tourism industries, it would be easy to assume that many of its products are *elastic*, i.e. as prices fall, demand will increase – if holiday prices fall, surely more holidays will be taken! However, there may be occasions when this is not true – a new, popular destination may be able to sustain higher prices – fashion may dictate that people will pay higher prices to visit the 'in' destination. Popularity, in this case, has rendered the destination inelastic.

Economic theory argues the elasticity can be measured. In fact, elasticity is the numeric value of the slope of the demand curve. Figure 9.3 shows two demand curves – for an elastic and for an inelastic product. As with knowledge of the state of supply and demand, managers are not often in a position to know mathematically the value of elasticity for a product – either they do not have access to all price and quantity data, or the product is new and therefore no historic data to derive the curve exist. Again, this does not necessarily make the concept redundant – pricing executives may have a 'feel' for elasticity. If their feeling is that the product is inelastic, they may tend to increase price.

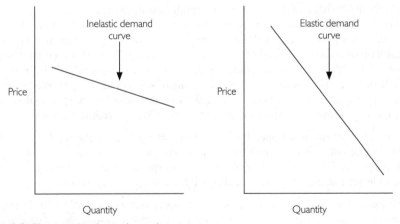

Figure 9.3 Elastic and inelastic demand curves

Features of the travel and tourism industry which may affect pricing

As already discussed, pricing decisions can be affected by, *inter alia*, demand, costs, the competition, supply, government policies on pricing, consumer legislation and competition, the economy (in particular, exchange rates and interest rates), profit margins and other corporate objectives.

In common with all marketing decisions, pricing decisions also need to be made in the light of the marketing environment for the particular product under consideration (see Chapter 3). The travel and tourism industry has its own peculiarities which have dramatic effects on pricing. These are as follows.

Marketing strategies in different destinations

Marketing strategies are often dictated by the differing environments in destination countries. A tour operator running packages to various European destinations and the USA may, according to exchange rates and the general climate of tourism in each country, have to vary their prices.

For example, if Spain and the Balearics have a favourable exchange rate compared to the UK, the operator may be able to increase volume and share by going for *economies of scale*. This might affect prices as follows: if in the previous year the average package price was £299, despite increased costs in hotels and transportation, the operator will incur some savings on a more favourable exchange rate. This is likely to increase demand for the destination. The operator may decide to reduce the average price to £275, thereby gaining competitive advantage by maintaining lower pricing and increased volume. The operator may also *capture market share* (remember, exchange rates are favourable and demand is likely to be high).

For the same operator running packages to the USA, an unfavourable exchange rate and news reports of attacks on British tourists in Miami may mean that demand is likely to be less favourable for Florida. The operator cannot go for growth, but wishes to maintain the product in the hope of more favourable conditions in the future. The objective here may now be to *maintain share* (or reduce loss of share) and look for *economies of scope*. To achieve this, the operator may look for lower costs of production in order to reduce prices and maintain demand (assuming price will affect demand). To do this they may look for suppliers who will reduce prices (who may do so in order to maintain their loyalty as a buyer). If the operator is able to secure the supply of services at cheaper rates, they may be able to pursue a reduction in price, and maintain share or reduce the loss of share. Similarly they may be able to sustain the lower volumes through reduced costs.

In this latter situation, some operators may decide to pull out of the market altogether, But this can be risky, as the supply of transport and accommodation may not be available to them when the market changes. Another alternative may be to accept lower volumes and lower margins, hoping that this will be a temporary situation.

In both examples, there are of course a host of other factors to consider, including the triggering of price wars and the risk of losing travel agent racking space if products are withdrawn from the market.

Controlling the supply of services

Tour operators may need to pay suppliers (such as a hotel chain) an adequate price and guarantee them the purchase of the volume of rooms demanded. This is necessary if the operator is to maintain supply in the long term.

Similarly, an operator's pricing policy can affect supply – cut-price operators may not be welcomed by some suppliers where it affects the supplier's own pricing or credibility. Consumers may find it strange if they are offered a hotel at a cheaper price through an operator than by booking directly with the hotel, leading to a reduction in the perceived quality of the hotel in the eyes of the consumer.

Some operators may seek to block the supply of successful products, like campsites and hotels, to other operators by pre-booking all the accommodation in a particularly popular hotel or destination.

Premium on popular travelling times

For a popular departure time, such as 11.00 a.m., a ferry company may have to decide between accepting a high volume/low price contract from a tour operator's coaches or risk waiting for individual car and passenger traffic, paying premium rates, to book later.

Predicting the demand for destinations and events

Predicting the demand for destinations and events is one of the primary tasks in achieving the correct pricing policy. For example, a coach operator who fails to gain an adequate supply of accommodation for a popular event, such as the Edinburgh Festival or Edinburgh Tattoo, may lose their foothold in the market.

Perishable product

The travel and tourism product is 'perishable', i.e. it cannot be stored and sold at a later date. In addition, suppliers may not wish the surplus to be sold through the same channels as the standard product, as this may affect future demand and pricing. This is why outlets exist which allow the supplier to remain anonymous, for example Teletext late offers which provide an outlet for major tour operators to off-load surplus holidays at reduced margins without affecting their main brochure. Similarly, flight-only specialists are the outlet for airlines with surplus.

Care must be taken with this opportunity – if a lot of spare capacity is available at short notice, then the consumer may learn to expect cheap/late deals. If too many people wait to book their holidays at the last minute, it can often lead to panic reductions in prices by operators and alter price expectation of package holidays.

Seasonal demand

Seasonality of demand leads to expectations on pricing. Demand for some UK hotels from commercial business tends to reduce in high summer. This leads to domestic consumers anticipating lower rates and availability mid-week. Conversely, many tour operators and ferry companies are able to increase prices in high summer when demand is at its peak.

Highly segmented industry

The travel and tourism industry is highly segmented, with varying elasticities of demand in those segments. This allows for discriminatory pricing, i.e. offering the same product at different prices to different consumers.

Where distinct segments exist, such as corporate business and tourist business, prices tend to be low, although generally this is tied to volume. The volume of such business tends not to change with price. This can be compared to holiday products which are generally more susceptible to recessions and changes in real income. Here, volume may well change a lot with price.

Market segments with different elasticity of demand

Some sections of the industry may experience different price elasticity of demand in the different market segments in which they operate. For ferries, premium peak business is the family holiday market with car and passengers, which is less sensitive to price than the day-trip market. However, pricing may also affect frequency of travel, and whereas changes in price would not affect the family and car market, it will affect the frequency with which day-trip travellers use ferries.

Considering the customer's total purchases

Some elements of the industry have to consider the customer's total purchases when considering prices and profits. Hotels should not consider room rates and restaurant prices separately. Selling a room cheaply to a guest who will use the restaurant and bars extensively may be more profitable compared to someone who pays full rate for the room but purchases nothing else. Tour operators need to consider the profit being generated by all aspects of the package, including, for instance, the contribution from the insurance policy. Greene (1987) provides a detailed insight into the complexity of pricing and selling of hotels and their restaurants.

Mass marketers and niche operators

The holiday industry is characterised by large, 'mass marketers' and specialist 'niche' operators.

Guaranteed standards may be directly associated with well-known brand names, but not necessarily smaller operators. However, specialisation is one advantage that some smaller operators have in increasing the perceived quality or standard of their product. A specialist tour operator to Greece may have a lead over one of the leading brand names like Thomsons on holiday packaging in Greece. This is how some independent operators are able to maintain distinct premium pricing, i.e. charging higher prices for products that are perceived to be superior.

The danger for small successful specialists is that larger operators like Thomsons may be able to charge low prices in order to break into the market. An operator with a lead in the market may wish to repel an attack on the market by another by instituting a penetration pricing policy first, i.e. they charge low prices such that the market does not appear attractive in terms of profit.

Operators are constantly looking for new destinations which will be the future growth areas – where many rivals are likely to emerge, penetration pricing may be necessary. Many smaller companies are reluctant to take the risk of higher volumes compensating for lower margins, or do not have the necessary resources to take these risks.

The effect of the product life cycle

Travel and tourism products and destinations are at different stages in their product life cycles (see Chapter 6). The theory of the product life cycle (should it prove to be valid) has a major impact on pricing decisions, i.e. prices tend to fall as products move through their life cycle – until the decline stage, when they may increase.

Pricing in travel and tourism's major sectors

Pricing for different sectors of the travel and tourism industry presents companies with different features or problems. Here the major influences on three of the sectors are considered in detail: the hospitality industry, tour operations and transport. Key considerations in these examples are the extent to which supply or demand influences pricing, and the extent to which perishability influences pricing.

The hospitality industry

The nature of demand is a primary influence on hotel pricing policy. Hotels may serve a number of market segments which range from business-based accommodation and conferences to tourism or leisure based-clients. The extent to which a hotel commits itself to each of these segments will determine the overall profitability of the hotel. Achieving the right mix of business is, therefore, an essential part of good yield management. Holloway (1997) defines yield as 'a measure of operating revenue per unit of output sold'. For example, a hotel room sold to someone staying on business may produce a greater yield than one sold to a holidaymaker. The difference may be because the business person will use the minibar, eat in the restaurant – perhaps entertaining a client. The holidaymaker, in contrast, may bring in their own drinks and regard eating in town as part of the holiday experience.

In general, most hotels want to achieve penetration in the market segment which provides the highest price. In a hotel serving both business and leisure, this is generally associated with business-based accommodation. Figure 9.4 shows the range of prices a hotel might charge. The highest price based on demand is generally termed *rack rate* and this usually provides the ceiling for pricing, i.e. the maximum price that can ordinarily be expected. This price will also reflect the peak demand for the product, i.e. mid-week, and according to the level of commercial activity (traditionally low periods being holiday periods like high summer and around the Christmas and New Year break). Other market segments generally reflect a discount off this rate based on either volume, for example where tour operators buy large numbers of rooms well in advance, or the packaging of total hotel services where there is commitment to spend on all the revenue generating activities of the hotel, i.e. conference packages and inclusive breaks (full-board or dinner, bed and breakfast rates). The floor, the lowest price (or highest discount), may be based on several factors.

Primarily it is important to predict the level of demand and to assess what surplus accommodation is going to be left for each market segment producing the lower revenues. This is generally near to the actual costs of providing the room.

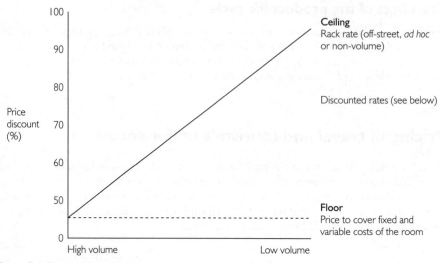

Figure 9.4 Demand-based pricing and discounting in the hotel sector

The most complicated aspect of hotel pricing is deciding on the contribution to fixed and variable costs that each segment makes. Additional spending by hotel guests on items like beverages or food can clearly contribute to overall profitability and therefore influence levels of discount on accommodation. The aim is to maximise the revenue from each guest, thereby maximising overall revenue. In this respect, each division within the hotel will have a vested interest in deciding how much each type of guest contributes to their departmental revenue or gross margin. Therefore chefs and food and beverage management will be interested in the level of food gross profit they can achieve from a packaged tour or leisure guest where the amount allocated to food is fixed, and they may adjust their menus accordingly by, for example, limiting choice to items which have a high return.

When assessing demand for hotels, the amount of supply and competitor activity are key to determining price. Where there are clear indications of undersupply of hotels, local authorities (who are concerned for the economic development of their region) will encourage the development of hotels and give a clear indication of that undersupply. Hoteliers, on the basis of average occupancy and room rates (usually supplied by tourist authorities), may well develop hotels or go for premium pricing.

The levels of discount offered to each market segment, whilst depending upon the levels of seasonality and periods of demand, may also depend upon the perishability of the product. The total long-term profitability of the hotel is dependent upon the fact that an unsold room night is lost revenue and cannot contribute to fixed costs. There is also a time-based factor of pricing. It would be unwise to assume that the closer it comes to the date of perishability, the cheaper the price will become. The key to yield management can be to hold back enough rooms to sell to off-street or ad hoc business prepared to pay full-price, and to pre-sell only a small amount of discounted accommodation. For instance, in the case of events like the Edinburgh Festival or major exhibitions, a shortage of accommodation may enable some hotels to sell rooms above the normal ceiling or rack rate and to maximise the sale of premium accommodation like suites.

In order to achieve target revenues or margins, the hotel seeks to maximise occupancy throughout the year with market segments which cover both variable and fixed costs. The average yield per room will vary seasonally or periodically as hotels are forced to take larger proportions of lower rated market segments. What is important is that the yearly room yield is on target and this is achieved by managing the correct mix of business in the correct volumes.

Figure 9.5 shows the time period that might apply when considering reducing room rates. Note that, with the hotel (and in particular where group sales people exist), there can be differences in approaches to pricing during this period. For instance, reception and reservations staff have a primary responsibility for maximising the room revenue. They are able to take many time-based decisions on pricing. However, for example, based on their knowledge of their hotel, they may refuse to discount prices for some rooms as they approach the last few days as their experience tells them they always get some high priced, walk-in trade each night. This might contrast with sales and marketing departments who are often responsible for volume sales and base prices on getting as much business as they can, well in advance of the 'sell by' date, they may inadvertently sell all capacity at low profit margins. The best way to maximise yield is for hotel managers, other department heads and sales staff to decide upon the optimum mix of business for that particular hotel.

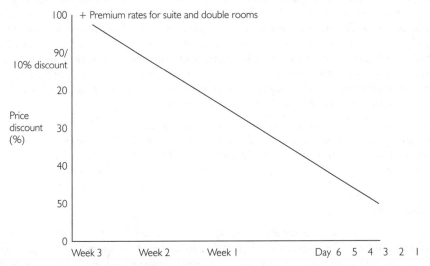

Figure 9.5 Time-based pricing and discounting

Tour operations

There are many different pricing scenarios in this sector, but one specific example should serve to demonstrate the complexity that might be encountered – tour operator pricing of coach holidays (for coaches with a capacity of 48 passengers).

Operators will generally undertake an analysis of contribution by analysing each tour, each brochure or each regional programme or destination. This will help to determine whether a particular tour programme will continue in the following year. It may be that some tours, whilst contributing lower levels to fixed costs, are guaranteed high volume sales and therefore continue to be offered. When tour sales double or triple on top of this, substantial profits are then made. These products may be seen as *cash cows* (see Chapter 6, page 145, on the Boston Consulting Group (BCG) product portfolio matrix, for more marketing implications of this phenomena).

As well as these 'bread and butter' products, the tour operator can then consider offering new – perhaps unusual and risky – products. They may now consider hiring a coach knowing that if there are 25 seats sold, the revenue will cover the cost of the coach (and the hotel accommodation for the passengers). Thereafter, they may regard further sales as making a contribution to fixed cost (which were covered by the cash cows anyway) or they may regard the revenue as pure profit (these products may be dogs, question marks or even stars – see Chapter 6, page 145).

Following the above, an operator can allow for variety within the programme – some tours selling at full-capacity and others selling at under that capacity. The anticipation will be that the total number of passengers on each tour will average at 40 or more in a successful year.

Whether the operator owns some, all or none of the components (for example, coaches and hotels) of the tour package produces key differences between the various types of operator. In general, at times where demand is high, operators who own accommodation, transport or similar elements are in a strong position to sustain growth by guaranteed supply, and adjust prices according to the level at which costs are covered. At times where demand is limited and an over-supply exists, operators who do not have fixed costs of ownership of accommodation or transport may be able to gain advantage by negotiating more favourable rates and making gains by volume sales. Neither case is always true, depending upon supply and demand in particular areas.

The essentials of tour operations, where the company does not own the components of the package, are good negotiation skills, established relationships (with suppliers) for price stability and supply flexibility, knowledge of the market and good environmental research.

Transport

Given that there is a wide variety of transport, no one method of pricing or costing is applicable to each. There are, however, certain similarities in transport marketing. Firstly, the vast majority of transport incorporates custom from several market segments and pricing is adjusted accordingly. Secondly, the demand or price elasticity for each segment may vary.

All elements of travel, tourism and hospitality tend to experience seasonal demand, therefore contribution, cash flow and seasonal elasticity of demand must be taken into account.

In many cases, transport and tour operators run programmes throughout seasons like autumn and winter with little or no contribution to overall costs, but must do so in order to maintain such things as cash flow, market presence or take-off slots at airports. It is often the creative relationships between hotels, transport and tour operators which enable them to stimulate demand in otherwise low seasons.

The majority of transport for tourism is similar to hotels in that it is the mix of market segments that determines the overall yield of each journey. In general, demand and price elasticity for each passenger type varies, and operators must juggle with the balance of each sector it accepts in order for each single or return journey to maximise revenue.

Similar to the hospitality industry, its most potent influence is its perishability. Arguably, unlike hotels, once transport has committed itself to operate it has less adaptability to manipulate costs.

Summary

The general approach to taking pricing decisions usually recommends drawing on a combination of the organisations' costs, what the market will bear and what the competition charges. It is further suggested that paying greater attention to market factors leads to greater profitability but it is recognised that understanding these factors is difficult compared to knowing costs and competitors' prices. This chapter initially follows that format. However, the travel and tourism industry probably has a greater claim than most industries that pricing is different for them. Issues such as intangibility, perishability and high fixed costs of the service make pricing difficult and more of a continuous process. Similarly, the packaging of several services (often provided by outside organisations) to produce holidays, can make decisions complex and unpredictable. This chapter has addressed the special circumstances of the industry directly by considering pricing in travel and tourism's major sectors.

  CASE STUDY
DAVID URQUHART (TRAVEL) LIMITED

Background
David Urquhart Travel is a private limited company which was founded in 1983 by its current owner and Managing Director, David Urquhart. Based in East Kilbride, the company produces coaching holidays to the UK and Europe with programmes from Scotland, Tyne Tees, Yorkshire, London, South Wales, the North West and Midlands.

In 1983, it employed two members of staff; by 1998 it employed 140 full-time staff, had six Board members, a turnover in the region of £25 million, and carried in excess of 150,000 people per annum. Whilst major policy decisions are still the province of the Managing Director and his Board, product pricing is largely the responsibility of the product management team headed by the Production Director.

The holidays are 'produced' by product managers negotiating and contracting hotel space with national groups and family-run hotels, and the company has recently invested in its own hotel in the north of Scotland. The company do not own any coaches, but sub-contract coach services from family-run or national groups who can provide vehicles to the required specifications – these may be in the coach operators own livery or, where scale permits, in David Urquhart livery.

The company is an important local employer, provides a valuable source of income for sub-contractors from the hotel and coach industries, and is a major contributor to the promotion of tourism-related income.

When the company was formed in 1983, it identified a gap in the market for packaged coach holidays offered on a local basis. The competition then was made up mainly of national operators like Wallace Arnold and Shearing, who started out as coach operators and typically owned their own fleet of vehicles. Urquhart Travel's main client base is still primarily Scottish, but they have developed further regional programmes, initially where less competition existed, for instance in north-east England, allowing the company quickly to become an operator of national significance.

Marketing

The aim of the company is to provide customers with an enjoyable value-for-money experience which exceeds expectations, thus ensuring customer loyalty, and a desire to travel on further tours offered by the company.

The company is largely a direct-sell operation – its main brochure (published in January) is mailed to a large database of customers and enquirers. In addition, it markets its programme via direct mail newsletters and promotional material, national newspapers (generally weekly throughout the year), and to a lesser extent regional newspapers. The company produce several regional brochures, one of which is distributed via Woodcock Travel based in Yorkshire, which is over-branded with the travel agent's name.

Telephone reservations are handled by a head office team which works seven days a week, and calls are routed according to geographical location to a workstation dedicated to the particular regional departure points, for example north-east England, Scotland. The company recognises the coach driver's role as a key area for developing and maintaining customer loyalty, and customer care training is undertaken to develop the drivers' skills.

The market

The market for coach holidays is primarily those aged 50+ with an approximate split of 60 per cent female and 40 per cent male. There is also a strong family programme based around holiday centre-type accommodation like Pontins. Three years ago Urquhart started a programme to continental Europe – by industry standards, this is a big programme. Equally large is the market for Ireland, although the largest percentage of business, around 60-70 per cent, is still for UK holidays.

The market for this type of package is highly seasonal, with peak earnings being reached in June, July, August and September. Although packages are offered all year round, carryings throughout the rest of the year are considerably smaller and the company must provide an incentive to travel by providing an imaginative and varied product and value for money.

The company tends to plan the size of the programme, or assess demand, on the general economic forecast and the previous year's demand. In order to expand or grow it would be logical first of all to look to increasing demand or producing more carryings (people per tour), or to expand the programme, i.e. growth tends to be achieved by increasing turnover as opposed to adjusting margin.

Current conditions and recent developments

The market for packaged holidays in the UK in the summer of 1998 showed a slight decline, with more people choosing to stay at home during the poorer weather. The decline in June of that year could also have been influenced by more people staying at home to watch football's World Cup. The company believes that past experience has shown that economic uncertainty has an effect on the market, particularly for those with invested or fixed incomes. Therefore, predictions of recessions and economic decline may affect demand. The company also believes that a particular aspect of the market is that as interest rates go up, people with invested income spend less, because they wish temporarily to take advantage of the increased income by leaving their money where it is.

In general, however, the future looks very bright for the company as they expand into new areas, employ more expertise in developing the product, and enhance their position with suppliers by increasing their programme and carryings.

(Caroline Barrass)

Questions

On the basis of Urquhart's operations, and in the light of the theory discussed in this chapter, consider the following questions.

1   In terms of deciding prices (and the associated mix elements), what do you feel are the relative strengths and weaknesses that Urquhart has compared to national operators?
2   As a member of the product management team, how would you go about pricing each package, i.e. which methods would you use, in which order and where should the emphasis lay?
3   For Urquhart, at roughly what capacity do you think a 48-seat capacity coach would break even? How would this compare to a national operator? Give arguments and cost considerations for your suggestion.

References and bibliography

Barrass, C. (1998) *The Impact of the Internet on Marketing Strategy in the Passenger Shipping Industry*, unpublished MA Marketing Dissertation, University of Northumbria

Bull, A. (1985) *The Economics of Travel and Tourism*, 2nd edition, Longman

Greene, M. (1987) *Marketing Hotels and Restaurants into the 90s*, Heinemann

Holloway, S. (1997) *Straight and Level: Practical Airline Economics*, Ashgate

Winkler, J. (1981) *Bargaining for Results*, Heinemann

10 Distributing travel and tourism products

Objectives

By the end of this chapter you should be able to:

- understand the role of distribution as an element of the marketing mix
- recognise the importance of careful selection and control of distribution channels
- identify the main distribution channels used by travel and tourism organisations
- appreciate the changing nature of travel and tourism distribution, especially the increasing use of information technology.

Introduction

This chapter is concerned with both the direct and indirect methods by which travel and tourism products reach consumers and potential consumers. Recent trends in distribution, particularly the increased use of information technology and direct marketing, are addressed. The chapter starts by looking at definitions of distribution and the importance of this to the overall marketing effort. This has not always been well-recognised in travel and tourism. Indeed, distribution has traditionally been associated with physical goods. There are, however, similarities between physical distribution and the distribution of services, albeit without the necessity for physical activities such as transportation and stock holding. The emphasis in travel and tourism is on the *distribution of information*. The distribution, or *place*, element of the marketing mix can be described using a number of terms.

The *Dictionary of Marketing* defines distribution as:

'the act of sending goods from the manufacturer to the wholesaler and then to the retailers.'

(Ivanovic, 1989)

Accepting this definition requires examination of the manufacturing and wholesaling function in travel and tourism. These are introduced in Chapter 1 and are well covered by Renshaw (1997).

Distribution undoubtedly involves a process of transfer of ownership from producer, or principal in the case of travel and tourism, to consumer. The importance of distribution lies in the fact that potential customers tend to buy those products which are available where and when they wish to purchase them. Availability and accessibility are central concepts to marketing success in any industry. This is an area in which organisations seek to differentiate themselves from the competition. The importance of distribution can also be seen by the expense that this element of the mix incurs. Whatever the product or service being marketed, if it is not successfully distributed there will be repercussions in the marketplace.

Distribution is no less *strategic* than are the other elements of the mix. Writers such as McDonald (1995) encourage readers to consider distribution in its widest sense as a critical aspect of marketing management. A narrow view of physical distribution often concentrates on the transportation of goods. This is clearly insufficient for travel and tourism where intangible products predominate and so concern should be placed more widely on the level of availability of products for consumers.

Traditional definitions of distribution emphasise the act of taking the product to the consumer. Where the product is not transportable this is not always applicable and, indeed, the customer is often transported to the product in travel and tourism. Distribution in these cases is concerned with the *provision of customer access to the product*.

The distribution of travel and tourism products was sometimes sacrificed to cost in the past. Organisations aiming to achieve maximum coverage at minimum cost often need to compromise in one of these areas. Costs may need to be balanced against the number of distribution channels used. Distribution has now become an area of much more central importance to organisations, partly in response to competitive market conditions and more demanding customers.

Distribution and the marketing mix

The distribution function plays an important part in the success of the other elements in the marketing mix. The product is of no use to those who desire it if it cannot be accessed and used by them at the required time. The nature of distribution can also influence the price of a product or service. A high price, for example, could be charged for exclusive availability. The cost involved in the use of different distribution methods varies. Availability can also influence promotional strategy to the extent that it may form part of the promotional message. The timing of promotional activities and distribution should complement one another. A tour operator advertising its new summer programme in advance of its brochures being distributed to travel agents may find potential customers, on responding to the advertisement and visiting a travel agent, book with a competitor instead.

The distribution of services

As mentioned above, much of the theory of distribution management is based on physical distribution which is not always wholly relevant to the distribution of services. Indeed, this area has been neglected by some authors as compared to physical distribution. It is, however, increasingly being recognised as an important area of both academic study and management practice. Some innovations in this area of services marketing are discussed later.

Shostack (1978) has suggested that the idea of place decisions for services is confused as people grapple with the concept of a distribution channel for items which are intangible, often inseparable from the person performing the service and perishable in the sense that inventory cannot be carried. The distinctiveness of services distribution can be examined by considering some of these characteristics of services, which are covered in more detail in Chapter 2.

Inseparability

In some cases, the person distributing the tourism product will not be an employee of the principal and so good co-ordination becomes vital. The consumer will see the activity of booking the holiday, perhaps in a travel agent which has no formal relationship to the tour operator providing the holiday, as part of the overall experience and so the service received at this stage will have a lasting effect.

Intangibility

As no actual physical product is distributed, the importance of communication and the distribution of information becomes paramount in services. Attempts are sometimes made to provide *tangible evidence* of the service through photographs in brochures or gifts representing a particular image which can be associated with the service.

Perishability

Having the means to distribute unsold services at the last minute becomes vital due to the inability to store services for future sale. A number of recent initiatives in services marketing have been aimed at selling remaining stock in the period prior to the commencement of the service provision.

Ownership

The importance of the service encounter at the point of sale is once again heightened in services marketing as consumption does not result in ownership of anything. The fact that no actual transfer of ownership takes place and services are only rented or consumed creates an additional challenge for those responsible for taking the service to consumers and making it accessible to them.

There are aspects besides the service characteristics of the tourism product that have implications for the distribution function. The fact that the tourism product is a fragmented one and the overall tourism experience likely to be made up of many component parts adds complexity to the issue of distribution. A tourist organisation or destination marketing company may be distributing the products of a variety of suppliers. This is not always an easy task. The principles of distribution and their application to travel and tourism are examined below.

The principles of distribution

Distribution channels

Products and services move from their original source to customers through marketing or distribution channels. This movement may be physical and it may involve the transfer of title. Many organisations will use more than one distribution channel. In many industries intermediaries can help organisations to reach a wide audience whilst holding stock and sharing financial risk. Channels of distribution can be simple or complex yet marketing channel decisions are among the most difficult a firm will have to make.

For the purposes of services, a distribution channel is still the sequence of firms involved in moving a service from producer, or principal, to consumer as it is with physical goods. Both direct sale and sale via intermediaries are used by service organisations and may even be used in combination. Services intermediaries tend not to hold stock, however, and so are less likely to carry any risk. In common with physical goods, services marketers need to conduct some sort of appraisal when selecting distribution channels, as each represents a unique blend of costs and benefits.

It is broadly accepted that there are three main choices in terms of channel network and these are as follows.

Intensive distribution
The principal uses as wide a network of distributors as possible to sell their products. Use by a tour operator of all ABTA travel agents in the UK would amount to this strategy. It is suited to products with broad market appeal and high volume sales.

Selective distribution
By using only a limited number of retailers or outlets a principal is adopting a more selective distribution strategy. Economies can be achieved, in certain markets, by concentrating on using those intermediaries which achieve the best results for the principal. There has been a slight move towards more selective distribution strategies shown by UK principals in recent years in an effort to improve efficiency.

Exclusive distribution
Selecting to restrict availability and accessibility for the purposes of image is crucial to the success of an exclusive distribution policy. This approach is suited to organisations with a highly specialised product and little competition. Some customers may even expect to have to search for such products.

The chain of travel and tourism distribution

Renshaw (1997) has compared the traditional distribution channels for manufactured products with those for travel and tourism as shown in Figure 10.1.

These models warrant detailed comparison in order to identify where parallels can be drawn between the respective forms of distribution. The first distinction to be made is that between *manufacturers* in the traditional model and *principals* in the model for travel. The latter, as suppliers of services, do not in fact perform any manufacturing function. Tour operators, although shown at a later stage in the chain of distribution, perform a role that more closely equates to that of the manufacturer in that they combine different elements for resale as a package. In some cases they can be seen to act as *principals* themselves whilst more often being described as *wholesalers*. This is, however, debatable. Although tour operators purchase individual elements of a package in bulk and sell them on, this is not undertaken in the same manner as for typical manufactured products.

Firstly, tour operators do not merely 'break bulk', they also add to the individual elements. For example, a unit of accommodation will be put together with an airline seat and other services to create a package. A second distinction is that the tour operator does not sell these elements of a package on to a retailer who then holds stock. Instead, it is *information* about the created packages that is distributed at this time. This crucial factor in the distribution of travel and tourism products is returned to later.

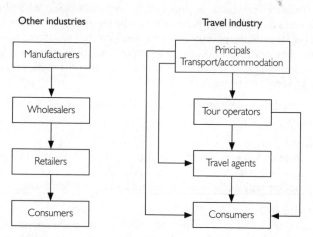

Figure 10.1 Distribution channels in the travel industry compared with other industries

Whilst the two models appear similar, the retail options facing travel and tourism principals, and tour operators if treated as a separate category, are presently limited. Essentially, in the UK, the retail option consists of a network of just less than 7,000 travel agencies. Recent legislative and technological changes are, however, likely to have influence in shaping a different structure to the retail sector of the future, with new forms of outlet emerging. This development is discussed in further detail later in the chapter.

The picture is not as straightforward as it may appear in that a slightly different set of distribution alternatives faces each different sector of the industry. Renshaw (1997) provides comprehensive coverage of these. He also details some of the complexities of travel and tourism distribution. Specifically, the dual role performed by tour operators is worthy of mention. Tour operators act as a form of wholesaler for principals, negotiating for different components of packages and assembling these. This function helps principals to distribute their products. A hotel, for example, could sell a block of rooms, for a season, to a tour operator and effectively remove the need to market these to individuals for that period. Consumers also benefit from having less need to search for information and only one purchase to make. Tour operators also act as principals themselves as they go on to distribute the packages they have created. Other organisations, which are not necessarily producers themselves, may be involved in obtaining distribution for principals. Tourist boards generally have a role in this and those in the UK are becoming increasingly commercial in this respect.

Central factors in distribution strategy are the position of an organisation within the overall market and the existence of any competitive advantage. Having decided upon an appropriate level of availability, a main concern will be the choice of marketing channels to be used to reach consumers. An initial decision therefore has to be the choice of distribution channel(s), or the route(s) by which the transfer of the title of a product or service moves from producer to ultimate consumer.

The end result will be a certain level of market coverage. Clearly it is in the supplier's interest to seek maximum coverage for minimum cost, bearing in mind the desired level of availability. Reciprocal referrals between different hotels, as well as links between organisations in different sectors of the industry, such as hotels and airlines, offer additional distribution alternatives in travel and tourism.

Direct versus indirect distribution methods

A distinction can be drawn between direct and mediated (indirect) distribution.

● Direct distribution involves selling to the consumer without making use of a 'middleman'. Methods include selling at the actual location of the product, such as a hotel reception, at an organisation's owned retail outlet, such as British Airways shops, or use of direct marketing methods such as direct mail.
● Mediated sales typically involve the services of a travel agent as there is currently little option in terms of the retail distribution of travel and tourism products. Travel agents, to date, have faced little competition other than from direct distribution. In order to fully understand the travel agency sector it is necessary to look at the structure of this and the role of travel agents as discussed in Chapter 1. A summary of this role is provided in Figure 10.2.

The role of travel agents in the distribution process

- To offer consumers a choice of products
- To undertake merchandising activities
- To provide consumers with information
- To distribute brochures
- To provide feedback on the marketplace to principals
- To handle complaints
- To make bookings
- To distribute tickets
- To offer a convenient location to consumers
- To offer ancillary products for sale (e.g. insurance, foreign exchange)
- To conduct joint promotions with principals
- To offer customers personal service
- To advise customers

Figure 10.2

Direct marketing methods are growing in popularity in business generally and the pace of technological advances may well facilitate yet more development. This is particularly relevant to travel and tourism where the *flow of information* is so vital.

The growth in direct marketing of travel products has been fuelled in part by the entrance of non-travel organisations, including credit card companies and newspapers, into this market. Financial considerations and increased competition have also been influential. Direct marketing also helps travel and tourism organisations to develop relationships with their customers and potential customers. The travel market in the UK has, to date, shown more willingness to purchase domestic products, including package holidays, directly from principals than they have done in respect of overseas travel. This was illustrated in Chapter 1.

Small businesses, a large sector of the tourism industry, often have little choice but to market themselves directly to consumers. These firms cannot afford the expense of providing a vast network of travel agencies with brochures and booking facilities. The volume of sales they are dealing with is also insufficient for them to attract the support of retailers. Some recent technological developments, notably the internet, could help smaller firms, but much depends on how the technology develops and the ways in which it is used. A further option, discussed later, is to join a consortium.

As direct marketing is an area where there is clear overlap between distribution and promotion, these methods are also examined in Chapter 11 on promotion. The chapter looks in some detail at the use of telesales in travel and tourism marketing.

Choice of direct or indirect distribution will vary with factors such as size of selling organisation, characteristics of the product and current marketing environment. The choice of method is a matter for constant review and evaluation. Valuable measures in this respect will be speed, efficiency, control, flexibility and cost. There are both costs and benefits to the use of middlemen. Evaluation of these is essential when selecting distribution channels.

Figure 10.3 lists the advantages and disadvantages of indirect distribution of travel and tourism products. It is recognised that generalisations are difficult, as precise methods vary. For the purposes of illustration, the middleman being considered is generally the travel agent.

Should a principal decide to distribute via the retail travel sector, the relative strengths and weaknesses of different agents will then need to be considered. The alternative is to market directly to consumers. The advantages and disadvantages of this approach are outlined in Figure 10.4. Once again each particular method will have its own strengths and weaknesses.

There is no one correct answer as to which of these key distribution methods to use. A process of application is required in every individual case and choices need to be constantly reviewed and evaluated.

The role of the sales representative

It is important to note that the sales representative forms another important link in the chain of distribution. Tour operators and principals often employ sales representatives in the hope that they will take the product to the middleman (usually in the case of tour operators, airlines and ferry companies) or direct to corporate clients (usually in the case of hotel chains and conference organisers). The role of field sales staff and the management of this function is covered more fully in Chapter 11, whilst Lancaster and Jobber (1994) provide detailed coverage.

The advantages of distributing via travel agents

- Specialist knowledge of the local market
- A nationwide network of outlets
- Consumer perceptions (of a choice of products being available and of travel agents as both unbiased and protective)
- The sale of ancillary products
- Shopping for a holiday can be viewed as pleasurable and part of the total holiday experience
- Atmosphere and environment are important to some consumers when making a purchase
- Marketing activities provided by travel agents (joint promotions and merchandising opportunities) can support the principals

The disadvantages of distributing via travel agents

- Brochure wastage (not all brochures sent to agents will be racked)
- Incentives (e.g. competitions) for agents can be required
- Commission and overrides can be expensive for principals
- Inflexibility (it is difficult to make brochure/product changes quickly when a middleman is involved)
- Communication between the principal and customers can be slow as they are more distant
- Feedback from customers is less direct
- There may be less product loyalty on the part of staff
- There may be less product knowledge on the part of staff
- There can be a loss of control (over areas such as service quality)

Figure 10.3

The advantages of direct marketing

- There is potential to exploit computer technology via the creation of databases and as a means of both reaching and researching consumers
- Two way communications with customers are possible
- Feedback on the marketplace is direct
- There is flexibility to change products and messages
- Test marketing can be carried out fairly easily
- A number of alternative direct methods of distribution exist
- This can be a useful way to reach international markets easily

The disadvantages of direct marketing

- Timing can be critical to success when contacting customers whereas travel agencies are available at all times
- The costs of starting up a direct sell function can be high especially investment in technology
- The use of direct techniques can upset middlemen (this is especially important to organisations using indirect methods for the same or other products)
- Some forms of direct marketing have a poor image (e.g. junk mail)
- Some consumers view direct marketing activities as an invasion of privacy

Figure 10.4

Customer loyalty programmes and additional channels

Customer loyalty programmes can be viewed as an additional channel of distribution which can be used to sell unsold capacity and add value for consumers. If managed properly, loyalty programmes can reduce the need to discount unsold capacity. These are discussed further in Chapter 11. There are also secretaries' clubs and other similar clubs and societies maintained by principals. Middleton (1994) also describes the allocation of product capacity to credit card companies, acting as tour operators, as an additional pipeline used by some travel and tourism operators.

Reservations systems

Reservations systems are used by most transport and accommodation suppliers as well as for booking theatre tickets, package tours, cruises and many more travel and tourism products. These tend to be less heavily used by visitor attractions and are rarely used by outdoor recreation facilities such as national parks. There are some examples of natural attractions and footpaths which implement a reservations system as part of an overall effort to curtail visitor numbers in the interests of preservation. It has become essential for hotels to encourage advance bookings from remote sources whereas they used to be able to rely on walk-in customers (Mintel, 1996).

Reservations systems are important in travel and tourism distribution as a method of controlling demand. Achieving a balance between supply and demand can be problematic in an industry typified by high seasonality. Reservations systems not only help to *manage demand*, but also to prepare for business peaks by increasing supply. Often this facility comes at a cost. Reservations systems represent an expensive aspect of distribution for principals. Equally travel agents view the use of a number of different systems as a financial burden. Implementation of a reservations system can however help a travel and tourism organisation to maximise their revenue. Large scheduled airlines, in particular, use highly sophisticated yield management systems linked to their computer reservations systems. A feature of reservations systems more generally is the ability to overbook. This accounts for the occurrence of 'no-shows' particularly amongst business travellers.

Both manual and computerised reservations systems are used in practice. Some smaller principals still encourage reservations from agents by phone or fax. The more sophisticated automated reservations systems are considered in the section on technology below. Tourist information centres (TICs) are becoming more involved in the commercial booking of travel and tourism products and are using reservations systems of their own.

Information flow

As Poon (1993) has noted, tourism is an information intensive business. Information is central to the successful distribution of travel and tourism products. This idea is supported by the role of information in helping to form the images and perceptions held by tourists. A growing variety of information sources exist and traditionally guide books, brochures, word-of-mouth communications and videos have all played a role in the transfer of information to both middlemen and customers. The characteristics of travel and tourism, particularly the importance of information flow and reservations, encourage the adoption of technology.

Finding adequate technologies has long been important in travel and tourism. There are several reasons for this including the omni-present difficulties of distributing intangible products. The complexity of the tourism purchase is a further factor. Holidays in particular are expensive, usually infrequent purchases which may have more than one end user and possibly an element of risk attached to their consumption. This all makes the need for clear and relevant information paramount. Traditionally, communications methods used by the industry have not been easily adapted yet the rate of change currently being experienced makes flexible communications methods essential. The competitive marketplace requires more information to meet consumer needs.

Technology and the flow of information

The technology that is available today can help travel and tourism organisations to be at the cutting edge of innovative development in terms of distribution. Technology has been rapidly diffused in the industry, especially amongst the larger organisations in the retail and air transportation sectors. Some of the more significant technological developments are discussed below, although space constraints prevent a more detailed consideration of this important and influential area.

Viewdata

The provision of information transmitted by telecommunications lines has been important to the distribution of travel and tourism products in many countries.

Inkpen (1998) describes *videotext* as the international term for what is referred to generically as *viewdata* in the UK. Other countries have their own systems, but most British leisure travel agencies and many others access tour operator and similar reservations systems using videotext networks. This is essentially a form of communication requiring a VDU, a keyboard, a telephone line and a modem. The first UK viewdata system was Prestel. Interestingly the companies behind these early systems were the Post Office and British Telecom. A number of travel and tourism operators introduced their own systems but the significance of viewdata in the distribution of package holidays was marked by the launch, in 1982, of 'TOP', Thomson's system. Viewdata quickly became a dominant technology in the UK leisure travel business and is still highly relevant today, albeit amid predictions of its demise as further technological advances are made. Viewdata is still popular in the tour operations sector, with many operators having their own network and others being connected to a major system. Travel agents access these via a computer terminal. The use of viewdata is not restricted to tour operators, with both accommodation and transport suppliers also using this form of distribution.

Viewdata technology has been described as redundant yet its continued popularity is partly explained by the widespread presence of the necessary technology. In the UK use of viewdata became so popular in the trade that the equipment used is now widespread. It is also relatively inexpensive and easy to use. Renshaw (1997) considers viewdata in more detail.

Computer reservations systems

Introduced as an aid to managing airline inventory in the USA, computer reservations systems (CRSs) have often been described as *intelligent* as they allow for two-way communications. Their use has become more widespread in travel and tourism in recent years. The past two decades, in particular, have seen their importance as on-line booking facilities in travel agents increase at a tremendous rate. CRSs have become more accessible as their costs have fallen and this has helped their penetration into the agency sector. The cost-savings potential of placing access to CRSs directly with agents via a VDU was recognised early on and CRSs are now used as an aid to sales and marketing as well as to control inventory. The first generation CRSs were single airline systems which were developed from the early 1960s onwards. Not all carriers could afford their own system, however, and some began to be 'hosted' on other carrier's systems.

CRSs have been adopted by the business travel agency sector where the need is very much one for speed and where itineraries can be more complex. Their penetration of leisure agents has been less impressive. Leisure agents were already used to viewdata technology and found this sufficient for their needs. Agents committing to CRS technology also faced the difficult choice of which system to select or the need to invest in several. To combat this, many single access CRSs were enhanced with multi-access technology. Essentially this involved a switching centre to enable agents to access several airlines' databases via one terminal and one set of instructions.

Deregulation of civil aviation in North America which occurred in 1978 led to a restructuring of route networks, the introduction of new products and a variety of air fares being offered. All of these areas had previously been restricted. CRSs were invaluable in managing the vast amounts of information created by deregulation and so their importance grew enormously at this time. This equally stimulated the development of European competitors. Airlines are still the dominant force behind CRSs, although their value is now also recognised by other principals including car hire companies, hotels and ferry companies. Some of the major CRSs currently operating are Apollo, Sabre, Amadeus and Galileo.

At the heart of any CRS is a continuously updated database which is accessed by a computer terminal. Subscribers obtain information on fares and conditions, schedules and availability and suchlike from the CRS, as well as which they can make reservations and print tickets using them. The extent to which these functions are available through a CRS will depend upon the level of 'functionality' that the participating airline, or other principal, has agreed with the CRS owners.

Despite the obvious advantages to using CRSs, criticisms have been levelled at them for a number of reasons. At one time display bias was an issue as airlines owning systems, or with a major share in one, could arrange to be displayed on the first page called up by an agent making an enquiry. This issue has subsequently been addressed both in the USA and Europe. The market power displayed by CRSs and their effect on airline distribution costs are current concerns.

CRSs have been attributed with revolutionising retail travel through their ability to instantly update availability information and to make on-line bookings. They can also be used to perform a number of back-office functions such as accounting tasks. It is however the move towards the creation of global distribution systems (GDSs) that is currently advancing the area of travel and tourism distribution.

Global distribution systems

Second generation systems, known as global distribution systems (GDSs), are created by partnerships between CRS companies and so are owned by different groups of airlines. These differ from CRSs in two key respects. The first is their global presence and the second their ability to access the product databases of many different principals. It is not only airlines that are involved but also hotels and car hire companies amongst others. Particularly in the field of business travel, with companies operating in an increasingly global marketplace, there is more demand by travellers to make and change travel arrangements from anywhere in the world. GDSs are ideally suited to these consumer demands. Consolidation of this sector has been evident in recent years and further consolidation is likely in the fight for domination.

It is not possible to examine CRSs and GDSs in further detail here, nor is it entirely relevant to do so given the pace at which they are developing. It is important to conclude, however, that these are a major force in the distribution and sale of both business and holiday travel. Their use is also expanding into new areas. Holloway (1997) provides useful coverage of the relevant background to CRSs.

The internet
The full potential of the internet as a travel and tourism distribution channel has yet to be exploited, but some significant steps leading to this have been taken. Many travel and tourism organisations and destinations have been developing internet sites in recent years. This can be useful as both a method of information provision and in some cases as a direct booking mechanism. It is not only principals and destinations who can benefit from the internet. Travel agents can use the internet as an additional means of information retrieval to help them in their advisory role. The uptake of the internet by agents has, at the time of writing, been limited. One view is that the trade needs to encompass these new developments as opposed to viewing them solely as a threat to their own continuation.

An important development for the trade has been the introduction of customised versions of the internet known as *intranets*. Access to these is generally restricted to password holders but they can offer more security and a more exclusive network.

The internet is suitable for use by many of the smaller travel and tourism operators who may not be able to afford large advertising campaigns and costly distribution systems. This is one area of marketing where success is not closely related to cost. It is also a means of reaching a widely distributed audience as it is a global medium. The characteristics of those consumers with access to the internet have much in common with the target markets for travel and tourism.

One travel and tourism organisation that has developed an internet site is ABTA. British Midland is widely reported as having the first internet airline booking and payment system. This emerged from a drive to cut distribution costs whilst differentiating themselves from the competition. The retail sector is also represented as seen by Sabre's internet travel shop, Travelocity. The site accepts bookings from both consumers and agents with the latter being paid commission for bookings. Travelnet was the first internet version of a GDS, offering access to 700 airline fare types, 480 of which are bookable. It also takes hotel and car hire bookings. New developments in travel distribution via the internet are often reported in the trade press.

Multi-media kiosks
A joint venture between NatWest and Thomas Cook led to the trial launch in 1995 of Touch, an electronic system enabling customers to obtain information and buy or apply for a range of banking and travel products. Customer access was through a network of self-service kiosks located in particular branches of NatWest and Thomas Cook. An extensive range of travel information was available including holiday and flight details. For holiday bookings, customers were linked to Thomas Cook Direct, the company's

telephone reservations service. Payment was possible by credit or debit card and receipts and bookings confirmations were provided.

CD-ROM technology

Although CD-ROM technology has been used for promotions, the uptake of this technology by UK travel agencies has been relatively slow. Developments including the testing, by Galileo, of Spectrum, a powerful hotel-mapping product aimed at helping clients to find products suited to their needs, have been significant to distribution. There is great scope for hotels, tour operators and other travel organisations, together with software houses, to distribute brochures in this way. Further discussion of CD-ROM technology and examples of its application are provided in Chapter 11.

Virtual reality

A further means by which travel organisations can position themselves favourably in the marketplace involves the use of virtual reality (VR) technology. Non-immersive VR technology, which has no requirement for hats or gloves for interaction with the interface, allows the 'virtual traveller' to explore sites, destinations and attractions. The potential for VR to aid the flow of information, particularly for the global market, whilst also creating competitive advantage for the sponsor, is great.

Teletext and digital television

Teletext distribution is heavily used for the sale of UK packaged holidays and other tourism products. This medium is particularly useful for advertising late availability holidays. The use of television for the distribution of travel and tourism products looks set to continue with the advent of digital television. This is an area where developments are likely to be rapid and could potentially be integrated with other technological forms. Inkpen (1998) covers this technology in detail.

Electronic ticketing

Commonly referred to as *e-ticketing*, electronic ticketing removes the paperwork from ticketing. This should impact heavily on some of the emerging distribution mediums. Although e-ticketing has been in existence in the USA for some time, it has only recently been introduced to Europe by airlines such as British Airways and Lufthansa. Both direct and indirect distribution methods can operate this function with CRS backup. The sale of e-tickets via travel agents could lead to difficulties in respect of commission levels as less work is required by the agent. There are other issues in relation to their use which are beyond the scope of this chapter. Once again Inkpen covers this area well.

Smart cards

A plastic card containing a miniature computer processor chip, including memory, known as a smart card, is being hailed as a key aspect in the development of many of the new technologies. These can be operated in a variety of ways and are currently the subject of much experimentation. Their use is not restricted to the areas of travel and tourism, but they could be used for checking in and out of hotels, recording loyalty reward points and such like, whilst reducing levels of fraud.

Disintermediation

Technologies such as those mentioned can be both a threat and an opportunity to the retail travel sector. However viewed, it is obvious that rapid change is taking place, affecting the ways in which travel and tourism products are distributed. As we have seen, the distribution of travel is becoming increasingly electronic. The technological revolution has been hailed as both an opportunity for retailers and a threat to their future. If viewed as a threat, technology may be seen to be more fearsome in the UK, which shows a higher propensity to use travel agents than many other countries. Many believe however that, whatever happens, there will still be a need for retail outlets at some level. Some consumers will continue to prefer to use agents, particularly for more complex purchases and some smaller agencies may concentrate on specialist areas. There appears to be no immediate change to the use of travel agents likely, but the retail sector would be well advised to prepare for an even more competitive marketplace in the longer term. The following section looks at some possible developments.

Travel distribution in the third millenium

The 1980s saw the exploitation of many new technologies. This has become a critical success factor in some competitive areas of travel and tourism. Improvements in speed, reduced cost and more user-friendly systems are now being exploited along with even newer technologies. There is basic agreement that IT will change travel and tourism distribution yet a great deal less agreement regarding what these changes will be and who will be the beneficiaries of change.

Experience to date suggests new forms of travel distribution will continue to evolve. The computer company, Hoskyns, has claimed the biggest threat to travel agents will be non-travel retailers launching electronic superstores (*TTG*, 1997). These superstores would be backed by electronic systems providing links to suppliers. The travel retailing sector may face yet more structural change as changes in the operating environment, including legislation as well as technology, impact upon organisations. All of this hints at a blurring in the distinction between travel retailing and retailing in other industries. An interesting example of cross-over is provided by Richard Branson's Virgin Bride store in London. Essentially a one-stop wedding shop, this store incorporates an interactive travel booking service for honeymoons. In addition to a touch screen facility, a number of tour operators' brochures are available for reference. The touch screen computer is linked to the travel company Page and Moy.

The concept of *one-stop shopping* for all holiday requirements can also be seen on the horizon with talk of department stores retailing holidays. Early developments have included the sale of travel insurance by supermarkets such as Tesco. The Post Office has also expressed an interest in travel retailing and has become involved in foreign exchange.

Whether non-travel specialists successfully break into the system and become dominant or travel specialists diversify and capitalise on their inherent strengths remains to be seen. In all probability, both will occur.

Expanding distribution

Clearly the more units a travel organisation, such as a hotel or visitor attractions opera-tor, has the more distribution outlets it also has. Increased size tends to lead to increased availability of the product. Methods of increasing availability, without direct expansion through ownership, also exist. Many of these methods have been growing in recent years and some of these are discussed below.

Integration

A highly topical issue regarding the travel industry is the extent to which organisations are integrated. Integration occurs when one organisation merges with another. This process can be either horizontal or vertical as discussed below. The concept itself is not new to travel and tourism, having long been evident in the tour operations sector in par-ticular. There has, however, been a phenomenal growth in integration in the industry in recent years. Many examples can be given from the UK, although this is not solely a British phenomenon. Indeed, some of Europe's largest travel groups have been expand-ing in this way, with many of the major European markets already dominated by large groups. Ownership of a retail distribution system is increasingly important to the large European tour operators. The phenomenon is not universal though, as restrictions are placed on integration in some countries.

Horizontal integration

Horizontal integration is that which takes place between organisations which are at the same level in the chain of distribution, as for example when one chain of travel agents purchases another. The 1980s saw much of this type of activity when the so-called 'march of the multiples' took place. This involved extensive take-over and merger activity in the retail travel sector and led to greatly increased concentration levels in the industry. As a result, the industry now has a network of more than 6,000 retail travel agents, domi-nated by a few key players, notably Lunn Poly, Going Places, Thomas Cook and Artac Worldchoice. This type of consolidation has clear implications regarding the power of the retailers and customer service. Renshaw (1997) provides a more detailed discussion of both the march of the multiples and the effects that this has had upon travel distribution.

Vertical integration

More recently it is vertical integration which has been a significant phenomenon within the travel industry. This has helped top operators to increase their market share, whilst provid-ing economies of scale and a guaranteed outlet for the organisation's products. Increased con-trol over distribution can also result as can opportunities for branding. There has been a trend towards industry concentration and vertically integrated companies at the mass market end of the spectrum of travel organisations. High levels of concentration can be observed in the UK tour operations market, as shown in Table 10.1.

Whereas the current trend is towards integration with airlines, ownership of hotels by tour operators was popular in the past. The impact of vertical integration is exemplified by Thomson, the UK market leader in the tour operations sector (at the time of writing) who own Lunn Poly, the market leader in the retail travel sector. There is obvious syn-ergy in the profiles of such companies.

This integration has been one issue under consideration by the Monopolies and Mergers Commission (MMC). This is not the first time the industry has attracted such attention.

Thomson's take-over of Horizon in 1988 was also investigated and ruled not against the public interest. Despite Thomson's major share of the outbound package holiday market, they still were not dominant in the overall outbound travel market. Events following this ruling, particularly the collapse in 1991 of International Leisure Group (ILG) and its tour operations arm, Intasun, increased Thomson's market share still further. The concern in such cases is that excessive market share amongst industry leaders could lead to price rises. Arguments are also offered in support of vertical integration. Figure 10.5 summarises the arguments for and against vertical integration.

Table 10.1 Market shares of top five AIT tour operators as part of the total market, by volume (%), 1993–7

AIT tour operators	1993	1994	1995	1996	1997*
Top five	63.5	64.0	61.5	57.0	57.0
Other operators	36.5	36.0	38.5	43.0	43.0
Total	100.0	100.0	100.0	100.0	100.0

* Key Note estimates

(Thomson Tour, before operations)

Arguments for vertical integration

- More control of the product at different stages in the process of distribution
- Increased financial strength possibly leading to less volatility
- Larger firms may be able to compete more easily in the global marketplace
- Many people believe travel agents and tour operators display preferences for one another even when they have no formal affiliation
- Brand loyalty can result
- Information sharing between companies can lead to improved marketing
- Increased bargaining power with principals can result for tour operators
- Increased bargaining power can lead to higher commission levels and incentives for travel agents
- There is still a wide choice of both travel agents and tour operators to choose from, in the UK market at least
- Independents and smaller chains have the option to form or join consortia
- Niche markets still exist that the larger players are not serving
- There are benefits of technological synergy
- Service quality can be more easily monitored
- Increased sales could lead to higher profits and ultimately lower prices
- Specialist product and market knowledge can be developed

Arguments against vertical integration

- Vertical integration makes it difficult for independents to compete with integrated companies
- New entrants may find it difficult to enter the market leading to a less competitive marketplace
- Vertical integration can restrict consumer choice
- Cost savings by larger firms could be passed on to consumers giving them a competitive advantage in the battle for market share
- Directional selling on the part of the integrated companies could result
- Smaller companies could lose bargaining power
- Less competition could in the longer term lead to price increases

Figure 10.5

Airline codesharing

Hanlon describes codesharing as:

'a commercial agreement between two airlines under which an airline operating a service allows another airline to offer that service to the travelling public under its own flight designator code, even although it does not operate the service.'

(Hanlon, 1996)

This is one example of a marketing arrangement between companies which are dealing with the same target markets yet which are not in direct competition with one another. Code sharing enables airlines to reach a larger market and is a prerequisite to airline franchising (discussed below).

Franchising

Franchising is a means by which organisations can expand their distribution systems far more quickly than through organic growth. Franchising operates as an arrangement whereby a business (franchisor), which may be a principal or retailer, allows another business (franchisee) to use their company name and market their products. This is usually in exchange for an initial fee and an on-going royalty payment. Typically, the latter will represent a percentage of the franchisee's turnover. An example of a franchised operation is that of the Pierre Victoire restaurant company (now out of business) which had a total of 101 units operating in 1996 of which the company owned only 18. The remaining 83 were franchises. Further details of the operation of Pierre Victoire are provided in Appendix 1.

Although franchisors are likely to grant these rights or licences to a number of different organisations, they usually guarantee each franchisee a minimum exclusive geographical territory. The exact terms of the franchise agreement vary, but it is usual to have precise obligations laid down for both parties to the agreement. This method of marketplace expansion has proved popular with organisations wanting to globalise their operations, as entry to overseas markets is possible without a great deal of risk or financial commitment. The creation of increased availability through franchising relates to the theory of both new product development and distribution. The past few decades have seen a tremendous growth in this form of business. Franchising on a large scale began in the USA in 1970s and has developed rapidly in many parts of the service sector, notably amongst fast-food businesses, such as McDonalds and Pizza Hut, worldwide. Franchising in general is well covered in the literature and useful sources include Price (1997) and Mendelsohn (1992). We will now go on to look at some of the main developments in franchising in travel and tourism.

A number of travel and tourism organisations, including car hire firms, hotel groups, travel agencies and airlines, have adopted franchising. Indeed, this has been a major influence on the international expansion of a number of well-known hotel chains, a popular example being Holiday Inns. Hotels are well suited to the concept, whereas the retail travel sector experienced problems with early attempts at franchising. Holloway and Robinson (1995) have pointed to a number of reasons for this, including the fact that IATA appointments for franchisees were not guaranteed and back-up facilities, such as training, did not always materialise. The latter was an important factor given the highly specialised nature of the product. Holloway and Robinson (1995) also suggest an additional legal hurdle in that commission could not then be split between different organisations which the payment of royalties effectively involved. However, this was made possible in the 1980s and the concept of franchising in the retail travel sector has re-emerged in recent years. Uniglobe, a Canadian company which focuses on business travel, has franchised more than a thousand branches worldwide since they were established in 1991.

The concept of franchising is being adopted by the major airlines, albeit in a modified format. This extends the distribution of the major's (franchisor's) product in an area where they would not otherwise be present. At the same time, the franchisee has an opportunity to distribute their services via the major's CRS.

FRANCHISING AT BRITISH AIRWAYS

Franchising is now an important aspect of British Airways' (BA) business, with significant benefits to the organisation both in terms of passenger feed into the airline's mainline network and also revenue contribution. Franchising is a strong element of BA's strategy for the future and is currently considered essential to their profitable growth.

Franchising activity at BA began in July 1993 with Cityflyer Express becoming the first franchisee. This agreement was followed, a month later, by the addition of Maersk Air Ltd and Brymon Airways. Loganair has been operating under the franchise agreement with BA since July 1994 and in January 1995 British Regional Airlines, formerly known as Manx Airlines (Europe) Ltd, signed an agreement.

GB Airways began operating as a franchisee in February 1995, effectively becoming the first BA franchise operator to span more than one continent. The next development saw the first franchise agreement with an overseas carrier, Sun Air, which began in August 1996. A further significant aspect of the development to date has been the inclusion of Comair – the largest privately-owned carrier in South Africa – in BA's franchised network in October 1996. Finally, BA's ninth franchised carrier, British Mediterranean, took over the BA routes to the Levant region in March 1997. In total, these nine franchise carriers currently contribute a fleet of 107 airlines to BA's operations.

(British Airways)

Consortia

Distribution can also be extended through membership of consortia. These represent one of the means by which some travel and tourism organisations, in common with other types of organisation, have chosen to market themselves collaboratively. This method is particulary suited to those companies wishing to remain financially independent. Retail travel agents, hotels, tour operators and visitor attractions have all formed consortia. First Business Travel International highlights the vast geographical spread that consortia can achieve. This is a worldwide consortium that includes Britannic Travel and has partners in Europe, Africa, Asia and America.

Individual companies, by forming or joining a consortium, can achieve far wider distribution of their products or services than they would be capable of achieving on their own. This can be a cost-effective way of reaching foreign markets. A main feature of the marketing activities undertaken by consortia is the production of a joint brochure. This highlights the overlap between the distribution and promotional advantages of consortia membership. There are also joint purchasing advantages for hotels and increased negotiating power for all sectors. The key distribution advantages are information dissemination, and increased access to reservation systems. A variety of types of consortia exist and these tend to consist of members with similar or complementary products which are not in direct competition with one another. The consortia Leading Hotels of the World is described in Chapters 1 (page 8) and 2 (page 39).

Site selection

Any discussion of travel and tourism distribution would be incomplete without reference to the fact that the place element of the mix covers not only distribution but also the location of travel and tourism facilities themselves. This is particularly important in sectors of the industry which benefit from passing trade as do some hotels, restaurants and visitor attractions. Tourists may walk in to these facilities and make bookings or stay for immediate consumption. The location of such facilities is clearly of heightened importance. Restaurants in areas which are attractive to tourists will benefit from passing trade more than other restaurants and may choose not to offer a booking facility at all on the basis that they can achieve a higher turnover by being available to passing trade.

Particularly for small businesses, choice of location is a most important decision as it determines both the site of their service production and also their main sales point. Such firms will concern themselves little with the complexities that influence the distribution strategies of the larger travel and tourism organisations, for whom this aspect is a major feature of the marketing effort.

Controlling the distribution function

There are different levels of control. Control over middlemen in particular is achieved in a number of ways. The criteria for *selection* of middlemen can be applied to ensure that middlemen are operating effectively on the principals' behalf. Valuable measures might also include the volume of sales achieved.

The inventory control process can be complex in some areas of travel and tourism. Airlines, for example, cannot easily adapt their production rates according to peaks and troughs in business. Scheduled carriers can, however, control the release of seats using yield management software and CRSs. Sophisticated systems use statistical techniques to forecast sales. This guides the release of inventory on a given flight and the price at which it should be released. Some airlines manage yield by having a variety of fare categories per flight with their CRS able to take account of different markets and marketing channels when releasing fares.

Control over distribution is one advantage of using direct marketing methods. Travel industry integration could also lead to more control over distribution as tour operators may have improved control of retail outlets owned by the same parent company.

Summary

The distribution of travel and tourism products is less concerned with fulfilling orders once these have been obtained and more concerned with ensuring the availability of timely information concerning products and ease of access to make bookings. These can be either direct from the customer or indirect bookings made through intermediaries. Increasingly this access needs to be available on a global scale.

Planning the distribution function is clearly important whether or not an organisation is physically involved in transportation of their products to customers or middlemen. It is still vital to ensure that the distribution plan stems from the overall marketing objectives and strategy. The type and number of outlets to be used should be decided and performance standards set for them. Measurement of performance should then help with control.

This chapter has concentrated on forms of tourism which are characterised by a need to book, such as holidays, transportation and accommodation. Having discussed the principles of distribution, the chapter examined their application to travel and tourism products. The importance of information flow was discussed and an outline of the technological advances in the management of this was provided. It was concluded that there is a very real threat of new entrants into travel and tourism provided by IT experts and retailers other than travel agents. New technology offers increased choice for both the industry and the consumer. It also lessens the distinction between the distribution and promotion elements of the marketing mix.

 CASE STUDY
SEAFRANCE

Background
Seafrance owns three ships and operates up to 30 crossings per day on the Dover-Calais short sea crossing. It is the largest employer in the Port of Calais, with over 1,000 employees. It is 86 per cent owned by SNCF (the French railways system), which also has a vested interest in the success of the Channel Tunnel by operating part of the rail service which links with the tunnel.

Like many ferry companies, Seafrance plays a major role in the social and economic fabric of the country and region, as both an employer and key transportation link. Seafrance must also prove its financial and strategic worth to its major shareholder, for instance, by being able to produce enough profits to up-grade their tonnage and service, by not being a burden on the national economy, by complementing or effectively competing with other national links, and by playing its part in the national and EU transportation policy and abiding by its laws.

Company history
In 1995 Seafrance entered the cross-channel market with experience in operating ships (they had previously been part of a pool of owners operating cross-channel routes), but as a newly formed company with 0 per cent awareness, no past passenger list and no reservations system, as Robin Wilkins, the company's UK director put it, 'We had a blank sheet of paper'.

In addition, the market was at its most turbulent; the Channel Tunnel having been open for just over a year, there was over-capacity, caused partly by the increased competition and partly by the preparations shipping had made in readiness for the tunnel. They had invested in new, faster and improved ships and had undergone some strategic positioning for market share on routes which had included some increases in capacity. A price war was raging, with downward pressure on both fares and duty-free. Because of lower revenues per booking, shippers were concerned about marginal revenue.

Within less than a year, Seafrance had established at least 4 per cent of the market, and in a peak month of 1997 they were reckoned to have at least 15 per cent of the total market (Travel and Tourism Analyst, 1997). Most onlookers have been surprised at the success they have had against great odds.

The market
The market for travel is highly seasonal, with peak demand for only two months of the year (July/August). Ferry companies must seek to provide incentives to travel in the rest of the year and balance capacities or sailings with the costs of owning and running ships. In some months demand can rely as much as 80 per cent on promotionally-oriented traffic.

On the Dover-Calais route, it is estimated that as much as 50 per cent of the traffic is promotionally-oriented, i.e. they are induced to travel by special short-stay rates, like day trips and 60-hour visits, or by other specially reduced fare offers, or by duty-free incentives.

Other business is often negotiated through third parties, like inclusive tour operators and general sales agents. Traffic inbound to the UK can include coach and rail tours of Europe and the UK, and includes many international travellers from, for example, Japan, Australia and the USA. Traffic outbound to Europe can include individuals on camping and caravan inclusive tours and holiday homes, or hotel packages, and onward traffic to other parts of Europe, with a variety of pre-booked camp sites or accommodation.

Other custom comes via travel agents booking with the operator on behalf of independent travellers, and travellers who prefer to make their own bookings direct with the shipping operator. This sector often includes business people with or without cars and small freight, home-owners in France, England and other European countries, and people on day trips, short breaks and longer vacations. It may also include independent travellers with or without vehicles and those taking onward coach or rail connections. Many consumers use the travel agents purely as a information source and book direct.

By 1997, the market was still somewhat turbulent, but increases in demand had occurred through the impact of the tunnel, faster and improved ships and the buoyant demand for shopping trips in particular. The Channel Tunnel had achieve duty-free shopping at its terminals (not onboard trains) and ferry companies had received permission from the Office of Fair Trading and the Monopolies and Mergers Commission to commence talks on mergers which would rationalise routes and capacity.

Recent developments
P&O European Ferries (Dover) and Stena have formed a merger to operate Dover-

Calais routes. They will be the largest shipper on the short sea routes. By some measures, the Channel Tunnel is calculated to hold anywhere between 40 and 50 per cent of the market for passengers, and the merged company many have similar levels of around 40 per cent or more, depending on rationalisation and the 1998 season. Seafrance, and the newly merged Sally Hollyman and Hoverspeed, provide the rest of the competition on the short sea routes, Seafrance having the largest capacity. The western Channel and North Sea routes also provide competition to France and the rest of Europe, and include the largest operator in the western Channel, Brittanny Ferries.

(Caroline Barrass)

Questions

1 As marketing manager, prepare a report on the particular problems Seafrance might have faced in achieving distribution.
2 What alternative methods of distribution may be relevant to Seafrance?
3 Discuss the internet as an alternative to retail distribution for Seafrance. Examine the advantages and disadvantages of each.

References and bibliography

Cowell, D. (1984) *The Marketing of Services*, Heinemann

Davidson, R. (1994) *Business Travel*, Pitman

Hanlon, P. (1996) *Global Airlines: Competition in a Transnational Industry*, Butterworth-Heinemann

Holloway, J.C. and Robinson, C. (1995) *Marketing for Tourism*, 3rd edition, Longman

Holloway, S. (1997) *Straight and Level: Practical Airline Economics*, Ashgate

Inkpen, G. (1998) *Information Technology for Travel and Tourism*, 2nd edition, Longman

Ivanovic, A. (1989) *The Dictionary of Marketing*, Peter Collin Publishing

Key Note (1998) *Travel Agents and Overseas Tour Operators*

Lancaster, G. and Jobber, D. (1994) *Selling and Sales Management*, 3rd edition, Pitman

McDonald, M. (1995) *Marketing Plans: How to Prepare Them, How to Use Them*, 3rd edition, Butterworth-Heinemann

Mendelsohn, M. (1992) *The Guide to Franchising*, 5th edition, Pergamon Press

Mintel (1996) *Hotels*, Mintel Marketing Intelligence

Poon, A. (1993) *Tourism, Technology and Competitive Strategies*, CAB International

Price, S. (1997) *The Franchise Paradox: New Directions, Different Strategies*, Cassell

Reinder, J. and Baker, M. (1998) The future for direct retailing of travel and tourism products: the influence of IT, *Progress in Tourism and Hospitality Research*, Vol. 4, pp 1–15

Renshaw, M.B. (1997) *The Travel Agent*, 2nd edition, Business Education Publishers

Shostack, G. (1978) The service marketing frontier, in Zaltman, J. and Bonona, T.V. (eds) *Annual Review of Marketing*, American Marketing Association, Chicago

TTG (1997) 3 July, *Travel Trade Gazette*

11 Promoting travel and tourism products

Objectives

By the end of this chapter you should be able to:

- understand the role and importance of marketing communications in travel and tourism
- appreciate the alternative budgeting strategies for marketing communications
- identify the elements of the promotional mix and the characteristics of the main alternatives
- recognise how the characteristics of travel and tourism influence the mix of promotional methods chosen.

Introduction

Marketing communications describes the combination of methods used to communicate with targeted consumers. The terms *marketing communications* and *promotions* are used interchangeably here. The chapter concentrates on those promotional techniques which are most suited to travel and tourism products.

We start by looking at the importance of communications and examining the communications process itself. The promotional mix is discussed, as are some of the factors which influence the success of marketing communications. We then look in more detail at the promotional categories which are most relevant to travel and tourism. Where a number of possible methods exist within a particular category, only the main ones are outlined due to limitations of space.

Promotion is often mistakenly referred to as marketing, although as we saw in the earlier discussion of the marketing mix, the promotional elements constitute only a subsection of marketing. Promotional activity is, however, extremely visible and so often attracts more attention than do the other marketing mix elements. Communication is implicit in product design, pricing and distribution, as these all portray something to consumers, but it is the main promotional methods of advertising, public relations, sales promotions and personal selling, and the specific tools within these categories, that we are concerned with in this chapter.

The promotional mix

Often described as a sub-mix of the overall marketing mix, the promotional mix consists of the variety of methods used to communicate with the target market. The combination of promotional methods chosen greatly influences the success of the marketing communications effort. Public relations activities are included in this chapter, although these often have a wider remit than the other promotional methods. In travel and tourism, the brochure has a significant role in communication and so can be treated as a separate promotional category, as it is in this book. Marketers essentially mix and match the promotional methods best suited to both their products and their promotional objectives. It is hoped that this will result in an appropriate marketing communications programme.

The importance of successful marketing communications

Successful management of an organisation's communications with its consumers, middlemen and other publics is essential. Without this, a well-designed and produced product or service may go unnoticed, however well distributed and priced it is. Some form of communications system is necessary in modern business, and organisations are constantly improving their skills in this area. The volume of messages now being aimed at consumers makes such improvements necessary. The cost of marketing communications also means that it is important to maximise the return on any investment in this.

The communications process

The essence of communication is to convey or exchange information. This is not always easily achieved. There is potential for any message to be rejected or incorrectly received. A communication is only successful if the message is received by the intended audience as the sender meant for it to be received. Anyone sending a message on behalf of a travel and tourism organisation should therefore be aware of how communications work. A popular model used to describe the many stages in the communication process is shown in Figure 11.1.

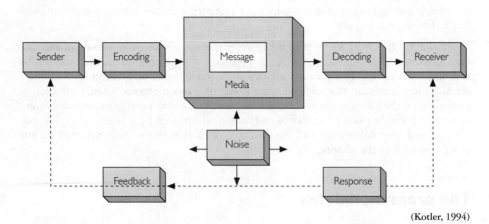

(Kotler, 1994)

Figure 11.1 Elements of the communication process

Each part of the model has a role to play in determining how successful an attempt at communication will be. The party sending the message to another party holds a great deal of responsibility for successful communication. They determine much of what follows in the communication process, such as who is to receive the message, the form the message is to take and the media to be used. This involves encoding the message – putting the ideas to be communicated into some other form for transmission through appropriate communications channels, known as media. The sender hopes the receiver will decode the message in an appropriate manner. The receiver's reactions to a message that they have been sent and which they have then decoded forms their response. Part or all of this reaction may be channelled back to the sender as feedback. Feedback may be invited by the sender, perhaps as part of their marketing research programme.

Extraneous conditions can distort the message. Other advertisements or anything else that detracts attention from the message are often referred to as 'noise'. Equally the receiver can be the cause of what is known as 'message misrepresentation', possibly by hearing only that which they want to hear or by forgetting the message. The existence of such interference can be a particularly negative influence on the success of any communication, for obvious reasons.

The organisation of an effective promotional campaign

The key to successful management of the communications effort is co-ordination, and there are a series of useful steps which organisations can take when preparing communications:

1 Identify target audience
2 Determine the communications objectives and budget
3 Select the message, method and media.

Identification of the target audience

Successful communications begin with a definition of the target audience. The target audience influences the message and its delivery. It is important to define the response that is sought from the identified target audience by firstly determining their current view of the product and its state of 'buyer readiness'. A number of authors, including Kotler *et al.* (1996), have described typical stages that a consumer may go through when making a purchase (see Figure 11.2). Progress through these stages should not however be treated as a foregone conclusion.

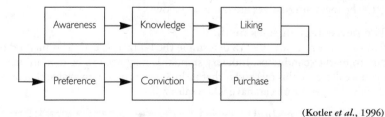

(Kotler *et al.*, 1996)

Figure 11.2 Buyer readiness states

The importance of each of these states will now be considered.

- *Awareness* The target audience must be made aware of the product.
- *Knowledge* Knowledge about a product does not necessarily accompany awareness of it and so it is important for organisations to communicate product knowledge also. A little known destination will need to ensure that the target audience is informed about what they have to offer.
- *Liking* Positive feelings can be developed towards products and it is important to try to encourage a degree of liking.
- *Preference* It is not always enough to like a particular product especially in competitive markets where other products may be viewed more favourably. In such circumstances, it is important to try to build consumer preference.
- *Conviction* It is possible for a potential consumer to develop preference without becoming convinced of the need to purchase the product. The challenge here for marketers is to convert a favourable attitude into conviction.
- *Purchase* Despite the presence of conviction, not all consumers will go on to purchase the product and so there is a need on the marketer's part to lead the consumer to purchase.

Determination of the communications objectives and budget

The overall objectives of a promotional campaign need to be considered. Promotional objectives stem from the broader marketing objectives which in turn stem from the organisational objectives. Without clear and precise goals, it is difficult both to produce promotions that are effective and to measure their success objectively. The importance of promotional objectives cannot be over-stated. A number of these may be identified by an organisation and need to be prioritised. Objectives should not be vague, but precise and measurable statements. The guidelines to objective setting given in Chapter 6 apply also to promotional objectives.

Travel and tourism organisations need to determine an overall budget, or appropriation, to cover all promotional activities. Budgeting aids both planning and financial control. Essentially, the budget is a plan, describing the sources and uses of funds for a future period, usually a year. The plan should allow for contingencies. Reserve funds can prove invaluable when unforeseen events create an opportunity for an unplanned promotion or an unexpected downturn in business suggests this would be appropriate. Many airlines increased their promotional spend following the negative effect of the Gulf War on their business. The budget will be proportionally allocated to the various elements of the promotional mix. This should provide some indication of the relative importance of the various promotional methods in the future period of marketing activity.

There are several methods that may be used to determine the overall promotional budget. The main alternatives are outlined below.

The percentage of sales method
Past or future sales are used to determine the budget. Clearly this method bears no relation to market conditions. Industry standards may need to be used for new products. A main weakness of this method is that it does not recognise the value that appropriate promotional expenditure can have when sales fall.

The going rate method
Budgets are determined by those of the competition. The main advantage of this is that

it can prevent advertising wars between companies, but it takes no account of the characteristics of the company or the reasons for using the promotions.

The historical method
This apparently simple approach looks at the promotional expenditure for the last budget period, yet bears no relation to the success of these. The obvious problem with this method is that it is not suited to markets which are in any way dynamic as tourism markets tend to be.

The affordable method
The financial position of the firm dictates the level of the promotional budget. Once again, this method does not take account of market conditions and so can be seen to be less than ideal.

The objective and task method
This is often described as a more strategic approach to setting the promotional budget as it determines what needs to be achieved before outlining how this should be done. The budget is then set at an appropriate level to support this.

In reality, budgets are often a compromise between the ideal and what is practical, especially for the smaller tourism organisations. Once the promotional budget has been determined, organisations need to decide how this can be used to maximum effect. Decisions about the message, method and media are all critical in this respect.

Selection of the message, method and media

The message
Having identified the target audience and the desired response from them, it remains for the marketer to design a message that will be effective. A variety of types of appeal may be adopted. A rational appeal, for example, could illustrate the benefits of using the product, whilst an emotional appeal will be based on stimulating an emotion, such as fear or guilt.

Once the message content has been decided upon, there are still a number of issues to be addressed regarding how to structure it. Should a one-sided or a two-sided argument be presented? At what stage in the message delivery should the strongest argument be presented? Is it necessary to draw any conclusions or should this be left to the audience themselves? Messages also need a format, the precise nature of which will depend on which media to be used. A typical print media format would involve a headline, copy and illustration, whilst for television it would be likely to involve sound, colour and people.

The message source and its credibility can greatly influence audience reaction and so experts in a field are often chosen to deliver messages. The Greater Glasgow and Clyde Valley Convention Bureau, for example, operates an 'Ambassador's Programme' whereby prominent local representatives of the academic, civic, cultural, business, professional and sporting communities are invited to pass on the message that the city provides an ideal conference venue. The programme aims to identify influential local contacts and then to encourage and motivate them to act as ambassadors by convincing their national or international colleagues that Greater Glasgow and Clyde Valley should be considered as a venue for future conferences. Promotions via the media often use highly credible sources in a similar manner. The presenter of a travel programme or a well-known explorer might be used to promote a travel organisation for example. In addition to credibility, likeability and trustworthiness can also enhance the value of a message source.

The method

It is highly likely that the organisation will select a variety of promotional methods in order to communicate their message to the target audience. This combination constitutes the promotional mix which was introduced above. We will now look at each of the main categories of the promotional mix in more detail. The role of direct marketing in promotions will also be discussed although this is considered more fully in Chapter 10. It is important to note that different authors and practitioners have categorised the many promotional methods in different ways. The precise categorisation is less important than the fact that appropriate methods are selected and used effectively.

The characteristics of the different promotional methods are important in determining the correct mix to be used. There are also a number of other influences on the make-up of the promotional mix, some of these are detailed below.

Product characteristics

Certain products do not lend themselves to some promotional forms. Aspects such as atmosphere, which are so important to travel and tourism products, are extremely difficult to portray through certain media.

The target market

The definition of the target audience, including buyer-readiness states as discussed above, will influence the choice of communication method. Different promotional tools will be more effective at different stages. Advertising and public relations are useful for creating awareness and knowledge whereas personal selling is more effective at creating liking and conviction. Sales promotions may help turn conviction into purchase. A number of techniques can therefore be utilised to try to propel the consumer through these different stages to ultimate purchase.

An important distinction exists in travel and tourism between consumer and trade markets. They use different media and require a different emphasis in messages, as the benefits each is seeking are very different.

The product life cycle

The effectiveness of the various promotional tools will vary at the different stages in the life cycle of a product. Advertising and public relations, for example, are helpful in the initial stages to encourage the trade to adopt a new product. Once a product has reached a certain level of sales, advertising need only be as a reminder communication. At the decline stage, sales promotions can play a valuable role in removing excess stock. Salespeople would no longer be concentrating their efforts on products at this stage.

The communications environment

No communications effort exists in isolation. Competitive communications can greatly influence the environment in which advertising takes place. Influence is also exercised by the prevailing costs of advertising. Furthermore, advertisers cannot ignore the legal environment.

Figure 11.3

(Reproduced with permission from Holiday Autos International Limited)

Push versus pull strategies

A clear distinction is often drawn between two alternative strategic approaches to marketing communications. A push strategy aims to push the product or service to the customer via any middlemen being used. This strategy is therefore often concerned with directing resources at the retail level. A principal which has a salesforce maintaining regular contact with the travel agency network and which advertises heavily in the trade press and offers sales promotions aimed at the middleman can be seen to be pushing their products through the trade. They might well highlight commission levels and potential agency profits in their messages. The advertisement shown in Figure 11.3 which was displayed in the *TTG* clearly focuses on the financial advantages, for the middleman, of booking the product.

A pull strategy, on the other hand, aims to pull the consumer to the distributor or producer. This can involve heavy expenditure on consumer advertising or other promotional activities to attract their attention and make them demand the product or service. Many tour operators advertising their brochure launches in the main media include an invitation to consumers to visit a travel agent and request the brochure or to request it directly from the tour operator. Messages may highlight consumer benefits offered by the product, such as rest and relaxation or family fun. Destinations may also adopt such an approach. Visit Florida, formerly known as Florida Tourism, have announced that they are targeting consumers in the UK in the hope of driving them into the travel agents. This involves the addition of consumer shows and the incorporation of consumer efforts into their UK marketing (*TTG*, 1998)

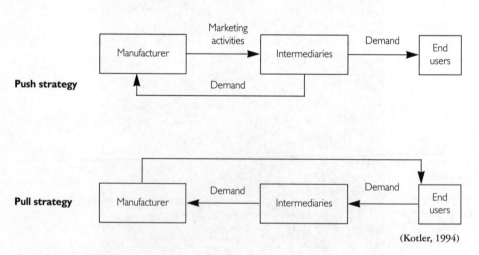

(Kotler, 1994)

Figure 11.4 Push versus pull strategy

We will now examine the main communications methods used by travel and tourism organisations. The model shown in Figure 11.5 attempts to illustrate indicative categories of promotions used by travel and tourism organisations.

Figure 11.5 Promotional categories used in travel and tourism marketing

Advertising

Possibly the most public of promotional methods, advertising has been described by Kotler as:

'Any paid form of non-personal communication and promotion of ideas about goods, or services, by an identified sponsor.'

(Kotler, 1994)

Advertising takes many forms and can be used for a variety of reasons. The advantages to this promotional method are that replication is possible enabling campaigns to build images over the longer term. Advertising in certain media can reach a large, widely dispersed audience. The cost per exposure in such cases can be relatively cheap, although some forms of advertising can be costly. Advertising is however impersonal and only provides one-way communication.

Advertising can be controversial and is often accused of increasing the cost of products. Proponents of advertising, on the other hand, would argue that it effectively prevents prices from rising by stimulating demand.

Agency relations

Marketers can create their own advertising in-house if they have the resources to do so. The use of advertising agencies is, however, popular, mainly because they employ specialists offering a degree of objectivity. Agencies have a great deal of bargaining power with media providers. A variety of types of agency exist, from full-service to more specialist agencies offering aspects such as creative services. Many advertising agencies specialise in the travel and tourism industry or have a number of travel and tourism organisations' accounts.

Client–agency relations revolve around the relationship between main contacts from each; typically an advertising manager or brand manager for the advertiser and an account executive for the advertising agency. These two individuals will liaise between the two organisations, ensuring that the relationship works effectively. Traditionally, advertising agencies earned commission on any advertising, which had to pay for the use of media space, whereas they earned fees only for other types of promotional activities they organised. Many agencies are, however, moving away from commission-based earnings altogether now.

Media selection

Media purchasing and scheduling issues assume great importance for advertisers. Numerous media options are available. For some types of product and promotional objective, the choice can easily be narrowed down. Factors to consider when choosing a media vehicle include the vehicle audience size and type, the budget, message objectives and ease of booking. Competitors' activities may also be taken into account. Computers are often used to evaluate alternative media costs. The expense involved in securing appropriate media can necessitate the employment of specialist media planners and buyers who are able to negotiate the best media deals.

Tourism marketers need to consider the characteristics of the available media types. These are often viewed as being either quantitative or qualitative. Essentially, quantitative characteristics are those which can be easily portrayed numerically, such as cost and coverage. There are too many media types available to enable us to look in detail at these characteristics for each within a chapter such as this. They are, however, summarised in Table 11.1, and information relating to most media in the UK is available in British Rate and Data (BRAD).

In the past much credence was given to these quantitative aspects in media planning. Increased emphasis on the more qualitative aspects has developed with the awareness that people use different media in different ways. Croisier (1987) describes the qualitative characteristics of media under four headings: usage, creative scope, vehicle effect and user-friendliness. These characteristics are summarised below.

Usage
This refers to the way in which the media audience uses the particular media vehicle. Media can be consumed in a variety of ways and under different circumstances. For instance, many people will leave the radio on as background, whilst others will read only certain sections of a weekly newspaper.

Creative scope
The visual and verbal effects of using different media vary. Television and newspapers, for example, have differing abilities to represent products visually whilst radio cannot do so at all.

Vehicle effect
The media itself can influence audience perceptions of the message and the advertiser. This can have repercussions for how the audience views the organisation and its products. For example, television can lend credibility to the advertising company as it is an expensive form of promotion and so the company can appear to be successful if it can afford to use it. The image of a particular newspaper or magazine could also reflect on the product being advertised.

User-friendliness
Whilst some media are easily accessible to advertisers, others may be difficult to buy or may have long lead times before time or space are available.

Table 11.1 Summary of media characteristics

| | TV | Radio | Cinema | PRESS | | | Posters | Direct mail |
				Daily, evening and Sunday	Regional	Magazines		
AUDIENCE Audience size	Some wastage, large and national (some international)	No national coverage	Small, no national coverage	Large and mostly national	Small, no national networks	Mostly national (and international)	National coverage is difficult	Large national and international
Audience type	Few, 15–24-year-olds	Mainly housewives, commuters	Many, 15–24-year-olds	Socio-economic	Geographic segments	Lifestyle segments	Commuters, car drivers, etc.	Any target available
Audience state of mind	Relaxed and passive TV couch potato = visual wall paper	Background/audio wallpaper?	Captive audience – willing suspension of disbelief	Deliberately read		Relaxed and involved with magazine		
COSTS Cost of production	High	Low	High	Low-med	Low	Low-med	Medi	Low
Minimum cost of space	High	Low	Low	Med	Low	Low-med	Low-med	High, but can experiment in small quantities
Average cost per thousand	Low, less than £2	Very low, less than £1		Low-med £8	Med £30	Med £12-70		High, £500
Extra advantages	Adds credibility to product or company	Transportable medium	High impact and captive audience					

Table 11.1 Continued

	TV	Radio	Cinema	PRESS			Posters	Direct mail
				Daily, evening and Sunday	Regional	Magazines		
MESSAGE								
Variable/ senses	Sight, sound, colour, movement, time constraint	Sound and time constraint	Big impact, enhanced sight and sound	Mostly black and white, some colour	Black and white	Four-colour	Four-colour big impact	Four-colour and 3-D possibility
Serial ad sequence	Viewed serially – no competition from other ads or editorial but zap	Serially, less zapping	Serially and no zapping	Must compete with the other ads and editorial on same page			Ad clutter	
Transitory	Highly transitory since you cannot refer back to ad once shown (unless taped)			Can keep clippings or refer back if desired			Can refer back/ walk back or drive past	Can refer back/ keep coupon
Demonstration	Ideal for usage and impulse purchases	Difficult	Yes	Benefits or results can be shown but not product usage demonstration			Only short image benefit	Yes
Detail/ technical	Viewer cannot absorb detail	No urgency and topicality	No	Yes	Yes	Yes	No	Yes
Urgency/ topicality rub-off	No	Unique immediacy, urgency and topicality	No	Yes	No	Magazine image spills on to ad	Cult image?	Yes
Flexible	Inflexible and pre-emptible	Flexibility		Flexible			Inflexible	Flexible
Lead times	Long	Short	Long	Short			Long	Short
EASE OF MEDIA BUYING								
Clearance	Script (1 week), finished film (1 week), ITVA	Same day clearance, ITVA	One week clearance, cinema ad. assoc.	Code of advertising practice (clearance is not compulsory)				
Audience research	BARB and TGI	RAJAR	CAVIAR	NRS	JICREG	NRS and ABC	OSCAR	
High frequency facility	Hourly and daily	Hourly and daily	No	Yes	Weekly	Weekly/monthly		
National coverage	Expert's job, but network exists and international cable/satellite	No national network	Yes	Yes	No national network		Difficult	

(Reproduced with permission from Smith, P. R., *Marketing Communications: An Integrated Approach*, Kogan Page 1993)

No single framework for media buying is adopted by all media buyers or indeed by all authors. Paul Smith adopts a different approach to Croisier whilst still summarising the key characteristics of the main media types effectively (see Table 11.1).

The media selection process will take into account not only the characteristics of the media but also those of the audience itself, as well as the budget, message objectives and the media used by competitors. There are, in some cases, legal restrictions on the use of some media forms by advertisers of certain products. Media research can greatly help with the selection process. Information about the media is available in a number of published sources and from trade associations and professional bodies. Yet another 'mix within a mix' can be seen where more than one medium is used in a particular campaign.

Media decisions are not merely concerned with which media to advertise in but also with the amount of time and space to purchase and the precise timing of advertisements. A media schedule may be produced for a particular campaign, specifying the exact media space and time to be booked.

Advertising by travel and tourism organisations

Many travel and tourism organisations will undertake no advertising whatsoever, whilst others have enormous advertising budgets. Airlines are big advertisers. According to Mintel (1996b) advertising expenditure by UK airlines increased by 44 per cent in the five years to the end of 1995. Growth in advertising expenditure was at its highest during the recession between 1991 and 1993 as airlines attempted to stimulate demand. Many of the major UK airlines segment their advertising across product groupings. For example, British Midland divided its expenditure between business and leisure products. Virgin Atlantic has used separate campaigns for its First Class and Economy Class products, and British Airways (BA) has previously split its advertising campaigns into the categories of BA, BA and Quantas, BA Club Europe, and BA Express. Airlines now also use the internet as a means of promotion as well as distribution. BA's web site is partly themed on its TV advertising campaign.

Airlines are not alone in the tourism industry in advertising their products. Main media advertising expenditure by tourist offices in Britain totalled £10.7 million in 1995, with the STB accounting for more than a quarter of total spend (Mintel, 1996a).

The STB's 1997 Autumn Gold poster campaign illustrates a highly targeted campaign. The series of six poster advertisements, one of which is reproduced as Figure 11.6), are aimed at commuters travelling to work on the London Underground. The campaign aims to bring visitors to Scotland whilst also tackling their short tourist season – it focuses on the shoulder months of October and November in order to extend annual tourism. Partnership is also evident as a number of transport providers – Air UK, Caledonian Sleepers, easyJet, GNER and Ryanair – contributed £170,000 to the costs of the promotion. This income helped towards the overall campaign costs. Annually, £1.5 million is spent on Autumn Gold.

The larger hotel chains also use advertising to differentiate their product and promote sales. The level of advertising expenditure depends on the preferred media and the form of promotion. The customer profile of the industry indicated that much activity must be targeted towards the business rather than the consumer market (Key Note, 1996a). Forte is the leading advertiser of short breaks in the hotel sector, spending £1.8 million in sup-

Figure 11.6

(STB)

port of its leisure breaks programme (Mintel, 1996c). Advertising and promotional activity is limited within the wider hotel sector. A large number of smaller operators carry out virtually no formal promotional work, relying on their location and listing in local directories to maintain business. Heavy media spends are the preserve of the larger chains who have the resources available to invest in advertising campaigns (Key Note, 1996a)

'Where smaller chains are involved in advertising activities, these take the form often of specifically targeted promotions.'

(Key Note, 1996a)

The attractions sector also undertakes limited media advertising. Media advertising can sometimes play a minor part in their marketing and promotional strategies. Advertising in tourist board literature is a common method of promotion for them. Alton Towers was the heaviest advertiser in the tourist attractions sector in the year 1995-6, spending £1.9 million on this (Key Note, 1997). Competition on the short sea crossing between Dover and Calais is reflected in the level of advertising which the three main operators on the route undertake. In the year to June 1995, P&O European Ferries, Stena Sealink Ltd and Hoverspeed collectively spent £13.9 m on advertising (Key Note, 1996b).

Advertising effectiveness research

Advertising is expensive and so expenditure on it requires justification. Advertising decisions are no different to other management decisions in that they are better if based on the results of reliable research. The risks involved in advertising need to be minimised. For example, the possibility that an advertising campaign could have a detrimental effect, by increasing the sales of a competitor's products instead, should be avoided at all costs. Advertising objectives provide criteria for the evaluation of advertising and these will often involve changes in mind-set, such as attitude, opinion and knowledge, rather than merely changes to sales performance.

Assessing advertising effectiveness can be problematic generally. The evaluation of travel and tourism advertisements presents additional challenges for marketers as it is difficult to isolate the influence of advertising from other influences such as currency, exchange rates and weather conditions. The complexity of tourist behaviour also means it is difficult to evaluate the effectiveness of one advertisement or one campaign. Accurate measurement of effectiveness can also be inhibited by the typically long time delay between the advertisement being shown and the travel taking place.

Advertising research can take place at any or all of a number of different stages in the advertising process. The initial concept may be tested and the advertisements pre-tested. The resultant campaign can then be tested throughout and followed-up with post-testing. Findings should then be acted upon. The importance of evaluating the success of any advertising campaign can be seen by the decision of Forte Posthouse to switch from TV advertising to press advertising believing that the TV advertising had not changed people's perceptions of the chain (Key Note, 1996a).

Brochures

The brochure is currently used as a principal marketing tool especially by tour operators, accounting for a significant proportion of most mass market tour operators' marketing budgets. One reason for the enduring popularity of the travel brochure is that it represents a form of 'tangible evidence' for the consumer purchasing a high risk product. Brochures tend to be highly structured and informative. The majority are aimed at two markets; the consumers themselves and the travel agents as middlemen. For many tour operators, the brochure represents their high street presence, even where the company is linked with the retailer. Where direct marketing methods are used, the brochure need only be aimed at the end consumers. This allows for a more creative approach as the size and style of the brochure need not conform to the restrictions of travel agents' racking spaces.

Tour operator brochures are attributed with performing a number of different roles, including:

- *Distribution* Brochures help the tourism product to reach consumers, either through retail travel agents or directly.
- *Packaging* As holidays consist of intangible combinations of a number of elements, packaging the total product becomes a concern of marketers. Brochures help with this and with the display of these packaged products.
- *Sales* Brochures can act as a sales tool if they are attractive, clear and easy to use, particularly if they stress any unique selling point (USP) of the product on offer.
- *Provision of information* The brochure communicates to the customers, contributing to the product and corporate identity at the same time. Prior to a holiday taking place, the brochure is often the only representation of that holiday for the consumer. Detailed information of holiday features such as destinations, accommodation, entertainment, travel, cost and timings can be provided.

The image portrayed by the brochure is clearly important. Design and production therefore need to create an image of a product that the potential consumer would wish to purchase.

Brochures may be distributed by specialist organisations which typically act on behalf of a number of tour operators. One such organisation, BP Travel Trade Services, distributes 140 million brochures a year on behalf of the industry. The company has more than 500 clients and supplies an estimated 44 per cent of the total market (*TTG*, 1997). Some of the larger tour operators may, however, select to undertake their own brochure distribution.

Brochure production and distribution represents a major expense for tour operators and so they now often analyse the previous years' sales figures for different travel agencies when deciding how many brochures to supply to them. The ratio of brochures distributed to the number of bookings made is referred to as the conversion rate. Tour operators today are more concerned with this than they were in the past.

As tour operators become more selective in terms of distribution, travel agencies are similarly becoming more discerning regarding which brochures they display on their shelves. A number of factors may be used to determine which brochures a particular agency will rack and position most prominently. Specialist agencies give priority to brochures which relate to their specialism, which could be activity holidays or cruises, for example. Vertically integrated companies may favour the display of their own company's products or those with which they are in less direct competition. The major vertically integrated companies claim to have differing policies in this regard. One common approach for those travel agents with no vested interest is to rack brochures for companies that have proved popular with their clientele in the past. Brochure display helps a tour operator to obtain market exposure and yet this is very much at the discretion of the travel agent. This has been a contentious area as 'racking rows' have resulted between some agents and operators. Racking decisions have become even more complex as a result of the trend for ever-earlier brochure launches – agents may have as many as three different seasons' brochures to rack at the same time.

In addition to racked brochures, a stock is usually retained of those brochures which have not been racked by the travel agent. It is normal to hold at least a file copy for most competitive brochures. Clearly this is not a significant means of increasing exposure for the selling tour operator.

Brochure design and production

In order to achieve sales, a brochure needs to be clear, persuasive and informative, with appropriate use of text and photographs. They therefore need to be well designed and produced. This process can be carried out in-house or contracted out to an agency. Computers are used heavily in brochure production, but this is a time-consuming process nonetheless, involving input from a variety of professionals, including graphic designers, photographers and copy-writers.

Before the process of designing the brochure begins, a great deal of market research needs to be conducted. Some of this research is concerned with the development of the product itself. Tour operators necessarily become involved in a process of negotiation with their suppliers – the principals. Further research will be undertaken in order to gauge the responses of targeted consumer groups to different brochure formats, front covers and content. This process will often involve the use of qualitative research methods including focus group discussions (see Chapter 5).

Those responsible will need to decide on the typeface to be used, the copy (the words) to be included and the layout of the text. Decisions are also needed regarding the use of colour, maps and photographs, as well as the overall quality of the brochure. The front cover requires careful consideration due to its importance in attracting the target audience to it. Where travel agencies are being used, design must allow for racking and possible overlap. Space restrictions can lead to fairly standardised brochure sizes. Format can also be highly standardised.

Information given in a brochure has to be accurate for a number of reasons. The legal factors pertaining to brochures are discussed in Chapter 12. The timing of brochure production is also important. It is usual for a brochure to be launched six months to a year before the relevant holiday season and so production could start the season before this. Tour operators have recently been experimenting with even earlier launch dates for their main holiday programmes. There has been some debate about the worth of this as consumers may become confused when several seasons' brochures are available at once. The market leaders tend to be the first to launch their brochures, other companies often prefer to see what price levels have been set by the leaders. Pricing panels therefore tend to be the last part of the brochure to be completed. This also allows for economic changes to be taken into account at the last minute. Brochure launches, especially those of the major mass market tour operators, tend to be surrounded by a great deal of publicity and are often supported by advertising. Care is needed to ensure no brochure is advertised before it is actually available, as this may lead the consumer to a competitor's already available brochure.

An important dichotomy facing large tour operators is whether to produce one holiday brochure encompassing all of their products, or whether to segment the market according to some established criteria. There are brochures offering different types of holidays, for example activity holidays and relaxing breaks, or particular geographic areas for example the Far East and North America, all offered by the same tour operator. Alternatively, a company could segment their brochures according to the price of the holidays. The method chosen is likely to depend upon the company, the market, the relative costs and estimated effectiveness.

Some tour operators complement their heavy reliance on the brochure with other activities. Specialist tour operators tend to involve themselves more in information provision than do mass market tour operators. Workshops or film evenings organised for customers and potential customers are just two of the methods used for higher risk purchases such as holidays to 'off the beaten track' destinations or those involving dangerous activities.

The use of brochures in tourism is not the sole preserve of tour operators. They are also used in the promotion and distribution of destinations. Hotels and other accommodation providers, transportation companies, museums and other visitor attractions all use the brochure to a greater or lesser extent as part of their promotional and distribution strategies. The size and quality of these brochures varies greatly. Forte Hotels has introduced a dedicated trade brochure for their Leisure Breaks programme replacing the dual-purpose brochure which is available to consumers. It is a 68-page directory covering 160 hotels (*TTG*, 1998).

Direct marketing is assuming increasing importance in the distribution of travel. The brochure continues to play a pivotal role here. It is not only the principals who are developing their direct sales business, travel agents are also becoming more involved with several of the multiples having opened large call centres recently.

The video age

Some tour operators now use the video to replace, or supplement, the holiday brochure. These provide detailed information regarding particular holiday types or destinations and can usually be viewed either on the travel agent's premises or at the customer's home. Like brochures, videos can be updated and re-issued as necessary. To date, video technology has not managed to destroy the popularity of the tour brochure.

The use of CD-ROM technology has recently been adopted for promotional purposes by the tourism industry, as evidenced by Virgin's Ski-D-ROM introduced in 1996. Their press release (Figure 11.7) describes the latest (1997) version of this.

press release

29th September 1997

Virgin's Virtual Reality ...

Last year saw the successful launch of our Ski-D Rom brochure, a first for the travel industry. After many rave reviews we are proud to introduce our Ski-D Rom for the 1998 ski season.

As previously, this interactive holiday brochure talks, move, bombards you with information and is of course lots of fun!

The Ski-D Rom guides you through a vast range of ski holidays in California, New England and Utah. All our holidays include flights with Virgin Atlantic Airways, accommodation, car hire or Virgin Buses for those customers who do not want to drive.

The disk features superb visual graphics, videos of all our resort areas including virtual tours of three areas by helicopter, 9 interactive ski trail maps, interactive street maps and photo galleries with full screen pictures of the resorts. New for '98 are on screen prices for all the holidays we offer including our popular 2 centres and "Vox Pop" videos of our holidaymakers in resort. Ski the Web! Automatically connect to our website from the CD and find links to all the top US ski resorts and much, much more!

We mustn't forget our brain teasing crossword puzzle, giving you the chance to win a ski holiday and a variety of games designed to capture everyone's attention.

Nigel Smith, Administration & Systems Director, Virgin Holidays says, "Following the introduction last year of the new Ski-D Rom, this new edition has been eagerly awaited. Advances in computer technology mean a growing number of people have access to a CD-Rom making this a very powerful marketing tool. We are confident that this is the way ahead and are delighted that our Ski-D Rom has been so well received."

The Ski-D Rom has been offered to our customers at a cost of £10 which is refunded only if they make a Virgin Holidays booking. To reserve your copy please call 01293 744 244.

(Gwyneth Markus, Public Relations Manager, Virgin Holidays)

Figure 11.7

Public relations

The British Institute of Public Relations (IPR) (revised 1987) defines public relations (PR) as:

'the planned and sustained effort to establish and maintain goodwill and mutual understanding between an organisation and its public.'

(Jefkins, 1989)

This definition seems to suggest that public relations has wide applicability within an organisation. Very often though it is seen to be the responsibility of marketing with the budget for public relations activities provided by the promotional budget. Public relations exist for all companies and the challenge is to manage these effectively so as to create a good public image. Concern should be for the overall corporate image as well as individual product images, as each can affect the other. The power of public relations is often underrated and yet this can be a highly effective communication tool for travel and tourism organisations. There is a popular, yet incorrect, presumption that all public relations activities are free. There are, however, costs involved in setting up and maintaining a public relations function within any organisation. Indeed, some of the activities involved may require fairly substantial financial outlay.

Successful public relations aim to create a positive image through the careful management of the relationships and communications with all of an organisation's 'publics'. Customers, shareholders, employees and the community at large can all be seen to be 'publics'. This is a creative sphere of marketing which may involve staging events, developing news stories or producing publications. The possibilities for the development of public relations techniques are both varied and extensive. At the same time good public relations skills are required to respond effectively to disasters and potentially damaging situations. Crisis management is discussed at the end of this chapter.

A great deal of attention has been turned to public relations amid increasing concerns about the environment and a general feeling that social responsibility on the part of organisations is becoming more important. The costs of public relations activities are often less than for other types of promotions and in addition they can have high credibility due to the lack of an obvious commercial sponsor. The apparent media endorsement that can accompany some forms of public relations activity is similarly helpful. For these reasons, public relations activities should be seen as an important part of the total marketing communications campaign. Balanced against the advantages of using public relations activities are a loss of control over the outcome, especially when the media are involved. Repetition is also unlikely in these circumstances, added to which there is the obvious danger of creating negative publicity.

Public relations activities

Activities involved in public relations may be concerned with the overall organisation or with a particular product. A variety of different methods can be used. These include activities such as courtesy magazines or other information sources, open days, public speaking, events, sponsorship, exhibitions, interviews, press relations and such like. Typically these techniques fall into the following categories.

Media relations
Media relations are a crucial aspect of an organisation's public relations. How the media portrays an organisation and their products greatly influences public perceptions. There are several aspects to media relations.

- Very newsworthy items often warrant calling a *press conference* whereby the company invites the media to a meeting, where a statement is likely to be made and there is an opportunity for questions to be asked.
- A less formal occasion is the *press reception* at which food and drink are likely to be available.
- The main method of communicating newsworthy information is the production of a *press release* containing a brief summary of the news (see Figure 11.7).
- *Feature articles* do not necessarily have the same requirement to be newsworthy, but usually contain relevant and topical information which may be exclusive to the publication. The *Travel Trade Gazette* for example has a feature article entitled 'View from the top'.
- *Press facility visits* involve inviting representatives of the media to attractions, destinations, hotels and such like in the hope that favourable media coverage will result.

Corporate communications

Corporate communications are a major area of public relations activity. These may be external communications, aimed at creating understanding about the organisation outside it, or internal, aimed at the provision of information to employees. Printed materials and videos are commonly used for each of these audiences.

Corporate identity

The identity of a company can be reflected in many ways, including the name and any logo. For example, British Airways has recently invested in changing its identity by redesigning its aircraft livery. The change from the use of a corporate colour scheme and national image on the aircraft to a far more international image reflects the company's global ambitions. The controversy that surrounded this change illustrates the importance of corporate identity.

A well-documented change in corporate identity has been the rebranding of the tour operator Owners Abroad to First Choice Holidays in 1993. This was part of a successful and far-reaching transformation of the company which had been prompted by an attempted hostile takeover bid by Airtours. Research indicated that the name Owners Abroad was not well known and, where it was known, it was sometimes seen to have timeshare connotations. A great deal of promotional support was given to the relaunch of the company as First Choice Holidays. Holloway and Robinson (1995) provide detailed coverage of the marketing campaign which was implemented.

Publicity

Publicity is non-personal communication usually in the form of a news story which relates to the organisation and its products. This story is transmitted free of charge, giving it credibility in the eyes of the consumer as it is not paid for by the sponsor. However, it cannot be guaranteed that the resultant copy (text) will be favourable.

Word of mouth

An important and often underrated element of travel and tourism marketing is word-of-mouth communication. Like printed publicity, word-of-mouth communication is highly credible. Organisations should therefore try to encourage recommendations as opposed to warnings. It is often said that bad news travels faster than good news and dissatisfied customers may tell others about their experience but will not necessarily tell the company concerned. There are implications here for researching tourist satisfaction levels and employing strict quality control measures.

Lobbying

Both organisations and individuals can achieve a high profile in the media by lobbying government or some other body in respect of some aspect of their industry. Some organisations have been lobbying government about the potential development of a fifth airport terminal at Heathrow, for example.

Sponsorship

Money or material support of an event, product, activity, person or organisation can draw attention to the sponsoring company. This is popular in the arts and sports, and can be a useful way of improving image or brand awareness. Holiday Inn for example was the official hotel sponsor of the 1996 Atlanta Olympic Games (Key Note, 1996).

Exhibitions

Exhibitions bring together buyers and competing sellers at one location. The essence of these is that they provide face-to-face contact with many people usually over a short period of time. There are a number of travel and tourism exhibitions notably the annual World Travel Market held in London.

The agency educational

Often known as 'familiarisation trips', agency educationals have long been used by principals as an effective means of promoting their travel and tourism products. There is a popular misconception that educationals are provided only by tour operators for travel agents in an attempt to improve their product knowledge and encourage their support. This is a narrow view of educationals which are also offered by transport providers, destination organisations or by a combination of different tourism suppliers. The beneficiaries may be travel agents but equally could be tour operators themselves being hosted by either national tourist organisations (NTOs) or carriers wishing to be featured in their packages. This is similar to the press facility visit and usually paid for out of the public relations budget.

The stated objectives of a particular facilitation visit may be to encourage free, hopefully positive, publicity or media coverage to increase knowledge or to encourage sales. In order that these objectives are met, the candidates need to be selected with care and the correct package prepared for them. The success of the trip should then be scrutinised as educationals are not cheap despite the fact that more than one principal may be sharing the cost.

Crisis management

Crisis management is a further responsibility which influences an organisation's public relations and so often falls upon the public relations executive or department. Any positive view held by an organisation's publics can quickly be lost should a crisis occur and be badly managed. Accidents, which occur all too often in the tourism industry, government investigations and other high profile problems can attract a lot of attention to an organisation. The preparation of guidelines for dealing with these eventualities can prove invaluable. Contingency plans should be prepared for any disaster which can be reasonably foreseen. In other circumstances, dealing directly with the problem can prove helpful. It is essential to be both honest with the media and considerate of any tourists or others affected. The role of successful press relations is paramount when disaster strikes. An already well-established and happy relationship with the media can greatly help an organisation in times of difficulty. Being proactive is as important as being reactive. Informing and updating the media during times of crisis is likely to be rewarded.

It is not possible in a chapter of this length to provide details of the many public relations methods available. Among those not considered are charitable donations, hospitality, seminars and the presentation of awards. The benefits of successful crisis management are exemplified by Sir Michael Bishop in the case study of British Midland in Clapper and Cunard (1990).

Evaluating public relations activities

The evaluation of public relations activities is a further important aspect of their management. It is usual for organisations to track the extent to which their public relations effort has led to media exposure by collecting clippings of all articles and noting the number of mentions on television and radio. This cannot guarantee that the communications were successful and so it is useful to supplement such activities with research into factors such as attitude change. The obvious difficulty here is that of isolating the public relations function from other promotional activities for this purpose.

The role of the media in promoting travel and tourism

Holiday and destination preferences are influenced by many factors that are not always easily controlled by the marketing organisation. Media coverage is one example of such an influence. This is not restricted to feature articles and travel journalism, but can be extended to include more general coverage such as documentaries relating to specific geographical areas, wildlife programmes, and so on.

The power of film

The power of film as a means of portraying destination image is increasingly being recognised by those with an interest in the promotion of places. A co-ordinated approach by all parties involved in order to capitalise on films can result in successful marketing activities.

Riley (1992) suggests that movies can influence the travel preferences and destination choices of some of those people who attend movies. Audiences are exposed to films for longer periods than they are to other broadcast communications and print advertisements. The importance of films in the promotion of particular locations has recently been recognised by the Scottish Tourist Board (STB) who implemented a number of marketing techniques to ensure that maximum advantage was gained from the films *Braveheart* and *Rob Roy*. These initiatives are discussed below.

FILM-LINKED INITIATIVES IN SCOTLAND

The success of the films *Braveheart*, *Rob Roy* and *Loch Ness* has attracted a great deal of free publicity for Scotland and formed the basis for several marketing campaigns during 1995-6. The challenge for the STB was to develop the awareness which resulted from the films into a propensity to travel. Recognising the potential for the films to expose the scenery of Scotland to an extensive international audience, a cohesive marketing strategy was launched for all three films. This was achieved by STB working with both area tourist boards (ATBs) and local enterprise companies (LECs). The resultant activities relating to *Braveheart* and *Rob Roy* are summarised below.

Braveheart
A £144,000 marketing campaign to position Stirling as 'Braveheart Country' was built around the film. Organisations involved in this included STB, Stirling District Council, Forth Valley Enterprise, Central Region Council, the National Wallace Monument and Twentieth Century Fox. Six national newspapers featured holiday competitions based on this theme and joint promotions with national cinema chains were undertaken. A 60-second film commercial was also made which was shown prior to the film around Scotland and the North of England. A further £100,000 was provided by the Scottish Office to extend the campaign to France and Germany.

A further joint marketing campaign with Fox Guild Video was developed to stimulate short holidays to Scotland. The aim here was to capitalise on the release of the *Braveheart* video by providing a 'two-for-one' offer with Independent Hotels of Scotland. STB invested £10,000 in this campaign and estimate that the incremental return on this was worth 2,000 bookings with a value of £480,000.

In addition, a documentary about *Braveheart* was made by Grampian Television, attracting yet more publicity.

Rob Roy

The STB, working with trade members and the distributor, UIP, designed an extensive public relations (PR) programme to position the Trossachs area as the real 'Rob Roy Country'. There were holiday competitions in five national newspapers and articles on Rob Roy in more than 30 local and national publications and broadcasts in the UK. Features were also published and broadcast overseas.

The campaign results

The audience attracted to the films far exceeded anything that an advertising campaign could have hoped to achieve. Furthermore, the audience had actually paid to see this form of promotion. Television repetitions and videos can continue to increase the audience size long after the release of the films. This can reinforce the image of the country in the viewers' minds. All of this is in addition to the press coverage of the films. The STB managed to build up a secondary form of publicity by building on the supposition that the growth of Scotland's tourism industry in 1995-6 was a result of the films.

The STB commissioned a study to assess the volume and value of press coverage gained through the PR strategies relating to the films. The study measured a total of 215 articles and 35 broadcast slots in 12 countries as a result of the campaign between April 1995 and June 1996. The advertising value of this exposure was estimated using details of media type and size of article or length of broadcast. This highlights the value of the STB's marketing campaigns.

Table 11.2 Estimated advertising equivalence April 1995 to June 1996 (by quarter)

Media type	Q1	Q2	Q3	Q4	Q5	Total
Articles	£210,904	£61,111	£113,643	£99,727	£127,578	£613,023
Broadcasts	£261,153	£26,426	–	£2,200,709	£7,154,568	£10,841,856
Total	£472,117	£87,537	£113,643	£3,499,436	£7,282,146	£11,454,879

The STB used the films as a basis for their campaign to sell Scotland as a tourist destination in 1995, using the line, 'You've seen the film, now see the country'. The campaign was reliant upon the global success of the films. The promotion of any location on the back of a film carries with it a clear element of risk. In addition to the possibility that a film will be unsuccessful, there is the chance that it will portray the wrong image of the destination.

The close co-operation between STB and the producers and distributors of the films was crucial to the creation of effective marketing campaigns. Close communications are essential if tourist authorities are to accurately predict whether a film is likely to provide the basis for a useful marketing campaign.

(STB and Hydra Associates)

Travel journalism

A more obvious form of media influence on destination choice results from specialist tourism feature journalism. This category includes dedicated magazines, such as Condé Nasts *Traveller*, as well as travel pages or supplements in more general interest magazines and newspapers. The increase in travel journalism is part of the growth in leisure journalism which has been occurring in recent years.

Travel journalism can lead to far wider exposure for a product than could otherwise be achieved by the company or destination in question. Sunvil Holidays believe that sending travel journalist Mark Ottoway to Namibia helped launch the destination for them. A two-page feature in *The Sunday Times* when Namibia was still a relatively unknown destination has helped the tour operator's Discovery Programme to sell 500 holidays a year to Namibia. It is not only these larger features that stimulate bookings, small 'snippets' in the media can be highly effective. Timely submission of a well-targeted press release can result in this sort of accessible publicity. Timing and content can be enhanced by successful portrayal of the atmosphere or the 'mood' of the destination.

In terms of television, there are a number of specialist travel programmes. Popular national travel programmes in the UK are BBC1's *Holiday*, BBC2's *The Travel Show*, ITV's *Wish You Were Here* and Channel 4's *Travelog* and *Lonely Planet*. In addition to national programmes, there are also a number of regional programmes broadcast throughout different areas of the country. Many other programmes, such as GMTV, also contain regular travel slots. Travel programmes are not confined to television however. There are both nationally and regionally broadcast radio travel programmes including Radio 4's long-established *Breakaway*.

The main strength of communication of this sort is that it appears to be unbiased, the independent source of the message suggesting credibility. This is a debatable point, however, as some journalists accept contributions, such as flights and accommodation, from principals. It is often suggested that credibility is compromised by such assistance.

Sales promotions

Sales promotions have been described by Kotler as consisting of:

'a diverse collection of incentive tools, mostly short term, designed to stimulate quicker and/or greater purchase of particular products/services by consumers or the trade.'

(Kotler, 1994)

Sales promotions are used to provide strong incentives to purchase and are often used to boost sales. There can be a strong element of immediacy inherent in their use. Sales promotions vary between being very subtle and extremely dramatic.

They act as an *inducement* or *incentive* to customers to purchase, usually in the shorter term. They are often used at irregular intervals to boost sales and are popular in travel and tourism due to the perishability of the products. Examples of the many forms that these can take include coupons, bonuses and contests. Both activity-based and material methods can be aimed at either the middleman or the final consumer. Techniques used by the travel and tourism industry include offers of free insurance and free child places. Both travel agents and tour operators use sales promotions heavily, not always with the desired effect. Indeed, the over-use of sales promotions can lead to consumer expectations of the additional benefits offered as the norm.

Categories of sales promotions

Sales promotions can be:

- economic incentives, such as discounts and special offers
- communications initiatives, such as point-of-sale materials or competitions.

Some forms of sales promotion are designed for physical products and are more suited to these. Many other types have been successfully adapted to services.

Discounts have been heavily used as sales promotions by the tour operations sector. The marketing communications and pricing elements of the mix can be seen to overlap here. Other sales promotion techniques involve adding value to products whilst keeping the price stable. Free excursions on a cruise, for example, mean more value for money for the consumer.

Sampling involves offering trial amounts of a product. In the case of travel and tourism products, this usually means consumers are offered free use of the product, such as a meal in a hotel restaurant, for a period of time.

Coupons offer savings when a purchase is made. In 1996, Novotel introduced a pan-European voucher scheme whereby guests could buy five vouchers (from £24), giving discounts of £12 per night at the chain's 200 plus European hotels (Key Note, 1996a). This sales promotion was backed by a £500,000 advertising campaign which illustrated their belief in the complementarity of different promotional forms.

Competitions are a popular form of sales promotion for travel and tourism products. Principals often run competitions aimed at the middleman and advertise these in the trade press. Prizes or entry to a prize draw may be offered as an incentive to salespeople to achieve a certain level of sales for the principal or product concerned. Alternatively, a competition may be based on trying to develop product knowledge on the part of the salesperson. The Eurostar competition shown in Figure 11.8, which was advertised in the *TTG*, is an example of the latter.

Frequent flyer programmes (FFPs) can be described as sales promotions since they offer consumer advantages in return for loyalty to the airline. These have become an important aspect in the marketing of business travel. British Midland operates an FFP known as Diamond Club which has three levels of membership – blue, silver and gold – dictated by membership points. The gold tier, for example, is for members who cross the threshold of 20 equivalent business class return flights per year. Pre-assigned seats, discounts on car hire, upgrades and a dedicated helpline are some of the benefits of membership of this elite tier, in addition to the opportunities to redeem frequent flyer points for free flights or accommodation.

Promotional gifts are used quite heavily in travel and tourism. A number of organisations advertise customised promotional gifts for the travel industry in the classified sections of the trade press. Popular items include customised passport holders, travel bags, luggage

(Reproduced with permission from Eurostar (UK) Limited)

Figure 11.8

tags and ticket wallets. These can provide a lasting reminder of the company for the middleman or final customer.

Point-of-sale materials are used to take advantage of an important promotional opportunity to capture 'late swing' consumers. These are used to promote products and services within or close to retail outlets and so can have a highly persuasive value. Examples include counter displays, hotel noticeboards, signs and stickers.

Tourist attractions often become involved in the provision of joint promotions with consumer goods companies. A typical example would be a promotion whereby the consumer is invited to collect tokens from breakfast cereal packets which can then be exchanged for part or full payment of the entrance fee to the attraction.

Poorly managed sales promotions can destroy the reputation or market position of a product or service. It is therefore sensible to test any sales promotion prior to running it to ensure that it is appropriate. As with other promotional methods, it is also important to evaluate the outcome of sales promotions. Comparing sales figures before and after a campaign is one method of doing this. A highly successful sales promotion campaign can display additional benefits, as occurred when BA offered free flights to anywhere in the world. This sales promotion was so newsworthy it also created a great deal of publicity for the company.

Personal selling

Selling is two-way, personal communication which takes place in travel and tourism at two levels. At the retail level, there are travel agencies dealing face-to-face with customers, whilst between the principal and the retailer there will often be a field sales representative. This chapter concentrates on the role of the latter. Personal selling is important to travel and tourism services due to the issue of inseparability, as there is a great deal of face-to-face contact between staff and customers. Kotler described personal selling as:

'oral presentation in a conversation with one or more prospective purchasers for the purpose of making sales.'

(Kotler, 1994)

The fact that two-way communication is possible is a main advantage of this method. Personal selling also allows for more flexibility in the design of messages, so these can be tailored to the customer. Negotiation with prospective customers may also be possible. Hiring and maintaining a salesforce can be expensive though and so it is not a method of promotion suited to all markets.

Salespeople can have responsibility for a number of functions, including the development of relationships with middlemen and key customers, increasing product knowledge, ensuring brochures are racked and collecting feedback from the marketplace. In order to perform this role successfully, they need to be knowledgeable not only about the products they are selling and those of the competition, but also about their customers and prospective customers. Salespeople typically need to display empathy if they are to meet their prospective customer's needs successfully and achieve their sales objectives. They need to be extremely well organised when planning their itinerary and reporting their activities. These attributes will not be effective without the presence also of appropriate selling skills. Central to successful selling is the sales sequence which takes place during a meeting with a prospect. Salespeople typically structure their sales situation in a sequence similar to that outlined below.

1 *Preparation* A call strategy should be designed around the objectives of the call and using information about the customer or prospect and their needs. Customer records may be used to gather information.
2 *Opening* Communication needs to be developed by gaining attention and then ensuring that all parties are at ease. The salesperson can then start to explore customer needs and identify any problems.
3 *Presentation* Having identified customer needs, the benefits of the product in relation to these can be presented.
4 *Objections handling* It is highly likely that the potential consumer will raise objections and if this is the case, these will need to be handled in an appropriate manner.
5 *Close* Poor sales technique at this stage can result in a lost order. The timing of the close is important. The salesperson will usually take their cue from the customer here. There are many techniques for closing a sale – these and other aspects of successful salesmanship and sales management are well covered by Lancaster and Jobber (1994).

Sales management

There are a number of issues facing sales managers. Their main role, however, is to offer leadership and support. Training and motivation of the salesforce constitute a significant part of this. As with other elements in the promotional mix, sales objectives are needed, together with strategies to achieve them. The evaluation of activities undertaken is a further important task.

Management of the sales function is in many respects similar to management of other areas, but it is particularly demanding due to the nature of the job. For example, sales managers of travel and tourism organisations are often geographically separated from their field salesforce leading to problems of communication, control and motivation. The last of these problems is heightened by the fact that salespeople often face rejections which can have a cumulative effect on their own attitude. Sales management has become a more central issue in companies as the importance of continued success to future sales is recognised. Some of the issues involved in managing the salesforce are referred to elsewhere in this book.

Evaluation and control of the salesforce

Particularly when a new sales manager has been appointed by a tour operator, airline, ferry company or some other tourism organisation, it is helpful to evaluate both the overall sales function and the individual salespeople within it. This may be carried out both on an on-going basis and periodically. Appraisal of sales staff is especially necessary as the nature of their job can lead to personality changes over time. Market conditions also change very quickly in the dynamic field of travel and tourism. Sales reports, expenses sheets and customer feedback can all supplement management observations and formal appraisal mechanisms when evaluating the salesforce.

Figure 11.9 lists some possible indicators of salesforce effectiveness. Assessing the effectiveness of the salesforce using these indicators does not always lead to accurate findings due to extraneous factors. There could be many reasons to explain the loss of an account, for example, which may be outside the control of the salesperson. Furthermore, direct comparisons between the success of different sales territories, or different products, are not always applicable due to the different characteristics that these may display. Care is also needed when looking at sales revenue or profits as measures of customer satisfaction in the longer term is important also. More qualitative aspects such as selling skills, product knowledge and customer relations should also be taken into account. One evaluatory method used by some tourism organisations involves a sales trainer accompanying a sales representative on visits.

Possible indicators of effectiveness

- The average number of calls per day
- The average length of a sales call
- The average revenue per call
- The average cost of a call
- The number of new customers per period
- The number of lost accounts per period

Figure 11.9

Use of the above measures should be cautious as factors such as length of call alone are insufficient to inform management of success or otherwise, yet this can be a helpful indicator when used in the correct manner. Use of evaluatory measures can in itself act as a control mechanism as staff are conscious of the fact that their performance will face scrutiny at some point.

Direct marketing

Direct marketing brings marketing activity to potential customers. This includes marketing directly to them in their home, office or even at a social environment. This marketing method crosses the divide between the distribution and promotional elements of the marketing mix. Direct marketing in travel and tourism has been developed greatly since the early 1970s when the tour operator Tjaerborg entered the market. At the time this company's approach was seen to be unique.

Forms of direct marketing include direct mail, telemarketing, door-to-door selling, computerised home selling and direct response advertising. Essentially each of these methods involves marketing the product directly to the consumer without the involvement of a middleman. It is important to distinguish between these main forms of direct marketing, each has its own advantages and disadvantages.

Direct mail

Direct mail in tourism involves sending brochures or letters to targeted consumers. Tour operators, travel agencies and hotels use this approach widely. Many of the larger tour operators today have a direct marketing division. Portland is the direct sell arm of Thomson. Other organisations rely solely on direct marketing methods.

Direct response advertising

Direct response advertising involves advertising to consumers in a way that will hopefully encourage them to enquire further about the company or product or even place an order. Contact details are included in advertisements to enable customers to make direct contact with the organisation.

Telemarketing

Telemarketing involves contacting prospective customers by telephone. It is more common in travel and tourism for markets to respond to calls from consumers. A number of call centres have been developed recently in the travel and tourism industry. Principals, such as airlines, have been developing their direct sales facilities in this way. British Airways has a nationwide telephone booking operation based in Newcastle. The retail sector has also entered this market recently with a number of significant developments.

Thomas Cook Direct opened a state-of-the-art call centre in Falkirk, Scotland in December 1997 to complement an existing site with 500 employees in Peterborough. This new centre has been designed to meet a number of challenges including that of attracting and retaining the right type of staff. One aim was to design a working environment that would motivate staff, support them and in doing so help to maximise their performance. Creating the right atmosphere was therefore crucial. John Morris, head of call centre operations, and his team worked on combining the excitement of travel with the needs of his staff. This involved the segmentation of work and non-work areas with the latter aimed at creating a *feeling* of travel. The two areas are literally separated by a flowing river. Staff enter through a 'sensorama' – a tunnel evoking a holiday feeling through the

Figure 11.10 A Thomas Cook call centre

sensations of light, sound and smell. The commitment to direct holiday sales resulted from the company witnessing expansion in all areas of the direct booking market – short haul, long haul, ski, teletext, cruise, flight and holiday money. Thomas Cook Direct has seen its business grow by over 300 per cent since setting up the Peterborough operation. The Falkirk site already handles over 1,000 calls a day. Television monitors throughout the building, used for communication, reflect the fun, fast-moving world of travel.

BP Travel Trade Services, the brochure distribution company mentioned earlier, has opened its own call centre which is operated by a staff of 30. It took more than 500,000 calls from consumers requesting brochures over the 12-month period ending in November 1997 (*TTG*, 1997).

Home selling by computer

This occurs when principals or agents are linked to consumers by computer. The discussion of technology in Chapter 10 looks at this in more detail. A further possibility is home selling by television, which looks set to increase in the future for travel and tourism products as digital television develops. Technology outside the home is also relevant, including multi-media kiosks.

Databases

Direct marketing is often concerned with databases and the data contained therein. Customer attributes, such as lifestyle or past purchasing behaviour, can be recorded and assessed to help forecast likely future consumer action. Details of all enquiries, purchases and transactions can be used to produce profiles which will be of use to marketers and may be supplemented with additional external information. Moreover, databases are concerned with the development of communication and ultimately relationships with customers.

Mailing lists
A mailing list represents the names and addresses of prospective customers for the product being sold. This will be a key component of any direct mail campaign. Mailing lists can usually be broken down into two main types:

- compiled lists – usually produced from static, generally published, information sources
- response lists – produced from live information, generally arising from actions taken by the person concerned. This could include such action as joining a club or making a purchase.

Theme parks in particular have increased their use of databases to target their marketing (Key Note, 1997).

Direct marketing is highly suited to products which have been carefully designed for targeted customer types and so is appropriate for package holidays. As direct marketing is arguably based on a narrow distribution channel, it is often adopted by smaller, specialist tour operators.

Relationship marketing

A direct extension of the concept of two-way communications with customers is the development of a longer term relationship with them in the hope of maintaining their custom. Many of the customer loyalty schemes adopted by the larger travel and tourism organisations, such as hotel chains and airlines, suggest an attempt to benefit from the cost economies of maintaining current customers as opposed to concentrating the communications effort on reaching new customers.

The regulation of promotion

The legislation which covers advertising is discussed in Chapter 12. This legislation operates alongside control by the statutory authority, which in the UK is exercised by the Independent Broadcasting Authority (IBA) Code of Advertising Standards and Practice. The IBA is concerned that broadcast advertising is legal, decent, honest and truthful. There are pre-clearance systems in place for these advertisements. There is also a system of control exercised by the Advertising Standards Authority (ASA). This amounts to self-regulation of the non-broadcast advertising by responding to complaints and judging them according to criteria laid down in their British Code of Advertising Standards.

Summary

Promotion constitutes a mixture of activities. The success of any combination of promotions depends on the skill with which it is selected and implemented. A number of factors influence promotional choices including the target audience, the promotional objectives, the available budget and the nature of the product(s) being promoted. Methods that are heavily used by travel and tourism organisations include advertising, proactive public relations activities and the brochure. Technology is becoming more important in the promotion of travel and tourism products.

Any promotional campaign should be continuously monitored to ensure that the stated objectives of the campaign are being met. We looked in particular at the evaluation of advertising and personal selling, but evaluation is important for all types of promotion.

 CASE STUDY
THE EDINBURGH INTERNATIONAL CONFERENCE CENTRE (EICC) RELATES TO ITS PUBLICS

EICC Ltd was set up as a company in 1991. Its remit was to construct an international conference centre. Although construction was still underway, marketing and public relations activities began in 1992 with the establishment of a team of marketing and public relations professionals. Their objective was to raise the profile of the EICC within the international conference industry prior to the opening of the centre. In other words, they were asked to market a building site. Some of the methods used are discussed below.

Provision of evidence

A brochure and a video incorporating CAD images were produced to convey to potential clients how the centre would look when complete. A pre-opening office was set up in Edinburgh which included a presentation suite to provide tangible evidence of the development. Audio visual equipment was used to portray the current status of the project by making use of an on-site camera. Videos, slides and details of the economic impacts were also provided.

Facilitation visits

Wellingtons and hard hats were provided for an on-going series of visits to the building site for potential conference organisers and other interested publics. Local hoteliers and other businesses which would be affected by the creation of a year-round tourism market were also key targets. The requirement to re-educate local suppliers of tourism products to enable them to meet the needs of a broader market was recognised. The creation of a positive image in the local community was of paramount importance. This theme was continued with the use of open days in the post-opening phase as well.

Countdown to opening

Edinburgh is twinned with nine other cities worldwide and an initial idea was to take the EICC message to these cities in the months leading up to the opening of the centre, but it was decided that the countdown campaign should target key conference cities in the world. The main locations the roadshow targeted were Hong Kong, San Francisco, Munich and Geneva.

Pictures of pictures

A local artist whose work depicts Edinburgh was asked to create a series of 6' by 3' pictures to present to local dignitaries in the cities visited. Presentations took place at receptions hosted for researched 'influencers' in both the marketplace and the media. Local media interest was generated at home by staging human interest photo-calls, including a picture being placed in a cab for the journey to the airport. EICC could be seen to be flying the flag for the city in this respect.

The cities visited created photo opportunities in themselves. In the case of Hong Kong, there was a photo-call with Chinese Dragons which led to media coverage both at home and in Hong Kong. Munich had been twinned with Edinburgh 40 years previously and so it was decided to host a dinner rather than a drinks reception there. The dinner was themed along the lines of a Burns' Supper, and a radio interview provided an opportunity to explain the traditions connected with this to the German market, so stimulating press interest at the destination. A Burns' Supper is now hosted in Edinburgh each year and there is an annual St Andrew's night in London.

Local initiatives

A competition was run in conjunction with the STV children's programme, *Skoosh*, asking viewers to suggest names for the conference rooms. The panel of judges included the Chief Executive of EICC and the architect of the centre among others. The suggestion of 11-year-old Laura Boyle that the centre adopt names of Scottish hill ranges won first prize of a trip to Disneyland with her family. Laura was then asked to present a bouquet to the Queen at the official opening of the centre. All of this created additional local publicity.

The mailing list

EICC established and now maintains a mailing list consisting of clients, prospects, suppliers and decision-makers in cities worldwide. Main media contacts are also included in the database. The centre's newsletter, *Conference Call*, is sent to all clients and prospects.

Partnership initiatives

The centre also works in partnership with the Scottish and Edinburgh Convention Bureaux and attended all key trade fairs in the run up to the opening. This enabled EICC to consolidate its positioning within the UK and European conference industry.

In addition, the centre secured sponsorship from the Bank of Scotland to produce a discounted shopping scheme for delegates, known as the Visitors' Passport. This Visitors' Passport lists transport providers, shops and other tourist attractions which discount their services for EICC delegates.

Exploring economic impacts

The economic impact that the centre generates is clearly of interest to many publics and this was especially the case during the early stages of operation. In order to maximise the attention that this could attract, an economic review has been produced every six months, providing facts and figures for the media. All enquiries, new wins and bids are made public in this way, together with statistics showing the number of delegates passing through the centre's doors and the economic impact they bring. Press briefings also take place in order that the press have an opportunity to speak to a representative from the centre.

Using its USPs

A particular feature of the centre is the catering which is provided by Leith's at the EICC. A photo-call was staged following the appointment of Leith's and all opportunities to generate additional publicity have been maximised. A food journalist was invited to witness the cook-chill operation, shadow an event and observe client tastings. Not only did this capitalise on a unique selling proposition, but it also created a point of interest for a wide audience.

Prolonging the opening

EICC had its 'soft' opening on 17 September 1995 and a gala opening in October 1995 with the Queen officially opening the centre the following July. Waiting for the Queen's visit to Edinburgh in order that such a high profile member of the Royal Family could open the centre effectively meant a long opening period resulting in more than one opportunity for media coverage.

A competitive marketplace

By the time EICC opened, it was in the unique position of having achieved 100 forward bookings. The centre has of course since lost the unique selling point of being 'new'. It now operates as an established centre in a fiercely competitive marketplace which in 1998 alone saw 12 new centres opening worldwide. The further development of EICC's supplier led public relations activities in this environment will be crucial to the centre's continued success. The emphasis on partnership and selling the EICC and the destination of Edinburgh as a package will be helpful in this respect, as will continued effective use of niche marketing and public relations. EICC will need to continue to be ahead of the pack in terms of innovative ideas.

(Edinburgh International Conference Centre)

Questions

1 If you had been appointed Marketing and PR Manager for the EICC, what measures would you have taken in the pre-opening phase and how would they have differed from the strategy adopted above?
2 Identify any further public relations initiatives that would now be appropriate given that the centre has moved from the pre- to post-opening phase.
3 EICC measures the effectiveness of its public relations activities. Suggest how this might be carried out in practice.

References and bibliography

Clapper, A. and Cunard, P. (1990) *The Public Relations Handbook: Major Campaigns in Action*, Kogan Page

Croisier, K., (1987) Promotion, in Baker, M. (ed.) *The Marketing Book*, Chartered Institute of Marketing/Heinemann

Holloway, J.C. and Robinson, C. (1995) *Marketing for Tourism*, 3rd edition, Longman

Jefkins, F. (1989) *Public Relations*, 3rd edition, M&E Handbooks

Key Note Market Review (1996a) *Hotels*

Key Note Market Review (1996b) *UK Travel and Tourism*

Key Note Market Review (1997) *Tourist Attractions*

Key Note Market Review (1998) *Travel Agents and Overseas Tour Operators*

Kotler, P. (1994) *Marketing Management: Analysis, Planning, Implementation and Control*, 8th edition, Prentice Hall International

Kotler, P., Bowens, J. and Makens, J. (1996) *Marketing for Hospitality and Tourism*, Prentice Hall

Lancaster, G. and Jobber, D. (1994) *Selling and Sales Management*, 3rd edition, Pitman.

Mintel (1996a) *Hotels*, Mintel Marketing Intelligence

Mintel (1996b) *Airlines*, Mintel Marketing Intelligence

Mintel (1996c) *Short Breaks in the UK*, Mintel Marketing Intelligence

Riley, R. (1992) Movies as Tourism Promotion: A 'Pull' Factor in a 'Push' Location, *Tourism Management*, Vol. 13, No. 3, pp. 267–74

Smith, P.R. (1993) *Marketing Communications: An Integrated Approach*, Kogan Page

TTG (1997) 5 November, *Travel Trade Gazette*

TTG (1998) 18 February, *Travel Trade Gazette*

12 The law affecting travel and tourism marketing

Objectives

By the end of this chapter you should be able to:

- appreciate the scope of the law as it affects the relationship between the marketers of travel and tourism products and services and their customers
- understand the distinction between civil and criminal law as it affects travel and tourism marketing
- know and understand the key legislation and cases concerning travel and tourism marketing
- know and understand the role of voluntary regulation in setting standards and resolving disputes in the travel and tourism industry.

Introduction

Travel and tourism make a significant contribution the UK economy, the importance of which has been dealt with elsewhere in this book. The industry involves many millions of transactions between customers, providers of services and the many different intermediaries, such as travel agents and tour operators. All these transactions are regulated to a greater or lesser extent within a legal or voluntary framework.

This chapter focuses on the legal framework, much of which is general to most business and consumer protection situations. Some law, however, such as the Warsaw Convention and the Package Travel Directive, is unique to travel and tourism. The chapter sets out to describe most relevant law which affects the relationship between providers, intermediaries and customers, including the law of contract, statutes which regulate what operators can and cannot do, and the legal status of travel agents.

The chapter does not look at general business law, such as company law, employment law, monopoly law or planning law, nor does it look at law such as aviation or maritime safety law. The focus is on the relationship between providers and customers.

What is the law?

Essentially, for the purpose of this book, the law has two main functions.

- The law provides a set of rules which oblige people to conform to agreed standards of behaviour. This is known as *criminal law*. The Trade Descriptions Act 1968 is an example of criminal law. Breaking the criminal law, for example by giving a misleading description, results in the convicted person being punished, usually through fines or imprisonment, or both.

- The law provides a set of rules for the conduct of a variety of transactions such as contracts. The law allows people to do business within a set of rules and to resolve differences when things go wrong.

In this chapter both the criminal and civil law will be looked at as each affects the travel and tourism industry.

Contract law

Virtually all business transactions are governed by contract law, and travel and tourism transactions are no exception. A good understanding of contract law is vital therefore. In English law, and in many other jurisdictions which are based on English law (for example, the USA and Australia), contract law is based on certain *common law* principles. Common law is that branch of law which has been established over hundreds of years through the decisions of judges, as opposed to *legislation* which is parliament-made law.

For a contract to be enforceable in most jurisdictions, there are several 'essentials of a valid contract'. These are:

- offer and acceptance
- consideration, i.e. something of value such as money
- intention to create a legally enforceable contract
- capacity of the person to enter into a contract
- legality of the objective
- possibility of performance.

If any of these essentials is absent, no enforceable contract exists. In this chapter we will look in more detail at the first of these essentials – offer and acceptance.

In all travel and tourism contracts, such as those for flights, package holidays, hotel accommodation and restaurant bookings, all of these essentials are normally present and a contract is enforceable upon both parties to any contract. Most contracts in English law do not have to be in writing and this applies to contracts for most travel and tourism services, although various Acts of Parliament and EU Directives and Regulations do specify that certain items have to be in writing. From an operator's point of view, however, it is advisable to have contracts recorded in writing.

Invitation to treat

In many businesses the goods and services available for sale are advertised, promoted or put on display in order to communicate their availability to potential customers. In most such cases this activity constitutes an *invitation to treat* which is different from an offer. Hotel brochures, airline timetables, car hire company tariffs, restaurant menus, self-service cafeteria displays are all examples of invitation to treat. A hotel brochure or a travel timetable fall short of an offer usually because they do not contain sufficient information to constitute an offer. For example, a hotel brochure, a car hire company tariff or an airline timetable does not usually state or imply that accommodation, a car or seats are available on a particular date. All the accommodation, cars or seats may have already been reserved.

⚖ In **Partridge v. Crittenden** (1968) it was held that an advertisement did not amount to an offer. The reasoning for this is that there is not enough information in an advertisement to constitute an offer – there may only be a limited supply of a particular item. (Partridge v. Crittenden [1968] 1 WLR 1204 [QBD])
See Grant and Mason,1995, and Pannett and Boella, 1996)

In some cases, however, an advertisement can possibly constitute an 'offer'. For example, advertisements containing vouchers offering free goods or services or price reductions can be an 'offer'.

⚖ In **Carlill v. Carbolic Smoke Ball Co.** (1893) the company published an advertisement agreeing to pay £100 to anyone who contracted influenza after taking their medicine. Carlill bought and used the medicine but still caught influenza. Carlill claimed the £100. Carbolic Smoke Ball Co. refused to pay saying that Carlill had not communicated her acceptance of the offer to the company. It was held that the purchase and use of the medicine was sufficient acceptance. (Carlill v. Carbolic Smoke Ball Co. [1893] 1 QB 256 [CA])
See Grant and Mason, 1995, and Pannett and Boella, 1996)

So if a restaurateur or hotelier wishes to attract trade at certain off-peak times, he or she may advertise free bottles of house wine or a free bedroom for every couple dining at his restaurant. As a result of the Carbolic Smoke Ball case the advertisement may well constitute an offer. To be safe in such circumstances, the restaurateur would be advised to put a limit on the offers, for example the first 50 to apply.

Hoover, the household appliance company, advertised holidays with the purchase of certain appliances, without limiting the number of holidays on offer. The consequence was a demand that was reputed to have seriously embarrassed the company.

Offer and acceptance

Under English law, it is the customer who *normally makes the offer*, in response to details in a brochure or an advertisement, or a feature in a guidebook. It is the provider of the service, such as the carrier, tour operator or hotel who *accepts* the customer's offer.

The actual offer made by the customer is normally made as a response to statements intended to *induce* someone to enter into a contract. Such statements may fall under a number of different definitions.

'Puffs'
Puffs include statements that make a product or service sound good. Words such as '*picturesque*', '*fascinating*', '*delightful*' and '*dramatic*' are all used, but are extremely subjective

and would be very difficult to prove or disprove in a court of law. Puffs, generally speaking, are allowed in promoting products and services, and any examination of advertisements will show that they are used extensively.

Representations

Representations go beyond puffs. They induce people to enter into a contract but do not, in themselves, become terms of the contract. Typical representations might describe local amenities which are not part of the contracted service itself. These might include neighbouring beaches, attractions and entertainments.

Terms

Terms may become legally binding. The terms of a particular contract will, in the main, be *express terms*, i.e. terms stated and agreed between the parties. Some terms, however, since the supply of Goods and Services Act 1982 (see below), are *implied* into a contract. There are different degrees of importance attached to terms in a contract. These include:

- *conditions* – a condition is an important term, for example payment of a deposit
- *warranty* – a warranty is of lesser importance than a condition, i.e. it is not vital to the contract, for example a hotel offers a trouser press in a bedroom
- *mid-terms or innominate term* – a term which might be either a condition or a warranty, dependent upon the exact circumstances.

Need for flexibility

From the business point of view, when negotiating contracts, it is vital to leave as much flexibility as possible. For example, if a customer books a single room, a hotel has total freedom to allocate whichever room it wishes. If, on the other hand, a customer has booked a room with a sea view, the hotel can only allocate the customer one of its rooms with a sea view. If the customer has been even more specific, i.e. he has booked a double-bedded room, with bathroom containing a shower and a seaview, the hotel's room for manoeuvre is further restricted. To allocate a room not fulfilling the customer's requests amounts to a breach of contract. This may be a breach of a term, a warranty or a mid-term also known as an innominate term (see above).

Most travel and tourism companies insert clauses into contracts which leave them with a degree of flexibility to maximise profitability. This might include the right to consolidate a number of undersold holiday destinations into one destination. A typical clause in a contract might be:

> *Although it is unlikely, the company reserves the right to make changes to the travel arrangements you have booked. Most changes are likely to be minor and you will be informed as soon as any information becomes available. If a major change is required, e.g. change of departure airport or time of more than 12 hours you will be given the option to accept the change or to cancel your arrangements without penalty. In addition compensation will be paid, as follows:...*

Such a clause gives the operator maximum flexibility, whilst generally remaining within the law (see also the Package Travel, Package Holidays and Package Tours Regulations 1992, below). Similar clauses would also protect companies from liability in the case of events such as the 1997 British Airways cabin crew strike or strikes of air traffic controllers.

Force majeure

Companies will also normally include a paragraph concerned with *forces majeure*, i.e. unpredictable circumstances such as natural disasters, political upheaval, disease, etc. In principle, such a clause protects the operator from liability in breach of contract should a *force majeure* prevent performance. The Association of British Travel Agents' (ABTA) code of practice contains a section on *forces majeures* defining them as circumstances such as war, riot, civil strife, industrial dispute, terrorist activity, natural or nuclear disaster, fire or adverse weather conditions which prevent the performance of a contract.

The question of *force majeure* is quite complex and beyond the scope of this chapter. Anyone interested in learning more about the subject should look initially at Grant and Mason (1995).

Frustration

A contract is frustrated where circumstances outside the control of one of the parties to the contract prevent it being performed. Generally frustration arises where the contract is impossible to perform through no fault of either party (Taylor v. Caldwell [1863] 3 B & S 826). In the travel and tourism context, frustration should be seen alongside *forces majeures* (see above) and the ABTA code of practice. Circumstances dictate which is most suited to a particular situation (see Grant and Mason, 1995, for more information).

Where a contract is frustrated, the customer does not have an automatic right to a refund of any monies paid in advance. The Law Reform (Frustrated Contracts) Act 1943 provides that any money already paid by the customer would be subject to a deduction for any expenses already incurred. If, however, no monies were paid or became payable prior to the frustrating event, the business will not be able to recover any expenses at all (see Pannett and Boella, 1996).

Deposits

In English law deposits, or advance payments, are not needed to confirm the formation of a contract. A contract will be binding if the essentials of a valid contract (listed above) are present. However, an operator can make it a condition of the contract that an advance payment or bank card number is provided. If the customer fails to meet this condition then the customer cannot sue for breach of contract should the accommodation be released.

Where an operator fails to perform a part of the contract, and the customer has paid a deposit, the deposit has to be returned, excepting in some cases were frustration of the contract may have arisen (see above). The customer, however, would be advised to accept such a refund with the condition that the acceptance does not prejudice any subsequent action on his part.

False statements and misrepresentation

False statements

Whilst negotiating contracts, a variety of representations may be made orally, in writing, by illustration, by sample and even by actions. In some cases, such representations may be false for a variety of different reasons. Wording of advertisements, brochures and other promotional and contractual material has to be considered very carefully as false statements, carelessness and recklessness can result in *torts* (civil wrongs) and even criminal offences being committed (for example, under the Trade Descriptions Act 1968 and the Consumer Protection Act 1987). In such cases, the person making the false statement can be sued in a civil court for damages or prosecuted in a criminal court for a criminal offence.

In some cases, travel agents, tour operators or other providers may make *false statements* which form a term of the contract (Jarvis v. Swan's Tours [1973] 1 All ER 71 [CA]). In such cases, the client may sue for *breach of contract*. We see, therefore, that false representations can lead to three different classes of action: an action in tort (a civil wrong, which is not a crime or a breach of contract), a criminal action and a breach of contract.

Misrepresentation

Misrepresentation occurs where a provider makes a statement of fact upon which the client relies, and as a result is induced to enter into a contract. Misrepresentation may arise under the common law of tort or under statute law, the Misrepresention Act 1967.

Where heavy overbooking occurs it is, of course, arguable that the operator knows that the booking may not be honoured. In English law this could be perceived as inducing someone to enter into a contract by deception or misrepresentation.

Withholding information

To withhold information (such as details of building works at a resort) from a potential customer, which may be necessary for him to make an informed offer or acceptance, may constitute a tort in English law and may well run foul of several statutes (parliament-made law) as well.

Fraudulent misrepresentation

Fraudulent misrepresentation occurs when a false statement is made. The definition of fraudulent misrepresentation is found in the case of Derry v. Peek (1889) 15 AC 337, in which the judge said:

'...fraud is proved when it is shown that a false representation has been made (1) knowingly, or (2) without belief in its truth, or (3) recklessly, careless whether it be true or false...'

(Grant and Mason, 1995)

Negligent misrepresentation

Negligent misrepresentation occurs where a person has suffered loss due to a representation (which is not fraudulent) being made by a person who cannot prove that he had reasonable grounds for making the representation. In practical terms, it appears that negligent misrepresentation occurs where statements are made carelessly and without using due diligence to check the relevant statements.

Negligent misrepresentation arises out of statute law, i.e. the Misrepresentation Act 1967. This statute gives protection to those who have entered into contracts, whereas the torts of deceit and negligent misstatement may arise before a contract has been entered into. In the case of misstatements, it is better to bring an action under section 2(1) of the 1967 Act, as it is for the defendant to justify his actions rather than the plaintiff to prove fault.

Innocent misrepresentation

Innocent misrepresentation occurs where a person making the representation had reasonable grounds to believe them true. This could be the case where false statements are made based on information provided by third parties who are believed to be reliable, for example a local tourist office. In English law, even if a provider is neither negligent or fraudulent, i.e. misleading information is given innocently, a customer may still have remedies under section 2(2) of the Misrepresentation Act 1967.

What to do in the case of misrepresentation?

People who have entered into contracts as a result of misrepresentation and who have suffered loss have two remedies available.

- *Rescission* This means that the contract can be cancelled and the parties returned to the position they were in before the contract was entered into. Rescission might occur where a customer discovers that statements about a hotel or resort he is contracted to go to are false. He can cancel the contract.
- Where a customer has already used some part of the contract, rescission is not normally available so *damages* may be the alternative remedy. This might occur where a customer arrives in a resort, having used part of the package, i.e. the transport element, to discover that the accommodation is not that contracted for. In this case damages, i.e. a sum of money as compensation, might be sought.

Damages

Damages are determined according to the nature of the misrepresentation. In the case of fraudulent misrepresentation, damages are aimed at putting the 'victim' in the position he would have been in if the statement had never been made. In the case of other misrepresentations, the 'victim' will be put in the position he would have been in if the statement had been true, for example if he had expected a luxury hotel but had been accommodated in an economy style hotel, he would receive the difference in the price of the two hotels.

Damages for consequential losses may also be awarded, for example when a misrepresentation leads to losses beyond those the direct subject of the contract. Examples in the travel business include compensation for distress and disappointment.

Supply of Goods and Services Act 1982

This Act is concerned with *implied terms* in a contract. Many contracts do not include specific terms about many of the services being offered, for example that a swimming pool will be clean and of a reasonable temperature. The 1982 Act implies into contracts what would be reasonable in the circumstances. In addition, the Act implies into certain service contracts that they will be provided with skill and care.

Pro-forma bookings – 'the battle of the forms'

In many cases bookings for travel, accommodation, banqueting, conference or restaurant services are made by companies using pro-forma orders. The booking may, in turn, be confirmed by a provider using a standard pre-printed confirmation. In many cases, the two documents differ in certain respects and the question often arises as to which of the two documents has legal effect. For example, a customer may make a booking from her office, using a standard order form. The order form may specify a particular type of room. The hotel may acknowledge the booking using their standard form which reserves them the right to allocate any room in the hotel. In English law *the last document* to be issued (so long as it meets the offer and is not in effect a 'counter-offer') is the legally binding one, so in the above example, it is the hotel which has the right to allocate any room.

Limiting liability

It is quite in order, as written above, to attempt, through the contract, to give oneself maximum flexibility and to minimise one's liabilities by writing in clauses which have that effect. However, not all limitation and exclusion clauses will have legal effect.

Unfair contract terms

Under the Unfair Contract Terms Act 1977, and the EU Unfair Terms Directive (93/13), certain unfair or unreasonable clauses in contracts and conditions of sale are void in law. The Directive applies to terms which have not been individually negotiated. Terms which have been determined in advance by the supplier, and where the consumer has not had the opportunity to influence the particular term, are covered. Unfair terms will not be binding on the customer. Operators therefore have to ensure that such terms are brought specifically to the attention of customers, either by highlighting them in contracts, and/or ensuring that staff bring them to the customer's attention.

Modifying contracts

Once entered into, contracts can only be modified should one of the two parties wish to modify the contract, by mutual agreement, i.e. both parties must agree to any new terms. Otherwise the contract must be performed within the terms of the contract or a breach of contract ensues.

Breach of contract

A breach of contract may occur in several different ways. Firstly, a business such as an airline may realise some time ahead that it can no longer fulfil its commitments. As a consequence it may write to the customer, or customers, attempting to modify or cancel the booking. This can constitute an *anticipatory breach*. An example, in another context, could be of a banqueting centre, having accepted a booking for a small party, receives a request for a much bigger and more profitable event. It may wish to cancel the earlier and smaller booking. It can only do so by mutual agreement.

If the contract is breached upon performance, for example if accommodation of a much lower standard than that agreed is provided, or no accommodation is provided, this constitutes an *actual breach*.

Where the breach is fundamental, i.e. breach of a *condition* which is at the heart of the contract, then the injured party (the customer) may refuse to perform his part of the contract, for example, to pay for or to accept a room. Where the term breached is a *warranty* (less than fundamental), then the injured party may have rights to a reduction of the price to be paid.

Criminal legislation

Whereas most of the law described above is civil law, there is also criminal law. Criminal law specifies what actions are criminal, such as assaulting someone or stealing. In the commercial context also, the law specifies what are criminal actions. For example, to knowingly make a misleading statement or claim regarding a product or service may not just make a contract unenforceable, or subject to rescission or damages, it also renders the person committing such an action liable to criminal penalties, such as fines or even imprisonment. The main criminal legislation is as follows.

Trade Descriptions Act 1968

The Trade Descriptions Act 1968 creates criminal offences, i.e. it provides for punishment of those guilty of committing offences under this Act. The main relevant provisions of the Act, are contained in Section 14 (1):

'It shall be an offence for any person in the course of any trade or business –

(a) to make a statement which he knows to be false; or
(b) recklessly to make a statement which is false; as to any of the following matters, that is to say –
    (i)   the provision in the course of any trade or business of any services, accommodation or facilities;
    (ii) the nature of any services, accommodation or facilities provided in the course of any trade or business;
    (iii) the time at which, manner in which or persons by whom any services, accommodation or facilities are so provided;
    (iv) the examination, approval or evaluation by any person of any services, accommodation or facilities so provided;
    (v)   the location or amenities of any accommodation so provided.'

For an action to succeed under section 14 of the Trade Descriptions Act it is necessary to prove that the defendant knew the statement to be false, or that he was reckless as to whether it was true or false (Sunair Holidays Ltd v. Dodds [1970] 1 WLR 1037 [CA]).

The case most commonly cited in this respect is British Airways Board v. Taylor [1976] 1 WLR 15 (HL). In this case BOAC (the predecessor to British Airways) confirmed a customer's reservation on a specified flight, on a particular time and day. BOAC operated an overbooking policy, i.e. more passengers were booked on flights than there were seats available. The passenger arrived to take up his seat, but BOAC could not carry him because there were more passengers than seats, as a result of their overbooking policy. BOAC were prosecuted for breach of section 14 (1) of the Trade Descriptions Act 1968 in that they recklessly made a statement about the provision of services which was false as to the time and manner in which the service was to be provided. Upon appeal, the

House of Lords held that BOAC's letter to the passenger and the ticket were a statement of fact that the passenger's booking on the flight in question was certain. This statement in view of section 14 (1) was false, since the passenger was exposed to the risk that he might not get a seat upon that particular flight.

Consumer Protection Act 1987: Misleading prices

The 1987 Act makes it a criminal offence to give a misleading price indication concerning accommodation, services, facilities or goods. There is a Code of Practice to the 1987 Act. The code covers the following points.

- Where a variety of prices is offered the brochure must state clearly the basic price and the optional extras.
- Non-optional extra charges for fixed amounts should be included in the basic price (for example, service charges).
- Non-optional extra charges which may vary (for example, fuel supplements) should be stated clearly in the brochure near to the basic price.
- Where prices can be increased after a booking has been made, details must be clearly stated in the brochure.

The Package Travel, Package Holidays and Package Tours Regulations (S.I. 1992 No. 3288) make it an offence to publish a brochure without 'legible, comprehensive and accurate' information about the price. The 1992 Regulations are discussed in greater detail below.

The Package Travel, Package Holidays and Package Tours Regulations 1992 (S.I. No. 3288)

For many operators in the travel and tourism industry, their objective is to create and market packages. For others, a major way to maximise profits from their existing products is to develop and promote products in conjunction with other products, i.e. to create a package. For some operators, the package may merely consist of adding an attraction such as a few visits or cultural activities to the main products of accommodation, food and drink. In other cases, packages may be extremely complex, consisting of different methods of travel and transfers, services of couriers and guides, accommodation, entertainment, sport, cultural and educational events and excursions, food and drink.

As the package travel industry developed, and as business failures left customers stranded, some authorities saw a need to harmonise the rules governing package travel so that operators from different countries (within the EU, in particular) operated within a similar legal regime. It also became necessary to introduce measures to give the consumer protection from abuses and from business failures.

The European Union Directive on Package Travel, Package Holidays and Package Tours (90/314) was adopted in 1990. A Directive is EU legislation directing a member state to introduce legislation with specific objectives, such as ensuring harmonised law throughout the EU.

The Directive was implemented in the UK by the introduction of the Package Travel, Package Holidays and Package Tours Regulations 1992. The 1992 Directive covers packages which consist of:

'the pre-arranged combination of at least two of the following components when sold or offered for sale at an inclusive price and when the service covers a period of more than twenty-four hours or includes overnight accommodation:

(a) transport
(b) accommodation
(c) other tourist service not ancillary to transport or accommodation and accounting for a significant proportion of the package;

and

(d) the submission of separate accounts for different components shall not cause the arrangements to be other than a package
(e) the fact that a combination is arranged at the request of the consumer and in accordance with his specific instructions (whether modified or not) shall not of itself cause it to be treated other than pre-arranged.'

From this definition it is apparent that a package may include a wide range of products offered by operators in the travel and tourism industry and not just the traditional package holiday. A conference which involves travel and excursions could fall within the definition, as would a weekend at a hotel with an inclusive activity such as tennis coaching. Business and educational services are excluded. The following is a brief description of the main features of the Regulations which cover a number of different issues including the following.

- The brochure must not contain any misleading information and where a brochure is provided it must contain information, where relevant, about transport, accommodation, meals, itinerary, passport and visa requirements for British citizens and any health formalities, deposit to be paid and method of settling the balance, minimum number of persons for the package to take place, arrangements for security of money paid over and for repatriation in case of insolvency of the operator (NB a brochure does not have to be provided).
- The consumer has an implied right to transfer his booking where there is some substantial reason preventing the consumer from proceeding with the package.
- Contracts providing for price revisions are automatically void unless they provide for decreases as well as increases. The term in the contract must state how the revised price is calculated and they must relate only to transport costs including fuel costs, taxes and fees such as airport taxes, exchange rate fluctuations.
- Where an operator is obliged to make changes to any of the 'essential terms' (due to factors outside the operator's control) the consumer must be notified as quickly as possible. The operator should indicate in the contract what might be considered 'essential terms' and what might be 'significant alterations'. Where a significant change has been made the consumer may cancel without penalty or accept a rider to the contract which states the alterations and any impact on price.
- Where an operator is obliged to cancel or to make significant alterations, the regulations entitle the consumer to take a substitute package, and where the substitute is cheaper to have the difference paid to him, or to have all moneys already paid refunded. The consumer may be compensated for non-performance of the contract except where the package was cancelled because the number required was not reached or where the package was cancelled for reasons beyond the control of the organiser.
- Where (after departure) a significant proportion of the services contracted for are not

provided or the operator knows that they will not be provided the operator must make suitable alternative arrangements, at no cost to the consumer, and provide for compensation for the difference between the two levels of service. Where alternative arrangements cannot be made or where the consumer has reasonable grounds for rejecting them the consumer must be transported back to the place of departure or another place agreed by the consumer.

- The organiser is liable for the performance of the contract whether or not he is providing the services directly himself or through other parties and the organiser is responsible for trying to remedy any defects in the performance of the contract.
- The organiser must provide evidence of security for the refund of moneys paid by consumers and for the repatriation of the consumer in case of insolvency. Such moneys should be secured by bonding, insurance, monies held in trust (or some variants of these) unless the moneys are secured in another member state or where the package is covered by the Civil Aviation (Air Travel Organisers Licensing) Regulations 1972.

From the above it is apparent that the Package Travel Regulations 1992 impose wide ranging legal responsibilities upon those offering packages.

Overbooking in the travel and tourist industries

Many argue that overbooking is an essential part of normal business practice in order that hotels, carriers and other similar types of business can maximise occupancy, load factors and profits, and maybe also offer lower prices to customers. It has been a part of many sectors of the tourism and hospitality industries for so long that few people within these industries question its ethical basis. It is argued that when conducted properly, i.e. based on sound knowledge of business patterns, it should not often result in having more customers than available capacity. However, there are occasions when the statistical forecasting necessary to underpin an effective yield management system does not run 'true to form' and more customers turn up than were predicted.

It should go without saying that staff concerned with handling overbooking situations should be carefully trained in how to select the 'unlucky' customers, what arrangements to make and in particular, how to inform them without giving grounds for legal action

What are the legal consequences of breach of contract?

Where an operator fails to provide the service contracted for, the customer may treat the contract as at an end. Furthermore, in seeking alternative services, for example if only a hotel of higher standard is available, the customer could sue for the higher cost.

In **Jarvis v. Swans Tours** (1973), Lord Denning said '... If the contracting party breaks his contract, damages can be given for the disappointment, the distress, the upset and frustration caused by the breach.' (Jarvis v. Swan's Tours [1973] 1 All ER 71 [CA])
(See Grant and Mason, 1995, and Pannett and Boella, 1996)

A customer may claim damages for disappointment incurred by the failure of the provider to meet the standards provided for.

In the case above, the plaintiff was awarded damages for disappointment and distress caused by loss of enjoyment of the holiday. Following from this case, a customer may be awarded damages greater than the contract price. In addition, as a result of another case, Jackson v. Horizon Holidays Ltd, a person who books for the benefit of others may be able to recover damages not only for their own disappointment, but also for the benefit of those for whom the contract was made.

⚖ In **Jackson v. Horizon Holidays** (1973), the plaintiff booked a holiday for himself and his family. The holiday failed to meet the description in the brochure. He sued for damages including a claim for his personal disappointment and that of his wife and children. The trial judge allowed, when assessing the amount of damages, for the plaintiff alone and not for his family as well. However the award was high so the defendants, Horizon, appealed. The Court of Appeal found that whilst the wife and children could not sue on the contract (they were not parties to it), the contract was made in part for their benefit. In this case the plaintiff, Mr Jackson, could receive damages for the loss of benefit sustained by his family as a result of the Horizon's breach of the contract. (Jackson v. Horizon Holidays Ltd [1973] 3 All ER 92 [CA])
(See Grant and Mason, 1995, and Pannett and Boella, 1996)

At the root of the case above is the principle of *privity of contract*. The doctrine of privity means that, as a general rule, a contract cannot confer contractual rights and obligations upon people who are not parties to the contract. However, as was shown above in Jackson v. Horizon, damages can be recovered where the contract was in part for the benefit of others who were not themselves parties to the contract.

The business's remedies when customers fail to show

Overbooking practices have arisen as a direct response to customer behaviour, i.e. making bookings and then not arriving to take up the service contracted for. In the worst cases customers, particularly airline passengers, make a number of bookings even though they need only one. In some such cases, the customer may be in breach of contract and the business concerned could sue for any damages suffered. The business however is still expected to mitigate the loss suffered.

⚖ In **British Westinghouse v. Underground Electric Railway Co.** (1912), the judge said: 'The fundamental principle is thus compensation...flowing from the breach; but this first principle is qualified by a second which imposes on the plaintiff (the injured party) the duty of taking reasonable steps to mitigate the loss...and debars him from claiming any part of the damage which is due to his neglect in taking such steps.' (British Westinghouse Electric and Manufacturing Company v Underground Electric Railway Co. of London [1912] AC 673 [HL])
(See Grant and Mason, 1995, and Pannett and Boella, 1996)

Whether to sue customers or not in such 'no-show' situations will depend upon the circumstances including the likely damages to be awarded by the court but also the adverse effects of publicity and loss of goodwill. For example, in the case of a restaurant the actual damages awarded are unlikely be the total costs to have been incurred by the customer but rather the actual loss suffered, maybe around 60 per cent of the anticipated bill.

Agencies

Much of the marketing of travel and tourism products is through agents. For the purpose of this book an agent is defined as a legal person (an individual or company) who is authorised to do certain acts on behalf of another person who, in the business context, is usually referred to as the 'principal'. When an agent is properly authorised through an agreement, a contract or a licence, the principal is bound legally by the acts of the agent – so if a travel agent overbooks an inclusive holiday, the tour operator is bound by the actions of the travel agent (see Grant and Mason, 1995).

In the travel business, it is apparent that the travel agent appears to be working for two parties – the customer (i.e. the traveller) and the principal (i.e. a tour operator). Grant and Mason (1995) conclude in general terms that up to the point the contract is made between the customer and the principal the agent works for the customer, and that once the contract is made the travel agent is working for the principal.

The customer–agent relationship

A special relationship exists between a customer and the provider of a service, such as a travel agent. A *special relationship* exists where a customer is trusting the provider of the service to exercise such a degree of care as the circumstances require, and it is reasonable for the client to rely on the provider's advice. So, if an agent gives advice which they know, or should have known the customer will rely upon, the provider may be liable should the advice be false. This liability arises out of the following case.

> ⚖ In the case of **Hedley Byrne & Co. Ltd v. Heller & Partners Ltd (1964)**, Lord Morris defined a 'special relationship': 'If someone possessed of a special skill undertakes (irrespective of contract) to apply that skill for the assistance of another person who relies on such skill he voluntarily undertakes the responsibility of so acting.'
> (Hedley Byrne & Co. Ltd v. Heller & Partners Ltd [1964] AC 465 [HL])
> (See Grant and Mason, 1995, and Pannett and Boella, 1996)

Most businesses acting as agencies, such as travel agents, set out to limit their liabilities making it clear that they are acting only as agents for the supplier. In most cases, this means that the contractual relationship is between the customer and the supplier of the service. An example of such a clause is:

Where the company acts as a retailer we act only as agent for the suppliers providing transportation, sightseeing, accommodation or other services comprising your booking. All coupons, receipts, tickets and other documents are issued subject to the terms and conditions specified by the supplier. By accepting the coupons, receipts and tickets and/or utilising the services, you agree that neither we nor any of our affiliated companies shall have any obligation to you whatsoever for the operation of the travel arrangements.

However, the case of Brewer v. Best Travel illustrates that in some circumstances the travel agents were working for the customer and were therefore responsible to the customer, not just to the tour operator.

⚖️ In **Brewer v. Best Travel** (1993), the customer, Mr Brewer had booked a specific type of accommodation. Best Travel however booked a 'late availability' holiday which enabled the tour operator to allocate whatever they had available. They provided accommodation which was not what Mr Brewer had specified. Mr Brewer sued the tour operator. It was found that the tour operator was not responsible and that the travel agent, Best Travel were liable because they had not made clear to the tour operator the accommodation which Mr Brewer had specified. (Brewer v. Best Travel [1993] 10 CL 10)

Disability Discrimination Act 1995

The 1995 Act makes it unlawful for the provider of services such as tour operators, travel agents and hoteliers, to discriminate against people with disabilities. The Act places a service provider under a positive duty to take reasonable steps to make it possible for people with disabilities to use their services.

Consumer protection

Up to this point this chapter has looked mainly at the law concerning the contractual relationship between organisations marketing their travel and tourism products and their customers. Many complaints about such products, particularly those that receive widespread media coverage, are concerned with the failure of the provider to ensure the health and safety of their customers. An outbreak of food poisoning, a fire in an hotel or a terrorist action can all have disastrous effects on demand for particular travel and tourism products and destinations. Health and safety is therefore of concern to the travel and tourism operator and should feature as a key part of the product development process. So in addition to a contractual relationship, the law is concerned with ensuring the health, safety and welfare of people who are being provided with services by businesses. The law is common to most businesses but it is summarised here with some specific cases drawn from the travel and tourism industry.

The Health and Safety at Work Act 1974 aims to secure the health, safety and welfare of employees but also customers and visitors using an undertaking's premises. The Act requires businesses to carry out risk assessment. In the tourism and leisure context, this could include risks to customers posed by facilities such as swimming pools and other facilities to which customers have access. In other cases, yacht charter for example, there are very precise regulations to be adhered to.

Details of the Fire Precautions Act 1971 (under revue at the time of writing) are beyond the scope of this chapter but sufficient to say that the Act specifies certain premises which are obliged to have a fire certificate. These include most business premises providing accommodation and premises used as a place of work. Most hotels therefore fall within the scope of the Fire Precautions Act .

Negligence

The courts do expect the providers of leisure services to ensure that reasonable precautions are taken to ensure the safety of users. In Farrant v. Thanet District Council (High Court, 11 June 1996), the judge found that the absence of warning notices contributed significantly to the injury sustained by Mr Farrant and found the District Council 80 per cent liable. The Court awarded interim damages of £250,000.

Furthermore, the responsibility of individual professionals providing services in leisure and tourism is extending constantly. A recent case illustrates this. A mountain guide was found responsible for the death of a client because the guide had been negligent in using only one icescrew where two should have been used (*Daily Telegraph*, 21 June 1997).

Dispute resolution

The ability to resolve disputes satisfactorily and with minimum publicity is vital to effective marketing. Resolving disputes in the courts can be very expensive and lengthy, particularly if professional legal advice is sought. As a consequence the travel and tourism industry has evolved a number of different ways of limiting their liability or settling disputes of various kinds. For example, ABTA has an arbitration scheme which enables customers of ABTA members to seek a simple and cheap remedy if and when things go wrong.

Intergovernmental agreements include the conventions of Warsaw (air carriers), Berne (rail) and Athens (shipping). The Warsaw Convention, for example, provides for compensation for death or injury of passengers, damage to or loss of baggage and delays to passengers or their baggage.

Other remedies include the simple expedient of reporting problems to the local trading standards officer who may intervene or whose threatened intervention may lead to a resolution of a dispute. The Consumers' Association also intervenes regularly on behalf of its members, many of its cases being reported in the association's monthly magazine *Which?*. Trading standards officers report that most such cases, where not settled under schemes such as the ABTA scheme are dealt with as breach of contract cases in the small claims division of the County Court.

Summary

This chapter has set out to introduce the main legal issues which affect travel and tourism operators. Many of the descriptions are by necessity very brief and readers interested in further detail should refer to the texts listed at the end of the chapter as a first step.

The chapter has shown that, in the context of this book, there are two main branches of law, civil and criminal. The civil law sets out to regulate relationships between people doing business together including customers, carriers, tour operators, hotels and travel agents. Civil law provides civil remedies (including damages) when things go wrong. Criminal law provides for punishment of those who break the law. The chapter also showed that the business of marketing travel and tourism services has a number of different stages at which the law intervenes. These include:

- the sales promotional, pre-contract stage which includes trade descriptions and representation
- the contract formation stage which includes an understanding of the differences between conditions, warranties and mid-terms or innominative terms and the liabilities and duties of the parties
- the delivery of the product, i.e. the performance of a contract and what may lead to rescission or making a contract void
- statutory duties imposed upon operators to provide information and certain economic guarantees
- the statutory responsibilities to customers concerning their health, safety and welfare.

Finally, it is important to bear in mind that business people and customers as well normally only use the law as a last resort. As a consequence, there exist several agreements and conventions which limit operator's liabilities and provide for simple dispute resolution. Going to law can be very expensive so other means, such as the ABTA arbitration scheme, are used to settle many disputes between customers and their providers.

    CASE STUDY
MIKE BEES TRAVEL COMPANY

The Mike Bees Travel Company sent its representative to a Mediterranean holiday resort in the early autumn to finalise contracts with hotels, including the Hotel Splendide, and to check out some details which were to be included in the next year's brochure.

The representative was informed by the Hotel Splendide, a three-star hotel, that certain works were to start shortly and would probably be finished by the start of the season.

The brochure was published and distributed by various travel agents including Happy Holidays. No mention of the building works was made in the brochure or subsequent communications between Mike Bees and its agents.

In March, Mr Smith purchased, for himself and his wife, a Mike Bees holiday at the resort from Happy Holidays, the travel agents. The holiday package included a scheduled return flight, seven days accommodation at the Hotel Splendide and transfer by coach to and from the airport.

The Smiths went to the resort in April. To their horror they found that building works were in progress right under their bedroom. Work started at 8 a.m. and went on until about 8 p.m. They complained to the Mike Bees representative, who was able to arrange a move within two days. Upon their return, the Smiths complained to Happy Holidays and asked for a refund. Happy Holidays said that the problem was not theirs, that the Smiths had to take their complaint to Mike Bees, the tour operator responsible for the Smiths' package holiday.

Shortly after the Smiths' complaint was made to Happy Holidays, Mr and Mrs Jones came to Happy Holidays and booked a 14-day Mike Bees holiday during the month of August, explaining that they wanted to go to the Hotel Splendide because it was the hotel where they had honeymooned ten years earlier. Happy Holidays accepted the booking on behalf of Mike Bees.

Mr and Mrs Jones' holiday did not go well. Firstly, they were unable to board their scheduled flight because the aircraft was overbooked resulting from an air traffic controllers' strike. The Jones caught another flight 24 hours later, having returned home between the two flights. Because they were not on the original flight, no transfer arrangements were made and they had to make their own arrangements to get from the airport to the hotel. The taxi cost £40.00. Upon arrival at the Hotel Splendide, they found that building work was still in progress. The work started at about 8 a.m. and went on throughout the day and into the evening. The Jones complained to the Mike Bees' representative, but because of the time of year the representative was unable to arrange a change of rooms nor to offer alternative accommodation. The Jones told the representative that if Mike Bees could not solve the problem that they, the Jones, would book themselves into a nearby four-star hotel, which did have accommodation, and they would expect Mike Bees to pay the bill.

Mike Bees' representative then offered alternative three-star accommodation on the other side of the island, about 40 miles away. The Jones refused, saying that they had specifically requested the hotel because it was in the town where they had honeymooned ten years earlier. They then informed the Mike Bees representative that they would move to the Excelsior, the nearby four-star hotel, the next day if he could not resolve the problem. The representative did not find alternative accommodation in the resort. The Jones moved to the Excelsior for the rest of their holiday. The hotel refused to invoice Mike Bees and insisted that the Jones pay their own bill. The Jones were told that their transfer coach to the airport would leave from the Hotel Splendide, but they chose not to use it, taking a taxi instead, the cost being £40.00. Otherwise their return journey home passed without incident.

Questions

1 In your opinion do the Smiths have any grounds for seeking redress?
2 If so, identify all parties who may be responsible for the fact that the Smiths' holiday did not come up to their expectations.
3 Identify and describe what legislation and case law exists which might provide the Smiths with the legal means to seek redress.
4 Which statutory authorities exist to enforce relevant law and who might have assisted the Smiths?
5 Which non-statutory authorities exist which may have assisted the Smiths to seek redress?
6 What action would you have advised the Smiths to take through the courts (identify the court) and against whom?
7 What differences, if any exist, between Mr and Mrs Smiths' legal rights in this case? Which case(s) might provide authority?
8 Identify all parties who may be responsible for the fact that the Jones' holiday was disappointing.
9 Identify and describe what law exists which might provide the Jones with the legal means to seek redress.
10 Which statutory authorities exist to enforce relevant law and who might have assisted the Jones?

11 Which non-statutory authorities exist which may have assisted the Jones to seek redress?

12 What action would you have advised the Jones to take through the courts and against whom? Are there any other actions they could have considered taking?

13 Itemise, using the case, the costs incurred by the Jones which you would suggest they attempt to recover in damages, with legal argument. Substantiate your proposal with legal argument.

14 Itemise, using the case study, the costs you believe that any of the travel and tourism operators:
a) should offer as compensation
b) would have awarded against them if the case went to court.

15 What international agreements or conventions, if any, provide for compensation for the Jones?

16 What is the fundamental difference between the cases of the Smiths and the Jones?

References and bibliography

Downes, J. and Paton, T. (1993) *Travel Agency Law*, Pitman

Grant, D. and Mason, S. (1995) *Holiday Law*, Sweet & Maxwell

Pannett, A.J. and Boella, M.J. (1996) *Principles of Hospitality Law*, 4th edition, Cassell

Yaqub, Z. and Bedford, B. (eds) (1997) *European Travel Law*, Wiley

Appendix 1: Case studies

Pierre Victoire in transition

Objectives

The objectives of this case study are to:

- demonstrate franchising and new product development as market growth strategies
- introduce the complexities associated with franchisor/franchisee relationships
- consider the impact these issue have for effective marketing planning and strategy
- illustrate the manner in which the vision of the founding entrepreneur influences every aspect of the organisation, including the marketing function.

Introduction

This case study provides an insight into a franchising organisation, which was one of Britain's biggest independent restaurant chains. It follows the organisation through four key transitional stages. These are the organisation's birth and early trading experiences, consolidation and growth, expansion, and strategic orientation. As Pierre Victoire the organisation is in fact embodied in the man, Pierre Levicky, it is understandable that the case study concentrates on the challenges which he faced.

Born in Lyon, Pierre Levicky moved to Edinburgh after training in Grenoble. He worked in up-market Edinburgh restaurants before deciding to branch out on his own in 1988, when he opened the very first Pierre Victoire restaurant. By 1996 there were approximately 100 Pierre Victoire units. The company owned 18 of them, and 83 were franchised. Together they employed 3,000 people, and served more than 110,000 meals per week.

What becomes clear from the case study is that a number of marketing planning and strategy issues are of import at each of the transitional stages. These are of particular significance given the nature of the core organisation requires co-ordinated action from a diverse grouping of franchisees in order to ensure effective marketing and the sustainability of the brand.

Organisation birth, critical illness and recovery

In April 1988, Levicky opened the first Pierre Victoire in a leased 780 sq. ft restaurant in Victoria Street (hence Pierre Victoire), Edinburgh, with a personal investment of £70, and a loan of £36,000 from the Royal Bank of Scotland. It was a restaurant designed to offer quality French food and wine at reasonable prices. The decor was simple – a financial necessity rather than choice – whitewashed walls, second-hand tables and chairs, and a wooden floor. This simple concept later became part of the group's brand image. It quickly established a reputation for serving inexpensive French cuisine, with the average spend per head being £7 for lunch, and £15 for dinner, including wine.

Levicky was totally immersed in his business, applying unlimited entrepreneurial energy, and his catering experience – 'This is what he had been made for'. It was a fun time. Consequently, within a year the restaurant had sales of £10,000 a week and a three-week waiting-list for bookings. Levicky recognised the potential to grow the company through franchising. He approached the Franchise Manager of the Royal Bank of Scotland who advised him to open a second Pierre Victoire and run it as a pilot franchise operation. Thus, the second restaurant in Union Street, Edinburgh opened in August 1989.

Despite market success, management controls were appalling, largely because Levicky was still cooking seven days a week in his restaurants. In September 1990, the company was £350,000 in debt and its accountant believed it could be insolvent within a month. The bank manager was asked for advice. She proposed a £96,000 overdraft facility to help clear all debts and the introduction of management controls. This set the company on a course of action that was to wipe out its borrowings in 11 months. The significant learning achieved as a consequence of this negative experience was voiced by Levicky: 'If we hadn't run into our troubles, there would be only three restaurants today, not 100'.

Consolidation and control

As part of the new regime, a business plan was prepared and computerised tills were introduced, along with weekly management accounts. Gross profit margins rose from 43 per cent to 65 per cent. Levicky sensibly surrounded himself with a knowledgeable Board of Directors who gave him support in the basic business skills he was lacking. Next, Levicky wrote a cookbook containing 500 recipes, enabling the chefs to keep prices down by buying what was fresh and cheap at the market that day and cooking it according to one of the recipes in the book. Indeed, Levicky was said to encourage his chefs not only to follow his recipes, but also his bartering skills in negotiating with local market traders.

Levicky was still very much in control of the business, in a very 'hands on' manner. The rewards of his efforts were shining through and he had never been happier. Confident that the concept was sound, the company had consolidated, and incorporated effective control systems. Levicky made the decision to expand the company in two ways. First, through launching two new brands, an even cheaper Chez Jules (1991), and the vegetarian Pierre Lapin (1992); and second, by means of franchising outlets.

Expansion

In 1992, Pierre Victoire began recruiting franchisees. They did not conform to any one stereotypical profile. According to Levicky: 'I think 90 per cent of us have dreamt of owning our own restaurants, so we have had people from all walks of life opening Pierre Victoires.' They were recruited on the basis of having some form of business, general management and/or financial acumen. Furthermore, they were required to be enthusiastic, energetic and fully understand the concept. The franchisees were usually new to the catering industry, and Levicky believed they were attracted to Pierre Victoire because it was a concept they could be proud of owning. Prior to signing contracts, potential franchisees were placed in an existing operating unit for 3–4 days to shadow the franchisee. This gave them exposure to the 'live' concept.

Franchises were usually granted for an initial period of five years. The contractual franchisor and franchisee obligations are presented in Tables A1 and A2 respectively. Associated franchisee financial information is presented in Table A3.

Table A1 Franchisor obligations to franchisees

Initial	Ongoing
• Locate suitable premises, investigate potential trading pattern and general viability, and acquire or lease premises • Refurbish, equip and fit out support and guidance • Opening and running advice and consultation • Provide training for franchisees and employees • Guidance relative to general stocking requirements • Support initial advertising and promotion campaign.	• Permit franchisee to carry out business • Update operations manual on a regular basis • Point-of-service advertising • Train substitute personnel and continuously improve the method • Consultation relative to operations • Provide staff training programmes and service • Refrain from positive/negative discrimination between franchisees • Computer system provision to support stock control and management information systems • Financial support service relative to cash flow development and bi-monthly accounts analysis • Calculate wages for each unit • Purchasing assistance for wines and products

Table A2 Franchisee's obligations

Initial	Ongoing
• Adequate training of key personnel • Conformity to the operations manual • Adherence to terms of the liquor licence • Adopt company norm for opening hours • Standardised menu, display of products and advertising material • Company approval of promotion and advertising activities • Keep accurate records and accounts in accordance with the operations manual and good accountancy practice in compliance with the franchisor's requirements • Compliance with laws • Pay suppliers promptly • If a franchisee makes or discovers any improvements to the business, the products or the method or the marketing they must notify the franchisor with all necessary details, and grant a non-exclusive licence to the franchisor and other users of the method in respect of	• Ensure financial payments to company as per contract • In all matters act loyally and faithfully to the franchisor • Pass on information and complaints • Protect the intellectual property of the company • Display the trade name • Maintain the condition and hygiene standards of the premises • Permit franchisor free inspection of books, computer data and premises • Not to engage directly or indirectly in any restaurant business venture in the territory other than at the franchised unit without the written permission of the franchisor • To indemnify the franchisor from and against any and all loss, damage or liability incurred by the franchisor arising as a result of any neglect or default by

continued overleaf

any such improvements
* Order all wine and other alcoholic beverages for resale in the business from the lists produced by or approved by the franchisor

the franchisee or agents.
* Ensure that there is sufficient stock of the products to ensure there will be no disruption of the business as a consequence of any shortage.

Table A3 Franchisee financial information

Minimum capital required to start-up	£30,000
Initial franchise fee	£12,500 plus VAT
Management fee for central follow-up and support costs	5% of net turnover
Financial support fee to cover central accounting service	£2,520
Average site-related franchisee costs	£46,000
Stock and working capital	£4,000
Average turnover	£400,000 p.a.
Average gross profit margins	60%
Pre-tax profits	11–18%

Franchisees underwent three weeks full training in a Pierre Victoire restaurant. In addition, the company acted as a marriage bureau for the chefs and franchisees. Levicky travelled to France, Holland and Belgium in search of chefs to bring back to the UK to staff both the franchised and company-owned outlets. As the majority of franchisees had no catering background, they were 100 per cent reliant on the chef. In this respect, the relationship between the chef and the franchisee was crucial to the success of the operation. The chef was seen by Levicky as the linch-pin, and to a large degree the kitchen was autonomous. Levicky noticed that a great deal of creative tension could build up between the owners and their employees when opening up a restaurant.

The regional director visited every two weeks to ensure that any problems were dealt with speedily and effectively. Regional meetings were held monthly, where performance, problems and success were discussed. Franchisees met at quarterly forums to discuss corporate strategy, promotions, new developments and all matters relating to running the franchises. If a franchisee deviated too far from the concept, in the first instance, attempts were made to resolve the situation. The company could appoint a manager to a unit at the franchisee's cost to sort out any problems. If it was not possible to turn the situation around, then the contract was terminated.

Thus, the company continued to grow market share in the UK through franchising. In addition, a third brand was launched in 1994, the Italian-based Beppe Vitorio. This expansion was fuelled through an injection of external funding. The Clydesdale Bank's venture capital arm paid £600,000 for a 10 per cent stake in the company in 1995. This phase had really tested Levicky's management and strategic ability. Furthermore, to a certain extent he was confused and unsure of his current role within the organisation. Was it time to disengage the 'engine' and let go? Sitting reflectively looking around the empty board room, he admitted: 'I have had to emotionally divorce Pierre the man from Pierre Victoire the company. Once the company was Pierre, now it doesn't need me.'

Strategic orientation

By 1996, the Pierre Victoire restaurant company had become one of the biggest independent restaurant chains in the UK. It was estimated that pre-tax profits would show an increase from £212,000 in 1995 to more than £900,000 with another big rise predicted for 1997. Turnover in 1995 for the company derived from estate-owned restaurants and franchise fees, amounted to £4.1 m. For the same year, the combined turnover of the company was £44 m.

Restaurants were opening at a rate of four per month. Franchised outlets were to be developed to reach the target of 300 over the period 1996-98. A new concept for the UK, the take-away kiosk, was being piloted in Edinburgh. In Brussels, a Scottish European theme brand was launched to appeal to the Belgian market. It was being test marketed prior to rolling it out in ten major continental cities, including Barcelona, Copenhagen, Amsterdam, Munich, Berlin and Lille in the north of France. Tackling the American market was still on the agenda, with the possibility of setting up a restaurant in Houston, Texas. Worldwide, Levicky claimed to have hundreds of willing restaurateurs throughout Europe, Australia, and South Africa interested in opening a Pierre Victoire.

The company was to be traded on the Alternative Investment Market (AIM) by the end of 1996 at a likely price of 10p a share. It was predicted that the share issue would be massively oversubscribed, and the value of the company was put at around £15 m. This would give Levicky a personal wealth of £8.5 million. The issue would have raised £2.5 m of new money for expansion of the chain, and to facilitate centralised buying, particularly wines, which could improve profit margins further. However, in October 1996 flotation was delayed, as Abtrust Scotland, the Aberdeen-based investment trust, took a 10 per cent stake at a cost of £1 m.

The company was rapidly moving through the fourth transitional stage of expansion. If Levicky was to continue to lead his company, he would be required to become a visionary with strong management and strategic capabilities. This was essential to ensure that Pierre Victoire was strong enough to combat competition, while strengthening its competitive advantage. Management would need to become even more professional, supported by an appropriate organisational structure, and increasingly formalised systems.

The Board of Directors consisted of Levicky, long-term employees who have been nurtured into the posts, and quality, corporate specialists who had been brought in more recently. Levicky drew attention to his own contribution to the Board in saying: 'The only reason I am on it is because I am the majority shareholder. Otherwise I don't think they would tolerate me.'

At a regional level, directors had been selected because they were the most successful franchisee within their respective regions. Sub-companies were set up for each of the regions. The parent company purchased the most successful franchise and gave the franchisee shares in the sub-company. The regional director continued to manage his unit, in addition to overseeing and growing the franchisees in the region. They ensured standardisation of operations. For instance, the daily menus at each of the units had to be faxed to the regional office each day.

In addition, there were six Executive Chefs. They were based at the Regional Directors' restaurant, were paid a premium by the parent company, and acted as executive chef for the region, training and standard monitoring. Each of the Executive Chefs were brought to the training centre, which was opened in 1996, to be trained personally by Levicky. The centre also enabled chefs and franchisees to be brought together for training for the first time. It was hoped that this would strengthen relationships and enhance communication.

In 1996, control systems were improved through the company supplying computers to all the franchisees. This enabled the use of a tailor-made software management information package, which updated information on a daily basis. This information could be accessed by regional directors and the head office. Bi-monthly, franchisees received a report which summarised the information, without naming units. This acted as an important benchmarking tool against which to monitor performance in terms of, for example, gross profit, wage costs, volume of turnover.

Pierre Victoire: Is the engine still on the rails?

The company's growth (Table A4) reflects Levicky's entrepreneurial qualities and ambitions. Furthermore, it appears that he successfully made the necessary transitions in pace with those of this company. It is important to emphasise that the rewards of such entrepreneurial achievement were tainted with frustrations. Indeed, Levicky was at a stage where he was seriously thinking that his job may well be over. He performed the essential role which germinated, gave birth and nurtured the company. It had now come of age. Moreover, 'it isn't as much fun anymore' he shrugged. During 1996, Levicky was at his happiest at the opening in Brussels, where he spent time working in the kitchen and front-of-house. Although he truly knew that this was what he was made for, and that was where he belonged, he proved himself to be undefeated by the seemingly unstoppable transition of Pierre Victoire. The 'engine' was still on the rails, it just might be found powering a different business interest in the years to come.

Table A4 Restaurant geographic locations and brands

Locations	Pierre Victoire	Chez Jules	Pierre Lapin	Beppe Vittorio
England	57	1	1	1
Scotland	16	3	1	2
Wales	1	0	0	0
Ireland	7	0	0	0
Belgium	1	0	0	0
Totals	82	4	2	3

Postscript

This case study was written before June 1998 when the Pierre Victoire chain went into voluntary receivership because it was unable to keep up with the necessary transition issues and challenges.

Questions

1 At each of the four phases consider what were the marketing implications, taking account of both the marketing planning strategy issues and the 'human' interface of the entrepreneur with the company?
2 The relationship between the franchisor and franchisee is crucial in sustaining the company's marketing strategy. What are the marketing strengths, weaknesses, opportunities and threats (SWOT) inherent in the Pierre Victoire organisation?
3 Discuss whether the marketing directions taken in the transitions were most astute, consider the range of alternatives, and consider how, if taken, they could have altered the course of the company.
4 On the basis of the analysis carried out in points (1) to (3) formulate a strategic marketing plan for the company for the five year period 1996 to 2001.

Further reading

Dewhurst, J. and Burns, P. (1993) *Small Business Management*, Macmillan

Falbe, C. and Dandridge, T. (1992) Franchising as a strategic partnership: Issues of co-operation and conflict in a global market, *International Small Business Journal*, Vol. 3, No. 10

Harrell, W. (1995) *For Entrepreneurs Only*, Career Press, Hawthorne, New Jersey

Hay, F. (1994) The dark side of franchising or appreciating flaws in an imperfect world, *International Small Business Journal*, Vol 3, No. 12

Mendelsohn, M. (1992) *The Guide to Franchising*, Cassell

Mendelsohn, M. (1994) *Franchising in Europe*, Cassell

Price, S. (1996) *The Franchise Paradox*, Cassell

Emirates flies into the market for global aviation

Objectives

The objectives of the case study are to:

- develop an understanding of the complex airline environment
- develop analytical skills
- illustrate the importance of new product development in the dynamic field of airline marketing.

Introduction

This case study provides information relating to both the current airline environment and to Emirates Airline, one of the fastest growing international carriers today. Emirates can be seen to be a niche player in the industry, yet one with a strong desire to become a global airline. The airline has introduced and developed both core and related airline products over the past 12 years. The innovation displayed by the company in developing these products provides a useful insight into this crucial aspect of marketing management. The case concentrates on both the issues surrounding the globalisation of an airline and the related area of new product development. The airline's cargo operations are not considered due to the tourism focus of this text.

To appreciate fully the central aspects of this case study, it is necessary to range more broadly and consider other elements of both the marketing mix and strategic marketing. This will also serve to illustrate the inseparability of these different elements of marketing.

The airline marketing environment

The airline marketing environment has been variously described as dynamic, turbulent, competitive and volatile. This environment has changed greatly since the early 1970s, when the industry was highly regulated. Historically, government involvement pervaded most areas of airlines' activities. Air fares and route entry were tightly controlled areas. Regulation of the industry was considered to be necessary for a number of reasons, including the maintenance of routes, safety standards and consumer protection.

The world airline industry is vast and displayed much growth during the 1970s and early 1980s. The industry reached a period of stagnation and decline from the mid-1980s, however, having been greatly influenced by the cyclical patterns of the world economy. Recession and the Gulf War have been cited as reasons for the cessation of growth in the global airline business in the early part of the 1990s (Horner and Swarbrooke, 1996). Average passenger journeys have, however, been increasing in length.

Deregulation of a number of the main domestic airline markets of the world has been taking place over the last two decades of the twentieth century. Two principal markets to effectively remove the regulation surrounding the operation of airlines have been the USA and Europe. Other countries or regions which have deregulated include Canada and Australia. The airline environment today is highly competitive, with liberalisation allowing airlines more freedom in their marketing than before.

Deregulation in the USA

The Airline Deregulation Act was passed in 1978, enabling carriers to operate under market forces. Initially, the US industry saw new entrants, lower fares and new routes. The industry later became more concentrated, however, as many of the newer airlines collapsed.

Liberalisation in Europe

Liberalisation in Europe has been a far slower process than was deregulation in the USA. Europe has never intended for liberalisation to be as far-reaching as deregulation in the US had been. Europe has preferred a more managed form of liberalisation. Essentially, this has come about, amid controversy, via three 'packages of measures'. The last of these, which came into effect in April 1997, allows airlines of any European country to treat another European country as its home base.

In essence, deregulation and liberalisation have freed airlines of restrictions on fare setting and marketing activities more generally. Many new opportunities for innovative air services and the establishment of new airlines have been created.

Privatisation

In the past, in many countries, state ownership of the national airline was common. More recently, however, there has been a move towards privatisation of these airlines. The privatisation of British Airways (BA) as been well documented (Horner and Swarbrooke, 1996; Morrell, 1997).

Globalisation

It has been argued that there is no global air transport market, merely individual domestic markets consisting of countries or regions (Axelsson, 1993). However, the development of global brands has recently become significant in air transportation.

Mergers and alliances

'The business strategy of airlines forming collaborative alliances with each other to extend market reach, control costs and – some argue – to limit competition is now the defining characteristic of the global air transport sector.'

(French, 1997)

Partnership involving the pooling of resources between two or more carriers has emerged as a central feature of strategic airline marketing in recent years. This development is not out of line with globalisation trends in other industries. To an extent, global mergers and alliances in the airline industry have been inevitable, partly as a result of liberalisation of domestic markets and partly because of restrictions on airlines' abilities to compete globally.

In order to be seen to be truly global, an airline should serve its own domestic market, foreign domestic markets and all major long-haul markets. This represents a significant departure for many aspiring airlines which may traditionally only have served their home market and the long-haul routes emanating from it. Air traffic rights are just one of the obstacles facing such airlines.

Axelsson has described the challenges for aspiring global airlines in the following terms:

'To build a global network whilst maximising brand yield and minimising production costs, and to create global awareness whilst meeting unique local needs.'

(Axelsson, 1993)

Given the above, it is hardly surprising that mergers and alliances have become a feature of the industry. A good example of this was the creation of the Star Alliance. The most significant period in the race to find partners was during the late 1980s, as airlines feared the emergence of a handful of mega-carriers, or galaxies as they are sometimes termed, becoming dominant.

BA has made no secret of its desire to form the first global airline network. Their global strategy involved the formation of partnerships in each of the world's major markets. Their alliance with Quantas has been significant in terms of their global reach in important growth areas, whilst investments in European airlines have strengthened their position more locally. At the time of writing, BA's global alliances offer a total of 492 destinations in 99 countries (British Airways, 1997).

Franchising is a growth strategy which has long been used by airlines in the US and which has been adopted by a number of European carriers, notably BA, in the 1990s. Franchising usually involves a major airline allowing a minor airline to adopt its brand image, including aircraft liveries, staff uniforms, service standards, and such like. In return, the franchisee will normally pay a royalty fee and provide traffic feed to the major airline.

The foundation stone of airline alliances is code-sharing – an agreement whereby an airline can sell a flight operated by another airline as its own. The main advantage of this is the increase in services offered, but there are further benefits such as traffic feed to the major airline.

Globalisation is also being portrayed by airlines' identities. British Airways has recently changed its image as seen by the aircraft liveries. This new image is reflected by what they term 'world images', celebrating and uniting the communities they serve (British Airways, 1997).

Amid all this global activity, there remain the niche players – airlines serving particular regional routes or offering a specialist type of product. The majority of airlines fall into this category and some will remain in niche positions in the future, undertaking a network 'feed' role. Others may disappear as the restructuring of the global industry continues.

Technological developments
CRSs are another etablished feature of the industry. These are also becoming more global, with the major systems increasingly being referred to as global distribution systems (GDSs). Other technological developments have also been important in the industry, including recent experiments with electronic ticketing.

Marketing initiatives
Frequent flyer programmes (FFPs) have become an expected part of the industry. First introduced by American Airlines as a short-term promotion, FFPs are now a highly influential aspect of airline marketing. In particular, they can help to develop longer term relations with customers and provide valuable marketing data. Despite a number of concerns about their use, FFPs are likely to continue to be important, in the eyes of the consumer, in the shorter term at least.

A number of high profile sales promotions have been used by airlines. BA used the highly publicised 'World's Biggest Offer' in which every seat on every flight on one day was given away free in order to increase sales following the Gulf War.

Airlines are generally big advertisers. According to Mintel (1996), advertising expenditure by UK airlines increased by 44 per cent between 1990 and 1995. Growth in advertising expenditure was at its highest during the recession of 1991–3, as airlines attempted to stimulate demand. Airlines now also use the internet as a means of both promotion and distribution.

Having attempted to summarise some of the major factors in the airline marketing environment, this case study now examines Emirates – one of the airlines operating within this environment.

Emirates: Background

Emirates is the international airline of the United Arab Emirates (UAE). The company began operations in 1985 with two leased aircraft and three destinations in the Indian subcontinent. The airline was launched to satisfy the high demand for increased air links with Dubai. The growth of the country had not initially been matched by a growth in airline capacity through the destination.

Emirates has grown rapidly, with a current fleet of 22 technologically advanced aircraft operating from Dubai to 44 destinations in the Middle East, West America, Europe, Africa and the Pacific Rim. The company now has offices in more than 40 cities worldwide. It has received a number of prestigious awards during the short period it has been operating.

Dubai's policy of free enterprise has been applied to its own airline and so there has been no money or government guarantees for the airline. The government of Dubai has an open-skies policy which has also remained intact.

The airline's mission statement, which is clearly reflected in their new product development, is:

'to offer the best service on every route it operates, to provide a link between UAE's main trading partners and to develop new ones capitalising on Dubai's pivotal geographical position.'

New product development at Emirates

Route networks
New destinations that are introduced reflect customer demand. The success of the first routes to the Indian subcontinent led to additional services within the Middle East and further expansion in West Asia. Europe was the next area to be developed with both London and Frankfurt becomeing Emirates' destinations in 1987. The focus then became the east, with locations such as Bangkok, Singapore, Manila and Hong Kong being introduced. In 1992, there was yet more development with the launch of services to Abu Dhabi, Paris, Rome, Zurich and Jakarta. The most recent addition to the airline's route network was Melbourne, Australia, in 1996.

Dubai's location and its historical position as a trading port between east and west has led to its natural developmemnt as a hub. New routes to be added shortly include Lusaka and Harare. Figure A5 shows Emirates' current route map.

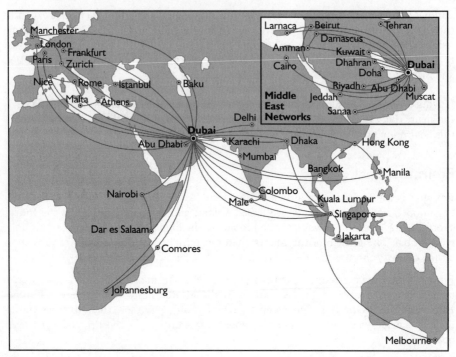

Figure A5 Emirates' current route map

Aircraft

To keep pace with the continuous network expansion detailed above, Emirates has steadily maintained an ambitious fleet building programme. It currently has one of the youngest fleets of aircraft in the world, consisting of 19 aircraft, nine Airbus A310-300 and six A300-600R as well as four Boeing 777s. Emirates set down new standards of cabin design when ordering new Airbus A310-300 and A300-600R aircraft. The resultant mock-up is used by Airbus Industrie to show to potential customers.

A major area of new product development at Emirates has been the addition of the four Boeing 777s to its fleet. This number was increased to a total of seven at the end of 1997. These aircraft are powered by Rolls-Royce Trent RB211 engines, the largest aircraft engines ever manufactured. The 777 is the world's largest twin-jet and one of the world's most technologically advanced aircraft, designed to offer new standards of comfort and spaciousness. Emirates' 777s have wider aisles and higher ceilings than usual. Emirates has been working with the Boeing Aircraft Company since 1990, participating in Boeing's Working Together programme which has enabled the airline to contribute to the design of the new aircraft.

The atmosphere of space has also been enhanced by fabrics and colour schemes selected by interior designers. First and Business class have ergonomically designed sleeper seats, with adjustable headrests, legrests and electronically-controlled lumbar support. Generous seat pitch is a further design feature – 63 inches in First Class, 46 inches in Business and 34 inches in Economy.

The 777 will allow Emirates to fly longer routes than it has been able to until now, so helping to expand its route structures and become a more global airline.

In-flight service

A main feature of Emirates in-flight service is the provision of multilingual crews. There are invalid toilets equipped with special doors, as well as wheelchair and stretcher facilities covering six Economy class seats on all aircraft. Baby bassinets, feeding bottles, disposable nappies, milk powder and a choice of baby food are all available, as is a baby changing table in a designated toilet, and entertainments for children, including Skyriders Club, soft toys and play packs.

Emirates provides an electronic typewriter, charging adapters in galleys for compatible PCs and there will be a fax modem in all seats in the future, so that passengers who have laptop computers with fax facilities can send faxes directly from their seats.

A further elements of luxury offered are freshly made capuccino and expresso coffee, piping hot towels to refresh passengers after boarding, and overnight amenity kits. Bone china dishes are used in every class and fresh flowers are placed in all three cabins. Both complimentary newspapers and Emirates' own in-flight magazine are part of the service offered. A polaroid camera is provided as a memento of the flight.

In-flight entertainment

In 1992 Emirates became the first airline in the world to offer passengers a personal video system on all seats in any class of the aircraft. The state-of-the-art Hughes Aviacom system costing US$1.4 m per aircraft and branded 'Emirates Television' offers six channels and more than 34 hours of in-flight entertainment.

A year later the airline installed user-friendly satellite telecoms equipment, enabling in-flight telephone calls by satellite anywhere in the world. Again, this facility was available to customers travelling in all three classes. Emirates was also the first airline to offer passengers an in-flight fax facility. Today, all Emirates' Airbus and Boeing 777 aircraft offer these consumer features.

The Boeing 777 aircraft has one video channel devoted to a new feature – the 'Flying Camera' – offering passengers the opportunity to view the world from any seat in the aircraft. Each aircraft has two cameras fitted, one provided a forward view and the other a downward view. Pictures are transmitted through the Flying Camera channel to each passenger's personal video screen, providing a bird's eye view of take-offs, landings, scenery, sunsets, and such like.

In addition, there are other important developments in in-flight entertainment, such as state-of-the-art handsets which allow for telephone calls to be made directly from the aircraft seats but which also can be used for video games and control of the entertainment system additional to touch-screen control.

Emirates Holidays

Emirates leisure division, which pioneered tourism in Dubai, expanded rapidly in 1993 with the launch of Arabian Adventures and Emirates Holidays. The former is a fully fledged destination management company, whilst the latter acts as a travel management company and tour wholesaler, promoting tours and developing travel across the network. Arabian Adventures offers a wide variety of tours throughout the United Arab Emirates, including city tours to the neighbouring emirates. Emirates Holidays offers holidays both in the UAE and throughout the airline's network. They design packages for holiday-makers and business travellers alike. These cannot, however, be sold in the UK.

The total product

Clearly, in a service-based airline, the development of new products is not on its own sufficient to meet consumer needs, and so Emirates has also made a conscious effort to develop its important staff resource. The Emirates Training Centre is tailor-made, equipped with modern facilities and staffed by expert instructors. The airline also recognises the importance of a close relationship with handling agents throughout its network in order to ensure consistency in customer service.

Further aspects that influence the total product experience include the rapid turnaround which is a key element in efficient aircraft scheduling. The engineering function at Emirates is thus important to the success of the product. The facilities at Emirates' technical centre, a modern complex at Dubai International Airport, include up-to-date equipment and technology. The stores department stocks range from entire engine assemblies to nuts and bolts. All are catalogued by an advanced computerised inventory system – EMPACS (Engineering Maintenance Planning and Control System). Emirates engineering is fully equipped to surmount the challenges of aircraft maintenance.

Equally important in terms of new product development has been the computer technology that drives and controls the inventory for all Emirates' flights. The system used is MARS which was purchased from Swissair. MARS is distributed to travel agents around the world through the world's leading central reservations systems, such as Galileo. This gives the travel trade instant access to the MARS database and the ability to make immediate bookings on Emirates flights. The company's development of state-of-the-art computer systems like EMIR is another example of its efforts to remain a market leader. It has also recently developed an internet site.

Market research and planning

A philosophy of careful planning pervades the airline. New routes are opened only after extensive research and new aircraft purchased to meet the needs of these routes. Emirates believes that planned expansion has been the key to their success to date. This targeted planning has centred around both pinpointing routes on which new business has been generated and maintaining a flexibility that can take advantage of new commercial opportunities.

Promoting the product

Television, radio and poster advertising are all used to promote the Emirates' product to the public. A variety of sales promotions are also used. These marketing activities help to promote the product and new product development at Emirates.

Distribution

Emirates employs approximately eight sales executives at any one time in the UK and their efforts are predominantly aimed at travel agents. The company does, however, also involve itself in direct marketing activities.

Price

In common with many other scheduled carriers, Emirates offers a variety of fares. These typically vary according to destination and ticket type.

Acclaim

Emirates has, to date, won more than a hundred awards for passenger services, food, marketing and advertising, magazines and entertainment.

The future

The airline hopes to continue to expand in the future and to widen its horizons in terms of its geographical reach. Emirates will continue to take a global view by adding more major gateways to their route network. Indeed, the airline's stated target is to become a truly global airline by the year 2000. It also aims to increase its flights to existing destinations.

As Emirates has stated: 'we do not intend to rest on our laurels'.

Questions ───

Note: When answering the following questions, please do not contact Emirates Airline.

1 Critically examine Emirates' mission statement.
2 Explain why Emirates should not 'rest on their laurels' as far as new product development is concerned, and suggest further new product development possibilities for Emirates.
3 In light of the information presented, critically evaluate Emirates' strengths and weaknesses.
4 In light of the information presented, critically evaluate the opportunities and threats facing the airline.
5 Outline the main alternative strategic options facing the company at present.
6 Suggest an appropriate strategy that Emirates should follow, providing justification for your choice.

References and further reading

Axelsson, R. (1993) Cloning a winner, *Airline Business*, September, pp 70–3

British Airways (1997) http://www.british.airways.com

French, T. (1997) Global trends in airline alliances, *Travel & Tourism Analyst*, No. 4

Hanlon, P. (1996) *Global Airlines: Competition in a Transnational Industry*, Butterworth-Heinemann

Horner, S. and Swarbrooke, J. (1996) *Marketing Tourism, Hospitality and Leisure in Europe*, ITP

Mintel (1996) *Airlines*, Mintel Marketing Intelligence

Morrell, P. (1997) *Airline Finance*, Ashgate

Norseman Travel Ltd

Objectives

The objectives of the case study are to:

- develop an understanding of the environment that travel agencies operate in
- examine how a small, independent travel agent can compete in the highly competitive retail travel sector in the UK
- introduce the importance of planning for changes that are likely to affect the organisation in the future.

Introduction

Amongst a small row of shops, midway between a council estate and an upmarket suburb of Newcastle upon Tyne is a travel agency of modest appearance. The smoked glass frontage bears no posters, special deals, discounts, last-minute bargains or free offers of any kind. Car parking is difficult and the agency almost seems to be trying to be insignificant and only obvious to those 'in the know'. Norseman Travel Ltd is one of a small, decreasing breed of independent travel agents.

The UK travel agency sector

Before looking at Norseman Travel Ltd, it is useful to examine the operating environment that independent travel agents face. As seen in Chapter 1, independents which have only one or a very small number of outlets operate alongside multiple travel agencies with many branches. There has been a strong move on the part of the larger multiples to become dominant in the marketplace and in the UK this sector is currently dominated by just a few major players.

This highly concentrated marketplace has resulted in part from a phenomenon which occurred in the 1980s and which was termed 'the march of the multiples' (MOM) by the trade press. MOM essentially changed the structure of the retail travel sector as the multiples expanded rapidly through take-over and merger activity. Prior to MOM, it was the independents who had collectively been the major part of the retail network, yet many of them disappeared or were absorbed by larger companies over a period of just a few years.

Consolidation of the industry continues today, and some of the effects for independents include reduced market share and pressure on profits as a result of excessive competition. A further consequence of integration has been that many of the larger multiples are now linked vertically also to tour operators and charter airlines. In response, some independents have joined consortia or franchise schemes.

In addition to operating within a highly concentrated marketplace, independents face a future in which technology is likely to be at the forefront of travel retailing. Technology can be seen as both an opportunity and a threat. Computer reservations systems, the internet, multimedia kiosks and interactive television all have potential to be influential in the field of travel distribution, as discussed in Chapter 10. There is already evidence of an increase in the use of direct marketing techniques by principals.

Norseman Travel: Background

Started 17 years ago, Norseman Travel has slowly and steadily gone from strength to strength to reach a turnover of £5 million. Managing Director, Bruce Ruffman, puts this success down to a simple company philosophy of trying to match the holiday to the customer. This is done by being willing to offer any holiday, and deal with any holiday company – big or small – that is felt to be good enough for his clients. Quality, flexibility and good service are the main company aims.

Whilst still offering the big book holiday, Norseman specialises in tailor-made holidays, particularly for the more independent traveller and those looking for long-haul destinations. The company deals a lot with BA, Kuoni and Abercrombie & Kent. It is a member of both Association of British Travel Agents (ABTA) and the Association of Independent Tour Operators (AITO). The latter provides access to a variety of good brochures for a minor cost of £200 a year. The role of ABTA was outlined in Chapter 1.

Company profile

Staff
Ruffman's experience in the travel industry spans 30 years. He started in a similar type of business, where he worked for 10 years, and then spent a further four years with another agent, before he decided he wanted to work for himself. Norseman Travel has become quite a family affair, with Ruffman's brother also having involvement in the business.

The family members are assisted by 14 sales staff, an expert in information technology (IT) and three other administrative staff. Most of the current staff have been with the company for years. Some of the most experienced female staff have, since joining Norseman, married and started families, and now work part-time. Ruffman is happy about this as he would rather keep quality staff with experience than have to train new employees. Any new employees have almost always gained previous experience elsewhere. Recognising that he is not in position to offer starter training in the travel industry, Ruffman freely employs staff who have gained their training with the larger travel companies. The advantage of this is that he does not have to do the groundwork, although staff do need to be trained in his way of doing things.

Product
Unlike the main high street travel agents, such as Thomas Cook, Norseman does not have a specific link with any tour operator. This gives the company a big advantage in that it can approach any tour operator it feels is suited to its clients. Whereas many large groups have been accused of preferring to deal with those operators offering them large discounts on brochure prices or commission overrides, negotiated for using their high turnovers, Norseman does not have the financial clout to benefit in this way.

Rather than try to compete on the same holidays as the big boys on the high street, Norseman tries to offer a wide range of 'different' holidays. There are about 150 facings in the travel shop, but it can deal with almost 800 other brochures. Norseman prides itself in being able to arrange almost any type of holiday requested. If one of its staff, who all have experience of a wide range of different types of holiday and destination, is unable to come up immediately with the organiser of a particular holiday, they will quickly get back to the client after making enquiries. Their main external sources of information are the tour operators themselves, the tourist offices at requested destinations or tour databases to which they have access.

Membership of AITO gives Norseman and about 100 other agents access to a wide range of small, specialist tour operators. Amongst these operators will be companies who can offer luxury villas in remote parts of Europe, historical tours of ancient ruins, white water rafting in New Zealand or scuba diving in uncharted waters. Initially, this type of tour operator would only have dealt directly with their clients through the classified sections of the quality Sunday papers. They are too small for the major high street agents to be interested in their holidays, but by linking to smaller agents through AITO they can access travel agents who have clients who are looking for something a bit different.

In summmary, the 'product' being offered by Norseman is made up of several parts:

- the experience of the staff directly through their own holidays
- the experience of the staff from their long service in the industry
- the tailor-made service available when required
- the high standard of service offered by the company, with a great deal of care and attention being paid to each client's holiday.

Customers

The agency has two main customer groups – the leisure group and corporate business.

The leisure or retail side is made up of customers from the more affluent parts of Newcastle upon Tyne and Northumberland, although almost one quarter of the business is from people living much further afield seeking a quality of service they feel they cannot access nearer to home. Repeat business is high and Ruffman feels customers come to him requiring a high level of service and easy access to someone who will take responsibility if things go wrong. Customers also tend to be those who are looking for something different, frequently because they have been to the more usual destinations earlier in their lives and with semi, or full, retirement approaching they have more time and possibly more money to spend on travelling. Many of the older clients are creatures of habit and will wish to book their holiday to the same destination year after year. There are also some clients with their own property overseas who merely use Norseman for flights or other methods of transport to get there. Others are more adventurous and will go into the travel shop looking for a new destination or different type of holiday.

The corporate business has grown almost of its own accord. Many corporate customers have previously used Norseman for their personal travel arrangements and, although not initially sought, these clients are dealt with through a different telephone number and a dedicated group of staff. It is difficult for such a small agency to deal with the large corporate travel agencies such as American Express and Hogg Robinson. They do not even try to compete on price, but concentrate instead on what they feel they do best – offering a good service. Corporate clients are told from the start that they will have to pay the published price as Norseman cannot afford to act any differently. Once again, the smaller companies do not have the bargaining power with the principals that the larger companies have.

A policy of never cold-calling and never tendering for corporate business has left Norseman with a surprisingly impressive list of household name organisations with annual travel budgets ranging from £5,000 to £240,000. Whilst the big ticket client is always welcome, Ruffman is wary of relying on a very small group of customers for too large a share of business. Another local travel agent had his fingers burnt when a large corporate client decided to move its business elsewhere and the agency immediately lost up to one third of its business.

Changes

The business has seen many changes over the last few years. There are many new products and destinations available, and technology has meant that the ways of doing things are completely different. The business has seen some ups and downs over the years, but surprisingly not in the same ways as some other types of business. Whilst a strong pound is good for business, Ruffman has also found that recessionary times can be good too. Since many of their clients have relatively large savings, higher interest rates mean a better return on investments and this extra investment may be spent on holidays. Another contrary factor is that when the big companies have over-capacity on airline seats, Norseman customers can get easy access to many different flights at reasonable prices. When seat numbers are cut and all charter flights full, it is harder to get Norseman customers a flight let alone one at a good price.

The customers also seem to be changing. With such a long-standing reputation, Ruffman feels that his customers tend to trust him and his staff. The average traveller, shopping on the high street for their holiday, is likely to be more demanding in terms of looking for a discount. Whilst Ruffman feels his company has the ability to satisfy both types of customer, the 'new' traveller is likely to book with a larger agent, having toured the high street.

Pricing

Discounts are something that Norseman does not offer due to their tight margins. Nor, however, does it try to bump up price for insurance. Indeed, for an expensive holiday this may be thrown in for free.

Promotion

With such a low profile shop-front, one might expect that the company has to make a big effort in terms of promotion, but this business is very much one which relies on word-of-mouth. This tactic may not be appropriate for a new business, but for one that has been going for this long it seems to be working. Many clients followed Ruffman and his reputation from his previous employers, and over the years the clientele has gradually built up. Having lived in an affluent area of Newcastle all his life, mixing socially and at the school gate with the likely client group, personal contact and recommendation have provided most new clients.

Advertising is something that Norseman does not do and to date the company has not felt the need. Two small advertisements are, however, positioned on the noticeboards of local rugby clubs and are targeted at the prospective customer group. Norseman do not benefit from stories in the local press who it believes favour those who have an advertising budget with them. It does not have a strategy of offering sales promotions, but will pass on any special offers or prices offered by travel companies, if applicable to a customer's requirements.

The future

Ruffman sees travel agencies, including Norseman, as making more use of the internet, although he is wary of how much emphasis to put on enquiries generated in this way.

Access and response to the pages is so easy that he feels many enquiries are not serious and time could be spent following up pointless leads.

Service is still felt to be the key to future success, and it is hoped that the introduction of the new computer system will help to facilitate this. Norseman already use the computer reservation system (CRS), Galileo, and have recently added 15 new PC servers which will link the telephone line into the customer database. Apart from customer service improvements, the new system is intended to make speed and efficiency gains in terms of bookings, invoices, etc. It will be easy to spot which customers come back with repeat business.

For the future, Ruffman is wary of the high street agents who can offer discounts, sometimes by selling high volumes of holidays, but at a loss. There are large pockets of business which will always go to these large competitors and they have the financial back-up to do this and the bargaining power to create competitive advantage in certain respects.

Norseman Travel Ltd is an example of how a smaller, independent travel agent can compete in the high discounting travel industry by finding their own niche and their own competitive advantage.

Questions

1 Norseman is a David amongst the Goliaths of the high street. Conduct a SWOT analysis for *both* a high street agent and Norseman Travel Ltd. Where do you feel Norseman has advantages over the bigger agents and where do you feel it is vulnerable?
2 How do you think a small business like Norseman Travel Ltd has managed to succeed in such a highly competitive industry?
3 Using segmentation variables, how would you define Norseman's leisure and corporate client base?
4 Ruffman feels his company is not particularly involved in marketing. What aspects of marketing do you feel Norseman currently carries out?
5 Ruffman hopes to market his company better in the future. What recommendations could you make to him?
6 Norseman's new computer system, which is linked to a database of past and present customers, would seem to offer the potential for direct marketing. How do you feel this could be best carried out?

Further reading

Inkpen, G. (1998) *Information Techology for Travel and Tourism*, 2nd edition, Longman

Renshaw, M.B. (1997) *The Travel Agent*, 2nd edition, BEP

Appendix 2: Organisations providing marketing research services for travel and tourism

The following are organisations who provide marketing research services in the areas of travel, transport and tourism, as listed in the Market Research Society's *Member's Handbook 1998*, and who have agreed to be listed here as such.

Applied Research and Communication
BDRC
Beaufort
Carter International Research
Makrotest
MBL
Market Profiles
MEW Research
MVA Consultancy
Numbers Research
The Oxford Research Agency
Pathfinder
Pickersgill
Pragma
Research Associates
RSL
Travel & Tourism Research
Harris Research Centre
Research Support & Marketing

Index

Page references in *italics* indicate figures or tables, those in **bold** indicate case studies.